Confronting Reification

Studies in
Critical Social Sciences

Series Editor
David Fasenfest (SOAS *University of London*)

Editorial Board
Eduardo Bonilla-Silva (*Duke University*)
Chris Chase-Dunn (*University of California-Riverside*)
William Carroll (*University of Victoria*)
Raewyn Connell (*University of Sydney*)
Kimberle W. Crenshaw (*University of California, LA,*
and *Columbia University*)
Raju Das (*York University*)
Heidi Gottfried (*Wayne State University*)
Karin Gottschall (*University of Bremen*)
Alfredo Saad-Filho (*King's College London*)
Chizuko Ueno (*University of Tokyo*)
Sylvia Walby (*Lancaster University*)

VOLUME 166

The titles published in this series are listed at *brill.com/scss*

Confronting Reification

Revitalizing Georg Lukács's Thought in Late Capitalism

Edited by

Gregory R. Smulewicz-Zucker

BRILL

LEIDEN | BOSTON

Cover illustration: "The Last Man: Imitator," Leonid Lerman, 2004. Plaster, pigment. 32.5" × 32.5" × 3.5".
Courtesy: McKee Gallery.

The Library of Congress Cataloging-in-Publication Data is available online at http://catalog.loc.gov
LC record available at http://lccn.loc.gov/2020025958

Typeface for the Latin, Greek, and Cyrillic scripts: "Brill". See and download: brill.com/brill-typeface.

ISSN 1573-4234
ISBN 978-90-04-35758-7 (hardback)
ISBN 978-90-04-43008-2 (e-book)

Copyright 2020 by Koninklijke Brill NV, Leiden, The Netherlands.
Koninklijke Brill NV incorporates the imprints Brill, Brill Hes & De Graaf, Brill Nijhoff, Brill Rodopi, Brill Sense, Hotei Publishing, mentis Verlag, Verlag Ferdinand Schöningh and Wilhelm Fink Verlag.
All rights reserved. No part of this publication may be reproduced, translated, stored in a retrieval system, or transmitted in any form or by any means, electronic, mechanical, photocopying, recording or otherwise, without prior written permission from the publisher.
Authorization to photocopy items for internal or personal use is granted by Koninklijke Brill NV provided that the appropriate fees are paid directly to The Copyright Clearance Center, 222 Rosewood Drive, Suite 910, Danvers, MA 01923, USA. Fees are subject to change.

This book is printed on acid-free paper and produced in a sustainable manner.

Contents

Acknowledgments   VII
Notes on Contributors   VIII

Introduction   1
   Gregory R. Smulewicz-Zucker

PART 1
Interpreting Reification: the Meaning and Origins of a Concept

1   Lukács's Theory of Reification: an Introduction   13
    Andrew Feenberg

2   Categorial Forms as Intelligibility of Social Objects: Reification and Objectivity in Lukács   25
    Christian Lotz

3   Reification in *History and Class Consciousness*   48
    Csaba Olay

PART 2
Philosophical Interventions in the Concept of Reification: Applications, Critiques, and Connections

4   Reification, Values and Norms: toward a Critical Theory of Consciousness   67
    Michael J. Thompson

5   Reification and the Mechanistic World-Picture: Lukács and Grossmann on Mechanistic Philosophy   91
    Sean Winkler

6   "The Nature of Humanity, or Rather the Nature of Things" – Reification in the Works of Georg Lukács and Walter Benjamin   116
    Andraž Jež

7   Lukács on Reification and Epistemic Constructivism   144
    Tom Rockmore

PART 3
Reification and the Idea of Socialism: Lukács's Contributions to the Renewal of Radical Politics and Their Limitations

8   The Project of Renewing the Idea of Socialism and the Theory of Reification   159
    Rüdiger Dannemann

9   Georg Lukács's Archimedean Socialism   186
    Joseph Grim Feinberg

10 Lukács's Idea of Communism and Its Blind Spot: Money   203
    Frank Engster

PART 4
Social and Political Interventions in the Idea of Reification: Gender, Race, Neoliberalism, and Populism

11 The Revolutionary Subject in Lukács and Feminist Standpoint Theory: Dilaceration and Emancipatory Interest   227
    Mariana Teixeira

12 Linking Racism and Reification in the Thought of Georg Lukács   252
    Gregory R. Smulewicz-Zucker

13 Reification and Neoliberalism: Is There an Alternative?   271
    Tivadar Vervoort

14 Populism and the Logic of Commodity Fetishism: Lukács's Theory of Reification and Authoritarian Leaders   289
    Richard Westerman

    Index   323

Acknowledgments

Many of the essays in this volume originated as presentations at "The Legacy of Georg Lukács" Conference held in Budapest in 2017. In the midst of the Hungarian government's assault on Lukács's legacy, a remarkable team came together in an effort to assert Lukács's significance as a philosopher, social theorist, and literary critic. Lukács scholars everywhere owe a debt to the main organizers, János Kelemen and Michael J. Thompson, for planning and realizing the conference. Cody Inglis, Ágnes Kelemen, and Jordan Skinner did the remarkable work of securing space and promoting the conference in Hungary. The late Ágnes Heller, who gave a wonderful talk on the closing night of the conference, played an indispensible role as a supporter of the event. The staff and faculty of Eötvös Loránd University and the Central European University guaranteed the success of the conference.

My thanks to Michael J. Thompson for suggesting I edit this volume based on talks related to the theme of reification. In his capacity as editor of the Studies in Critical Social Sciences series, David Fasenfest helped turn this idea into a book. He has been an incredibly supportive and patient series editor. Though they were unable to attend the conference, I thank Tom Rockmore and Christian Lotz for turning the talks they would have presented into essays for this book. I am grateful to all the contributors for their participation in the conference and commitment to this book. Finally, I thank Leonid Lerman for generously granting permission to use an image of one of his magnificent sculptures for the cover of the Brill edition of this book.

Notes on Contributors

Rüdiger Dannemann
is President of the International Georg Lukács Society. He studied philosophy, German and history in Bochum and Frankfurt/Main. He received his doctorate in Rotterdam for *Das Prinzip Verdinglichung*. His numerous publications cover social philosophy and political philosophy, especially on Lukács, Western Marxism and Critical Theory, as well as on literary studies and music aesthetics. He is editor of the Lukács Yearbook (since 2012) and the Lukács selection of works in individual volumes (at Aisthesis). Selected Publications include *Georg Lukács – Jenseits der Polemiken* (ed., Sendler Verlag, 1986); *Das Prinzip Verdinglichung* (Sendler Verlag, 1987); *Georg Lukács zur Einführung* (Panorama Verlag, 2005; Junius Verlag, 1997); *Lukács-Schule* (in HKWM 8/II (2015) (with Michael Löwy); *Lukács and 1968. Eine Spurensuche* (ed., Aisthesis Verlag, 2009); *Zur Aktualität von Georg Lukács* (forthcoming in 2020); and *Staat und Politik bei Georg Lukács* (ed., together with H.E. Schiller, forthcoming).

Frank Engster
wrote his Ph.D. thesis on the subject of time, money and measure and was subsequently a junior fellow at the Post-Wachstumskolleg (Degrow-College) in Jena. He works for several political institutions and foundations and is active in political groups in Berlin. His areas of interest lie in the different readings of Marx's critique of political economy and especially money as a technic and its connection with measurement, quantification, time and (natural) science. Some publications are available on academia.edu.

Andrew Feenberg
served as Canada Research Chair in Philosophy of Technology in the School of Communication, Simon Fraser University, where he continues to direct the Applied Communication and Technology Lab. His books include *The Philosophy of Praxis: Marx, Lukács and the Frankfurt School*, (Verso Press, 2014), *Technosystem: The Social Life of Reason* (Harvard University Press, 2017), and *Technology, Modernity, and Democracy*, co-edited with Eduardo Beira (Rowman and Littlefield, 2018) *Critical Theory and the Thought of Andrew Feenberg*, edited by D. Arnold and A. Michel, appeared with Palgrave Macmillan (2017).

Joseph Grim Feinberg
is a research fellow at the Philosophy Institute of the Czech Academy of Sciences. His current research involves the history of critical social thought in

East-Central Europe, the problem of citizenship and non-citizens, and the notion of internationalism. His book *The Paradox of Authenticity*, on problems of performance and the reconceptualization of "the people" in post-Communist Slovak folklore, was released in 2018 (University of Wisconsin Press).

Andraž Jež
is a Ljubljana-based literary historian. He received his Ph.D. (2015) from the Postgraduate School of the Research Centre of the Slovenian Academy of Sciences and Arts (ZRC SAZU), his thesis dealing with questions of dissemination of (proto)nationalism in *Vörmarz* Habsburg Monarchy by analyzing work of Slovenian-Croatian poet Stanko Vraz (1810–1851) on whom he also wrote a book published by the Research Centre of the Slovenian Academy of Sciences and Arts (ZRC SAZU). Jež works as a Research Fellow of the ZRC SAZU's Institute of Slovenian Literature and Literary Studies and as a Teaching Assistant of the Department of Slovenian Studies at the University of Ljubljana's Faculty of Arts (FF UL). His articles have appeared in numerous academic publications such as the *Encyclopedia of Romantic Nationalism in Europe* (ed. Joep Leerssen, Amsterdam University Press, 2018). He is currently researching social, political and economic history of the 19th and 20th century literature and arts. He is also an experimental jazz musician.

Christian Lotz
is Professor of Philosophy at Michigan State University, working in critical theory and Post-Kantian continental philosophy. He is the author of, among other books, *The Capitalist Schema. Time, Money, and the Culture of Abstraction* (Lexington Books, 2014); *Karl Marx: Das Maschinenfragment* (Laika, 2014); and *From Affectivity to Subjectivity. Revisiting Edmund Husserl's Phenomenology* (Palgrave Macmillan, 2008). In addition, he co-edited a volume on critical theory, reification, and Heidegger entitled *Ding und Verdinglichung. Technik- und Sozialphilosophie nach Heidegger und der Kritischen Theorie* (Fink, 2012). His current research interests are in contemporary European political philosophy, Marx's critique of political economy, phenomenology, and philosophical anthropology.

Csaba Olay
studied philosophy, mathematics, and physics at Eötvös Loránd University Budapest. He obtained his Ph.D. in philosophy at Freiburg University (Germany). He has been teaching at Eötvös Loránd University since 2001 and is currently Head of the Department of Modern and Contemporary Philosophy, where he was appointed as full professor in 2015. His main research areas are 19th–20th

century continental philosophy, hermeneutics, Heidegger, Gadamer, Hannah Arendt, and Frankfurt School. He has published books and articles, and edited collections of essays in these fields, and taught courses in Berlin, Dijon, Oldenburg, Cluj, and Oradea.

Tom Rockmore
is the Distinguished Humanities Chair Professor and Professor of Philosophy in the Institute of Foreign Philosophy at Peking University and was formerly a McAnulty College Distinguished Professor at Duquesne University. He is the author of numerous books.

Gregory R. Smulewicz-Zucker
holds graduate degrees in history, philosophy, and political science. He has taught in the City University of New York system and currently teaches at Rutgers University where he is pursuing his Ph.D. in political science. His most recently published edited books include *The Political Thought of African Independence: An Anthology of Sources* (Hackett, 2017) and (with Michael J. Thompson) *Anti-Science and the Assault on Democracy* (Prometheus, 2018). He is co-editor of *An Inheritance for Our Time: The Principles and Politics of Democratic Socialism* (OR Books, 2020) and editor of *Jonas Mekas: Interviews* (University Press of Mississippi, 2020).

Mariana Teixeira
is Associate Researcher at Cebrap (Brazilian Centre for Analysis and Planning) and Scientific Coordinator of Mecila (Merian Centre for Advanced Studies: Conviviality-Inequality in Latin America). She received her Ph.D. in philosophy from the University of Campinas, Brazil, and was a Visiting Researcher at the Free University Berlin, Germany. Mariana Teixeira was a Visiting Lecturer at the University of São Paulo and at the University of Campinas, Brazil, and is Managing Editor of *Dissonancia: Critical Theory Journal*. She has published on critical theory, Marxism, post-/decolonial studies, and feminism.

Michael J. Thompson
is Professor of Political Theory in the Department of Political Science, William Paterson University. He is the author of *The Politics of Inequality* (Columbia University Press, 2007), *The Domestication of Critical Theory* (Rowman and Littlefield, 2016) as well as the forthcoming *The Specter of Babel: A Reconstruction of Political Judgment* (SUNY Press, 2020).

Tivadar Vervoort

studied philosophy in Amsterdam and Berlin and finished his research masters in political philosophy at KU Leuven with a thesis on Foucault's and Adorno's modes of critique. He is preparing a Ph.D. proposal enquiring into the dynamics of repolitization by combining Lukács's focus on intersubjectivity and late Foucault's conceptualization of subjectivation. He is an editor at *De Nederlandse Boekengids* (The Dutch Review of Books) and the editorial secretary at *Krisis – Journal for Contemporary Philosophy*.

Richard Westerman

is the author of *Lukács's Phenomenology of Capitalism* (Palgrave Macmillan, 2019). He has published extensively on Lukács, the Frankfurt School, and philosophical aesthetics.

Sean Winkler

completed his Ph.D. in philosophy at KU Leuven in Belgium and currently works as a postdoctoral research fellow at the National Research University – Higher School of Economics in Russia. He specializes in early modern philosophy and the sociology of science/technology, with competences in 20th-century French philosophy, classical Chinese philosophy, phenomenology and Russian philosophy. His main publications include "'The Bartleby Effect': Deleuze's Critical-Clinical and Melville's Bartleby, the Scrivener" (in: *Psychoanalysis, Culture and Society*, ed. David Henderson, Cambridge Scholars Publishing, 2012), "Self-Identity in Spinoza's Account of Finite Individuals" (*Graduate Faculty Philosophy Journal* 39(1), 2018), "Practice and Ideology in Boris Hessen's Newton Paper" (*Telos* 190(Spring), 2020). He was the invited editor and contributor for a recently released special issue of *Societate si politica* entitled *Boris Hessen and the Dialectics of Natural Science* (*Societate si politica* 13(1), 2019).

Introduction

Gregory R. Smulewicz-Zucker

With the publication of *History and Class Consciousness* in 1923, the Hungarian philosopher, Georg Lukács (1885–1971), can be credited with revitalizing Marxist thought. Nearly a decade before the release of Marx's *Economic and Philosophic Manuscripts of 1844*, Lukács unearthed the philosophical sophistication embedded in Marx's work through an innovative reading of his later works. One of the furthest reaching implications of this was the reestablishment of the depth of Marx's debt to Hegel. He also provided a Marxist position that at once drew from and responded to advances in social theory, especially the work of Georg Simmel and Max Weber. Certainly, others, particularly Karl Korsch and Antonio Gramsci, who along with Lukács are recognized as the forefathers of Western Marxism, helped to identify and build on Marx's significance for philosophy. Today, when compared to Lukács, Korsch's influential works appear less philosophically innovative. There is no philosophically rich concept in Korsch's work equivalent to Lukács's reification or Gramsci's hegemony. And, though Gramsci remains wildly popular among leftist theorists, his important *Prison Notebooks*, written while imprisoned by Mussolini's fascist government, lack the systematicity of Lukács's work. Nevertheless, the analysis of Lukács's work and application of his ideas lags far behind that of contemporary work drawing from Gramsci's insights.

This collection of essays contributes to a growing renewal of interest in Lukács and his work. It focuses on the explication and relevance of one of the core concepts of *History and Class Consciousness*, reification. Through an original synthesis of Marx's notion of commodity fetishism and Weber's understanding of the tendency toward rationalization in modernity, Lukács uses reification to analyze the ways capitalism distorts human subjectivity and turns humans into objects. The commodity form, as Lukács explains, "stamps its imprint upon the whole consciousness of man; his qualities and abilities are no longer an organic part of his personality, they are things which he can 'own' or 'dispose of' like the various objects of the external world."[1] To be sure, in one sense, Lukács, independent of any knowledge of Marx's early writings, was pointing to the existence of something resembling the young Marx's theory of alienation. By the same token, reification perhaps resonates more deeply with

---

[1] Georg Lukács, *History and Class Consciousness: Studies in Marxist Dialectics*, trans. Rodney Livingstone (Cambridge: The MIT Press, 1971), 100.

our hyper-technologized and hyper-commodified society than Marx's description of alienation ever could. Far beyond a description of the condition of working people under capitalism, reification points to the ways the entire structure of society is redesigned to meet the imperatives of capitalism, including individual consciousness itself.

It was the humanistic ethos undergirding Lukács's argument that would make it an animating force for the formation of what we now know as the first generation of Frankfurt School thinkers. For those who had survived the horrors of World War I, it explained the automatization of warfare. More importantly, it could explain why the working class had largely failed to mobilize against capitalism in the aftermath of the War. It injected new insights into Marxist thought at a time when Marxism could often sound more like dogma in the hands of party theoreticians. It was no accident that interest in *History and Class Consciousness* would enjoy a revival of interest by the generation of 1968. This generation had, in its own way, experienced the vapidity of life in the Western world, which Herbert Marcuse so aptly characterized as "one-dimensional," while witnessing the atrocities committed in the suppression of anti-colonial struggles as well as the struggle of the Civil Rights Movement.

In *History and Class Consciousness*, Lukács lay the groundwork for a self-critical Marxism that privileged Marx's method over the economic determinism espoused by so many Marxist parties. Indeed, for a younger generation of intellectuals, the analysis of reification could be applied to the purportedly actually existing socialism of the Soviet Union. Soviet totalitarianism exemplified all the most pernicious attributes of reification. Lukács's Marxism was one that could combat all the self-proclaimed prophets of Marxism. Of course, Lukács seemed notoriously unable to resist orthodoxy. Unlike Korsch, who left the Party after Grigory Zinoviev condemned his position at the Fifth Comintern Congress, Lukács recanted his argument and seemingly surrendered to orthodoxy.[2] So the story went until the rediscovery of later pamphlets in which Lukács persisted in defending his work.[3] The simplistic account of Lukács as kowtowing to party disciplinarians is further challenged by his participation in the Hungarian Revolution of 1956 against Soviet control.

Whatever the motivations for Lukács's alleged periods of political acquiescence, Lukács was and remains a philosophical gadfly. There is no greater

---

[2] This episode is discussed in Arpad Kadarkay's thorough biography of Lukács. See: Arpad Kadarkay, *Georg Lukács: Life, Thought, and Politics* (Oxford: Basil Blackwell, 1991), 280–282. Kadarkay's biography remains an indispensable resource for Lukács scholarship.

[3] See: Georg Lukács, *A Defence of History and Class Consciousness: Tailism and the Dialectic*, trans. Esther Leslie (New York: Verso Books, 2000).

testament to this fact than the release of this volume and its companion volume on Lukács's contributions to social ontology. Both have their origins in the 2017 conference, "The Legacy of Georg Lukács". Held in Budapest, the conference itself was a response to the effort of Viktor Orbán's far-right government to close the Lukács archive housed in the philosopher's former apartment.[4] Since the conference, the Hungarian Academy Sciences has closed the archive and a statue of Lukács has been torn down. There is a sad irony that Lukács, nearly fifty years after his death, is once again targeted by an authoritarian regime. His ideas clearly continue to be dangerous.

Despite recent efforts to erase his memory, Lukács has undeniably left his mark on the history of philosophy. Without him, we would likely be without what we now call critical theory in all its guises, but, most importantly, that of the first generation of the Frankfurt School. It was, in part, through the critique of Lukács that we have the second generation of the Frankfurt School's Jürgen Habermas and his democratic theory. There is a strong case to be made that we would not, for better or worse, have Martin Heidegger without Lukács.[5] This is to say nothing of Lukács's influence on French thought as Jean-Paul Sartre, Maurice Merleau-Ponty, and Louis Althusser all developed ideas in argument with Lukács.

His historical impact aside, Lukács persists because his ideas remain provocative. By examining the way social conditions distort consciousness, his work constitutes a unique bridge between social theory and philosophy. Our increasingly technological society appears to increasingly incapacitate critical thought as we turn more to our cellphones and social media than to one another. Our every habit is tracked and quantified to determine how better to sell us things we do not need. Our values are ever more commodified as our society worships wealth of staggering proportions. Class distinctions have become more pronounced as wages stagnate and wealth becomes more concentrated at the top. A resurgent nativism across the globe attests to the stubbornness of groupthink. But complaints about these phenomena become hollow and platitudinous without theory. Lukács, in general, and his theory of reification, in particular, retains contemporary appeal because it offers new avenues for confronting these problems. Still, the dormancy of interest in Lukács following the

---

4 For more on this controversy, see: G.M. Tamás, "The Never-Ending Lukács Debate," *Los Angeles Review of Books*, March 6, 2017, https://lareviewofbooks.org/article/the-never-ending-Lukács-debate/.

5 The connections between Lukács and Heidegger is the subject of Lucien Goldmann's *Lukács and Heidegger: Towards a New Philosophy*, trans. William Q. Boelhower, (London: Routledge & Kegan Paul, 1977).

renaissance his thought enjoyed in the late 1960s and early 1970s has left its mark. Philosophy, social theory, and our economic and political contexts have changed since his death. A new Lukács revival requires serious reassessments of his work.

It is only in the last decade that we have witnessed a resurgence of publications dealing with Lukács and the concept of reification. At the same time, there is a history of noteworthy, but sporadic, efforts to appropriate the concept while shedding it of its moorings in Marxism. Even before the rediscovery of Lukács's work by intellectuals influenced by the New Left, the sociologists, Peter Berger and Stanley Pullberg, recognized the usefulness of the concept and endeavored the resuscitate it.[6] Though they argued the concept was useful to the agenda of a sociology of knowledge, their account gave only passing acknowledgement to Lukács's in formulating the concept. Even as they argued that the analysis of reification might inform a critique of consciousness, their approach dismissed the significance of reification as part of a radical critique of social systems. Two decades later, the political theorist, Hanna Pitkin, attempted her own retrieval of the concept with far greater consideration for Lukács's role in developing the concept. Pitkin admitted, "There really is something going on among us that we urgently need to think and talk about, and that Lukács's and Berger and Luckmann's conceptions of reification were meant to address."[7] She concluded, however, that too many definitions of reification exist to make the concept useful – even if the concept responded to "something going on among us that we urgently need to think and talk about."

In the years that followed, it seemed that Lukács's work would become the preserve of intellectual historians. For the most part, the scholars who helped revive interest in Lukács and *History and Class Consciousness* in the 1960s and 1970s largely turned their focus to the social theory and philosophy of late twentieth century German and French theorists. Of course, astute readers can still detect Lukács's influence on the Anglophone scholars as well as the fact that the problems Lukács first formulated remained an important, but sometimes obscured, source of much of the German and French theory that rose to prominence. Yet, it was undeniably Jürgen Habermas's critique of Lukács in his *Theory of Communicative Action* that seemed to do the most to render Lukács irrelevant to contemporary theory. Even as Lukács's influence remained

---

6 Peter Berger and Stanley Pullberg, "Reification and the Sociological Critique of Consciousness," *New Left Review* 35 (Jan/Feb, 1966). For more on the place of reification in Berger's sociology, the reader should also see Peter L. Berger and Thomas Luckmann, *The Social Construction of Reality: A Treatise in the Sociology of Knowledge* (New York: Anchor Books, 1966).
7 Hanna Fenichel Pitkin, "Rethinking Reification," *Theory and Society* 16, No. 2 (Mar., 1987): 286.

implicit in the work of many scholars who came to political and intellectual maturity in the lead-up to and aftermath of 1968, the task of an explicit, sustained, and theoretically sophisticated engagement with Lukács fell to the few. Three of those scholars who remained committed to that project – Andrew Feenberg, Tom Rockmore, and Rüdiger Dannemann – are included in this volume.

The rediscovery and publication of *Tailism and Dialectic*, a short rebuttal to Lukács's Soviet critics and defense of *History and Class Consciousness*, provided the beginnings of an opportunity for a Lukács revival. On the one hand, it showed the old story of Lukács's submission to Soviet dogma was significantly more complicated. On the other, it opened new avenues for scholars seeking to reassess Lukács's argument.

Further signs of a reemerging interest in Lukács and the concept of reification came with two renewed attempts to give the concept contemporary relevance. In a study that incorporated analyses of poststructuralist thinkers, literature, and cinema, the literary theorist, Timothy Bewes, focused on the anxieties surrounding reification. He explains,

> The truth, as the present study seeks to show, is that a profound anxiety towards reification may be unearthed behind every piece of serious writing on the subject. Thus, the second major proposition of this book is that such feelings are *constitutive* of the experience of reification, that the latter is incomprehensible without taking into account the consciousness of the perceiving subject who creates it; that the anxiety towards reification suggests a static, frozen conception of the relation between reality and its representation; that the anxiety towards reification is *itself reifying*.[8]

Bewes's book was followed by an attempt by the philosopher, Axel Honneth, to incorporate the concept into his influential theory of recognition. Breaking with Lukács in significant ways, Honneth states,

> I have made clear that we can use the term 'reification' in a direct sense only when referring to our relations to other persons, whereas our relation to nature can be called 'reified' only in an indirect or derivative sense of the term. When our relation to other persons is at issue, 'reification' means that we have lost sight of our antecedent recognition of these same persons; whereas when we speak of our relation to the objective

---

8 Timothy Bewes, *Reification, or The Anxiety of Late Capitalism* (New York: Verso, 2002), xiv.

world, the term signifies our having lost sight of the multiplicity of ways in which the world has significance for those we have antecedently recognized.[9]

Both works reinterpreted Lukács's ideas in ways that distanced the concept from Lukács's major concerns, but they had the major merit of making both Lukács and his concept part of contemporary theoretical discourse. Honneth's book, in particular, helped to spur the publication of two edited volumes (one by Bewes and Timothy Hall, the other by Michael J. Thompson) on Lukács's work that included essays by both seasoned and younger Lukács interpreters. It had become evident that a return to the texts themselves was in order.

The last five years has witnessed the publication of four major studies of Lukács's work. János Kelemen's collection of essays, *The Rationalism of Georg Lukács*, is particularly valuable for its discussion of less prominent currents in Lukács's thought. The recent work of Andrew Feenberg, Richard Westerman, and Konstantinos Kavoulakos stand out for their specific contributions to our understanding of reification. These three works have in common some of the most original and insightful discussions of the origins of Lukács's theory of reification we have seen in decades (in this volume, Christian Lotz's piece contributes to this agenda). Less intellectual histories, however, their historical forays serve as correctives to the work of Lukács's critics, both sympathetic and unsympathetic, to demonstrate the contemporary relevance of Lukács's concept of reification on Lukács's terms. The major hurdle for such an enterprise is overcoming the commonplace charge that, for all his aspirations to revolutionary social transformation, Lukács's theory is ultimately an idealist one. And, if Lukács's theory is indeed idealist, then it is one too rife with contradictions to earn a place in the pantheon of the great idealist philosophers, Kant, Fichte, and Hegel.

A major influence on Westerman and Kavoulakos, Feenberg's *The Philosophy of Praxis* is a reworking of his important early study, *Lukács, Marx, and the Sources of Critical Theory*. Countering the criticism that Lukács's theory lapses back into the very idealism it sought to escape, Feenberg interprets Lukács as one of the most significant thinkers of a tradition of praxis-oriented philosophy. "Idealism," Feenberg explains, "attempted to resolve contradictions between subject and object, value and fact, freedom and necessity, life and thought. The idealist resolution of these 'antinomies' took the form of a speculative play with concepts. Philosophy of praxis demands a real resolution

---

9 Axel Honneth, *Reification: A New Look at an Old Idea*, ed. Martin Jay (Oxford: Oxford University Press, 2008), 63–64.

through the practical transformation of the social basis of the antinomies."[10] Crucially, Feenberg reestablishes the connection between philosophy and practical political change. From such a standpoint, the problem of reification, with its preoccupation with consciousness, necessitates practical resolution through social and political transformation.

Westerman's *Lukács's Phenomenology of Capitalism* similarly responds to critics who charge that Lukács's theory is a thinly veiled idealism by tracing the origins of Lukács's argument in *History and Class Consciousness* to drafts of an unfinished work on aesthetics that relied on Edmund Husserl's phenomenology and its emphasis on intentionality. Westerman argues "that by incorporating intentionality into social practices themselves, Lukács includes subjectivity as a determinative moment within objective structures: it is integral to social practices that they include this dimension of meaning. The subject is in turn defined as part of the objectively meaningful practices it partakes in."[11] This has direct bearing on reification insofar as "Reification is not a misrepresentation; it is the actual existence of objects in a society governed by the commodity structure. Such meanings are embodied in intentional practices that determine objects by the way we are oriented towards them."[12] Like Feenberg, Westerman stresses Lukács's place as a philosopher of praxis rather than as the vulgar idealist who imagines a messianic proletariat standing outside of history. Yet, Westerman arrives at this conclusion by tracing a different intellectual inheritance within Lukács's thought.

Following a different path from Westerman, Kavoulakos's *Georg Lukács's Philosophy of Praxis* focuses on the neo-Kantian roots of Lukács's thought. Even as Lukács turned to dialectics to overcome the antinomies of bourgeois thought, Kavoulakos emphasizes the place of neo-Kantianism in setting up the problem: "Lukács attempted to find a way to overcome the so-called antinomies of bourgeois thought through his shift to the dialectical mediation of subject and object in history. However, he conceptualized this mediation in terms of the primacy of the content over the form, as well as the primacy of praxis over theory."[13] By revisiting Lukács's path from neo-Kantianism to Marxism, Kavoulakos presents an interpretation of Lukács that cannot fall back on an idealist metaphysics. As Kavoulakos argues, "From Lukács's viewpoint, the goal

---

10   Andrew Feenberg, *The Philosophy of Praxis: Marx, Lukács, and the Frankfurt School* (New York: Verso Books, 2014), 204.
11   Richard Westerman, *Lukács's Phenomenology of Capitalism: Reification Revalued* (Cham, Switzerland: Palgrave Macmillan, 2019), 18.
12   Ibid., 277.
13   Konstantinos Kavoulakos, *Georg Lukács's Philosophy of Praxis: From Neo-Kantianism to Marxism* (London: Bloomsbury Academic, 2018), 220.

of emancipatory praxis could never be the establishment of a metaphysical realm of the achieved identity of subject and object – an idea from which he explicitly distanced himself – but on the one hand breaking their false identity and, on the other hand, consciously-practically liquidizing their relation."[14]

These summaries hardly do justice to highly sophisticated works of Lukács's scholarship, but they do evidence a renewed enterprise to retrieve Lukács's work after decades of calcified dismissals. Such innovative scholarship helps to explain why the proponents of a Lukács revival are not only drawn to the reconsideration of Lukács because his ideas remain so compelling, but because there are sound reasons to question whether the critics had correctly characterized Lukács and his work. Naturally, this also begs the question as to whether or not Lukács was right to ultimately abandon his theory. Lukács's defenders are left to defend the theory in spite of the author's disavowals.

It is important to keep in mind that what we now know as the critical theory that predominates in the academy has largely been able to take its current form through the dismissal of Lukács. Despite Honneth's appropriation of reification, it is one that takes the criticisms of Lukács as a settled matter and, thus, contends that the concept can only be recovered through a fundamental reconceptualization. Yet, even this critical theory that is willing to re-admit Lukács back into its canon on the condition that he be severely reconstructed is a critical theory that Michael J. Thompson has provocatively charged with domesticating and de-radicalizing the original project.[15]

Neither Thompson's criticisms of contemporary critical theory nor those of other critical theorists who remain attuned to Lukács's thought are motivated by some nostalgia for Lukács. On the contrary, it is because Lukács's critique of capitalism and its wider implications for understanding the persistence of forms of oppression and exploitation remains a vital resource. There is, quite simply, no philosophical substitute for him. He comes with baggage and it is the task of his defenders to determine what is living and dead in his thought. Yet, on the whole, the problems that Lukács was among the first to identify have only become more pronounced.

Recent years have displayed a growing awareness of capitalism's consequences. But there is good reason to question whether or not there can be a revitalized and analytically potent critique of capitalism without the assistance of Lukács's thought. Lukács's thought provided a refreshing criticism of Marxist orthodoxies. By pointing to the tendency of capitalism to reification,

---

14 Ibid., 221.
15 Michael J. Thompson, *The Domestication of Critical Theory* (London: Rowman and Littlefield International, 2016).

he provided a philosophical explanation with political relevance for the difficulties confronted by emancipatory efforts. A radical politics that does not heed Lukács insights might very well allow for struggles against capitalism to play out more as farce than tragedy. Accepting Lukács's discomfiting conclusions, especially the extent to which reification threatens notions of agency, will certainly disturb simplistic assumptions about what counts as resistance, particularly in the context of a left that too readily identifies every act as a form of resistance. There is all the more reason for a left willing to engage in self-reflection to confront the problem of reification.

PART 1

Interpreting Reification: the Meaning and Origins of a Concept

∴

CHAPTER 1

Lukács's Theory of Reification: an Introduction

Andrew Feenberg

Lukács's theory of reification is central to his 1923 book *History and Class Consciousness*.[1] That classic work of Marxist philosophy had a great influence on the Frankfurt school. There are frequent references to reification in Lukács's sense in Adorno, Horkheimer and Marcuse.[2] Although many aspects of Lukács's early work are no longer applicable, the concept of reification is relevant to struggles around technical and bureaucratic systems today, such as environmental struggles or struggles over medical practices. It is also useful for thinking about the meaning of the fall of Soviet style socialism.

According to Lukács reification means taking social relations for things. This definition follows from the etymology of the word: *res* is the Latin word for thing, hence thing-ification. The original German, *Verdinglichung*, incorporates the ordinary German word for "thing," "*Ding*." The concept is critical. An institution, for example, a university, appears as a solid and substantial thing like a natural object but in reality it is a complex of social relations. Breaking with the illusory thinghood of social institutions and recovering their contingency is called "dereification."

Although reification is often interpreted as a theory of ideology, it is also a theory of social practice and a social ontology. Implied in the contrast between social relations and things is a deeper argument concerning the nature of action, or practice as Lukács calls it. Reification and dereification describe different types of practice, individual technical practices aimed at adaptation, survival, and success, and collective transforming practices with the potential for establishing a solidary socialist society. Reification provides structure through determining a specific type of practice that stabilizes and reproduces the institutions, while dereification involves agency, another type of practice with the

1 This chapter is based on a talk given at the 2017 Budapest conference on The Legacy of Georg Lukács. For more on Lukács's early Marxism, see Andrew Feenberg, *The Philosophy of Praxis: Marx, Lukács and the Frankfurt School* (London: Verso, 2015), and Kontantinos Kavoulakos, *Georg Lukács's Philosophy of Praxis: From Neo-Kantianism to Marxism* (London: Bloomsbury, 2018).
2 For a discussion, see Andrew Feenberg, "Why Students of the Frankfurt School Will Have to Read Lukács" in *The Palgrave Handbook of Critical Theory*, ed. Michael J. Thompson (New York: Palgrave Macmillan, 2017).

power not only to penetrate the reified appearances but to transform the structures they establish.

I will illustrate this correlation of reification and dereification with a story about the medieval Japanese sword maker, Masamune, reputed to make the sharpest blades. This account is from Suzuki.

> Masamune flourished in the latter part of the Kamakura era, and his works are uniformly prized by all the sword connoisseurs for their excellent qualities. As far as the edge of the blade is concerned, Masamune may not exceed Muramasa, one of his ablest his disciples, but Masamune is said to have something morally inspiring that comes from his personality. The legend goes thus: when someone was trying to test the sharpness of a Muramasa, he placed it in the current of water and watched how it acted against the dead leaves flowing downstream. He saw that every leaf that met the blade was cut in twain. He then placed a Masamune, and he was surprised to find that the leaves avoided the blade. The Masamune was not bent on killing, it was more than a cutting implement, whereas the Muramasa could not go beyond cutting, there was nothing divinely inspiring in it. The Muramasa is terrible, the Masamune is humane. One is despotic and imperialistic, the other is superhuman, if we may use this form of expression.[3]

This charming story illustrates the difference between reifying and dereifying practice. The sword of the disciple obeys the law of war under which the techniques of killing stand. Technical practice is based on respect for the law of the object. The technical actor learns the law and applies it in his or her practice. In a social context the technical actor thereby reproduces the law under which the practice stands. The sword of the master, Masamune, acts on the law of war itself rather than simply acting under its horizon. The Masamune illustrates action on the logic of action rather than technical action in conformity with that logic.

The laws of nature are not changed by Masamune's sword, but it can change the human world in which the laws regulating behavior are contingent on human action. For example, the laws of the capitalist economy presuppose individual subjects acting in their personal self-interest through buying and selling. Absent any of these conditions, capitalism dissolves. But this is precisely

---

3 D.T. Suzuki, *Zen and Japanese Culture* (Princeton: Princeton/Bollingen, 1959), 91–92.

what class consciousness achieves. By breaking down the barriers between individuals and moving them to challenge the economic laws, class consciousness effects change in those laws themselves.

As this account shows, reification is a form of social appearance, a particular way in which things give themselves to consciousness in capitalist society. Appearances in this sense are not merely in the mind. Marx's critique of political economy explains the ontological status of appearances. According to Marx capitalism is generalized commodity production. He treats the phenomenon of the commodity as a puzzle to be unraveled in the early chapters of *Capital*. He writes, "a commodity is therefore a mysterious thing, simply because in it the social character of men's labor appears to them as an objective character stamped upon the product of that labor, because the relation of the producers to the sum total of their labor is presented to them as a social relation, existing not between themselves but between the products of their labor."[4]

Marx calls this the "fetishism" of commodities because commodities appear to be alive with a will and power of their own. The world of commodities is an autonomous realm which moves according to its own laws. This is unprecedented in human history. Until the capitalist era goods were primarily produced for use. But capitalism is a system in which the use value of goods is subordinated to their exchange value. Everything acquires a price under capitalism, and price, a mere number, governs design decisions, moves things from place to place, and determines whether they exist at all. The decision about what to produce, how much to produce, where and how to produce it, is made in function of salability on the market rather than human need. And since exchange value is expressed as a quantity, the social world is for the first time quantified. What is real under capitalism in the sense of having significant effects on the world, are quantities not qualities. Lukács's concept of reification generalizes this critique of the quantification of social reality from the market to society at large.

This generalization gains another dimension from Marx's critique of capitalist technology. In *Capital*, Marx discusses the relation of the worker to the machine in considerable detail. Under capitalism technical innovation aims to deskill labor and to reduce the worker to a mechanical part of the production system. Craft workers are gradually replaced by machines tended by unskilled women and children. The worker is now external to the process of production rather than its center and organizer. The machine has its own logic, its own law

---

4   Karl Marx, *Capital*, Vol. 1, trans. E. Aveling (New York: Modern Library, 1906), 83.

of motion and the worker simply maintains or services it. The worker becomes an external manipulator of a self-acting mechanism. The relation to the machine parallels and confirms the relation to the economy. In both cases action is reduced to individual technical manipulation of a world with its own unchangeable laws. As the story of the two swords shows, this describes the general form of technical action: the actor accepts the law of the object and uses it to advantage.

In his early work Marx had described this relationship to the world with the concept of alienation. The *Economic-Philosophical Manuscripts* of 1844 in which this concept is developed were not published until nearly 10 years after *History and Class Consciousness*. But Lukács reconstructed the essential idea from other references in Marx's writings. By alienation Marx means that the common creation of the working class becomes a dominating power over its creators. Workers build the very system that dominates them. Dead labor, the accumulated product of past work, dominates living labor. Revolution is the re-appropriation of the alienated world by and for life.

Lukács's concept of reification recapitulates this idea of alienation with the proviso that the domination takes the form of rational institutions and impersonal laws. What Lukács adds to this original Marxian notion is the idea that the appearance of the fetishized economy resembles nature, as science understands it. Workers do not simply build the machines and institutions that dominate them, but in so doing constitute them in the forms of reified rationality as subject, like nature, to individual technical control. Reification is a type of alienation characteristic of a "rational" society.

This interpretation of Marxism situates Lukács's concept of reification in the context of the discussion of science and technology in German thought at the end of the 19th and the beginning of the 20th century. This was a time of rapid industrial development accompanied by the rise of scientistic ideology. In reaction philosophers and social theorists tried to save something human from the technological flood. This was the atmosphere in which German thinkers developed an elaborate theory of the difference between the humanities and natural science, two different ways of understanding the world. They distinguished the fields by their method.

The philosopher Dilthey, for example, distinguished between the interpretive methods suitable to social and cultural artifacts and the explanatory methods of the natural sciences. In the one domain, meaning prevails, in the other, causality. This distinction was politicized by certain right-wing thinkers. To the epistemological difference between the literary and artistic domain and nature corresponded the social distinction between culture and civilization. According to these conservatives, Germany was a culture nation, dedicated to art and beauty, while England and France were characterized by a materialistic civilization interested only in machines and money.[5]

The great German sociologist Max Weber elaborated a more theoretically interesting version of the distinction with his concept of rationalization, the growing significance of calculation and control in the administration of modern society. Weber contrasted this with the pre-modern reliance on custom and tradition. Rationalization brought together features of both the market economy and bureaucratic administration. Technology appears as an obvious corollary for Lukács.

Lukács was the first to appropriate the methodological distinction between the forms of understanding for the left. This was explicit in his early critique of capitalism, formulated in cultural terms. But in this period cultural critique was so closely tied to right-wing politics that he soon abandoned the reference to culture and replaced it with categories drawn from contemporary neo-Kantianism and Marxist theory. Today "culture" no longer has the conservative associations that troubled Lukács. In the modern anthropological sense, reification is a cultural pattern based on the generalization of scientific-technical rationality to society as a whole. Reification is the encroachment on society of an attitude toward the world appropriate to nature. Lukács writes, "what is important is to recognize clearly that all human relations assume increasingly the form of objectivity of the abstract elements of the conceptual systems of the natural sciences and of the abstract substrata of the laws of nature. And also, the subject of this action likewise assumes increasingly the attitude of the pure observer of these artificially abstract experiences, the attitude of the experimenter."[6]

With the theory of reification Lukács joined the critique of science and technology to the Marxist critique of capitalism. Weberian rationalization was the bridge between the two aspects of his theory. This background shows that Lukács's theory of reification is not, as some critics argue, an attack on thinghood as such, which would be silly. He is not even criticizing the existence of stable social objects which resemble the things of nature insofar as they endure through change. Rather, what concerns him is the lawful form of institutions and especially of markets. Individual subjects relate to these institutions technically just as they would to natural objects. It is the specific form of thinghood that is in question, a form of thinghood that resembles nature. Not only

---

5 Jeffrey Herf, *Reactionary Modernism: Technology, Culture, and Politics in Weimar and the Third Reich* (Cambridge: Cambridge University Press, 1984).
6 Georg Lukács, *History and Class Consciousness*, trans. Rodney Livingstone (Cambridge: The MIT Press, 1971), 131.

does the society become a kind of second nature, but the individuals begin to relate to it in a purely technical manner, with the detachment and disinterest of a scientist engaged in an experiment.

I want to now dig a bit deeper into Lukács's concept of form. Lukács calls the appearance of capitalist society a *"Gegenstandlichkeitsform,"* a "form of objectivity." He writes, "The structure of commodity relations can be made to yield a model of all forms of objectivity of bourgeois society and all the corresponding forms of subjectivity."[7] The concept of form of objectivity refers to the way in which objects present themselves to a specific look. For example a physicist looks at the world in his or her work as matter in motion. That is the type of object-ness with which physicists are concerned. The physicist has to leave out a lot of other aspects of nature in order to focus on the interesting one. This way of constructing objects of concern is not confined to physicists, but rather characterizes all perception. We all look at objects from a certain angle that corresponds to the type of object they are for us.

This way of thinking about perception belongs to Kantian philosophy, which was very influential at the time Lukács was writing. According to Kant we impose a form on the raw materials of experience, which in themselves lack order and meaning. Our perception and understanding of objects depends on a priori forms and categories of the mind. These a prioris shape a content, namely, the flow of experience. They make sense of what would otherwise be pure chaos. Thinghood, for example, as the distinctive identity and durability of objects, is imposed by the mind on the flux of sensation. Similarly, causality is an a priori category imposed on the succession of events. We always assume that what happens has a cause in the past even when we do not know what it is. Now, thinghood and causality, as forms in this Kantian sense, are definitely not in the world like the contents they form. They are not related practically and materially to their contents. The very idea would seem absurd to Kant. In Kant and his neo-Kantian followers the forms are purely logical. Here is where Lukács innovated.

In the theory of reification, this form-content distinction is transformed into a social distinction. This changes the relation between form and content. Capitalist economic practice is the origin of the a prioris, the meanings, which form social content. The forms are such things as profits and wages. But these are entities within the world and not simply logical a prioris. Now the reified forms are actual social phenomena and not merely a conceptual apparatus of the mind. This has bizarre implications for the life of the worker: wage labor is the form and a life process is the content. That content is the human beings

---

7   Ibid., 83. Translation modified.

whose relations and activities sustain the forms in being. But, Lukács argues, the reified forms fail to fully embrace their human content. This results in crises and class struggle.

> The quantification of objects, their subordination to abstract mental categories makes its appearance in the life of the worker immediately as processes of abstraction of which he is the victim, and which cuts him off from his labor power, forcing him to sell it on the market as a commodity, belonging to him. And by selling this, his only commodity, he integrates himself into a specialized process that has been rationalized and mechanized, a process that he discovers already existing, complete and able to function without him in which he is no more than a cipher reduced to an abstract quantity, a mechanized and rationalized tool.... The quantitative differences in exploitation which appeared to the capitalist in the form of quantitative determinants of the objects of his calculation, must appear to the worker as the decisive, qualitative categories of his whole physical, mental and moral existence.[8]

What Lukács calls the qualitative categories: the physical, mental and moral life of the worker, overflow the quantitative form of wage labor. The gap between form and life is known to the worker if not to the capitalist. It is obvious to the person who actually lives it when, for example, the rate of wages is too low to support a family. This knowledge of the gap between form and content is a kind of self-knowledge. The worker knows that he or she is more than a worker. In this sense the worker is the "self-consciousness of the commodity." Simple existence places the work in an essentially critical relation to the forms of the capitalist economy. This is the basis for class consciousness, the precondition of revolution. Lukács shows that class consciousness is not simply a matter of belief or interest, but rather a tension between form and content, appearance and reality, in the structure of capitalism. Lukács calls this the "unity of theory and practice": the proletariat changes the meaning of its own existence in becoming class consciousness and thereby changes the structure of society itself.

This involves a process of dereification that overcomes the logic of capitalism. Lukács conceives class consciousness as a kind of self consciousness in which the proletariat transcends its own reified form of objectivity. That reified form condemns it to an individualistic, technical relation to social reality, which reproduces the capitalist system. But once it conceives itself outside the

---
8 Ibid., 165–166.

framework of reification as the living human basis of the system in solidarity with other workers, it is capable of transforming the logic of the system. Instead of merely acting on the given laws of the system the class-conscious working class can change those laws.

Dereification makes possible a new system with different social laws from those of capitalism. Under this socialist system goods are produced to fulfill human needs rather than according to market demand. Individuals no longer have to act individually in a technically manipulative manner on an alienated society but can combine to change the social laws under which they live. Lukács thus conceives the Marxist concept of socialist revolution as the shattering of the reified forms of capitalism by their proletarian contents.

Now I can show how Suzuki's story fits the case. This concept of revolution corresponds to Masamune's sword. It is not technical action under the horizon of the established laws but action on the laws themselves. Dereification is thus a different kind of action from the instrumental action determined by capitalism. It implies a different subject of action, a collective subject oriented toward human needs rather than an individual subjects in pursuit of profit and personal advantage.

Lukács's theory of reification has applications even today, long after the decline of the proletarian revolutionary movement that inspired him. Certainly, reification has not gone away. We are if anything ruled even more imperiously by capitalist logic than before. The notion that there is no alternative to capitalism in its present form and the correlated notion that all we can do is adapt to the system reflects the continuing reification of the society.

In Marx's time and even when Lukács wrote most technology was found in factories. Workers were assembled in large masses by the technologies they used. They could therefore resist capitalism collectively as they became class conscious. Since 1923 things have changed. Marcuse's *One-Dimensional Man* argued that advanced capitalism was a system based on technological rationality, another way of expressing the idea of scientific-technical rationality achieving cultural generality. But his target was not simply capitalist economic relations but the technocratic order which supports those relations. "When technics becomes the universal form of material production, it circumscribes an entire culture; it projects a historical totality – a world."[9] Technology is no longer to be found mainly in a single institution, the factory, but is now involved in every aspect of social life. The generalization of technical mediation has extended reification well beyond its earlier economic limits. Reified

---

9   Herbert Marcuse, *One-Dimensional Man* (Boston: Beacon Press, 1964), 154.

technical disciplines of all sorts reflect and determine every aspect of life, and not just the economy.[10]

The economic logic of capitalism is not the only reified form against which people protest. We live in a technologized world and so even though the proletarian revolutionary movement has declined, other movements have arisen which resemble it. In these new movements too masses are assembled by technology in reified forms. The designs of technology and administrative systems have similar effects and provoke resistances. These movements around technical issues cannot replace the proletarian movements of the past, but they are of fundamental importance in any society based on modern technology.

Dereification continues although it is no longer confined to traditional class struggle in the factory. The environmental movement is an example of resistance to reification. Environmentalists are told that their demands contradict the requirements of a prosperous industrial society, the so-called "imperatives" of technology and economics. The demystification of this proposition requires the dereification of institutions and technologies, the demonstration that they are human products that can be changed.

Technological design is often the reified form against which people struggle. This is more difficult for the users and victims of technology to understand today than the failure of the economic forms in the life of a factory, but the potential is there. For example, awareness of pollution can reveal a mismatch between technological form – the design of polluting technology – and human life processes. The members of the community are all connected by the polluting technology even if they are unaware of that fact. When the consequences become known, the community can become self-conscious in Lukács's sense. This is the basis of local environmental protests such as the one at Love Canal, which launched the anti-toxics movement in the U.S. The established form cracks as its limits are revealed. Pollution can activate a latent collective in the affected community.

Other examples can be found in the field of medicine, for example, the women's health movement, or the movement of AIDS patients to obtain access to experimental drugs in the early stages of the struggle with the disease. The feminist movement shows the force of self-consciousness in transforming apparently rigid, permanent social relations. The "standpoint epistemology" that is associated with feminism traces its roots back to Lukács.[11] Today the Internet

---

10   See Andrew Feenberg, *Technosystem: The Social Life of Reason* (Cambridge: Harvard University Press, 2017).
11   Nancy Hartsock, "The Feminist Standpoint: Developing the Ground for a Specifically Feminist Historical Materialism" in *Discovering Reality: Feminist Perspectives on*

is the object of struggle over network neutrality. The theory of reification is thus not exhausted.

Examples like these show the emergence of what Foucault called subjugated knowledges among ordinary people subjected to various forms of technological alienation. Just as workers in the original Marxist schema were said to gain insight into the limitations of capitalism from their subordinate vantage point, so do ordinary people engaged as users or victims of technology today. As Fred Jameson writes, "We need to make an inventory of the variable structures of constraint lived by the various marginal, oppressed, or dominated groups – the so-called new social movements fully as much as the working class – with this difference that each form of privation is acknowledged as producing its own specific epistemology, its own specific view from below, and its own specific and distinctive truth claim."[12]

Lukács failed to elaborate some of the most important implications of the theory of reification. These implications concern the nature of socialism conceived as "human control of history." Where human control is interpreted as it was in the Soviet Union in terms of state planning by experts, the outcome is the substitution of reification through bureaucracy for reification through the market.

Soviet socialism is usually criticized with normative arguments about democracy that Marx himself rejected as historically ungrounded. But how can we justify the preference for a bottom up socialism without such arguments? The theory of reification helps to understand the failure of technocratic versions of socialism that rely on political controls and economic planning rather than democracy. Missing from the technocratic arguments against democratization is understanding of the world-shaping character of technical decisions for those who must live inside the technical systems, whether they be patients, workers, victims of pollution, or Internet users. Once that is recognized, it is obvious that more than technique is involved, that technical decisions are also social decisions and so should be subject to review by those whose lives they affect.

In recognition of this fact, some radical Marxists advocate a politics of direct democracy, but it is difficult to see how it can sustain a modern society. Modern life requires far more stability and expertise at the helm than a direct democracy can supply. Industry requires extensive delegation of authority to

---

Epistemology, Metaphysics, Methodology and Philosophy of Science, eds. Sandra Harding and Merrill B. Hintikka (Dordrecht: Reidel, 1983), 283–310,

[12] Frederic Jameson, "History and Class Consciousness as an 'Unfinished Project.'" *Rethinking Marxism* 1, No. 1 (1988): 71.

experts qualified through their knowledge of technical disciplines. There is no way around this requirement which means that the imposition of forms on the content of the life process is an inescapable feature of modern society.

There is thus something more basic than economic and political institutions and this is the mode of action favored or excluded by the system. Capitalism and Soviet style socialism depend on the reification of the society. They individualize the members of society and force them into a manipulative relation to the system. The dereification of the society would open other possibilities.

Lukács did not explore those possibilities consistently or in detail. Like most Marxists, he placed too much emphasis on the ability of the revolution itself to transform society. He occasionally remarks on the difficulties ahead, noting that reification will not simply disappear with the abolition of capitalism, but that it will persist in many areas a social life long after the revolution. But he does not offer a clear and convincing account of the difference between the relation of reification and dereification under socialism and capitalism.

His argument hints at the institutionalization of democratic delegation and intervention wherever tensions between the forms and contents arise. This would not abolish reification but it would remove the armoring that protects it from popular initiatives under capitalism and bureaucratic socialism. This suggests far more continuity between capitalism and socialism than Marxists usually concede, but it also answers the most common objections to the idea of radical transformation.

A third alternative is possible, which is neither capitalism nor Soviet style socialism. This alternative addresses the persistence of both reification and resistance. State institutions must be much more responsive and responsible to mass participation than they are under capitalism or Soviet style socialism. This alternative version of socialism would not end the principle of representation as direct democracy demands but would extend democratic forms of representation into regions of social life previously ruled by bureaucracy and the economic laws of capitalism.

Experts and administrators responsible to those they serve would make different decisions and gradually reconstitute the technical disciplines they implement to better reflect human needs. This would require not only the "workers councils" favored by democratic socialists, but also openness to many forms of democratic intervention by dissatisfied publics of all sorts. So far this alternative has not had a fair test, but nor has it been disproven by the few experiments in workers' control that have occurred.

Could such a democratized system function effectively in a technologically advanced society? This raises the question of citizen agency in a wide range of technically based institutions currently managed bureaucratically.

The assumption that technical experts possess all the knowledge necessary to operate such institutions comes up periodically against resistances that force revisions in procedures, technical disciplines, and designs. We are increasingly aware that such cases have had a significant impact on medicine and technology in recent years.

Lukács argues that workers are situated in a social position from which they can understand the impact of the economic system on their own lives far better than can the capitalists who think in economic terms. Something comparable goes on today as individuals confront the limitations and harms of the technical systems in which they live. Knowledge from below of those limitations and harms can inform technical work and technical disciplines and improve the fit between the form and content of social life. This is a dialectic of lay and expert, which is already engaged under capitalism although it is still almost always treated as exceptional. It must become normal to open up communication across this gap but that implies a redistribution of the existing power relations and their economic foundations. This is why socialism is still an important democratic concept.

Let me conclude. Lukács's concept of reification gives us a powerful way of thinking about social struggle. His concepts of reification and dereification enable us to understand the different modes of action involved in living under and resisting institutions and technologies. We are constantly between the swords of Masamune and Muramasa and we need to be clear on the difference between them. But learning to wield Masamune's sword is difficult. We are a long way from such mastery.

CHAPTER 2

Categorial Forms as Intelligibility of Social Objects: Reification and Objectivity in Lukács

Christian Lotz

1   Introduction: Categorial Forms

Although it is well known that Lukács's emergence as an important philosopher for the European Marxist tradition was only possible because of his neo-Kantian background, with notable exceptions, not many scholars have paid much attention to this background of Lukács's thought.[1] The myth that Lukács made a sudden radical turn away from cultural philosophy towards Marx and Hegel in 1918 was taken for granted, although even in the central essay on reification, the influence of Weber and Simmel is apparent. Though Lukács seems to make a turn towards Hegel in his speculations on the "subject-object" in history, the Fichtean undertones of the claim that the proletariat unites both knowledge and being of history are overwhelming. Moreover, these Fichtean tendencies point back to Lukács's interests in ethics. In addition, many scholars focus exclusively on the reification essay alone, without connecting the essay to the other essays collected in *History and Class Consciousness*, and to the other writings from the previous period of Lukács's thought. In particular, as

---

1   Exceptions are Andrew Feenberg, *Heidegger and Marcuse: The Catastrophe and Redemption of History* (New York: Routledge, 2004), Chapter 3; Andrew Feenberg, *The Philosophy Of Praxis: Marx, Lukács And The Frankfurt School* (London: Verso, 2014), Chapter 4; Konstantinos Kouvelakos, *Ästhetizistische Kulturkritik und ethische Utopie. Georg Lukács's neukantianisches Frühwerk* (Berlin: De Gruyter, 2014); Jürgen Habermas, *Theorie des kommunikativen Handelns*, Erster Band (Frankfurt/M.: Suhrkamp, 1988), pp. 474–488. Habermas clearly acknowledges Lukács's debt to Neo-Kantianism and, as a rare exception, he focuses on the concept of *Gegenständlichkeitsform*; however, he criticizes Lukács for remaining tied to the concept of instrumental rationality, an epistemological position and a theory of society that is structured by the subject-object schema. Instead, Habermas works out a new concept of communicative rationality. Though I cannot deal with Habermas's critique of Lukács in this paper, I agree with Thompson that "from a Lukácsian perspective, Habermas's move towards communicative rationality is insufficient for such a task because it does nothing to deal with the problem of constitution." (Michael J. Thompson, "Ontology and Totality: Reconstructing Lukcas' Concept of Critical Theory," in Michael J. Thompson, ed., *Georg Lukács Reconsidered*, (London: Continuum, 2011), p. 237).

I will indicate in this essay, Lukács's understanding of categories, as introduced in the important essay *What is Orthodox Marxism?*, provides a fruitful perspective for a proper philosophical understanding of the concept of reification, especially since it can provide us, beyond Lukács, with a transcendental and phenomenological conception of social reality. Lukács himself never gave up his early concept of categories. Even in one of his last interviews he points to the central importance of his concept of categories as a concept central for understanding being. I will come back to this point.

Before we go into more details of Lukács's conception of social objects and social reality, we would do well to recall that the intellectual situation in Germany at the beginning of the 20th century was characterized mainly by schools that came out of Kantianism, but tried to move away from his epistemology, such as neo-Kantianism, life philosophy, hermeneutics, and phenomenology. The emerging non-dogmatic Marxism (initiated by Korsch and Lukács) and Frankfurt School critical theory (such as Horkheimer) tried to develop theories though which epistemological and ontological questions can be grounded in social philosophy. All of these attempts to move away from Kant, however, were characterized by a deep suspicion and skepticism about the metaphysical underpinnings of Hegel's thought as it is presented in the *Science of Logic,* as well as about his system, as it is presented in the *Encyclopedia* (which Hegel, leaving aside the early *Phenomenology of Spirit*, later in his life took to be the true introduction to his philosophy). This skepticism regarding absolute idealism and a metaphysics of thought and being, however, drove all of these schools back to struggling with and further developing Kantianism, the philosophical starting point of which presented itself as the only true alternative to Hegel's absolute metaphysics. Accordingly, the intellectual mindset was somewhere located between Kant and Hegel, insofar as most philosophers denied both the subjectivist position of Kant as well as the objectivist position of Hegel. What was needed, then, was a theory that could function as a mediator between a subjectivist conception of knowledge and reality that was localized in human reason alone (as in Kant) and an objectivist conception of knowledge and reality that was localized in some kind of absolute being (as in Hegel).[2]

---

2 Andrew Feenberg offers a clarification: "Lukács calls this mode of perception/structure a 'form of objectivity' to get away from any subjectivist notion of mere illusion. Capitalism has a reified form of objectivity which is perceived and acted upon in a reified disposition, closing the circle of social construction" (Andrew Feenberg, "Reification and its Critics," in Thompson, *Georg Lukács Reconsidered*, p. 107).

Given this overall picture, I propose that we should read Lukács through such a lens. For what he tries to develop is a social philosophy that moves towards a new understanding of social being in which epistemological and ontological questions come together and are synthesized. This synthesis of anti-subjectivism and anti-objectivism in Lukács is mediated trough two aspects, namely, on the one hand, through a strong "methodological" take on Marx's concept of categories as Marx outlined it in the introduction to the *Grundrisse* (and to which Lukács always refers when it comes to reflections about fundamental social questions) and, on the other hand, through a transformation of Lask's concept of categories as Lask developed it in his work *The Logic of Philosophy*. One commentator nicely summarizes Lask's position as being somewhere between Kant and Hegel:

> Lask[...] opposes Kant's 'purely logical' deduction of the categories, because they are after all 'not logical through and through ... but arise from alogical material' and so find their order in a material logic; 'we can determine their place only by way of a detour across this matter, persistently looking at it and regarding its stufflike nature' (11, 62f). Also, contrary to Hegel's panlogism, the individual forms are not intertwined by reciprocal logical relations. They stand before us in a reciprocal heterogeneity and irreducible multiplicity. The pure forms in which we stand at most give us the inner light by which to regard their matter, since it is also being reflected from the impenetrable surface of matter's brute facticity. In our encounter with this interface of facticity, we can only accept its alogical order of being and resign ourselves to the limits of reason.[3]

In what follows I will outline a few signposts for such a (Laskian) reading of Lukács between Kant and Hegel that help us understand the concept of reification as the central concept for a theory of social reality and social objects as objects that can be neither reduced to subjective nor to objective dimensions alone and which push us towards an understanding of history that is neither historicist nor essentialist. It is important to note, however, that despite the

---

[3] Theodore Kisiel, "Why Students of Heidegger will have to read Emil Lask," *Man and World* 28 (1995), p. 210. For a superb reading and interpretation of the relation between Lask and Heidegger that opened up the entire intellectual field as well as my own reading of Lukács, see Steven Galt Crowell, *Husserl, Heidegger, and the Space of Meaning. Paths toward Transcendental Phenomenology* (Evanston: Northwestern University Press, 2001), and Steven Galt Crowell, "Emil Lask: Aletheiology as Ontology," *Kant Studien* 87 (1996), pp. 69–88.

rejection of Kant's subjectivism, this understanding is transcendental.[4] This transcendental viewpoint can be defined in the following way: what a social object *is*, is determined by what makes it possible as this or that kind of object; i.e., as its social form or its "being." This social form, however, is neither directly derived from some inner structure of reason; instead, it is itself something that we can only find "at" or "on" the objects and in their relation to us, which, in turn, transforms the classical Kantian question of the "condition of the possibility of 'x'" into a phenomenological and genetic question, insofar as categories are the condition of the possibility of experiencing (social) objects, but they no longer can be generated and "applied" to reality through human reason alone. Instead, they are *historical*. Put differently, the form of objects is found

---

[4] I would like to focus on this methodological conception of history, since Lukács's concept of history remains problematic in the light of contemporary (post-colonial) critiques of progress and history as a unified "super concept" in the sense of "human history" (Erich Hahn, *Lukács und der orthodoxe Marxismus. Eine Sudie zu 'Geschichte und Klassenbewusstsein* (Berlin: Aurora Verlag, 2017), p. 121). Lukács clearly has no awareness of his own Euro-Centrism and rarely asks whether he is justified in speaking of one history or "the" history. As Kavoulakos rightly points out, though, the initial motive of Lukács's turn to Marxism is not a somewhat metaphysically distorted concept of history; rather, it is the "*experience of the crisis* of modern culture and society" (Konstantinos Kavoulakos, "Back to History? Reinterpreting Lukács's Early Work in the Light of the Antonomies of Contemporary Critical Theory," in Thompson, *Georg Lukács Reconsidered*, p. 159); for this, also see Hahn, "Lukács und der orthodoxe Marxismus," p. 98, 104, 118. Kavoulakos argues that Lukács's concept of history is based on "the adoption of a radically presentist perspective" (Kavoulakos, "Back top History," p. 160). We might add that this "presentist perspective" is unfortunately lacking in contemporary critical theory, such as Honneth and even Habermas. For example, the ecological devastation, the looming total control of individual behavior by state power and bio-industries, the global dynamics of capital, the establishment of new walls, the return of the nuclear threat, the re-emergence of European nationalisms, and the emergence of a totally irresponsible managerial class that runs the world together with the most irrational leaders ranging from Berlusconi, Le Pen, to Trump, never comes up in their work. As a consequence, on some level, this perspective remains a-historical and society is no longer seen as changeable. Against this, Kavoulakos argues the following: "In reality, the philosophical problem that Lukács sought to address concerns the way in which we could conceive of a nonmechanistic emergence of a qualitatively new form of consciousness and a corresponding social practice as the concrete embodiment of effective human freedom. On his view, this prospect requires an irreducible manifestation of the authentic objective structure" (ibid., p. 162). As Kavoulakos further points out against Habermas's charge that Lukács's falls back onto a metaphysical conception of history, Lukács did not hold that the change will be an immediate rupture; instead, Lukács is aware that change is "a long process of rupturing a repeated ossification of social reality" (ibid., p. 82). In addition, for an elegant reconstruction of the critiques of Lukács's concept of reification by Adorno, Habermas, and Honneth, see Konstatinos Kavoulakos, "Lukács's Theory of Reification and the Transition of Critical Theory," in Michael J. Thompson, *The Palgrave Handbook of Critical Theory* (London: Palgrave Macmillan, 2017), especially pp. 80–83.

and needs to be traced back to what Marx calls in the chapter on primitive accumulation its "origin."[5]

The key term that Lukács uses for all of this is *Gegenständlichkeitsform*, which is a concept by means of which both the unity of objects as well as the form of the unity of objects is addressed.[6] The social sphere, now understood via the *Gegenständlichkeitsform* or the "form of objecthood," unites both epistemological and ontological aspects of social reality. Reification is precisely the name for the reflexive category of (capitalist) objecthood as being applied equally to social subject and social reality. As Kouvelakos has it, "the *Gegenständlichkeit*, as the primordial relation between form and material, is the foundation for understanding its correlated subjective position";[7] i.e., the position of the knower is correlative to her position in the social reality. It is important to note that Lukács affirms this point in his *Chvostismus and Dialectic* (1926). He underlines there that the abstract concept of history is overcome by materialist dialectic because it "reveals the concrete, real, historical genesis of the historical structure";[8] i.e., Lukács does not speak of a historical genesis of certain empirical phenomena; instead, he is concerned with the structural and categorial aspect of social reality. Put differently, the essence of history is to be found in the history of categorial forms. Consequently, a social change in the "real material also changes the entire structure [*Struktur der Zusammenhänge*],"[9] since the categorial structure or the social form of the social reality under capitalist conditions defines both how objects *are* and how they are *known*.

---

5 For this, see my interpretation in Christian Lotz, *The Capitalist Schema: Time, Money, and the Culture of Abstraction* (Lanham: Lexington Books, 2014), pp. 96–103.
6 As Andrew Feenberg has remarked, Lukács's relation to Kantianism is obscured by the problematic translation of one of his key words, not only in *History and Class Consciousness*, but also in his later writings (Andrew Feenberg, "Rethinking Reification" in Timothy Hall and Timothy Bewes, eds., *Georg Lukács: The Fundamental Dissonance of Existence: Aesthetics, Politics, Literature* (London: Continuum, 2011), p. 118). Most crucially, the following terms are problematic: "Gegenstand" is often translated as object (what gets lost is that "Gegenstand" means that something stands positioned towards against us); "Gegenständlichkeit" is translated with "objectivity" and "Gegenständlichkeitsform" with "forms of objectivity" (instead, I translate it with "forms of objecthood"); finally, the term "Wechselwirkung" has been translated with "interdetermination" or "reciprocal determination" (I translate it with "mutual determination"). For more on this term see my own attempt in Christian Lotz, "Gegenständlichkeit. From Marx to Lukács and Back Again," in Arnold Darrell and Andreas Michels, eds., *Theory and Practice: Critical Theory and the Thought of Andrew Feenberg* (London: Palgrave Macmillan, 2017), pp. 71–89.
7 Kouvelakos, *Ästhetizistische Kulturkritik und ethische Utopie*, p. 65 (my translation).
8 Georg Lukács, "Chvostimus und Dialektik (1925/26)," Jahrbuch der Internationalen Georg-Lukács-Gesellschaft (1998/1999), p. 133.
9 Ibid.

Accordingly, the problem of how to overcome capitalism *must* be a problem of both knowledge and reality.

This middle path between historicism and naturalism or between constructivism and essentialism is based on what Lukács calls a "methodological" understanding of Marx, insofar as Marx provides us with exactly such an outlook. For, on the one hand, the categorial system of commodity form, money, capital, interest, etc. is not something that can, as a form, change every day, but, on the other hand, it can only be understood if we interpret these categories as historical categories whose content can be traced back to an emerging historical field (origin). Consequently, Marx thinks of the structural form of capitalist social reality as laying both beyond historicist relativism and essentialist naturalism. The methodological position, then, implies a position by means of which we are able to argue that despite the categorial form of social reality it is nevertheless historical because the social form is tied to the *real* and historical being of social objects. Consequently, revolutionizing social reality must mean to revolutionize the categorial form of this reality. Accordingly, for Lukács history is not a process in which a multiverse of social mediations are, to use a Sartrean term, totalized; instead, he has an overall transcendental idea of totality, insofar as the totality is not constituted by the relational network of social objects or social actions.[10] Rather, social totality is constituted by the relational network of the *categories* united under one form.[11] As we know, this form is

---

10   Menninghaus has charged Lukács with a wrongheaded universalization of the concept of reification. As he argues, Lukács concept of reification refers to the contents and not to its form; Lukács confuses the forms of objectivity with the objects themselves (Winfried Menninghaus, "Kant, Hegel und Marx in Lukács's Theorie der verdinglichung. Destruktion eines neomarxistischen 'Klassikers,'" in Norbert W. Bolz and Wolfgang Hübener, eds., *Spiegel und Gleichnis. Festschrift für Jacob Taubes* (Würzburg: Königshausen und Neumann, 1983), p. 321). I do not think that Menninghaus' charge is convincing, since a neo-Kantian reading of the concept of *Gegenständlichkeitsform*, as I argue in this paper, shows that with this concept of reification, Lukács refers to the *unity* of form and matter.

11   Though the influence of Simmel and Weber is visible everywhere in *History and Class Consciousness*, the decisive difference between Lukács and them (including contemporary critical theory) is that Lukács assumes that all social systems and social "spheres" follow the same underlying rationality or social form (which is reification). For this, see Mariana Teixeira and Arthur Bueno, "Spectres of reification: Weber and Simmel on History and Class Consciousness," *Journal of Classical Sociology* 17, 2 (2017), pp. 101–115. Additionally, Rüdiger Dannemann argues that reification is the negative expression of a totality that did not exist before capitalism. In this sense, totality is itself a result of the historical process. This thesis deserves more discussion, since, at least to some extent, it clashes with my interpretation of totality as a *categorial* concept and as a concept for the closure of categorial systems; for this, see Rüdiger Dannemann, *Georg Lukács. Eine Einführung* (Wiesbaden: Junius Verlag, 2005), p. 61.

referred to as "reification" and it seems to me that many commentators overlook this quasi-Kantian dimension in Lukács's thought and therefore tend to misconstrue the original motives and problems in critical theory to which, I submit, we need to return if we want to overcome the contemporary deadlock in critical theory of the Frankfurt School tradition.[12]

2   History as History of Structural Forms

In order to clarify the transcendental horizon of Lukács's understanding of social reality and its possible change, in what follows, I reconstruct and clarify the problem of method and categories in Lukács in some detail. Despite its length, I need to quote the following passage in its entirety since it is a crucial passage for Lukács's re-reading of Marx on the basis of his neo-Kantian background. It should be noted that the quote is taken from one of his last interviews, which demonstrates that his theory of the categorial aspect of social reality is central for his entire oeuvre.

> Marx established – and in my estimation, this is the most important part of Marx's theory – that historicality is the fundamental category of social being, and as such of all being [*Sein*]. In the Paris Manuscripts, Marx says that there is only one science, the science of history, and he even adds, 'a non-objective essence is not an essence' [*ist ein Unwesen*]. This is to say, something [*Sache*] without categorial attributes cannot exist. Existence means, therefore, that something exists as a determinate form of objecthood [*Gegenständlichkkeit von bestimmter Form*]; i.e., the determinate form of objecthood makes up the category to which the essence in question belongs. It is this that distinguishes my ontology clearly from earlier philosophies. Traditional philosophy conceived of a system of categories

---

12   For a critique of the "formalist" reductions in contemporary critical theory, see Kavoulakos, "Lukács's Theory of Reification and the Transition of Critical Theory," p. 82; for an application of the concept of reification to contemporary issues, see Rüdiger Dannemann, "Das unabgeschlossene Projekt der Verdinglichungskritik. Verdinglichung als Leitbegriff der Gegenwartsdiagnose," in Hanno Plass, ed., *Klasse, Geschichte, Bewusstsein. Was bleibt von Georg Lukács's Theorie* (Berlin: Verbrecher Verlag, 2015), pp. 140–145; For a different position and different idea of critical theory as (re-)centered around concepts of political economy, see Werner Bonefeld, *Critical Theory and the Critique of Political Economy: On Subversion and Negative Reason* (London: Bloomsbury Press, 2014), as well as my comments on Bonefeld in Christian Lotz, "Critical Theory and the Critique of Political Economy: On Subversion and Negative Reason," *Radical Philosophy Review*, 18/2, 2015, 337–342.

which included the categories of history along with others. In the Marxist system of categories each thing is furnished from the outset with a specific quality, with a specific thinghood and with a categorial being. A non-objectified essence is not an essence [*Unwesen*]. And in what exists [*innerhalb dieses Etwas*] is the history of the changing categories. Accordingly, the categories are components of objective reality. Nothing can exist which is not in some sense category. In this respect there is an extraordinarily sharp difference between Marxism and earlier world-views. In Marxism the categorial being of a thing constitutes its being, whereas in the old philosophies categorial being was the fundamental category within which the categories of reality were constituted. It is not the case that history unfolds within the system of categories; rather, history is the changing system of categories. The categories are therefore forms of beings [*Seinsformen*]. To the extent that they also become ideas, they become mirror forms of reality; however, primarily they are forms of being. In this way completely different groups of categories with their various contents come into being.[13]

The following three points are important: Lukács argues [1] that the existing reality is constituted socially and, as such, historically, [2] that existing reality has a categorial structure (its form of objecthood or *Gegenständlichkeitsform*), [3] that the categorial structure determines both existing reality and history. Accordingly, the essence of the historical has to be localized in the categorial form of social objects and not, as one might think, on the level of the objects. Put in Heideggerian language, the categorial form belongs to the being of beings.[14] The problem of reading this highly suggestive passage is partly a problem of how to translate Lukács's terms. For example, the translator of the English translation translates "Kategorie" with "concept" and not with "category." Furthermore, he translates "Sein" one time with "beings," and another time

---

13   Georg Lukács, *Autobiographische Texte und Gespräche*, Werke, Band 18 (Münster: Aisthesis Verlag, 2009) p. 196; in English: Georg Lukács, *Record of a Life* (London: Verso, 1983), p. 142; translation altered; one of the very few commentators who points to this passage is Werner Jung, "Zur Ontologie des Alltags. Die späte Philosophie von Georg Lukács," in Werner Jung, ed., *Objektive Möglichkeit: Beiträge zu Georg Lukács's Zur Ontologie des gesellschaftlichen Seins. Frank Benseler zum 65. Geburtstag* (Opladen: Westdeutscher Verlag 1995), p. 260.

14   For this, see Martin Heidegger, *Being and Time*, tr. John Macquarrie and Edward Robinson (Oxford: Basil Blackwell, 1962), p. 6: "Being lies in the fact that something is, and in its Being as it is; in Reality; in presence-at-hand; in subsistence; in validity; in Dasein; in the 'there is.'"

with "existence," which is confusing, given that Lukács uses the term coherently (though in line with Hartmann and not with Heidegger). Categories are determinations of reality *as* reality; accordingly, they are not comparable to concepts in general. What Lukács wants to say is that something cannot exist *as* this or that without its categorial determination, and the historicality of beings is to be sought in their categorial constitution. In fact, true history for Lukács is the history of categorial determinations since the categories make beings accessible. Lukács, then, connects Marx's claim in his early work that something only exists in an objectified manner [*gegenständlich*] with what he says later in the introduction to the *Grundrisse*, namely, that categories are forms of existence [*Daseinsformen*]. For Lukács, something that exists in an objectified manner is accessible to us only because of its objective status; i.e., something that stands opposed and in relation to us. This means that an object exists historically and socially only insofar as it is constituted categorially.

All of this becomes clearer when we connect Lukács's claim about the categorial structure of social reality to his critique of Hegel in *History and Class Consciousness*:

> Hegel's enormous intellectual achievement consisted in making theory and history dialectically relative to each other, conceiving them in terms of a process of dialectical interpenetration. But even this attempt finally failed. Hegel was never able to advance to a real unity of theory and practice; instead he merely either saturated the logical arrangement of the categories with a wealth of historical material or rationalized history into a succession of sublimated and abstracted forms, alterations of structure, epochs, etc., which he raised to categories. Marx was the first to see through this false dilemma: he did not deduce the order of sequence of the categories from either their logical arrangement or from their historical succession, but he recognized that 'their order of sequence [*Reihenfolge*] is rather determined by the relation which they bear to one another in modern bourgeois society.' [...] The critique of political economy no longer stands as 'one' science alongside the others, nor is it merely ranked above the others as a 'basic science'; but rather it comprises the entire world-history of the 'forms of existence' [*Daseinsformen*] (the categories) of human society.[15]

---

15 Georg Lukács, *Geschichte und Klassenbewusstsein*, Frühschriften II, Werke, Band II (Münster: Aisthesis Verlag, 2013), p. 684; for this, also see ibid., p. 342; English: https://www.marxists.org/archive/Lukács/works/1926/moses-hess.htm (last accessed February 26, 2018).

What Lukács points out here is that the relation between categorial structure and reality should be seen as the crucial hinge for understanding historical progress and change. Whereas Hegel, at least in Lukács's understanding, remains tied to a metaphysical juxtaposition of logical form and social reality, Lukács argues that the "logical" form of social reality must be found *in* it as a historically-specific type of social reality that is constituted by its categorial relations. To be "methodological," then, means that we reconstruct the categorial form in their order of sequence. This order of sequence is dialectical because, as Lukács underlines, the "higher" categories are needed for grasping the "lower categories." For example, although money existed before capitalism, what money is under capitalist social conditions can only be revealed through it being determined and formed by capital. Accordingly, capitalist social reality only exists *as* this reality because in it all social reality is constituted by a categorial form in which money is a lower expression of capital (even when it *seems* to function exclusively as money in market exchanges). Furthermore, we are only able to understand simple everyday objects, such as tables, as *social* objects (i.e., not as objects of the natural sciences or as aesthetic objects) because their categorial determination make them "meaningful" for us, which, in this case, would be an explicit or implicit relation to wealth accumulation and growth.[16] To give another example, in relation to machines, Lukács argues that the "actual form of objecthood [*wirkliche Gegenständlichkeit*]"[17] should not be seen in an ahistorical essential core; instead, with its inclusion in the capitalist organization, it receives what Lukács calls its "structural form" [*Strukturform*],[18] which, in turn, determines the uniqueness of a historical epoch as well as machines as actually existing objects.[19] Machines can therefore only be understood *as* social objects by means of their structural form. Put differently, only if we ask what makes machines *capitalist* machines, do we understand their historical structure.

> There must be clarity about the fact that the so-called simple categories are not trans-historical elements of the system, but are just as much products of historical development as the concrete totalities to which they belong, and that, therefore, simple categories are correctly grasped

---

16   In Laskian terms: "It is only because I live in the validating element that I know about the existing element" (quoted in Kisiel, "Why Students of Heidegger will have to read Emil Lask," p. 206).
17   Lukács, *Geschichte und Klassenbewusstsein*, p. 335.
18   Ibid., p. 336. Note that the term Lask uses in his theory of judgement is "Strukturkomplikationen."
19   Ibid.

from higher, more complicated, more concrete ones. That is to say it is only the comprehension of the concrete whole, to which the simple categories belong, that makes possible knowledge of the simple ones and not the other way round, even if – as has already been outlined – its exposition must often take a reversed path.[20]

Consequently, by "totality" Lukács refers exclusively to the categorial determination of social reality, and not, as one might think, to the totality of the entire historical process or the totality of all social mediations. *Comprehending* a totality requires a reconstruction of the categorial relations as determinations of social reality. "Concrete analysis," as Lukács puts it, "means: relation to the society as a whole."[21]

Accordingly, the status of the categories changes from being applied to a historical process (as in Hegel) to being the essence of the historical itself, insofar as the categories themselves *are* constitutive for the historical dimension of reality.[22] Categories are the *forms* in which and through which societies exist as this or that society. For example, the movement from feudalism to capitalism can no longer be (simply) explained by causal connections of historical events; in addition, what has to change is the categorial unity of the society, which then leads to a new social configuration of reality and, finally, to a new framework under which social objects *are* social objects and are knowable *as* these objects. In categories, we can recognize, as Lukács says, "what *is specific and new*, grasped in thoughts":[23]

> And the nature of history is precisely that every definition degenerates into an illusion: history is the history of the unceasing overthrow of the forms of objecthood [*Gegenständlichkeitsformen*] that shape the existence [*Dasein*] of man. It is therefore not possible to reach an understanding of particular forms by studying their successive appearances in an empirical and historical manner. This is not because they transcend history, though this is and must be the bourgeois view with its addiction to thinking about isolated 'facts' in isolated mental categories. The truth is rather that these particular forms are not immediately connected with

---

20 Lukács, "Chvostimus und Dialektik" p. 136.
21 Lukács, *Geschichte und Klassenbewusstsein*, p. 223; for this also see Dannemann, *Georg Lukács. Eine Einführung*, p. 61.
22 Lukács, *Geschichte und Klassenbewusstsein* p. 306. Lukács argues that being should not be understood as an abstract formal concept; instead, in addition to the formal and empty level, we need to take into account "additional levels [*Stufen*] of actuality" (ibid., p. 306).
23 Lukács, "Chvostimus und Dialektik," p. 136; emphasis mine.

each other either by their simultaneity or by their consecutiveness. What connects them is their place and function in the totality and by rejecting the idea of a 'purely historical' explanation the notion of history as a universal discipline is brought nearer. When the problem of connecting isolated phenomena has become a problem of categories, by the same dialectical process every problem of categories becomes transformed into a historical problem. Though it should be stressed: it is transformed into a problem of universal history which now appears-more clearly than in our introductory polemical remarks-simultaneously as a problem of method and a problem of our knowledge of the present.[24]

Although the consequences of this way of thinking are enormously problematic, it should be clear why Lukács's further thinking about the proletarian revolution is directly linked to his concept of *Gegenständlichkeitsform* and, as its central expression, to reification. Since Lukács does not operate with a concept of rupture and "event" a la Heidegger or Badiou, he needs to locate the rupture on both the productive capacities of the agents and knowers of social reality. The capacity to change the course of history lays in changing the categorial form of reality and not this or that aspect of reality. Not only is it the case that "history becomes the history of the forms of objecthood from which man's environment and inner world are constructed and which he strives to master in thought, action and art, etc.,"[25] but it is also the case, we might add, that man needs to destroy the existing forms of objecthood if new thoughts, actions, and art are to be discovered. Seen from the point of practical theory, the proletariat is "the transformation of the form of objecthood of the objects of action."[26] Accordingly, everything changes because everything changes its form, and since form and matter cannot be separated, knowledge and reality can also not be separated insofar as the reality is known *through* its categorial structure. In addition to Fichte, the influence of Lask on Lukács should not be underestimated, as for Lask knowing [*Erkennen*] means that one lives through *and* grasps the categorial form within which the material is given.[27]

---

24   Lukács, *Geschichte und Klassenbewusstsein*, p. 372; English: Georg Lukács, *History and Class Consciousness*, tr. Rodney Livingston (Cambridge/MA: MIT Press, 2000), p. 186.
25   Ibid., p. 375; ibid., p. 188.
26   Lukács, *Geschichte und Klassenbewusstsein*, p. 359.
27   Emil Lask, *Die Logik der Philosophie und die Kategorienlehre. Eine Studie über den Herrschaftsbereich der logischen Form* (Tübingen: J.C.B. Mohr, 1993), p. 82.

3   Categories in Lask and Heidegger

At this point, we already know that Lukács's concepts of categories and social form are opposed to Kant's and Hegel's concept of categories, insofar as he is searching for a middle ground between a subjectivist theory of categories as something belonging to human reason alone and an objectivist theory of categories as something belonging to an absolute reality. The reality of society is, then, sought by Lukács (and other early critical theorists), as the region of reality that can function as the constitutive level for all other regions, such as mind and nature, without turning society into a replacement region for Hegel's logic.[28] This move brings Lukács closer to a phenomenological approach to reality since neither questions about "absolute reality" are addressed nor is a dialectics of nature developed. Marxism, at least seen from this angle, cannot be developed into a new super theory for everything. Be that as it may, it should be clear by now that Lukács's approach to the problem of categories is distinctively anti-Hegelian since the categorial relations are the precondition for a historically specific form of social reality, and they are not understood in some metaphysical fashion as determining absolute thought as absolute being, which, in turn, brings him back to Kant. However, Lukács's position is anti-Kantian, too, insofar as categories are no longer "implanted" in mind or reason on the side of the subject; instead, from the beginning the identity, they determine type, and kind of object that the subject *can* encounter; i.e., they are part of what can be experienced. Accordingly, in a sense they function, similar to Heidegger's phenomenology of assertion and judgement in *Being and Time*, "before" judgements, insofar as they make subjective references to them possible. The objectivity of objects is prior to reason, which is now understood as a rather passive element of receiving these forms. Logic, or in the case of Lukács, with the help of Marx's critique of political economy, social logic is rethought as the condition for objects to be "discovered" by subjects. In this way, transcendental philosophy is transformed into a social and ontological philosophy in which the togetherness of categorial form and reality make up what Lask calls "sense" [*Sinn*]; i.e., the framework of meaningfulness under

---

28   For the sake of this paper, I am unable to go into any details of Lukács's later ontology; however, Lukács's position towards nature is, with the exception of issues related to his concept of the proletariat, most problematic. For this topic, see the classical study by Alfred Schmidt, *The Concept of Nature in Marx* (London: Verso, 2014); and, more recently, John Bellamy Foster and Brett Clark, "Marxism and the Dialectics of Ecology," *Monthly Review*, 68/5 (2016). Foster and Clark demand a return to the idea of a dialectics of nature.

which assertions about and the experience of objects *as* social objects are possible. Sense is both structural form and social reality. The consequence of the indivisibility between structural form; i.e., forms of objecthood, and social objects, is that subjects do not "make" or constitute these forms. They are precognitive and, to use a phenomenological expression, need to be *read off* from reality. This point is very important because Lukács's position, despite all talk about dialectics and logic, pushes him away from contemporary Hegelian approaches to Marx and his critique of political economy.[29] This is also the reason for the Weberian and Simmelian elements in his (early) thought, inasmuch as these thinkers are equally skeptical about reconstructing social reality in logical terms. Instead, *interpretation* is the key term. To be sure, the categories must emerge in history, within an "original" field, but the decisive insight of Lukács is that this emergence of a new shape of historical development is in truth the emergence of a specific structural form, instead of it being simply the emergence of new things, institutions, ideas, or actions. For example, the emergence of the steam engine was certainly important for the development of modern industrial capitalism; however, the decisive event in history that led to a new preconfiguration of the social reality as a new *reality* is the emergence of the structural form under which steam engines are possible and become meaningful things to their operators and inventors. In a rather complex manner, this goes back to the instrumentalization of nature, a functionalist metaphysics, the exploitation of the earth and labor power, and a socially abstract accumulation of wealth. As we know, the term that unites all of this, at least for Lukács, is reification.

In order to make Lukács's concept of categories as "structural form" even clearer, we should briefly look at two other authors who were struggling with the same problem as Lukács (albeit not in relation to social reality), namely, Lask in his *Die Logik der Philosophie und die Kategorienlehre* (1910) and Heidegger in his early text *Die Kategorien- und Bedeutungslehre des Don Scotus* (1916).[30]

---

29 For this, see Chris Arthur, *Dialectics of Labour. Marx and his Relation to Hegel* (Oxford: Basil Blackwell, 1986); Tony Smith, *The Logic of Marx's Capital. Replies to Hegelian Criticisms* (New York: State University of New York Press, 1990); and Helmut Reichelt, *Zur logischen Struktur des Kapitalbegriffs bei Karl Marx* (Freiburg: Ca Ira, 2001).

30 The influence of Lask on Lukács has been debated before. Whereas Lukács himself in his late self-reflections as well as in his Lask obituary, denies that he was *deeply* influenced by Lask, others, such as Rickert and Szilasi, argue differently (for this, see Elisabeth Weisser-Lohmann, *Georg Lukács's Heidelberger Kunstphilosophie* (Bonn: Bouvier, 1992), p. 86). Be this as it may, it is undeniable that the reflections on the role of categories and the shift from epistemology to ontology plays a crucially equal role for neo-Kantianism, phenomenology, and Marxism; i.e., for Lask, Heidegger, and Lukács respectively.

4   Lask

One of the most important moves regarding the problem of categories in Lask's work, insofar as it is relevant for Lukács, is his claim that "the objecthood *of* the objects is category [*Die Gegenständlichkeit an den Gegenständen ist Kategorie*],"[31] which Lukács transforms from a theory of being into a narrower theory of social being in *History and Class Consciousness*. Lask's newly established logic is based on the claim that "contents stand *in* the form";[32] i.e., "the form of objecthood *of* the objects is category, is identical with the categorial form *of* the realm of truth."[33] Lask makes a distinction between objects [*Gegenständliches*], form of objecthood [*Gegenstandsform*], and object sense [*gegenständlicher Sinn*], whereby the intertwinement of form and material, as the realm of truth, is called *sense*.[34] Additionally, as Lask underlines, this concept of sense differs from sense as "sense of," given that it is pre-predicative and objective *before* a judgment *about* it. The realm of the object *is* the realm of truth. It is what makes it possible for judgments to be judgments about something as judgments of something. *Sinn* is both form and material; whereas the categorial form determines the form of objecthood, the objects are identical with their theoretical sense.[35] As a consequence, the two separate realms of truth (about an object) and the object *as* object are no longer separated. Lask gives Kant's theory of categories an ontological reading, which foreshadows the readings of Heidegger (and Adorno) years later.[36]

As to Lukács, reification becomes the determinate form that determines the way in which an object is accessible to us as an object as *being* an object. We do not simply encounter things in our world; neither do we encounter simply social things in our world; rather, we encounter things in our world of a *specific* historic quality, which, at least in our case, is that which makes objects *capitalist* objects.

As one commentator has it, "the object [*Gegenstand*] already shows up before judgement-based knowledge in an 'openness' [*Offenheit*]; i.e., it stands in

---

31   Lask, *Die Logik der Philosophie und die Kategorienlehre*, p. 33.
32   Ibid., p. 33.
33   Ibid., p. 33.
34   Ibid., p. 34.
35   Ibid., p. 40.
36   For this, see my comparison of Adorno's and Heidegger's reading of Kant's *Critique of Pure Reason* in Christian Lotz, "Warentausch und Technik als Schematisierung von Gegenständlichkeit bei Adorno und Heidegger," in Christian Lotz, et al., eds., *Verdinglichung. Technik- und Sozialphilosophie nach Heidegger und der kritischen Theorie* (München: Fink 2012), pp. 191–211.

relation to be possibly known by the subject."[37] In other words, Lask transcends the Kantian position by introducing a realist interpretation of the transcendental realm as the pre-predicative openness of being that is related to the knowing subject, and, in addition, it is *presupposed* for any kind of active epistemological engagement of the subject. The categorial form, we might say, opens things up to us so that we can encounter them as meaningful for us. Their objecthood is the way in which they stand opposed to us. Lask is the decisive author for this new way of looking at objects, insofar as he argues in *The Logic of Philosophy* that "the object [*Gegenstand*] is always already *object for*; i.e., is always already material in definite meanings. For the knowing subject, the material is always already part of and stands in the meaning bestowing *logos*: the object is always already 'immanent to the logos.'"[38] As a consequence of Lask's synthesis of neo-Kantianism and phenomenology, we no longer need to assume that the subject "creates" or "makes" the object in front of it. Reason is conceived in Lask rather as a passive openness and relation towards something that makes the reception on the side of the objects possible.[39] In Lukács's reading of Marx' concept of categories this passivity is turned into a historical and genetic concept. Sense makes objects transcending and "real" entities, before the subject judges or reflects about these entities, thereby allowing them to be encountered with new categories that belong to the reflexive realm. Accordingly, according to Lask, theoretical reflection is secondary and establishes a new level of categorial forms.[40] With this position, Lask prepares Heidegger's analysis in *Being and Time*, which states that the epistemological attitude establishes its own relation to the non-reflexive primary everyday life of *Dasein*. Reflection isolates elements and abstracts from the original unity of what we are living through. As a consequence, judgement (in Lask) and assertion (in Heidegger) are taken to be secondary and are taken to be derived modes of what is already accessible and transparent on a deeper level. In Heidegger's terms, assertions and judgments are not the primary way of disclosing the world; on the contrary, judgments can either "cover up" or "uncover" our

---

[37] For this, see the excellent article by Konrad Hobe, "Zwischen Rickert und Heidegger. Versuch über eine Perspektive des Denkens von Emil Lask," *Philosophisches Jahrbuch* 78 (1971), p. 364.

[38] Ibid.

[39] In his Duns Scotus book, Heidegger already uses "to heed to something" [*Hineinhören*]; for this, see Martin Heidegger, *Frühe Schriften* (Frankfurt/M.: Klostermann, 1972), p. 343.

[40] For this, see Kouvelakos, *Ästhetizistische Kulturkritik und ethische Utopie*, pp. 71–72.

being-in-the-world, which is primarily characterized by concern. Logic and truth are now understood as something that belongs to the immanence of the objects, which can only be grasped and articulated through devotion, specifically, "as devotion [*Hingabe*] of the subject to the categorially encompassed material."[41] It comes of no surprise, then, that Lukács points to the receptive concept of the subject in his obituary of Lask. "This subject," as Lukács remarks, "is purely receptive [*hinnehmend*], its cognition is never the activity of predications, but, instead, the simple [*schlichte*] receiving of the object [*Gegenstand*]" (363). In fact, Lukács himself uses the notion of devotion. For example, what is needed in philosophy, according to Lukács, is a "devotion"[42] towards the objects of thought, which are now conceived of by Lukács via a "new concept of the 'given'"[43] coupled by an acceptance of the facticity of the starting point[44] for every social analysis.

According to Lask, the "*Gegenstand* is truth as being positioned *towards against* us [*entgegenstehende*]."[45] Put differently, the "being there" of the objects belongs to the objecthood of the object and is a character *of* them; i.e., it is that which makes the object a *possible* object of judgement. Objects already stand in certain relations to us before we get cognitively or practically engaged with them. However, the categorial form is not a natural property of the object; rather, it is that which "gives" the object *as* object. As Weisser has it, "it means that the given object is not, as in Kant's conception, the product of a synthesis that the subject brings about. On the contrary, the object is encountered from the outside as a task for the cognizing subject."[46]

We can easily see how Lukács transforms Lask's ideas into a Marxian position by arguing that the structural *social* form can only be found *in* social reality and that it is precisely this form that makes them historical objects, insofar as history is now understood as a structural form of a reality in which each element needs to be traced back to its origin. Reification is the expression for the way in which objects always already stand in relation to us and, correlatively, we to them, insofar as categorial form and content open up the social space in which we know these objects.

---

41 Lask, *Die Logik der Philosophie und die Kategorienlehre*, p. 80; see also 85; see also Kouvelakos, *Ästhetizistische Kulturkritik und ethische Utopie*, 65.
42 Georg Lukács, *Heidelberger Philosophie der Kunst*, Frühe Schriften zur Aesthetik I, Werke, Band 16 (Frankfurt: Luchterhand, 1974), p. 238.
43 Ibid.
44 Ibid., p. 239.
45 Lask, *Die Logik der Philosophie und die Kategorienlehre*, p. 30.
46 Weisser-Lohmann, *Georg Lukács's Heidelberger Kunstphilosophie*, p. 72.

5 Heidegger

Heidegger's interpretations of Kant's philosophy and his philosophy in *Being and Time* are heavily influenced by Lask and his early work on scholastic philosophy in which Heidegger delivers an astonishing reading of Duns Scotus via terms that he takes from Laskian neo-Kantianism and Husserlian phenomenology. Heidegger follows Lask by arguing that Kant's transcendental logic is primarily not an epistemology; instead, it is in truth an ontology and it is based on a logic of objecthood. In a central passage Heidegger writes:

> A category is the most general determination of objects. Objects and objectivity [*Gegenständlichkeit*] have, as such, sense only *for* a subject. In this subject, objectivity [*Objektivität*] is built up through judgments. Consequently, if we want to conceive of categories in a decisive manner as determinations *of objects,* then we must establish their essential relations to the forms that build up objectivity [*Gegenständlichkeit*]. Thus it was no 'accident' but rather grounded in the innermost core of the problem of categories that this problem arose in both Aristotle and Kant in some sort of connection with predication, i.e., with judgment. This might mean that the categories would have to be reduced to mere *functions of thinking,* but the possibility of such a move does not make any sense at all for a philosophy that has acknowledged *problems having to do with sense.*[47]

We can see that "sense" is offered by Heidegger as the key term for moving beyond both Aristotle and Kant, insofar as it brings us to a new concept of categories as something (at least primarily) independent from thought. Heidegger connects the concept of objecthood [*Gegenständlichkeit*] to the concept of form, which Heidegger defines as determinateness [*Bestimmtheit*] and specificness of an object [*Gegenstand*].[48] The form of an object makes up the objecthood of the object. One consequence of this is that the world of categories is more complex than Aristotle, Kant, and Hegel conceive of them; for from now on form and objects are indivisible and are always encountered as "meaningful" before they can be reduced to objects of logic and reason. For example, the categorial form makes it possible that I have something like one object *in front* of me, which means that the phenomenon of "being in front of me" is already

---

[47] Heidegger, *Frühe Schriften*, p. 345; English: Martin Heidegger, *Supplements: From the Earliest Essays to Being and Time and Beyond* (New York: Suny Press, 2002) p. 64.
[48] For Heidegger's determination of the concept of form, see Heidegger, *Frühe Schriften*, pp. 164–166.

something that belongs to the object *as* object. The "being in front of me" makes it possible that I can address the object in predications, assertions or other reflective activities. Form is that through which something is revealed to me as something that I can grasp as this or that kind of object. Lukács reads Marx' concept of categories thorugh the same theoretical lens. Form determines the object's objectivity; i.e., how it is posited towards the subject. Form is, as Heidegger points out, the *respect* through and in which I grasp the object.[49]

> If we conceive of the categories as elements and means for interpreting the sense of what is experienceable – of what is an object [*Gegenständlichen*] in any sense – then what ensues as a basic requirement for a theory of categories is *characterizing and demarcating the different domains of objects into spheres that are categorially irreducible to one another*.[50]

The problem of how to demarcate regions of the reality, which is already prominently featured in Husserl's attempt to transform ontological questions into phenomenological questions, is precisely the problem that Lukács struggles with, insofar as Lukács tries to introduce the concept of reification as a concept for demarcating capitalist social objects and capitalist social reality as a region of *sense* in which this reality is disclosed as a capitalist reality.[51] As such, Lukács underlines that Lask's position no longer allows us to deduce all realms of objects via one principle;[52] the different "spheres"[53] have "their own laws" [*eigengesetzlich*] and due to their immanent status, theoretical reason is left with "revealing" [*aufdecken*] their different qualities and making them transparent, as Lukács puts it (astonishingly close to Heidegger). Another consequence of this position that is equally important for phenomenology and critical theory, is that different spheres of experience and reality neither can simply be reduced to or be subsumed by the logical sphere as such,[54] nor can they be

---

49 Heidegger, *Frühe Schriften*, p. 165.
50 Ibid., p. 342; Heidegger, *Supplements*, p. 63.
51 It is rather surprising that not even Goldman in his groundbreaking study on Lukács and Heidegger seems to be aware of this connection.
52 Hartmut Rosshoff argues that this position has consequences for the concept of actuality, insofar as the actuality dissolves into a multiverse of separate and distinctive objects; for this, see Hartmut Rosshoff, *Emil Lask als Lehrer von Georg Lukács. Zur Form ihres Gegenstandsbegriffs* (Bonn: Bouvier, 1975), p. 41.
53 Georg Lukács, „Nachruf auf Emil Lask," *Kantstudien* XXII, January (1918), p. 357.
54 For this, also see Weisser-Lohmann, *Georg Lukács's Heidelberger Kunstphilosophie*, p. 90, 191.

subsumed to an overarching metaphysically defined system as we find it, for example, in Hegel's *Encyclopedia* (1830). Instead, each sphere receives its own "positioning character" [*Setzungscharakter*] and, hence, its own *Gegenständlichkeit*. Reification is Lukács attempt to interpret and reveal the form of objecthood of one sphere, namely, the social sphere.[55] Spheres, because they are unities, are independent from each other, and have a "structure."[56] As Lukács puts it, the task is

> to uncover the genuine structure of each sphere, to which the problematic object belongs, and to grasp it as something unified [*Einheitliches*] and self-contained [*Abgeschlossenheit*], so that each thing that becomes an object of knowledge [*Gegenstand der Erkenntnis*] can be returned to its original and implicit contained objecthood [*Wesenheit*].[57]

It comes as no surprise, then, that Heidegger, at least in the *Duns Scotus* book, also refers to history and culture as the main stepping stones for developing a richer theory of categorial forms:

> History and its teleological interpretation in philosophy of culture *must become a determining element for the meaning of the problem of categories* if we want to think differently about working out the *cosmos* of categories in order to go beyond an impoverished schematic table of categories.[58]

Despite his lack of properly understanding phenomenology, Lukács would wholeheartedly agree with this position, although he would have added that this goal can only be achieved through a Marxist interpretation of categories.

---

55   Kisiel clarifies: "each with its own governing regional category (especially validity versus reality) differing in meaning from other such region-constituting forms; if these different domains have their own logic, then there must be a logic which unifies and differentiates them, and this 'logic of logic' will in turn have its own categories." (Kisiel, "Why Students of Heidegger will have to read Emil Lask," p. 206). Lukács, *Geschichte und Klassenbewusstsein*, p. 335. The claim that the Aristotelian categories are no longer universal, but can only be applied to a specific sphere and specific respect of reality is also argued by Heidegger in regard to Duns Scotus in his early work (for this, see Heidegger, *Frühe Schriften*, p. 205).
56   Lukács, *Heidelberger Philosophie der Kunst*, p. 236.
57   Ibid.
58   Heidegger, *Frühe Schriften*, p. 350; Heidegger, *Supplements*, p. 67.

6   Conclusion: Reification as Intelligibility

As we indicated, philosophers such as Lask and Heidegger re-interpret the concept of truth as an ontological concept, in close connection with the concept of meaningfulness or sense. As Kavoulakos has it, "aletheiological questions are related to the discovery of 'sense structure and categorial form-content,' which is the central topic of a theoretical doctrine of sense."[59] Sense allows social agents to experience social objects in a meaningful way as historically specific objects. To give an example, a table is a table with certain natural properties that are put to use through the process of objectification and labor. The table is also a social object, insofar as it functions not only within different social worlds, such as family or school, but also in different use value contexts. However, a hand crafted middle age table or an industrially produced table in the 20th Century are not simply social objects because people in the middle ages or people in the 20th Century can use them for eating or learning; rather, they are historically specific objects because they are meaningful within a broader frame that, at least in our contemporary epoch, determines the table as a table used and produced within our capitalist social organization. The table *is* something and has a specific form of objecthood since it was produced under certain circumstances, is categorially formed though its monetary form, and contributes to the overall wealth production in our world – independent from whether we reflect on its categorial structure. This fact, that even a simple breakfast table is what it is by means of it being an expression of surplus value, is no longer visible for most consumers. Nevertheless, despite its intransparency, nothing can change the fact that, if we intend to understand the table as a social *and* historical object, we need to address its capitalist categorial forms that disclose the object as an object of our time period. During this process of theoretical clarification, with Lukács, we might come close to concluding that the categorial forms can be unified by the concept of reification.[60] What the table *in truth is* cannot be exhausted by its natural and a-historical social properties; the aletheiological "showing" of *capitalist* society occurs *through* its specific *Gegenständlichkeitsform*. This form of objecthood reveals that the table is

---

59   Kouvelakos, *Ästhetizistische Kulturkritik und ethische Utopie*, p. 54.
60   I have argued in Lotz, *The Capitalist Schema,* that reification is not satisfactory; instead, we need to argue that money is the central category; for a similar point and direct critique of Lukács see the excellent study by Frank Engster, *Das Geld als Mass, Mittel und Methode: Das Rechnen mit der Identität der Zeit* (Berlin: Neofelis Verlag, 2014).

only understandable *as* a table of our times if we understand it as already being constituted through *value*.

As a final point and in order to conclude this set of reflections, we should remind ourselves that with the publication of *History and Class Consciousness*, Lukács's Laskian and phenomenological understanding of categories and categorial form receives a Marxian twist. For the concept of reification is not only developed in close connection with Lask, but also with what Marx says in the first chapter of *Capital*[61] and the introduction to the *Grundrisse*. In two central passages Lukács writes the following:

> The mutual determination [Wechselwirkung] we have in mind must be more than the interaction of otherwise unchanging objects. It must go further in its relation to the whole: for this relation determines the form of objecthood [*Gegenständlichkeitsform*] of every object of cognition. Every substantial change that is of concern to knowledge manifests itself as a change in relation to the whole and through this as a change in the form of objecthood [*Gegenständlichkeitsform*] itself. Marx has formulated this idea in countless places. I shall cite only one of the best-known passages: 'A negro is a negro. He only becomes a slave in certain circumstances. A cotton-spinning jenny is a machine for spinning cotton. Only in certain circumstances does it become capital. Torn from those circumstances it is no more capital than gold is money or sugar the price of sugar.' Thus the forms of objecthood of all social phenomena change constantly in the course of their ceaseless dialectical mutual determinations with each other. The intelligibility of objects develops in proportion as we grasp their function in the determined [*bestimmte*] totality to which they belong.[62]
>
> Thus the economic categories become dynamic and dialectical in a double sense. As 'pure' economic categories they are involved in constant mutual determination with each other, and that enables us to understand any given historical stage of the evolution of society.[63]

Consequently, revealing the form of objecthood means that we analyze each thing under a totality of categorial relations, which means that we analyze the

---

61 For this see my attempt to relate Lukács to Chapter One of Marx' *Capital* in Lotz, "Gegenständlichkeit. From Marx to Lukács and Back Again," especially pp. 81–86.

62 Lukács, *Geschichte und Klassenbewusstsein*, p. 185; Lukács, *History and Class Consciousness*, p. 13 (translation altered).

63 Ibid., p. 187; Ibid., 15 (translation altered).

object as one that belongs to a specific historical stage and a specific determination of its categorial unity.[64] Accordingly, this unity is finite and cannot be universalized – and this is precisely why the critique of political economy is *critical*: for it demonstrates the limits of the capitalist world. Something that is limited can change. Accordingly, only a theory that demonstrates that social objects in capitalism have a specific form of objecthood would allow us to imagine a new, even a revolutionarily new, categorial form for encountering objects; i.e., an altogether different frame of meaningfulness, which would also mean that we "know" the social reality in a different sense.

Therefore, the assumption of a radical social change, whether it is a realistic position or whether it is not, necessarily follows from Lukács's concept of reification as the expression of the unity of the structural form of capitalist social objects. Rejecting Lukács's concept of history as speculative nonsense is therefore not as easy at it sometimes seems.

---

64   Hartmut Rosshoff argues that Lukács's introduction of the concept of totality as the idea of a new historical configuration stems from Fichte; for this, see Rosshoff, *Emil Lask als Lehrer von Georg Lukács*, p. 32.

CHAPTER 3

Reification in *History and Class Consciousness*

Csaba Olay

Huge masses suffer in capitalism, but do not know why. Is lack of talent the reason for this? Is it personal misfortune? Or is it capitalism's fault, which brings about this suffering? George Lukács's answer is clear: it has to do with the inevitable and total structure of capitalism that he calls reification. In what follows I shall examine a sub-question of this issue, namely the problem how we face, how we experience reification, how and in terms of which characteristics do we meet reified or objectificated relations? In asking these questions I shall partly disband reification from the framework of Marxian revolutionary dialectic as elaborated by Lukács. More precisely, I detach the treatment of reification from the standpoint and revolutionary praxis of the proletariat. My interest is above all descriptive, motivated by the accusation of Lukács (and Marx) that capitalism inescapably and in various ways puts human beings into an inhuman predicament, which could and should be swept away through proletarian revolution. This descriptive interest is also the reason why I neglect here the problem whether the detachment of reification and revolution is justified or not, viz. the problem of the unity of Lukács's point of view.[1]

As to Lukács's analysis of reification, his famous conception in *History and Class Consciousness* has proved to be one of his most influential ideas. His contribution to the theory of alienation has also often been seen in his concept of reification (*Verdinglichung*). It is under this heading that present paper discusses Lukács's critique of capitalist society. With his concept of reification Lukács not only "found out," as it were, what came to be published in Marx's *Economic and Philosophic Manuscripts* only nine years later, but continued at the same time to develop his "romantic anti-capitalism" from his pre-Marxist period which had been elaborated in the writings before Lukács's Bolshevist turn. In addition, the argument will also focus on the clarification of how non-reified or dereified conditions are, rather implicitly, described by Lukács. The presupposition of a concept of non-reified or non-alienated conditions lies at the heart of every theory of reification or alienation including Marx' conception, too. The paper begins, thus, with a discussion of the concept of reification as developed in the chapter entitled "The Phenomenon of Reification" in the

---

1 See a discussion of different possible conceptions in Timothy Bewes, *Reification, or the Anxiety of Late Capitalism* (London: Verso, 2002), pp. 85–88.

central essay of *History and Class Consciousness*, in "Reification and the Consciousness of the Proletariat." It will be examined, then, how Lukács proposed to overcome reification by way of a revolution, and what sort of problems are implied in overcoming reification. I conclude with the claim that Lukács's contribution to the theory of reification lies not in a proposed solution, but rather in a differentiation and extension of the phenomenon or reification along broader social dimensions. At the same time, Lukács, as Marx before him, still owes an answer to the question how non-reified relations and non-alienated conditions should be conceived of. The fragility of his proposal manifests itself in the idealistic, highly implausible description of the allegedly non-reified Communist Party.

Three preliminary remarks should be made here, the first of which concerns terminology. Reification (*Verdinglichung*), as Georg Lohmann and Axel Honneth among others emphasize, can be taken in an active or passive sense of the process of *Verdinglichung*: either we make out of something which is essentially not a thing (e.g. human being) a "thing," or it happens to something which is essentially not a thing that it comes to be treated as a "thing."[2] The difference between the two meanings lies in the aspect of conscious treatment and of responsibility. If it depends on us that we treat someone or something as mere objects, than we would be responsible for that; correspondingly, to reverse this situation also lies in our capacity. If there are external factors that facilitate or create such a situation, the responsibility cannot be ascribed to us. We will return to this after having outlined Lukács's theory. As we will see, Lukács regards reification to be a process beyond individual will and intention.

Second, it is perhaps one of Lukács's most important presuppositions while approaching the Marxist tradition that late capitalist society needs more than political ameliorations, amendments. It is not easy to isolate where and for what reasons he develops this conviction. Lukács possibly takes over the conviction from Marx himself who was persuaded of the inevitability of revolution, too.[3] For Marx, the idea depends on the structural problems of capitalist production he considers to be not reparable be a step-by-step procedure or evolution. Accordingly, the fundamental opposition between gradual amelioration and radical break by revolution is at stake here. It is worth noting that Lukács's paper "Bolshevism as a Moral Problem" clearly articulates Lukács's awareness of basic assumptions in the Marxist approach, primarily the moral problem that in order to achieve liberation evildoing and violence are unavoidable. The

---

2   Axel Honneth, *Reification. A New Look at an Old Idea* (Oxford: Oxford University Press, 2008), p. 22; Georg Lohmann, *Indifferenz und Gesellschaft. Eine kritische Auseinandersetzung mit Marx* (Frankfurt am Main: Suhrkamp, 1991), p. 30.
3   Thesis 11 on Feuerbach.

revolutionary change, in his eyes, is a must which should bring about fundamental change in the whole way of life: culture, community as well as political life must change, if we are to avoid final crystallization of ossified structures. As we shall see, the revolutionary impulse doesn't immediately follow from his diagnosis of reification.

This being said, third, the critical tone against late modern society is not a new perspective in Lukács's work. The collection of essays, *The Soul and the Forms,* as well as two books on the history of the literary genres of drama and novel were deeply saturated with a critique of capitalist society. György Márkus, member of the Budapest School around Lukács, highlighted in an essay on the early Lukács that the problem of culture had meant from the very beginning the problem of the possibility of *human life without alienation*.[4] In analyzing this search for non-alienated life, Márkus observed that Lukács had taken a too harmonistic view of ancient Greek "integrated civilizations," best portrayed in *The Theory of the Novel*. There are even passages that seem to articulate a precursor-conception of alienated conditions, and so seem to anticipate the description of reification. The modern individual, i.e. the hero of the novel, faces "the strangeness of the non-human world" and is "the product of estrangement from the outside world." Modern man is no more at home in the world, the modern soul does not find everything it needs and has to create and animate everything out of its own self.[5] A sketchy look at the young Lukács, thus, verifies that he could partly ground his theory of reification on his "romantic anticapitalism" from the pre-Marxist period which had been influenced by cultural critics (*Kulturkritik*), philosophy of life, and Neo-Kantianism.[6]

Turning now to the explicitly Marxian *History and Class-Consciousness*, the first point to underline is that Lukács declares to revive Marx's method in Hegelian spirit. As explained in "What is orthodox Marxism?," Lukács takes as the center of Marx's thought the demand of revolutionary transformation of the world. With this move against the main line of the Second International,

---

4 György Márkus, "Life and the Soul: The Young Lukács and the Problem of Culture," in György Márkus, *Culture, Science, Society. The Constitution of Cultural Modernity*, (Leiden – Boston: Brill, 2011), pp. 521–552, p. 526: "from the beginning of his development as a thinker the question of culture meant for Lukács the question of whether it is possible to live a life free from alienation. But behind this question lay his passionate diagnosis of the hostility to culture, the "crisis of culture," that characterized modern bourgeois existence, and his own determined rejection of it."
5 George Lukács, *The Theory of the Novel* (London: The Merlin Press, 1974), pp. 64–65.
6 Georg Lohmann, "Authentisches und verdinglichtes Leben. Neuere Literatur zu Georg Lukács's *Geschichte und Klassenbewußtsein*," *Philosophische Rundschau* 30, 3/4 1983, p. 255.

the core of Marxism is grasped as an activist, revolutionary attitude towards the existing conditions, instead of the scientific-economic self-interpretation of the late Marx. Lukács touches here a sensible point, viz. the tension of economic analysis of capitalism and class-struggle in Marx's conception. The ambiguity of an activist-voluntarist strand and an economic-scientific strand could be traced back to the early writings of Marx. On the one hand, he seeks to show that private property – being ossified and alienated human labor – is the key to the misery of contemporary capitalism (*Economic and Philosophic Manuscripts of 1844*). At the same time, the proletariat is depicted as a force which would inevitably change the world (*Critique of Hegel's Philosophy of Right*). The precise connection of these two motives in the structure of Marx's thought is far from being clear. However, in *History and Class Consciousness* this twofold structure appears as the connection between reification and revolutionary class consciousness.

Lukács's collection of essays is basically a reaction to the theoretical crisis of Marxism after World War I. The crisis is caused by the fact, roughly put, that the proletariat, against predictions by Marx, does not seem to bring revolutionary changes, and even less to move towards a revolution. Still worse, social democracy appears as an alternative, both theoretical and practical, reaction to the fact that revolution does not arrive. In this vein, Löwy reminds not to forget that this work is, "perhaps above all, a *political* work, the central problem of which is *the proletarian revolution against capitalist reification*."[7]

Even if we deal here with the descriptive content of reification, it should be noted that Lukács's understanding of Marxism has its special characteristics. First of all, the significance of dialectics as primacy of the whole against the parts needs to be underlined. As Lukács puts it, "[t]his absolute primacy of the whole, its unity over and above the abstract isolation of its parts – such is the essence of Marx's conception of society and of the dialectical method."[8] In terms of this reading of dialectics, Lukács takes the Marxist method as the attempt to consider the social world as a single whole of "totality".[9] In doing so, his underlying premise is "the belief that in Marx's theory and method the

---

7 Michael Löwy, *Georg Lukács – From Romanticism to Bolshevism*, (London: NLB, 1979), p. 171.
8 Georg Lukács, *History and Class Consciousness. Studies in Marxist Dialectics*, (Cambridge (MA): MIT Press, 1971), p. 27.
9 "His view that this is the key to Marxist theory did not alter from 1919 to 1971. [...] Marxism, according to Lukács, would be impossible if it did not involve the principle that the social 'totality' cannot be reconstructed by accumulating facts. Facts do not interpret themselves: their meaning is only revealed in relation to the whole, which must be known in advance and is thus logically prior to the facts." Kolakowski: *Main Currents of Marxism*, III (Oxford: Clarendon Press, 1978), p. 265.

true method by which to understand society and history has finally been discovered." The Marxist method serves for Lukács, then, the pre-eminent aim of the "knowledge of the present."[10]

Secondly, the explicitly revolutionary aspect of Lukács's reading of Marxian dialectics should also be accentuated. To understand society and history, the "knowledge of the present" is not merely theoretical and contemplative, as clearly indicated by Marx's eleventh thesis on Feuerbach chosen as a motto for the study on orthodox Marxism: "The philosophers have only interpreted the world in various ways; the point, however, is to change it."[11] Correspondingly, a revolutionary action is prepared by "a dialectical knowledge of reality, which discovers the tendencies pointing towards the ultimate objective not in isolated facts, but in the dynamic totality."[12] It is within this theoretical framework that the central essay should be understood the title if which showing the two major components of the concept: "reification" as the description of the crisis of capitalist society and "the consciousness of the proletariat" as the revolutionary impetus which needs to be actualized. Marxist orthodoxy, among others Bukharin, regarded Marx as a Darwin of history with no methodological awareness. Lukács's approach, on the contrary, tried to revitalize the revolutionary impulse he thought necessary for society's escape from capitalism. In his view, this impulse could only be conceived of as the action of the identical subject-object of history, viz. of the proletariat, but it cannot be considered as an automatic result of historical processes: "A situation in which the 'facts' speak out unmistakably for or against a definite course of action has never existed, and neither can or will exist."[13]

Lukács's concept of reification (*Verdinglichung*) has often been seen as a contribution to the theory of alienation in Marx and Marxism in general. It is, for sure, a theory of objectified or reified relationships that relies on Marx's theory of commodity fetishism. Gajo Petrovic, for example, defines reification as "[t]he act (or result of the act) of transforming human properties, relations and actions into properties, relations and actions of man-produced things which have become independent (and which are imagined as originally independent) of man and govern his life."[14] Reification, then, appears to be a special case of alienation, as a widespread form characteristic of modern capitalist society.

---

10   Lukács, *History and Class Consciousness*, p. xliii.
11   Ibid., p. 1.
12   Löwy, *Georg Lukács*, p. 174.
13   Lukács, *History and Class Consciousness*, p. 23.
14   Tom Bottomore, Laurence Harris, V.G. Kieman, Ralph Miliband (eds.), *A Dictionary of Marxist Thought*, (Cambridge, MA: Harvard University Press 1983), pp. 411–413.

One could, however, challenge the idea that Lukács's theory of reification is simply a variation of Marx's account on alienation. The most important argument against such an identification is the fundamentally different scope of alienation and reification. Alienation is clearly a much wider phenomenon than reification, since there are cases of alienation not being necessarily cases of reification, e.g. alienation from other human beings. This thread was even developed further by e.g. Fredric Jameson who considers reification to be more important in understanding late capitalism than Lukács thought it in the 1930s. Jameson theorizes the emergence of global late capitalism in the sense of the extension of capitalism all over the world as a process which implicates a more fundamental *commodification* than ever before.[15] An additional problem of the identification of reification and alienation would be the problem of the continuity of alienation in the thought of Marx, which was notably disputed among others by Louis Althusser.[16] To clarify the complex relationship between alienation and reification let us turn to Lukács's description in *History and Class Consciousness*.

Lukács begins the explanation of reification with an analysis of commodity-structure, which he regards to be *the* basic problem of capitalist society. With a surprising universality he declares that in the age of capitalist society "there is no problem that does not ultimately lead back to that question and there is no solution that could not be found in the solution to the riddle of commodity-*structure*."[17] Lukács not only stresses the central character of commodity-structure, but assumes its model-character for all aspects of capitalist society. The commodity-structure is the central, structural problem of capitalism, because it yields a "model" of objective and corresponding subjective forms in bourgeois society.[18] The description of reification is, thus, grounded on the commodity-fetishism described by Marx in *Capital*. What complicates matters is that Lukács's argumentation exhibits deep affinity also with Marx's early theory of alienation, even if he could not know it. The question must be suspended here whether the perspective of *Capital* carries on

---

15   See Adam Roberts, *Fredric Jameson*, (London: Routledge, 2000), pp. 38–40.
16   "The whole fashionable theory of 'reification' depends on a projection of the theory of alienation found in the early texts, particularly the 1844 Manuscripts, on to the theory of 'fetishism' in *Capital*. ... An ideology of reification that sees 'things' everywhere in human relations confuses in this category 'thing' (a category more foreign to Marx cannot be imagined) every social relation, conceived according to the model of a money-making ideology." Louis Althusser, *For Marx*, (New York: Vintage), p. 230.
17   Lukács, *History and Class Consciousness*, p. 83.
18   Ibid.

the early writings on alienation as some think.[19] In our context, however, it is worth noting that the theory of alienation in the young Marx made essential assumptions concerning a "human being," whereas the theory of commodity fetishism doesn't need such assumptions. At this point, a cursory look at the young Marx's doctrine of alienation is needed.

Famously, in Marx's work we find a shift from alienation in the early manuscripts (*Economic and Philosophic Manuscripts of 1844*) to reification/objectification in the later work (*A Contribution to a Critique of Political Economy*). It is debated whether this means a break in the treatment of, or even abandoning the issue, or rather implies the presence of the topic in the whole work.[20] Be it as it may, the normative basis of alienation in the early Marx is the concept of man's self-realization in the working process. The self-realization takes place in a double movement of a prior objectification and a following re-appropriation, and thus it follows that labor is the self-realizing human activity.[21]

As is well known, the early Marx claimed that in capitalism labor cannot be but alienated. Alienation is in his eyes a drawing-away, a distanciation in

---

19   See for example Karl Korsch's claim that what Marx baptized "self-alienation" in his early philosophical period, became "commodity fetishism" in his later critical-scientific period. See also Leszek Kolakowski's comment: "Although the word 'alienation' occurs less often, the theory is present in Marx's social philosophy until the end of his life; 'commodity fetishism' in *Capital* is nothing but a particularization of it. When Marx writes that commodities produced for the market take on an independent form, that social relations in the commercial process appear to the participants as relations among things over which they have no control (exchange value being falsely represented as inherent in the object and not as an embodiment of labour), and that the supreme type of this fetishism is money as a standard of value and means of exchange – in all this Marx is reproducing the theory of self-alienation that he had formulated in 1844." (Kolakowski, *Main Currents*, I, p. 173).

20   On various positions see Kolakowski, *Main Currents*, I, pp. 263ff. An obvious point of divergence in Marx's oeuvre is the treatment of revolution. Kübler remarks that we do not find any justification of the refusal of capitalism in the later work, only in the *Manuscripts* (Lukas Kübler, "Marx' Theorie der Entfremdung," in: Rahel Jaeggi – Dainel Loick (eds.), *Karl Marx – Perspektiven der Gesellschaftskritik* (Berlin: Akademie Verlag, 2013), pp. 47–66.). Barbara Zehnpfennig, however, sees no strict separation of the alienation-theorem and the later critique of capitalism: "Seine im Kapital entwickelte Kapitalismuskritik und seine Revolutionstheorie lassen sich im Grunde gar nicht verstehen, wenn es nicht die in der Entfremdungstheorie beschriebenen Defizite wären, die durch die Revolution behoben werden sollen." (Barbara Zehnpfennig, "Rousseau und Marx: das Ende der Entfremdung." in: Hidalgo, Oliver (ed.), *Der lange Schatten des Contrat social. Demokratie und Volkssouveränität bei Jean-Jacques Rousseau* (Wiesbaden: Springer VS, 2013, pp. 177–209, p. 185).

21   Lohmann, *Indifferenz und Gesellschaft*, p. 23.

various respects. Marx talks about alienation of the worker in four different senses: he is alienated from (a) the product of his work, (b) the process of his working, (c) from species-being (*Gattungswesen*) – i.e. man is not exercising activities proper to true human nature and capacities –, and finally (d) from others. Considering the inner dependence of these forms, the essential point, in my view, can be found in the second form, since the first alienation is a consequence of the alienation within the activity of work itself, which is a kind of self-alienation (*Selbstentfremdung*) of the worker. Self-alienation means that the working activity is "external" (*äußerlich*) to the worker, it does not belong to his essence, it is forced labor, so that it is the exact opposite of work as self-realization in the sense of "free psychic and intellectual energy."[22] Let us put aside the question whether everything we call labor or work must have these features or not.[23]

Marx's conception of work as a counter-conception of self-realization contains the characterization of work as "abstract." He follows in this context Adam Smith's description of the poverty of workers, and considers his identification of work with pain as a naturalization of alienated work.[24] Marx regarded property as something that should be explained, not simply accepted, as Smith and Locke did. Whilst he explicitly acknowledges categories and "laws" of national economy, he refuses it as being an ahistorical perspective without offering a basic principle for the explanation of property.[25]

Without getting lost in the complexities of Marx's conception of alienation, it can be stated that he thinks the transformation of alienated work into a non-alienated situation possible.[26] The main purpose of the process of history, in

---

22 "Der Arbeiter fühlt sich nicht wohl, sondern unglücklich […], […] fühlt sich daher erst außer der Arbeit bei sich und bei der Arbeit außer sich" (MEW Vol. 40, p. 514).

23 It is not here to discuss an alternative conception to this that could be developed along the Aristotelean conception of *energeia*. See my paper "Alienation in Rousseau."

24 As to Marx's relationship to Rousseau, one could accentuate the refusal of the construction of an original non-alieneted position.

25 "Die Nationalökonomie geht vom Faktum des Privateigentums aus. Sie erklärt uns dasselbe nicht." (MEW Vol. 40, p. 510) Economy fixes thus "die *entfremdete* Form des gesellingen Verkehrs als die *wesentliche* und *ursprüngliche* und der menschlichen Bestimmung entsprechende" (451).

26 Kolakowski regards a series of "critiques" of Marx – including among others the *Paris Manuscripts* and *Capital* itself – as more and more elaborated versions of the same basic idea which he formulates as follows: "We live in an age in which dehumanization of man, that is to say the alienation between him and his own works, is growing to a climax which must end in a revolutionary upheavel; this will originate from the particular interest of the class which has suffered the most from dehumanization, but its effect will be to restore humanity to all mankind." (Kolakowski, *Main Currents*, I, p. 262).

his view, is nothing else than a situation without private propriety, viz. Communism. In the present context, it is enough to emphasize that even if the realization of Communism might be regarded as problematic, the fact that it would mean a non-alienated state cannot be doubted. For our argument it is also important that the core of Marx's idea of alienation is not an objectifying relationship that would make an object out of human skills, properties or human beings. However, the point of reification in Lukács's sense is exactly this move of making something/somebody into an object or considering something/somebody as a mere object.

Even more important is the extension of the analysis of reification as compared to Marx. In Lukács's view it is not only market and exchange processes, but all dimensions of capitalist society that show reification processes. In other words, he broadens the scope of the reification structure processes in capitalism that are, he adds, infinite in tendency. By extending reification to all aspects of society, he gives an overall diagnosis of his time. If his description of reification can be regarded as a continuation of alienation, then its novelty lies less in new forms or variations, but in the universality of reification in all social forms and dimensions of capitalist society.

The core of the phenomenon of reification is that a relation between human beings "takes on the character of a thing and thus acquires a 'phantom objectivity,' an autonomy that seems so strictly rational and all-embracing as to conceal every trace of its fundamental nature."[27] As already indicated, Lukács does not confine his analysis to the economic sphere, but tries to show that it is necessary "for the commodity structure to penetrate society in all its aspects and to remould it in its own image."[28] Although he seems to promise here a kind of justification of this penetration, it is not clearly explained why the thing-structure should become pervasive in every dimensions of capitalist society. The lack of explicit explanation is particularly unfortunate, since the connection of the economic sphere with other dimensions of society, the one-sided dependence of the latter on the former was an often criticized idea in Marx's oversimplifying base-superstructure scheme.

Lukács's comment on the famous Marxian passage on the fetishism of commodity helps to highlight his position: "a man's own activity, his own labor becomes something objective and independent of him, something that controls him by virtue of an autonomy alien to man."[29] The argumentation, then, differentiates between an objective and a subjective side of the phenomenon. In

---

27   Lukács, *History and Class Consciousness*, p. 83.
28   Ibid., p. 85.
29   Ibid., p. 87.

terms of his example of the unchangeable, but knowable laws of market, Lukács suggests that his problem is not the strange character of reified phenomena, but the independence of reified phenomena and man's loss of influence upon them. In contrast to this, as we saw above, alienation in Marx is a kind of distanciation from different aspects of the working activity, but not an objectifying relationship that would make an object out of human factors or human beings.

The specific negative evaluation of this objectifying relationship is not really explicated by Lukács. The single fact that we regard human capacities, performances as properties of objects could not yet justify a negative evaluation. Axel Honneth also stresses that the type of reification is unclear, since Lukács misses to specify whether it is an epistemic category mistake, morally wrong behavior, or a distorted form of praxis. This underdetermination is in fact a consequence of the lack of detailed explanation of the negativity of reification.[30] Lukács's point on the negativity of reification is that the worker loses its organic relationship to his or her own skills and capacities: "With the modern 'psychological' analysis of the work-process (in Taylorism) this rational mechanization extends right into the worker's 'soul': even his psychological attributes are separated from his total personality and placed into specialized rational systems and their reduction to statistically viable concepts."[31] The following key passage shows the finer structure of how Lukács thinks the rational fragmentation of "the subjects of labour" both individually and collectively:

> On the one hand, the objectification of their labour-power into something opposed to their total personality (a process already accomplished with the sale of that labour-power as a commodity) is now made into the permanent ineluctable reality of their daily life. Here, too, the personality can do no more than look helplessly while its own existence is reduced to an isolated particle and fed into an alien system. On the other hand, the mechanical disintegration of the process of production into its components also destroys those bonds that had bound individuals to a community in the days when production was still 'organic.'[32]

Georg Lohmann reconstructed the basis of special negativity of the objectifying relationship as follows. Contrary to properties of objects, human capacities can only be actualized in accordance with the will of the person possessing them.

---

30   Honneth, *Reification*, pp. 25–27.
31   Lukács, *History and Class Consciousness*, p. 88.
32   Lukács, *History and Class Consciousness*, p. 90.

Therefore when treating human capacities as properties of objects, we ignore the decisive moment of will and deliberation. This disregard is the essentially problematic move in the objectifying relation of the worker to his or her capacities and skills.[33] Let's consider the universality of the commodity-structure.

As already indicated, the universality of the commodity relation is a basic claim of Lukács, although the spread of reification doesn't get explained in the book. Even if there are already remarks of Marx on the dynamics of commercialization,[34] expansion of reification is rather declared than clarified by Lukács. His argumentation for the expansion of reification might perhaps be conjectured as follows. The main reason of reification is the spreading of commodity exchange, which becomes in capitalist society the dominant form of intersubjective actions and relationships. Causes or motivations of this dominance, however, are not identified beyond the intensive presence of commodity exchange. It could, of course, be proposed that through the prevailing presence of commodity exchange the capitalist self is tempted to a reifying attitude towards his or her environment. This reifying attitude is the calculation solely on the basis of utility and profit which in Lukács's view can appear in various forms of reification, e.g. perceiving objects merely as "things" that one can potentially make a profit on, or regarding other human beings solely as "objects" of profitable transaction, or regarding one's own abilities as calculable "resources." Nonetheless it is unclear what exactly makes these forms of reification appear and why each of the three forms (a person's attitude towards the objective world, society, and himself or herself) can be treated in the same way.

What makes Lukács's analysis distinctively different from the commodity-fetishism is an additional essential aspect, which had been inspired by Max Weber. Weber connected the process of rationalization with specialization, and this connection is especially important for Lukács: "the principle of rationalisation based on what is and *can be calculated*."[35] It is rationalization that intensifies the process of reification: "the principle of rational mechanisation and calculability must embrace every aspect of life. Consumer articles no longer appear as the products of an organic process within a community [...] They

---

33   See Lohmann, "Authentisches und verdinglichtes Leben," pp. 260–261.
34   „[A]lles, was die Menschen bisher als unveräußerlich betrachtet hatten, Gegenstand des Austausches, des Schachers, veräußert wurde. Es ist dies die Zeit, wo selbst Dinge, die bis dahin mitgeteilt wurden, aber nie ausgetauscht, gegeben, aber nie verkauft, erworben, aber nie verkauft: Tugend, Liebe, Wissen, Gewissen usw., wo mit einem Wort alles Sache des Handels wurde." (MEW, Vol. 4, p. 69).
35   Lukács, *History and Class Consciousness*, p. 88.

now appear, on the one hand, as abstract members of a species identical by definition with its other members and, on the other hand, as isolated objects the possession of which depends on rational calculations. Only when the whole life of society is thus fragmented into the isolated acts of commodity exchange can the 'free' worker come into being."[36] It is interesting to note that Lukács doesn't really justify the necessity of rationalization in the production process; he simply claims it, and goes on to an argument we already find in Marx about the anarchic nature of capitalism, viz. that capitalist production seeks profit and doesn't follow real needs of a real community.

While integrating Marx and Weber, Lukács claims that commodity production revolutionizes the production process. He combines here two traditions, in so far as he adds to the Marxian critique of capitalism the dimension of philosophy of life in the form of a rather unorthodox reading of Weber's rationalization thesis.[37] This combination is the more strange, the more clear we see that Weber attempted an alternative explanation of capitalism. What is even less clear is how the two threads of argumentation intensify each other. To put it otherwise, it is undecided which explanatory factors stem from Marx and which from Max Weber. Timothy Hall interestingly proposes a double focus of Lukács who in his view discusses in *History and Class Consciousness* not only reification as the source of injustice in capitalism, but at the same time the problem of nihilism as a result of social rationalization and good life. Hall claims that the Frankfurt School concentrates only on the first problem. However, he doesn't succeed in showing that the problem of good life could be discussed in the light of an individual's perspective, since the domination of class-point-of-view is not questioned by him.[38]

The central claim of Lukács is, then, that in capitalism reification becomes the second nature of man. He asserts that human beings in capitalism inevitably get accustomed to perceive themselves and their environment as mere objects. Lukács concentrates here on transformations on the subject's side, especially on transformations under the pressure of commodity exchange. Persons under conditions of permanent commodity exchange, he suggests, change their basic attitude to their whole environment, in so far as they acquire a contemplative stance, they become "detached observers" of their own existences, which are "reduced to an isolated particle and fed into an alien system."[39] By

---

36 Ibid., p. 91.
37 Rüdiger Dannemann, *Georg Lukács* (Wiesbaden: Panorama Verlag, n.d.), p. 51.
38 Timothy Hall, "Justice and the Goog Life in Lukács's History and Class Consciousness," in: Timothy Bewes and Timothy Hall (eds.), *Georg Lukács: The Fundamental Dissonance of Existence* (London: Continuum, 2011), pp. 121–137.
39 Lukács, *History and Class Consciousness*, p. 90.

contemplative attitude Lukács means to the aspect of passivity of the observer who is contemplating the independent processes, and he or she does not grasp himself or herself as an active participant of what happens.[40] Interestingly, Lukács considers the structure of detachment, viz. "the split between the worker's labour power and his personality" a pervasive feature of every field of capitalist society.[41]

Andrew Feenberg challenges this interpretation, while arguing against Axel Honneth's reading: "Honneth draws out the implications of this notion of the reified subject as fundamentally an observer rather than an authentic actor." Feenberg claims that the worker's "contemplative" attitude towards his or her own performances should be understood in a different manner: contemplative for Lukács in 1923 simply means to accept the laws of a field and to follow them in action without changing them.[42] In terms of his reading, however, Feenberg has problems in specifying the problematic character of reification. Especially unclear is in his interpretation reading who would be able to "experience" reification, since he situates it on the level of social events.

With the claim that capitalist society has arrived into a final stage of reification, Lukács reproduces a similar diagnosis to that of Marx. The criteria to judge that society has entered into a final stage are *eo ipso* precarious, even if they carry a heavy burden of proof. In fact, the final, irreversible character of capitalist society is the reason why Lukács, as already mentioned at the outset, doesn't even consider the possibility of a step-by-step or piecemeal improvement of society. There is no other way out of this situation than a revolution of the proletariat, and Lukács's efforts are directed from this point on to solve theoretical difficulties with regard to this revolution. Two main difficulties arise for him. First, the proletariat in its reified status should be revolutionized, and secondly, in opeacerder to solve the first problem a non-reified point of departure is needed. Lukács presupposes that it is impossible to change society's reified status from within, so that a factor not touched by reification has to initiate the process of dereification. For this purpose he follows Lenin's proposal concerning the role of a political avant-garde embodied by the Communist Party. Let us turn to this conception.

---

40 See Honneth's remarks: "Unlike Martha Nussbaum, Lukács isn't interested in determining the point at which the reification of other persons becomes a morally reproachable act. Instead, he sees all members of capitalist society as being socialized in the same manner into a reifying system of behavior, so that the instrumental treatment of others initially represents a mere social fact and not a moral wrong." (Honneth, *Reification*, p. 26)

41 Lukács, *History and Class Consciousness*, p. 99.

42 Andrew Feenberg, "Rethinking Reification," in: Timothy Bewes – Timothy Hall (eds.), *Georg Lukács: The Fundamental Dissonance of Existence* (London: Continuum, 2011), p. 105.

Lenin was for Lukács a source of life-long inspiration both practical and theoretical. Lenin embodied the revolution in Lukács's eyes, even if Lenin's Marxism can be questioned.[43] The Communist Party plays an eminent role in the conception of both:

> The conscious desire for the realm of freedom can only mean consciously taking the steps that will really lead to it. [...] this desire must entail the renunciation of individual freedom. It implies the conscious subordination of the self to that *collective will* that is destined to bring real freedom into being and that today is earnestly taking the first arduous, uncertain and groping steps towards it. This conscious collective will is the Communist Party.[44]

It is not a hard task to find idealizing formulations with regard both to the Communist Party and to its members. "Every Communist Party represents a higher type of organisation than every bourgeois party or opportunist workers' party, and this shows itself *in the greater demands made by the party on its individual members*."[45] Lukács apparently overestimates and romanticizes Communists assuming them not to be so reified than the rest of society. At this point, his argumentation becomes dubious. On the one hand, he acknowledges with Lenin that the revolution cannot be made but with "men who have been brought up in and ruined by capitalist society."[46] He maintains, on the other hand, that organizational structures and guarantees can alleviate the consequences of reified consciousness men acquired by having been grown up under capitalism.[47] In other words, if there is a constant threat of rigidity and ossification with regard to every activity and theory in capitalism, then it is not

---

43 See Pannekoek's remark: "Der Marxismus Lenins und der bolschewistischen Partei ist eine Legende. Lenin hat den wirklichen Marxismus nie gekannt. Wo hätte er ihn hernehmen sollen? Den Kapitalismus kannte er nur als Kolonialkapitalismus, die soziale Revolution nur als den Sturz eines Grundherren- und Zarendespotismus. Der russische Bolschewismus konnte den Weg des Marxismus nie verlassen; denn er ist nie marxistisch gewesen." Anton Pannekoek, *Lenin als Philosoph* (Frankfurt/M.: Europäische Verlagsanstalt, 1969), p. 121.
44 Lukács, *History and Class Consciousness*, p. 315 (italics are mine). Cf. also: "[t]he Communist Party is an autonomous form of proletarian class consciousness serving the interests of the revolution." (Ibid., p. 330.).
45 Ibid., p. 316.
46 Ibid., p. 335.
47 There are some who think that Lukács ascribed only secondary significance to the institutionalized leaders of the Communist Party, and so he could be critical of party bureaucracy as a remnant of capitalism. See on this Fritz J. Radditz, *Georg Lukács* (Reinbek bei Hamburg: Rowohlt, 1972), pp. 54–55.

at all clear how Lukács thinks the members of the Communist Party could escape this threat. He cannot explain why members of the Communist Party should be able to exercise their activity *"with the whole of their personality,"* "so that they cease to be mere specialists necessarily exposed to the danger of ossification."[48] Lukács can but dogmatically claim that the Communist Party somehow "tears away the reified veils that cloud the consciousness of the individual in capitalist society."[49]

To conclude, this paper has highlighted major aspects of Lukács's theory of reification. It has also indicated general assumptions underlying the analysis of reification in capitalist society. This paper has argued that on the premise of the primacy of economy Marx conceived other non-economic spheres or fields as serving the maintenance of the economic order, whereas Lukács claims the spreading of a specific economic structure, i.e. the commodity structure into other social spheres or fields. It has also been stressed that the justification of reification spreading into other fields was not sufficient. Consequently, it is up to further inquiry to evaluate the descriptive import of Lukács's theory of reification.

Furthermore, it has been shown that the presupposition of a non-reified island in the profound reification of late capitalist society is seen by Lukács in the Communist Party that he depicts in terms of Lenin's party theory. The obvious irreality of Lukács's description of the Communist Party as non-reified community makes it hard to decide whether it goes back to his factual lack of experience with political parties or rather results from the theoretical necessity of a cornerstone serving as basis for dereification of society. For these two reasons this paper neglected the problem of what kind of normative consequences could have been drawn, if at all, from the diagnosis of reification.

Finally, it has also been pointed out that the difference between alienation and reification cannot be simply stated in Lukács's *History and Class Consciousness*. Although there are conceptual possibilities to distinguish the two, the structural description of reification in Lukács is fairly near to that of alienated work in the early Marx. Since Lukács doesn't intend to shape the contour of reification in a more detailed manner, it doesn't seem possible to make a difference with regard to alienation.

This paper has elaborated two major conclusions. First, it has been shown that Lukács vainly tries to solve a problem implicit in Marx's thought, which can be called the supremacy of the economic sphere. Lukács didn't succeed in

---

48   Lukács, *History and Class Consciousness*, pp. 335–336.
49   Ibid., p. 339.

establishing how the economic ways of thought spread over into other spheres, e.g. cultural or interpersonal ones. Secondly, this paper has pointed out that Lukács could not clarify how non-reified conditions should be conceived of. That said, it should be stressed that this problem arises even for recent descriptions of reification.[50]

---

50 See for example: Rahel Jaeggi, *Alienation* (New York: Columbia University Press, 2014).

PART 2

Philosophical Interventions in the Concept of Reification: Applications, Critiques, and Connections

CHAPTER 4

Reification, Values and Norms: toward a Critical Theory of Consciousness

Michael J. Thompson

1   Reification Revisited[1]

It has been fifty years since the apex of the student and social movements of the late 1960s. These movements embraced both western and communist societies, from San Francisco to Paris to Prague. An awakening of the dullness and the injustice of modern, administered societies – both capitalist and communist – were among the central the focuses of these movements. Viewed long range, these movements evince a very different kind of political agency and moral awareness than contemporary societies. Whereas movements for racial, class and gender justice have by no means disappeared, there has been a deepening of the acceptance of liberal-capitalist institutions. The tacit consensus that pervades our world is rooted in a degradation of moral awareness and political dissent. Add to the passive acceptance of these institutions the fact that we are also witnessing a decline of democratic institutions, values, and practices. How can we confront and explain these trends in modern society? I think that a core thesis is to expand the idea of reification to encompass the core spheres of the personality, consciousness and the self that provide for the continued political and cultural stability of a society based on exploitation, domination, inequality and alienation. In short, I want to show how the theory of reification can be expanded to provide an account of subjectivity that accepts as legitimate and as basic the pathological consequences of capitalist society.

Another aspect to the argument I want to explore here is what reification actually inhibits in one's social agency. In this sense, the theory of reification must not only be diagnostic with respect to the problems of rational reflection within subjects, but it must also be normative in the sense that it can make evident that which is being blocked by reified consciousness itself. This second aspect of the argument is rich with possibility insofar as we see

---

[1]   An earlier version of this paper was delivered at the bi-annual meeting of the International Sociological Association on 16 July 2014 in Yokohama, Japan.

reification as hiding from view or even distorting our cognitive capacity to grasp the social-ontological structure of our world. What I mean here is that reification is not only a process whereby things that are human become non-human objects, but, more importantly and, I think, more accurately, it distorts and misshapes our cognitive capacity to see our world as cooperative, interdependent, and constituted by our actions. In this sense, it robs from us a crucial aspect of what Marx saw as crucial for any sense of social transformation: a conception of our species as self-conscious of our own socio-poietic capacities. In this sense, reification renders consciousness non-dialectical.

It is true that reification cannot be – indeed no concept can ever be – exhaustive in its diagnosis of the problems of capitalist society. But reification comes as close as any of its competitors to such a category. Nancy Fraser, for one, has argued that, "we must replace the view of capitalism as a reified form of ethical life with a more differentiated, structural view."[2] I do not believe this observation is correct. More than any other time in capitalist society we can see our world as sustained by a culture of internalized, implicitly valid norms and world-views with respect to the social goals posited by capitalist imperatives. More than any other time in the history of capitalism, we are witnessing a decrease in class conflict and an increasing stability of the system's legitimacy; all of this despite obvious and well-publicized accounts of corruption, inequality, social pathologies and other social defects. I want to suggest a widened conception of reification that is still rooted in the basic thesis put forth by Lukács in 1923: that consciousness has become colonized by heteronomous patterns of social life that have themselves been saturated with quantification, administrative reason, and exchange value. But as I see it, this basic thesis must be enlarged in order to confront what I think is a core pathology in modern cultures, namely, the degradation of agency and the self and its incapacity to articulate concrete alternatives to the prevailing social order.

The central thesis of this paper is that the concept of reification has to be expanded and cultivated into a richer theory about the nature of defective social consciousness in order for us to come to terms with the acute erosion of moral and political agency in modern societies. The idea is not that reification follows simply from the logic of commodification. Rather, my argument is that capitalist society as a social formation consisting of certain kinds of social relations larded thickly with norms and value-orientations has a strong constitutive

---

2 Nancy Fraser, "Behind Marx's Hidden Abode: For an Expanded Conception of Capitalism." In Penelope Deutscher and Cristina Lafont (eds.) *Critical Theory in Critical Times: Transforming the Global Political and Economic Order.* (New York: Columbia University Press, 2017), 141–159, 153.

power in forming the consciousness and personality of subjects. Norms are where much of the action is in the problem of reification because of the ways that norms underwrite our conceptual and evaluative dimensions of the self. Norms are, as I see it, capable of structuring our cognitive powers and conceptual fields to the extent that they are routinized by social institutions and systems and then internalized by agents who are "successfully" socialized by those institutions and systems. These norms carry with them what I call an "implicit validity," by which I mean they require no justification to be accepted by the subject, but are accepted by them as a second nature. Reification is not only a concern of this problem, but also the consequences of the acceptance of these norms on our reflective and cognitive powers as a whole.

What I would like to explore therefore is the impact that reification has on moral consciousness or, more generally considered, the capacity of individuals to reflect and judge their world from a rational, critical perspective. The essence of the problem that I want to diagnose is the demise of the rational capacities of autonomous individuals in modern, mass societies. One reason that we should consider this an important concern is that it constrains and distorts the ability of individuals to come to critical consciousness of their social world. A basic reason for this is that, as I see it, at the root of our cognitive faculties lie value-orientations that are embedded within our consciousness due to socialization. These value-orientations can be residues of traditional or conventional forms of morality on the one hand, but they are also, most certainly, absorbed from the value systems put forth by modern administrative capitalist institutions. Values of efficiency, of technical progress, of profit, of possessive individualism and consumption can serve to undergird the ways we think cognitively through our world. If these values were not successfully absorbed by social actors, there would be an erosion of the legitimacy of institutions that operate according to those imperatives. The problem here is that the more secure and more consolidated any system of socialization becomes, the more successful that it becomes in securing its values and aims within the personality structure of the subject and, as a result, the more heteronomous will be the subject's moral-political consciousness.

But another reason for taking this seriously is the current emphasis in philosophy and in critical theory as well on norms and moral consciousness as the mode in which critique occurs. The postmetaphysical and normative turn in moral philosophy more generally and critical theory more specifically is premised on the capacity of individuals to participate in a community of reason-givers and reason-takers that can obtain objectively valid values and norms via agreement and the project of justification. On this view, critique is seen as a means by which we ask for reasons and justifications for the social norms that we are asked to accept.[3] But this approach takes no account of the effects of reification and the ways that it serves to frustrate, if not totally block, such a capacity. Indeed, what this approach misses entirely is the fact that essential to any system of modern dominance is the capacity of that system to deploy norms and values that render its activities legitimate in the minds of its actors. This is the essential problem of reification and why it remains such an essential category for any critical theory of society. Without a diagnosis of this pathology of consciousness and social cognition, there will be no way for us to comprehend the ways that culture is the handmaiden to other systems of power and dominance.

My purpose here is to reconstruct reification and place it on a very different trajectory. As I see it, reification ought to be seen as the result of capitalist forms of social relations, as determined by the productive forms of social structure and function that pervades under a commodity-based production and consumption system. However, reification is the result of the ways in which consciousness is shaped by these relations in such a way that individual subjects become unable to grasp the objective context within which they live their lives; an objective context that is determined by a hierarchically structures system of extractive social relations that come to be for the interests of a small, elite segment of the community as a whole. Reification is unique to capitalism, however, because it does not rely on a value system that is transcendental or in any way but rather is entwined with the ontology of our social relations and social processes. As Andrew Feenberg has remarked: "In modern societies, the reified formal rationality of the technical disciplines and experiential knowledge of the technical achieve a partial separation at the level of discourse, but in the material reality of artifacts and systems they interpenetrate through and through."[4]

The centrality of reification for critical theory becomes more evident when we see that its central aim is the raising of critical consciousness. The withering of this capacity under the conditions of modern and late capitalism are without question, but the insights that Lukács was able to elicit from his theory of reification require development if they are to maintain their theoretical and practical salience for any critical theory of society. The basic problem becomes the inability of subjective consciousness to find appropriate mediations for self-understanding. A false totality is impressed on consciousness that

---

3 See specifically Rainer Forst, *The Right to Justification*. (New York: Columbia University Press, 2012).
4 Andrew Feenberg, *Technosystem: The Social Life of Reason*. (Cambridge, Mass.: Harvard University Press, 2017), 133.

represses and distorts reflection on the actual and potential ways we can structure and shape our social life. This is where the theory of reification ties in with the project of a critical social ontology: for the same norms that restrict critical consciousness also shape our social actions and orient our collective intentionality toward articulating specific kinds of social forms and social facts.[5] Robbed from us is the capacity to imagine let alone re-shape the reality of our social world. Again, this is because of the role played by norms in consciousness: they orient the intentional structures of consciousness that in turn shape social action and the meaning we attach to those actions. Since the thinking subject becomes unable to find a critical means by which to cognize world and self, *thought is collapsed into the object*. In this sense, since social facts – unlike natural or brute facts – are dependent on our intentions, on the normative meaning we ascribe to them collectively (think of Pierce's concept of the *legi* here as well as Searle's theory of collective intentionality) it follows that if social institutions can shape these forms of normative-intentional meaning, they can also orient our cognitive capacities and endow social facts with a second-nature-like objectivity.

But the theory of reification has been seen as superseded, in many senses of the term. Attempts at a reconstruction of the theory of reification have recently come into vogue. Axel Honneth's attempt to reconstitute reification as a pathology in recognitive relations misses a crucial aspect of the problem: namely that reification, as I interpret it, is becoming increasingly total. There are fewer and fewer social spaces where the culture of capitalism and the values and norms that orbit it are excluded. But in the end, I think that the basic principles and tenets of the theory of reification as laid out by Georg Lukács retain their salience today, albeit in different philosophical and social scientific language. A renewed theory of reification can enable us to see the continued salience of reification no only for a revived formulation of critical theory, but for a more critical understanding of the ways that social processes are able to shape, in a pathological way, the reflective capacities of individual subjects. I therefore want to defend the thesis that Lukács's understanding of reification is of paramount importance for any brand of critical social theory.

This does not mean that I seek no modification of what we might call the classical formulation of reification. Lukács's theory was constructed using the language of German Idealism; it was meant to intervene in the debates of neo-Kantian and Marxist theories of consciousness and social theory. I want to defend Lukács's totality thesis that states that reification results form a patterning

---

5 I have explored this thesis with more technical depth in my paper "Collective Intentionality, Social Domination and Reification." *Journal of Social Ontology* 3, No. 2 (2017): 207–229.

by the economic system of other spheres of social and cultural life. This patterning of the totality is a gradual but increasingly penetrating phenomenon and it results in a deep distortion of the subject's capacity to gain critical cognition of what we can call the "false totality" of capitalism. One reason I believe that this thesis needs to be taken seriously is that it nullifies, or at the very least seriously calls into question, alternative logics of critique that believe an immanent critique of capitalism can come about through the intersubjective practices either of language, justification, reason-giving and reason-taking, or recognition. What Lukács's theory implies is that logics from these kinds of social action cannot carry over into a critique of the totality.

At another level, I want also to show that only a cognitive and evaluative grasp of the totality as a social ontology of relations and processes can we achieve critical knowledge of modern society. At the heart of the theory of reification is that insight that certain ways of thinking, of being able to perceive and cognize one's place within the social system and the causal nature of its processes on subject formation. My basic argument is that reification can be further understood as the colonization and rigidification of these spheres of consciousness. Emancipating these spheres and enabling them to achieve critical awareness can only come about when we question the totality, and place capitalism once again at the heart of any theory of social criticism. Any approach that leaves this out will, as I see it, be doomed to reproduce the reified categories and practices that already exist. Although Lukács formulates his argument through the philosophical language of German Idealism, I maintain that we can construct a more compelling, more satisfying account of reification through the development of the extensions that I propose.

2 The Classical Theory of Reification

Lukács introduces his concept of reification as a result of a prolonged attempt to understand the problem of the crisis of culture that he witnessed during the late nineteenth and early-twentieth centuries. He also saw that the precepts of orthodox Marxism – which posited a mechanistic form of consciousness that would propel working people to revolutionary praxis – as misguided. What was lacking in Marxist theory was a theory of mind and consciousness that was adequate to grasp the problems of cognition under industrial capitalism. To do this, Lukács read Marx's theory of the fetishism of commodities through several important sources. First, there was the philosophical problem of Idealism raised once again by neo-Kantianism. According to this view, a separation of facts from values was needed to be able to construct a conception of science that was free from the moral baggage of normative claims. Empirical facts could only be grasped rationally, on this view, through being cleansed of normative value judgments, which were to be resolved not through the analysis of facts, but through discursive domain of culture. In terms of its epistemic theory, neo-Kantianism also broke with the Hegelian view which saw that rational knowledge could only be approached through the dialectic of essence and appearance: I come to know what something is not through an analysis of empirical facts, but through the teleological end that any object holds within a system or totality. To return to empiricism in social theory would therefore mean a reifying of consciousness in the sense that objects disappear from cognitive view. Lukács therefore saw one root of reification as the return to subjective Idealist models of mind as well as an epistemology that privileges empiricism over coherence theories of truth.

Another source for Lukács's concept of reification came from his sociological studies with Weber and Simmel. From Weber he took the thesis of rationalization seriously which maintained that modernity was being characterized by a methodical calculation of means and ends and that this was coming to affect the subjective capacities for judgment and knowledge of the social world. Since modern industry was characterized by a heightening of rationalization, or a "methodical attainment of a definitely given and practical end by means of an increasingly precise calculation of adequate means," its ability to shape consciousness according to its patterns of operation were increasing their dominance.[6] From Simmel, Lukács took seriously the thesis of the "tragedy of culture," which saw a growing inability of modern individuals to be able to comprehend the totality of social life and its many mechanisms and forces – a rift between what Simmel termed "subjective" and "objective" culture respectfully.

Lukács saw Marx's theory of the fetishism of commodities as the prism through which these theories could be made concrete. Both Weber and Simmel saw their diagnoses as essentially fatalistic and pessimistic; there would be no way out of the dilemmas of modernity and they were consequently unable to locate an agent of transformation. But for Lukács, reification is a theory that brings together the theory of mind as well as the theory of society: it seeks to reconcile the problems of subjectivity and objectivity from the abstractions of neo-Kantianism by positing their relation within a totality. As with Marx, the fetishism of commodities is the expression of the fragmentation of a consciousness that can no longer grasp the whole process that produces it, for

---

6 Max Weber, "The Sociology of the World Religions," in Hans Gerth and C. Wright Mills (eds.) *From Max Weber*. (London: Routledge, 1970), 293.

Lukács, reification is the inability to grasp totality, to see the internal relations that undergird reality itself. The ability to know the essence of reality is to be able to grasp dynamic process as opposed to isolated particulars. It is the ability to conceive of the processes that shape objective and subjective life – it is the very groundwork of what allows capitalist institutions to maintain their legitimacy in an age of legal-rational authority.

Central to Lukács's concept of reification is the notion that objects of consciousness – most specifically, those things that are human – become "thing-like." What Lukács has in mind here is the thesis that the social world loses its inherently human character and ceases to be seen as created by human praxis. But also, it turns human beings themselves into objects for manipulation and into extensions for one's own projects. Think of a waiter in a restaurant, a cashier at a store, or a cab driver. All are transformed from human subjects to practical objects that can be utilized via the cash nexus. The social bonds between people become reified, dehumanized. Since humans make the world not only materially through the labor process and the shaping of nature through work but also cognitively via the intentional structures of consciousness, to lose the human character of the world means that it becomes estranged from our comprehension of it as collectively formed and re-created.

The commodity form under modern forms of capitalist production is responsible for this change in consciousness. What occurs through the division of labor and the rationalization of mass production is the fragmentation of the object. No longer do we see the objects created by human labor as human, but increasingly as inert objects. As Lukács notes: "this fragmentation of the object of production necessarily entails the fragmentation of its subject. In consequence of the rationalization of the work process the human qualities and idiosyncrasies of the worker appear increasingly as *mere sources of error* when contrasted with these abstract special laws functioning according to rational predictions. Neither objectively nor in his relation to his work does man appear as the authentic master of the process; on the contrary, he is a mechanical part incorporated into a mechanical system."[7] The "thingness" of reification (recall the German term is *Verdinglichung*, literally, "to become thing-like") is now also a cognitive problem insofar as a "thing" (*Ding*) in Kantian terms, is an object that fails to become an object of cognition. It literally disappears and is taken for granted, not thought about, not reflected upon.

As a result, the subject encounters not a world that he has shared in making, but rather as an already-formed totality to which he must fit himself and

---

7 Georg Lukács, *History and Class Consciousness: Studies in Marxist Dialectics*. (Cambridge, Mass.: MIT Press, 1971), 89.

conform: "He finds it already pre-existing and self-sufficient, it functions independently of him and he has to conform to its laws whether he likes it or not."[8] The effect of this is the deterioration of the subject's will as he increasingly surrenders his autonomy and power of judgment to the functional imperatives of the system: "As labor is progressively rationalized and mechanized his lack of will is reinforced by the way in which his activity becomes less and less active and more and more *contemplative*."[9] The subject now becomes divided against himself. Reification renders one's consciousness passive to the activity of the system. The system is, of course, re-created by us, by those rendered passive. Hence, one is still active in the sense that one labors, one purchases, one lives one's life according to the structures and norms shaped by the system. But now, each of us does this without reflecting on the purposes and ends of that system. We take it for granted, as basic, as the basic background conditions for our lives. As such, it is rendered outside the scope of critical consciousness.

But what this means for Lukács is more than a mere cognitive defect. He argues that reification effectively hides from view the very purposes and legitimacy of the social order as a whole. We become unable to critique the totality and to see it as the cause of any of the particular subjective pathologies we may experience. We are unable, in effect, to move beyond the phenomenological experience of social pathology and question the system as a whole. "The question why and with what justification human reason should elect to regard just these systems as constitutive of its own essence (as opposed to the 'given,' alien, unknowable nature of the content of those systems) never arises. It is assumed to be self-evident."[10] The key issue here is, once again, a question of drilling down into the "essential structure" of the system itself, the system *as totality*. The core property of critique now can be seen in Hegelian and Marxian terms at once: as the penetration beneath the phenomenological, empirical manifestation of the system and its products into the essential structures and processes that are constitutive of it: "The question then becomes: are the empirical facts – (it is immaterial whether they are purely 'sensuous' or whether their sensuousness is only the ultimate material substratum of their 'factual' essence) – to be taken as 'given' or can this 'givenness' be dissolved further into rational forms, i.e., can it be conceived as the product of 'our' reason?"[11]

Reification now is further revealed to be our incapacity to rationally comprehend the essential structure of the system. By essence is meant not some

---

8   Lukács, *History and Class Consciousness*, 89.
9   Lukács, *History and Class Consciousness*, 89.
10 Lukács, *History and Class Consciousness*, 112.
11 Lukács, *History and Class Consciousness*, 116.

inflated metaphysical substance but the basic structure of the system as a whole and the way it structures social relations, social processes and social ends or purposes that constitute the social whole and our subjective orientations as well. The key idea here is therefore one of critical metaphysics: de-reified consciousness is not some mystical, special power to which only a select few have access; it is the result of an ability to thematize the nature of the social system as a whole. There is an ineliminable social-ontological component to this thesis. Lukács sees in Hegel and in Marx a need to understand that social reality is the product of our practices, practices guided by ideas. Hence, the nature of social reality corresponds to the nature of the ideas we possess about it. Indeed, if we go back to the Aristotelian conception of *praxis*, it is not simply a matter of activity, but it is *thought directed to an end*. As Aristotle says in his *Nicomachean Ethics*: "thought (διάνοια) alone moves nothing, but thought directed toward an end (πρακτική) does; for this is indeed the moving cause of productive activity (του ποιεῖ) also since he who makes something always has some further end (τέλος) in view."[12] This means that for a practice to change, it entails a transformation in the end toward which that practice is organized.

Now we can glimpse a richer idea of what reification is about. Once we connect our powers of cognition with the idea of social practice, we can see what the social totality means as an ontological category. The totality is not an entity external to us, but one that is constituted through us – through us as practical beings. It is an ontological category because it embraces the total world of social facts that we as members of any community create and endow with meaning and significance. As Lukács see it, what is special about capitalism is its ability to constitute the entirety of the totality; it is a capacity to reshape and reorient all social practices toward ends that it posits as valid. Once we see practice as consciously directed activity, reification now presents itself as a corruption of praxis; it is the supplanting of heteronomous ideas about what the ends of our activities should be that re-orients our world-creating powers toward heteronomous ends and purposes. These ideas are normative ideas, for

---

12   Aristotle, *Nicomachean Ethics*, VI.ii.5. Lukács will seek to develop this idea more fully in his *Ontology*, but even in *History and Class Consciousness* we can see he has this insight in view: "In his doctoral thesis Marx, more concrete and logical than Hegel, effected the transition from the question of existence and its hierarchy of meanings to the plane of historical reality and concrete praxis. 'Didn't the Moloch of the Ancients hold sway? Wasn't the Delphic Apollo a real power in the life of the Greeks? In this context Kant's criticism is meaningless.' Unfortunately Marx did not develop this idea to its logical conclusion although in his mature works his method always operates with concepts of existence graduated according to the various levels of praxis." *History and Class Consciousness*, 127–128.

they express ways that we should orient our activities, our practical lives, as well as the ways that we rationalize and legitimate those regimes of practice. Capitalism as a total process, indeed, as an "inverted world," as Hegel would have called it, is not only an economic, but a total social system once it is able to absorb not only our time and labor, but our practices as a whole.[13] It has absorbed our capacity to see that the ends toward which our activities are oriented possess class character – that capital is material force insofar as it has the capacity to colonize our practices by supplanting *its* ends as *our* ends. The key idea here is that reification is not epistemic in nature, but rather (social) ontological: it is re-organizes the very reality of the social world via this shaping of our consciousness and the norms that underwrite it and our practices. What I want to show now is how this shaping of consciousness is a matter of the shaping of norms and values that are absorbed through socialization processes before returning to this theme of a critical social ontology that can provide us with a means to shatter the effects of reification.

3   An Expansion of the Model of Reification

Central to my project of reconstructing reification is the thesis that it is a complex concept, covering three distinct areas of human thinking and feelings. As I suggested above, the main thesis that Lukács puts forth is the idea – taken heavily from the project of German Idealism – that the subject's impulses for ethical and political obligation and, implicitly, of dissent rests on the ability to comprehend the social reality within which one lives. This is a theme taken from Hegel's phenomenological understanding of the ways in which the thinking subject transitions to absolute knowledge: one is able to comprehend one's

---

13   As Michael E. Brown notes: "the fact that capitalist political economy defines and therefore can be said to operate hegemonically across the entire terrain of economically relevant and economically dependent social life makes it difficult to speak sensibly in ways that are inconsistent with it.... The comprehensiveness of capitalist production, and the inevitable moral vacuum in the local settings it inevitably leaves behind, are findings of the Marxian critique of ideology." *The Production of Society: A Marxian Foundation for Social Theory*. (Totowa, NJ: Rowman and Littlefield, 1986), 101, 103. This is one reason to accept the implications of Lukács's thesis that the totality is re-patterned around the imperatives of capital once it penetrates the domain of culture. Andrew Feenberg notes that: "'Culture' now refers to the unifying pattern of an entire society, including its typical artifacts, rituals, customs, and beliefs. The concept of culture points toward the common structures of social life. It assigns the researcher the problem of discovering the overarching paradigms of meaning and value that shape all the various spheres of society." *The Philosophy of Praxis: Marx, Lukács and the Frankfurt School*. (London: Verso, 2014), 65.

world and as a totality, but also, if one is free, one sees that this totality is rational, i.e., that it serves the rational, universal interest of the social whole rather than elevating a particular part of it over the whole. The Marxian twist on this is a critique of capitalist society that distorts the social-ontological structures and processes of society to run counter to the common social interest and instead valorize private surplus over social, human ends and needs. Reification is a lack of the kind of cognitive power to penetrate the *appearance* of capitalist society as "natural" and justified based on its mere existence. Reification is the defective form of reasoning that limits this power of reflection.

But there is also a neo-Kantian trace in Lukács's thesis in that he is claiming that the central capacity – indeed, the *critical* capacity – to be able to perceive the world as a proper object of knowledge disintegrates and we are left with the problem of the reified subject relating to the world as mere appearance, where essence (or the space of causal reasons) is veiled beneath a haze of "natural" processes and forms. The neo-Kantian separation between fact and value means that it is unable to see the connection between the way that values are constitutive of the world; that there is in fact a unity between the norms and values we possess and the nature of the social facts that are generated and then interpreted by us. By insisting on a separation between these two spheres, consciousness is rendered unable to see that this distortion in consciousness is the result of the transformation of norms that are generated by rationalized forms of production, consumption and social coordination that are successfully internalized by subjects. At the core of the phenomenon of reification, it can be said, is this mechanism of the generation and internalization of norms and its effects on consciousness and cognition.

Think of reification therefore not simply as a transposition problem within consciousness but as a re-coding of the norms that shape and structure our cognition and our practices. What this thesis entails is the idea that any norm is not simply value but is also a routing of cognitive and epistemic capacities in such a way that they are unable to work outside of the boundaries set by the system of norms that are ambient within the community. In this sense, norms take on a kind of social power in that they can orient action and the reasons for such actions. As Joseph Raz has pointed out: "Generalizing, one may say that normative power is the power to effect a normative change. A normative change can be interpreted to comprise every change in the reasons for action that some person has."[14] If we explore this idea, we find that the idea of normative power is the capacity of our norms to be shaped and oriented by others. But going further, it entails the shaping of our intentionality, the very way that

---

14   Joseph Raz, *Practical Reason and Norms*. (London: Hutchinson and Co., 1975), 99.

we endow meaning and significance to the world – i.e., the very creation of social facts itself. Since social facts are created by our intentionality, the power to shape norms is also the power to shape social reality itself.

This, in turn, leads to a deeper problem in that social power now operates within the normative valences of consciousness. Raz calls this "influence" and argues that it "includes the power to affect the goals people have, their desires and aspirations. Beliefs in the desirability of pursuing certain styles of life are induced through educational institutions and the mass media."[15] Reification, on this view, can be seen as the result of this kind of power and social dominance. Elsewhere I have called this *constitutive power*, or the power to shape and orient our norms and value-orientations that in turn transforms not only our consciousness, but also our social practices.[16] But what reification adds to this discussion is that it is not simply a neutral shaping or orienting of consciousness. More specifically, it is shaped according to the logics of the dominating social systems and their imperatives. Historically speaking, under rationalized capitalist forms of social production and consumption, it means that these new norms and values absorb subjective life into the system of production and consumption that generates private surplus. But what is particularly problematic here is that the different dimensions of subjectivity are shaped and formed by this reification of consciousness. Pointing to three different dimensions of subjectivity, we can say there exist cognitive, evaluative and cathectic dimensions of the self and that each are underwritten by the normative structure of consciousness.

Now, this means that the phenomenon of reification runs much deeper than the cognitive layer alone. Hence, the extent to which subjectivity gets folded into the fabric of the social order is more deeply rooted than a cognitivist framework can account for. Going back to Raz for a moment, we can see that norms have a deeper impact on how we see and how we judge and evaluate the social world. Any norm can shape our evaluative capacities. Think of the simple argument that says: *it is right for you to* φ, which leads to the logical consequence: φ-*ing is good*. Once successfully internalized by the subject, the personality system may also come to invest itself cathectically in φ: *It feels good whenever I* φ. This is, to be sure, an overly simplistic argument about the effect of norms on consciousness and personality, but it captures much of how the norms that shape systems can also reify consciousness. Norms and values therefore constitute a crucial means by which reification can serve to hide

---

15 Raz, *Practical Reason and Norms*, 99.
16 See Michael J. Thompson, *The Domestication of Critical Theory*. (London: Rowman and Littlefield, 2016).

from view a more critical account of the social world. It also goes a long way in demonstrating that phenomenological and pragmatist arguments concerning critical reasoning are unable to overcome the problem of reification. Indeed, as much as communicative and discursive theories of judgment may appeal to some, they are unable to explode the structures of reification that fuse subject and object in capitalist society.

Norms are therefore more than simply structures of practice, they are also structures of meaning in that they serve as the ways that we as subjects and members of a collective form of life assign meaning to objects and phenomena that occur within the lifeworld.[17] In this sense, the alteration of social practices necessarily entails a transformation of norms. Since a practice is, as Aristotle and Marx agree, thought-directed activity, then once we change the meaning and purpose of any activity, we also change the thought behind it. Capitalism patterns meaning just as it patterns practices; it therefore becomes constitutive of new norms and value-patterns that form into coordinated webs of norms that shape social action and subjective dispositions. But these norms are rooted not in the spontaneity of the lifeworld, or according to some democratic consensus about how we should organize our world, but according to the imperatives of productive and consumptive demands of an economic system oriented toward private surplus and the means to the expansion of that surplus. These imperatives gradually reorganize the very ontological structures of the social world and create a new social reality. Reification therefore constitutes a deeper pathology not only of consciousness and itself, but those structures of meaning that orient practices and the very reality that our social practices create.

The key idea here, taking after Parsons, is that there is a sense in which "successful" forms of socialization are understood to be the extent to which individuals take up the norms of the social systems and institutions around them. But the key issue here, as Parsons points out, is that these norms cannot simply be acquired in mature adulthood. There must be some background basis for

---

[17] Andrew Feenberg notes, on this point, the common avenue of departure for both Lukács and Heidegger: "it inspired Heidegger and Lukács, who both accepted Lask's breakthrough to a new kind of transcendental account of meaning that borders on ontology. Meaning is the 'being' of the phenomena through which we gain access to them as what they 'are.' Heidegger and Lukács went on to attempt to ground being on practice rather than subjectivity." *The Philosophy of Praxis*, 75. I think the key idea here is that we need to move into the next stage, to that of a social ontology where meaning, as structured by normative frames of cognition, is the nexus of consciousness which is infiltrated by social practices and the norms that ground them thereby serving as the location of reification since that is the meeting point between fact and value as well as thought and being.

the acquisition of more complex social norms. For Lukács, the thesis of reification holds that it is the activities of the workplace – of the technical transformation of production, of the collapsing of time into space in terms of the expansion of productive capacities, and rational forms of bureaucratization, and so on – that serve as the soil of reification. This may have been true in the early twentieth century, but as these norms of production and consumption, or rationalization, the legitimacy of the capitalist economic life and culture penetrated more deeply into the layers of culture and social institutions as a whole, reification became more trenchant since the acquisition of the values of capitalist life are acquired at younger ages. Hence, Parsons notes that

> [I]t may be concluded that it is the internalization of the value-orientation patterns embodied in the role-expectations for ego of the significant socializing agents, which constitutes the strategic element of this basic personality structure. And it is because these patterns can only be acquired through the mechanism of identification, and because the basic identification patterns are developed in childhood, that the childhood structure of personality in this respect is so stable and unchangeable.[18]

Once the social order is seen as, essentially, a collection of norms that guide and coordinate social action, we must also see that for this to be successful it is required that it be absorbed or internalized by the ego structure of the individual. This leads, as Herbert Marcuse insightfully points out, to a crippling sense of reification as one-dimensionality, literally as a folding of the ego into the social structure itself, unable to distinguish itself from the social reality:

> The mediation between the self and the other gives way to immediate identification. In the social structure, the individual becomes the conscious and unconscious object of administration and obtains his freedom and satisfaction in his role as such an object; in the mental structure, the ego shrinks to such an extent that it seems no longer capable of sustaining itself, as a self, in distinction from id and superego.[19]

Hence, we can see that reification can be expanded to understand the ways that norms and value-orientations fuse the subject to the objective domain of

---

18   Talcott Parsons, *The Social System*. (New York: The Free Press, 1951), 228.
19   Herbert Marcuse, "The Obsolescence of the Freudian Conception of Man." In Herbert Marcuse, *Five Lectures: Psychoanalysis, Politics and Utopia* (Boston: Beacon Press, 1970), 44–61, 47.

the world of social facts. The more that capitalism as a social formation, as a economic-social-cultural formation is able to make its web of norms efficiently internalized by the ego, the more that reification will be deeply rooted in the subject. As Andrew Feenberg points out concerning the analysis of reification, "The focus must shift from the mechanistic 'influence' of social conditions on consciousness to the generalized patterning of all dimensions of society."[20] This internalization of the web of norms deployed by social institutions is what causes the reification of subjects, what essentially explains their relative lack of awareness of the defective nature of the social order of which they are a part and which their practices have been oriented to re-create. It also quells the antagonism of class conflict. This is one reason why industrial and post-industrial societies have witnessed a sharp decline in the politicization of economic inequality: the normative webs of the system have penetrated deeply into the culture that socializes its members to such a degree that critical reflection has been stunted.

But again, norms are more than mere normative "A should φ" statements. They are also constitutive of facts as well in the sense that they endow our practices with a social-ontological facticity.[21] Here reification takes on a more pernicious and more deeply rooted course. Parsons was correct that successful internalization was a means to the stability of any social system and that the ego had to internalize social norms for it to stabilize the ego. But this also means that it has the capacity to create new social facts as well; hence, the link between norms and consciousness. At a more technical level, we can see that the collective-intentional structure of consciousness shared by any community is active in the ways that it articulates their social reality. This is because, as John Searle has argued, the norms we adopt coordinate collective forms of meaning by assigning objects "status functions," or forms of meaning with which we endow objects based on collective forms of intentionality, or collective forms of meaning-giving. In this sense, social facts are the result of this collective intentionality and the ability to control the norms that shape that intentionality is also a power to shape the structure of social reality. In this sense, reification and social ontology are deeply entwined and constitutes a theory not only of defective consciousness but also a theory of power.[22]

---

20   Feenberg, *Philosophy of Praxis*, 66.
21   As Joseph Raz notes: "Statements of facts which are reasons for the performance of a certain action by a certain agent are the premises of an argument the conclusion of which is that there is a reason for the agent to perform the action or that he ought to do it." Raz, *Practical Reason and Norms*, 28.
22   See John Searle, *Making the Social World: The Structure of Human Civilization*. (New York: Oxford University Press, 2010), 145ff. Also cf. Thompson, "Collective Intentionality, Social Domination and Reification."

4   Value Heteronomy and Cognitive Distortion

I have been arguing that an extension of reification as a concept for critical theory should focus on a particular conception of cognition that sees epistemic capacities as tied to value-orientations. I have also argued that these value-orientations have the ability to shape cognitive and epistemic powers. Most importantly, they are able to form the basis not only for the *content* of reasoning – both normative and cognitive ideas that individuals carry with them and use to understand their world – but also the *formal* aspects of thought, given in terms of isolated, episodic thinking styles as opposed to holistic and dynamic and relational forms of thought. The latter was considered critical in the objective Idealist sense since it was concerned with the actual, objective features of thought and reality. Whereas for Kant, and Enlightenment thinkers more generally, cognition was conceived as an independent process, contemporary psychological models of mind show that it is more correct to see it as a function that is embedded in the personality system of individuals. According to this view, the problem of cognition is linked to the kinds of value-systems that individuals possess.

Lukács echoed this view in the sense that he saw the central problem of reification as residing in the ways that practices were reordered by new normative regimes that patterned the background conditions for our reflective and evaluative judgments about the world.[23] Reification can now be seen as a pathology of consciousness, but one which is itself linked to the pathology of personality. Since norms come to socialize agents, the nature of the norms will come to shape value-orientations that also give form to the concepts used to understand the world. Reification is the result not of the rationalization of society alone – i.e., of the techno-industrial order and of forms of strategic action – but of the values that are required to secure legitimacy of a system of extractive social relations. Here, Lukács seems to me to lay a foundation for an extension of reification, which goes beyond techno-industrial forms of social integration and toward one that can capture the intricacies of social power and domination in a systemic sense. A society that is able to *routinize* particular norms and values therefore has the ability to shape the powers of cognition as well. Reification is a pathology of the whole self; a problem that affects the total personality of the subject, not simply forms of reasoning. As such, it presses itself

---

23   By background conditions, I mean, as Searle does: "The Background consists of all of those abilities, capacities, dispositions, ways of doing things, and general know-how that enable us to carry out our intentions and apply our intentional states." Searle, *Making the Social World*, 31 and *passim*.

onto the powers of reflection and critical judgment by ensconcing the subject in a web of norms from which it is difficult to escape.

What I mean by this is that as the web of norms are increasingly rooted in the systemic imperatives of the social order, and the more that this social order is articulated by rational, administrative-capitalist purposes and goals, the more that this web of norms will exert pressures on different spheres of agency. The social field, where the web of norms is located, exerts four kinds of pressure: internalization, routinization, rationalization and socialization pressures. In the first level, the ego must absorb the value-patterns (web of norms) that are ambient within the social world. This becomes more efficient in modern societies by routinizing them so that they become part of the background *hexis* of the subject. As these value-orientations and the practices that they shape become more routinized and internalized, they carry with them their own rationalizations. This is because they become increasingly self-referential as the system becomes more imbued by those value-patterns and more and more spheres of life and institutions are colonized by the logics of rational authority tied to economic imperatives. Last, we can see that these lead to the socialization pressure where our active forms of judgment and reasoning are pressed into the structural constraints imposed by the social system but also, once it has been successfully internalized by the subject, imposed from within as well. Consider the schematic version of my thesis summarized in Figure 4.1.

According to this scheme, reification is the result of the constraints placed upon cognition by the value systems resulting from the inculcation of social norms. It is also a diachronic and synchronic process, which affects multiple levels of consciousness and social action. This means that the powers of reason, as well as of judgment, in the model are affected by the types of value-orientations that the subject has absorbed. The goal of social norms under capitalism is to maximize the efficiency of its goals; to this end, it is crucial that subjects accept the goals of such institutions as their own, to see that the only real purpose of their own actions, values, and ideas are in some kind of conformity with the world around them. Hegemonic values and norms therefore are the starting point for the deformed kind of consciousness that constitutes reification. These values are increasingly heteronomic in that they emanate from institutional worlds that do not require nor do they ask for any form of rational justification. Rather, they increasingly are taken as basic and form the background condition for the various forms of deontic power that hold social action together.

As I have been arguing, norms affect consciousness in a straightforward way. They have the ability to shape our practical activities as well as the rationalizations for those activities and their effects. This occurs through the problem of

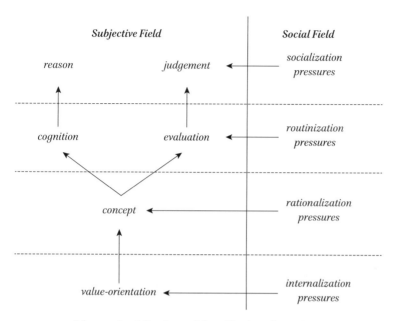

FIGURE 4.1 Scheme of socialization and the reification of consciousness

value heteronomy, where the socialization process has been able to successfully inculcate a basic value system that orients the evaluative capacities of the subject. Value heteronomy is the condition where modern forms of authority express themselves as interior to the subject. Recall that for Weber, authority or domination is "the chance of commands being obeyed by a specifiable group of people," and on in which "the content of the command becomes the maxim of their conduct for its very own sake."[24] The reification of consciousness therefore begins with the inculcation of routinized and rationalized value systems and concepts which shape normative orientations toward the world. But they also, as Weber points out, solidify and legitimate the social relations that serve as the conduits of authority and socialize the sense of self that constitutes the personality of the individual.

Reification of consciousness therefore begins with the uncritical acceptance of heteronomous value systems, which legitimate ideas, norms, values, social relations, institutions and goals. Crucial in this sense is that the norms be accepted as they are presented; that they become part of the subject's interior structure of attitudes. But it is not possible to do this if the norm is questioned, or if some rational basis is sought for its acceptance. When this occurs,

---

24   Max Weber, *Wirtschaft und Gesellschaft*. (Tübingen: J.C.B. Mohr, 1972), 532.

there is generally some form of deviance involved. But more importantly for my purpose here, it also implies an affect of the rational faculty of cognition: to accept norms without rational justification means to accept its conception of the world. Rationalized social and institutional norms that serve the powers of elites and their economic ends – norms about labor, about inequality, about income and wealth, about education, about the purpose of social goals, and so on – are imposed on consciousness which results in a lack of consistency between the different values within the subject. This lack of logical consistency, over time, requires that the subject's cognitive powers be weakened in order to accept the particularistic norms of capitalist institutional logics. Rational consciousness and evaluative consciousness are therefore dialectically linked.

Recall that the reification thesis has at its core the insight that consciousness is shaped by norms and value-orientations. What this means is that since norms are constitutive of social facts, as I have demonstrated, it also means that such social facts carry with them their own validity, what I call *implicit validity*. This is because the mechanism of value-acquisition does not come as a result of rational justification but because it is embedded in the practices and norms that constitute the social world. As a result, reified consciousness is able to split reality into particulars. It lacks consistency and can only know isolated, static forms of reality as opposed to dynamic and processual forms of reality. It is unable to grasp internal relations and to connect the logic of the social world with the pathologies one experiences, at a social and existential level. Since value systems establish a basis for the evaluative capacity of the subject, it can also be shown that they form the basis for the cognitive capacity of subjects in the sense that knowledge about the world requires the suspension of critical cognition. As Milton Rokeach claimed in his investigation of "open" and "closed" minds, "Isolation between parts reflects a tendency not to relate beliefs to the inner requirements of logical consistency, but to assimilate them wholesale, as fed by one's authority figure."[25] As a result, reified consciousness not only shapes cognitive but also evaluative capacities about the relative rightness and wrongness of things, irrespective of the "reasons" given for them.

The reification of consciousness – conceived as the concealment of dynamic social reality behind the façade of isolated, episodic consciousness – therefore implies that the mind is somehow constrained from grasping the essential nature of the world. And this only makes sense since the value systems that constitute subjectivity under capitalism exert the pressure of partial, immediate forms of reasoning. They offer for the subject simple scripts for understanding the world; not in terms of how it actually works, but how they must work

---

25   Milton Rokeach, *The Open and Closed Mind*. (New York: Basic Books, 1960), 61.

within its conception of how the world should be. Hence, the relation between the value system and cognition becomes manifest: a critical, mediated relation to the world is displaced by an immediate relation to the world. The values that steer consciousness also deter the subject from rational inquiry, from being able to see the world in its actuality. As Lukács argues: "As long as man adopts a stance of intuition and contemplation he can only relate to his own thought and to the objects of the empirical world in an immediate way. He accepts both as ready-made – produced by historical reality. As he wishes only to know the world and not to change it he is forced to accept both the empirical, material rigidity of existence and the logical rigidity of concepts as unchangeable."[26]

Reification of consciousness therefore is not simply to be understood as the inability to conceive of the social world properly, but at its root, it is the result of specific forms of values and norms that stultify the forms of socialization that make individuals critical, open, and to see social praxis and civic life as an essential aspect to their individuality. As Lukács wrote much later in his "Literature and Democracy": "If we are not aware of this relation, or if we do not wish to take notice of it, then our so-called external destiny, that is, our economic, political, and social destiny appears, in our creations, to be stripped of every human element. The 'we' do not experience and imagine this destiny as being our social interactions with other people, but, rather, in our self-consciousness, we fetishistically transform it into external objects and lifeless things. Instead of the concrete economy of life, the colorful web of our interactions, an abstract, impoverished, oppressed 'I' stands opposed to an external world that has become an abstract, fetishized, dead thing."[27]

5 Overcoming Reification through Critical Judgment

So is there a way out? If critical theory is to serve any useful end, it must move beyond the merely diagnostic and into the political where we can perhaps use rational reflection to mitigate against reification. Even though the argument I have elaborated above seems complete and totalizing, this can never be the case. Rather, any social system suffers from its own imperfections, as subtle as they may be. Pathologies of society and self still emerge in the process of our lives and it is only when those pathologies are experienced in some way can we have an entrée point into the possibility for social critique. To combat and

---

26 Lukács, *History and Class Consciousness*, 202.
27 Georg Lukács, "Literature and Democracy II," in Tyrus Miller and Erik Bachman (eds.) *The Culture of People's Democracy*. (Leiden: Brill, 2013), 75.

dissolve reification is therefore only possible when we are open to questioning the basic value-orientations that shape the social reality of which I am a part. This must be a political act, or the result of a political challenge to the culture that perpetuates the forms of social power that pervade our lives. For this reason, combatting reification must be a central role of any political critique of power. For reification to become the object of political critique once again, it is necessary to understand the inherently social-ontological structure of Lukács's argument.

With this in mind, let me return now to how we can reconstruct a theory of critical judgment from the reflections I have laid out here. As I see it, the essence of critical judgment must be expressed in an expanded form of thinking that can encompass the social totality as the basis for understanding any particular expression of social or political power. Reification becomes increasingly difficult to combat the more that it penetrates into cultural and personality structures. But the reality it creates is one that is always open to critique because it is a false totality – i.e., it is a totality that is irrational because it does not serve universal ends and purposes. The contradictions generated by such an irrational system are the necessary cracks that forces us back to re-theorize the totality. In this sense, we must ask about the purpose and end of the social totality – we must inquire into the validity of ends and purposes of our lives as interdependent, cooperative social beings. Now, this is precisely, I think, what Lukács urges in critique of reified consciousness. His idea of "expressive totality" may seem to us to be out of date politically; I want to suggest that it has been dismissed too soon without proper theoretical treatment.

What Lukács argues is that it is only when working people discover that they are the "subject-object" of history that reification will be overcome. This kind of consciousness, though, is not a contemplative form of consciousness, but an active one. He has in view here the need to change the practical relations we have with one another and with nature, and this means, as I have been arguing here, a transformation of the normative structure of consciousness that orients our activities. As Lukács puts it: "the consciousness of the proletariat must become deed ... namely, since consciousness here is not the knowledge of an opposed object but is the self-consciousness of the object *the act of consciousness overthrows the objective form of its object*."[28] What this means is that consciousness must become a new self-consciousness that sees the immanent ontology of our sociality and the ways that this has been shaped and formed according to the interests of others, directed and oriented toward

---

28   Lukács, *History and Class Consciousness*, 178.

private needs, ends and purposes as opposed those of all. A rational universal is therefore discovered through a new form of self-consciousness. But this self-consciousness is to know ourselves as social beings, as practical beings and as members of a totality entails a new way of thinking and judging.

For this reason, Lukács maintains that three aspects of critique must be in play. First, we must become aware of the contradictions that plague the system as a whole. If we are able to do this, then it is necessary, second, for us to have "an aspiration toward totality, that action should serve the purpose, described above, in the totality of the process." What this means is an ability to grasp the truth of the totality – "the truth that in the dialectical totality the individual elements incorporate the structure of the whole."[29] In this sense, we need to be able to see any particular contradiction or norm or practice part of a total process. Last, if we are to be able to judge any given norm or practice, "it is essential to relate it to its function in the total process."[30] If we are able to do these three things then the hold of reification can be loosened. The reason is that thinking in terms of relations, processes, and ends or purposes is the grammar needed to think the totality as an ontological reality. Once we see this, we can begin to grasp the ways that uncritical practical activity helps to re-create and sustain the false totality that generates the contradictions in the first place and push us toward embracing a "critical practical activity."

This may seem overly philosophical, but we can make this more concrete by casting it in terms of a social ontology. Once we gain self-consciousness of ourselves as social beings, whose existence is interdependent on, and within relations with, other beings; that these interdependent relations are embedded in processes of change and activity; and finally that these processes and practices have ends and purposes, we can glimpse the essential structure of any given social reality in ontological, as opposed to empirical, form. The totality of social reality begins to expose itself. I go to work each day to bring home money to pay my bills and purchase things. But as isolated "facts" these things taken independently render critical reflection inert. Once I ask about the purposes or ends of that work, or the things I purchase, or about the kinds of relations that are needed to bring about the things for which I work or which I purchase, and the other institutions, norms and practices that uphold such a social reality, I begin to inquire into the legitimacy of such a system. Is it rational? Does it exist for the benefit of all? Reification only begins to break down at such a point, when the question of the ontology of my social world and my place within it is

---

29   Lukács, *History and Class Consciousness*, 198.
30   Idem.

raised to consciousness. This is why Lukács argues that "Marxist theory is designed to put the proletariat into a very particular frame of mind."[31]

Once we see this as an alternative mode of critical judgment, we can also see the severe errors of the post-metaphysical, discursive and phenomenological approaches to judgment that are current in theory today. Relying on thinkers such as Hannah Arendt, Jürgen Habermas, or Axel Honneth cannot get us past the blockages posed by reification. Indeed, as I see the matter, such theoretical projects do little more than refract reified consciousness back onto the judging subject. Indeed, their emphasis on a noumenal conception of intersubjectivity shears off the deeper normative, practical and social-relational structures and processes that constitute our social reality. It is this, after all, that Marx really meant by the term "material": that our sociality possesses a thick ontology of practices, norms, processes and relational structures and these structures are embedded within a social totality with its own imperatives. Without access to this totality, as Lukács importantly points out, there is no way to overcome the pathology of reification and come to terms with the deeper, core dynamics of our social world and the way it shapes its members. Perhaps a return to this concept and its critical implications for culture and political judgment can help us return critical social theory to its original Enlightenment political aspirations for a rational, free form of sociality. And perhaps it can also enable progressive social movements to disclose a rationally valid emancipatory interest to overcome the dehumanizing, reifying tendencies of capitalist modernity.

---

31   Lukács, *History and Class Consciousness*, 262.

CHAPTER 5

Reification and the Mechanistic World-Picture: Lukács and Grossmann on Mechanistic Philosophy

Sean Winkler

1   Introduction

For George Lukács, reification is the defining predicament of the modern condition. Next to "class consciousness," it is the central concept of his magnum opus, *History and Class Consciousness* (1923). The English translation of the original German term, *Verdinglichung*, and the portmanteau of the Latin term "*res*" [thing] and "-ification," reification refers to "thing-ification" or "objectification," or the process by which "truth" manifests as "objectivity." Lukács maintains that it has taken on a totalitarian form in modernity under the auspices of capitalism, as all spheres of life—subjective, objective and intersubjective[1]— have come to be subsumed by the logic of one kind of object in particular, namely, the "commodity-form." But, while Lukács treats the commodity-form as paradigmatic of reification in modernity, he coincidentally accompanies every reference to reification with an analogy to machines; attributing the objectifying aspects of, for instance, labor, bureaucracy, the state, jurisprudence, etc., to their being "mechanical." This raises the question: what is the relationship between reification and the "mechanistic world-picture"[2] for Lukács?

In this paper, I would like to respond to this question by providing a Lukácsian account of the emergence of so-called "mechanistic philosophy." Mechanistic philosophy provides the ideal object of study to answer this question, because it marks the point at which the commodity-form and machine

---

1   Axel Honneth, "Reification and Recognition: A New Look at an Old Idea," in *Reification: A New Look at an Old Idea (The Berkeley Tanner Lectures)*, ed. Martin Jay and trans. Joseph Ganahl (New York: Oxford University Press, Inc., 2008), p. 75.
2   By "mechanistic world-picture," I mean the view that all causation is analogous to mechanistic processes; that is, that causal processes are divisible into parts and forces. The mechanistic world-picture need not apply only to proponent accounts of mechanistic causation. It may also encompass those schools of thought that reject the notion of causation or of the capacity for human beings to have adequate knowledge of causation, but based on the assumption that causation be conceived as inherently mechanistic.

analogies appear to converge as reifying agents; subject, objects and intersubjective relations are treated as equally quantitative and mechanistic in this school of thought. Moreover, its emergence corresponds with the rise of the world market and early capitalist manufacture, which saw the increased use of machinery in production.

Unfortunately, Lukács alludes to, but does not provide a thorough account of mechanistic philosophy in his own works, and so, I will complement his remarks with the more robust account of Henryk Grossmann. An economist, historian and, like Lukács, Marxist revolutionary of a Leninist persuasion, Grossmann was a member of the Institute for Social Research, which was the home of the "Frankfurt School" and "Critical Theory." He is best known for his work entitled *The Law of the Accumulation and Breakdown of the Capitalist System*, which was published only a few months before the Stock Market crashed in 1929. But he also wrote several historiographical studies of early modern philosophy, most of which have only recently attracted attention, namely, "The Social Foundations of the Mechanistic Philosophy and Manufacture" (1935), "Descartes and the Social Origins of the Mechanistic Concept of the World" (1946), a letter to Friedrich Pollock and Max Horkheimer (23 August 1935) and a book review which discusses G.N. Clark's *Science and Social Welfare in the Age of Newton* and George Sarton's *The History of Science and the New Humanism* (1938).[3]

From Lukács and Grossmann's combined insights, I propose the following thesis: the commodity-form and the machine analogy are both reifying agents, but the former is more fundamental than the latter. The machine analogy marks part of the effort to make intelligible particular subjective, objective or intersubjective phenomena, which are already reified by the commodity-form. The machine analogy abstracts an intelligible moment of capitalist production and seeks to apply it to the anarchic whole or its elements. In doing so, the analogy fails to articulate the totality or its elements at the same time that it conceals its true nature. To develop this claim, I will proceed as follows. In Section 2, I establish a common ground between Lukács and Grossmann through the revolutionary tradition of Leninism. In Section 3, I show that Lukács tries to remedy certain limitations within Leninism through his

---

3   See Gideon Freudenthal, "The Hessen-Grossmann Thesis: An Attempt at Rehabilitation," *Perspectives on Science* 15, No. 2 (2005): 166–193; Gideon Freudenthal and Peter McLaughlin, "Classical Marxist Historiography of Science: The Hessen-Grossmann Thesis," in *The Social and Economic Roots of the Scientific Revolution: Texts by Boris Hessen and Henryk Grossmann*, ed. Gideon Freudenthal and Peter McLaughlin (Dordrecht: Springer, 2009), pp. 1–40; Rick Kuhn, *Henryk Grossman and the Recovery of Marxism* (Urbana/Chicago: University of Illinois Press, 2006).

concepts of class consciousness and reification. In his presentation of reification in *History and Class Consciousness*, however, he appears to waver between treating the commodity-form and the machine analogy as the dominant reifying agent. In Section 4, I argue that in "Technology and Social Relations," Lukács gives some indication that because technological progress rests upon social relations, the commodity-form is more fundamental than the machine analogy. In Section 5, I show how Grossmann complements Lukács's account, through his demonstration that the universalization of the machine analogy appears in mechanistic philosophy as part of an effort to grasp a world system already commodified. To develop my arguments, I will draw support from the works of Lukács, Grossmann and Lenin, as well as from the secondary literature. Finally, Section 6 offers my conlusion.

2   The "Leninist" Critique of Mechanistic Materialism

Before addressing Lukács's and Grossmann's works directly, I will provide some background as to the significance of causal mechanism for "Leninism"; Leninism being a Marxist revolutionary tradition based on the strategies and tactics of Vladimir Lenin, to which both Lukács and Grossmann subscribed. There is no easy way to summarize Leninism, but Lukács and Grossmann can be described as adherents to it insofar as they, like Lenin, maintain that "[w]ithout revolutionary theory there can be no revolutionary movement."[4] The defining feature of this revolutionary theory, as Lukács and Grossmann saw it, can be found in their citation of the same, noteworthy quote; Lukács in *History and Class Consciousness* and Grossmann in *The Law of the Accumulation and Breakdown of the Capitalist System* cites the following passage from Lenin's "Report on the International Situation and the Fundamental Tasks of the Communist International (19 July 1920)":

> [c]omrades, we have now come to the question of the revolutionary crisis as the basis of our revolutionary action. And here we must first of all note two widespread errors. On the one hand, bourgeois economists depict this crisis simply as 'unrest,' to use the elegant expression of the British. On the other hand, revolutionaries sometimes try to prove that the crisis is absolutely insoluble. This is a mistake. There is no such thing as an absolutely hopeless situation. The bourgeoisie are behaving like bare-faced

---

4   Vladimir Lenin, *What Is To Be Done?*, in *V.I. Lenin: Collected Works*, 45 vols., ed. Victor Jerome and trans. Joe Fineberg and George Hanna (Moscow: Progress Publishers, 1977), 5: 369.

plunderers who have lost their heads; they are committing folly after folly, thus aggravating the situation and hastening their doom. All that is true. But nobody can 'prove' that it is absolutely impossible for them to pacify a minority of the exploited with some petty concessions, and suppress some movement or uprising of some section of the oppressed and exploited. To try to 'prove' in advance that there is 'absolutely' no way out of the situation would be sheer pedantry, or playing with concepts and catchwords. Practice alone can serve as real 'proof' in this and similar questions. All over the world, the bourgeois system is experiencing a tremendous revolutionary crisis. The revolutionary parties must now 'prove' in practice that they have sufficient understanding and organisation, contact with the exploited masses, and determination and skill to utilise this crisis for a successful, a victorious revolution.[5]

"There is no such thing as a hopeless situation"; in the conflict between the bourgeoisie and the proletariat, no outcome is guaranteed. To whom the future belongs will not be decided by fate, but by the strategic and tactical competence, as well as the sheer will of one side over the other. Lenin's quote boils down to one essential point: those among the Communist Party who maintain that capitalism will collapse under its own weight await conditions that will never come to pass, as capitalism's fate can only be decided through struggle. In *History and Class Consciousness*, Lukács adopts this position with respect to the ideological crisis of capitalism and in *The Law of the Accumulation and Breakdown of the Capitalist System*, Grossmann with respect to the economic crisis of capitalism.

Lenin attempts to lay the theoretical groundwork for this position in his two major philosophical works, *Materialism and Empirio-Criticism* (1908) and *Philosophical Notebooks* (1929), both of which defend historical materialism as the revolutionary theory of the proletariat. *Materialism and Empirio-Criticism* was, for better or worse, essential in codifying historical materialism as the ideological dogma of the Soviet Union, while his *Philosophical Notebooks* were instrumental to the composition of some of his most important texts such as the *April Theses* (1917), *Imperialism, the Highest Stage of Capitalism* (1916) and *The*

---

5 Vladimir Lenin, "Report on the International Situation and the Fundamental Tasks of the Communist International (July 19)," in *V.I. Lenin: Collected Works*, 45 vols., ed. and trans. Julius Katzer (Moscow: Progress Publishers, 1974), 31: 226–227. See also Georg Lukács, *History and Class Consciousness: Studies in Marxist Dialectics* (Cambridge: The M.I.T. Press, 1971), p. 306; Henryk Grossmann, *The Law of the Accumulation and Breakdown of the Capitalist System, Being also a Theory of Crisis* (London: Pluto Press, 1992), Online. https://www.marxists.org/archive/grossman/1929/breakdown/.

State and Revolution (1917).[6] While "idealism" often serves as the object of Lenin's criticisms in these works, he is no less critical of so-called "metaphysical" or "mechanistic materialism," as he saw this as an emerging tendency within Marxism to accept "evolutionism" or "gradualism," which he took as the indefinite postponement of revolution altogether. Because the *Philosophical Notebooks* were not published until some six years after *History and Class Consciousness*, I will focus exclusively on *Materialism and Empirio-Criticism*.

Materialism and Empirio-Criticism is best known as a polemic against so-called "empirio-criticism" (as well as its counterparts such as "empirio-monism" and "empirio-symbolism"), which had garnered prominence among Russian Marxists at the beginning of the 20th century. Empirio-criticism is an extension of the principles of the philosophy of Ernst Mach, who developed the theory as a response to the perceived crisis of contemporary physics. Like many other theorists at the time, Mach held that due to the rising prominence of the so-called "electron theory of matter," according to which "atoms are composed of very minute particles, charged with positive or negative electricity, called electrons and 'are immersed in a medium which we call ether,'" matter had effectively disappeared. That is, "matter" and "motion" had ceased to be acceptable principles upon which physics could be based.[7] In their place should be stood the principle foundation of "experience."[8] According to some Russian Marxists in the early 20th century, Marxism was not immune from this crisis in physics and, to retain its scientific character, should incorporate empirio-criticism as its new foundation.[9]

For Lenin, however, despite pretenses to originality, empirio-criticism did not offer a solution to the crisis. In fact, empirio-criticism simply recycled tried and failed solutions to previous crises that had occurred throughout the history of philosophy.[10] As he writes, "Ernst Mach's doctrine of things as complexes of sensations, is subjective idealism and a tedious repetition of Berkleianism."[11] Nor was Mach the first philosopher to repeat Berkeley's strategy:

---

6   Antonio Negri, *Factory of Strategy: 33 Lessons on Lenin* (New York: Columbia University Press, 2014), pp. 162, 165–166.
7   Vladimir Lenin, *Materialism and Empirio-Criticism*, in *Collected Works of V.I. Lenin*, 13 vols., ed. Alexander Trachtenberg and trans. David Kvitko (New York: International Publishers Co., Inc., 1927), pp. 213, 218–225.
8   Ibid., pp. 115–121.
9   Ibid., pp. 1–2.
10 Ibid., p. 102.
11 Ibid., pp. 23, 46–47, 102. See also Louis Althusser, "Lenin and Philosophy," in *Lenin and Philosophy and Other Essays*, trans. Ben Brewster (New York/London: Monthly Review Press, 1971), pp. 54, 64.

> [t]he different ways of expression—by Berkeley in 1710, by Fichte in 1801, or by Avenurius in 1892 – 4—do not in the least change the fundamental philosophic position of subjective idealism.... [T]his is the same old trashy stock-in-trade of subjective idealism under a newly painted signboard.[12]

Philosophy's history, then, has really been a series of repetitions through, what Engels refers to as, "'two great camps'—materialis[m] and idealis[m],"[13] which are sometimes punctuated by a third, "agnosticism."[14] Lenin defines materialism as that camp according to which "nature is primary and spirit secondary," idealism as the reverse[15] and agnosticism as "deny[ing] the possibility of knowing the world, or at least of fully knowing it."[16]

These three camps, however, are not all made equal. Materialism, Lenin argues, is superior, as it is the only philosophical tendency that can account for pre-organic and pre-historic existence. The crisis of physics does not do away with one notable discovery in the sciences, namely, the Earth's pre-existence to all human and other forms of organic life. He writes that

> [n]atural science positively asserts that the earth once existed in a state in which no men or any other living creature existed or could have existed. Inasmuch as organic matter is a later appearance, a result of a long evolution, it follows that there could have been no perceiving matter, no 'complexes of sensations,' no self which is 'inseparably' connected with the environment.... Hence, matter is primary, and mind, consciousness, sensation are products of a very high development. Such is the materialist theory of knowledge, which natural science instinctively holds.[17]

No other philosophical tendency can account for this reality without descending into absurdity.[18]

Materialism's past failures in staving off idealism and agnosticism do not refute materialism as such, but rather show the demand for a new kind of

---

12 Ibid., pp. 46–47.
13 Ibid., p. 14.
14 Ibid., pp. 14, 74.
15 Ibid., p. 14.
16 Ibid.
17 Ibid., pp. 52, 96, 104, 154, 290.
18 Ibid., pp. 52–62.

materialism. Material reality had not disappeared, only a certain conception of material reality had become untenable. "'Matter disappears,'" he writes,

> means that matter in the form of the limit which we have known up to now vanishes, as our knowledge penetrates deeper; those properties of matter which before seemed absolute, immutable, and primary (impenetrability, inertia, mass, etc.) disappear, and now become relative, belonging only to certain states of matter. For the sole 'property' of matter—with the recognition of which materialism is vitally connected—is the property of being *objective reality*, of existing outside of our cognition.[19]

Moreover, Marxism need not cede its materialist foundations to empiriocriticism, as neither Marx nor Engels ever committed to any particular conception of matter, only to the existence of objective reality. They acknowledged that materialism would always have to be adapted to new scientific discoveries, but as a philosophical tendency, it was irrefutable.[20]

To liberate materialism from its former shortcomings requires a rejection of "metaphysical" or "mechanistic materialism" in favor of the more robust "dialectical materialism." He distinguishes the two as follows:

> [t]he metaphysical, that is, the anti-dialectical, materialist may posit the existence of matter (be it 'temporary,' 'prior to' the 'first impetus,' etc.) without motion. The dialectical materialist, however, not only regards motion as the inseparable property of matter but rejects even the simplified interpretation of motion.[21]

And while the former prioritizes a theoretical approach to epistemology, the latter prioritizes a practical approach; practice, for Lenin, referring to industry, or the transformation of things in-themselves into things for-us.[22] So long as materialism prioritizes theory over practice, it is destined to stand in a contemplative gaze toward nature, never understanding how human knowledge is possible in the first place, and leaving it preyt to the critiques of idealism and agnosticism.[23] Prioritizing practice over theory, however,

---

19 Ibid., p. 220.
20 Ibid., p. 201.
21 Ibid., p. 83.
22 Ibid., pp. 77–78, 83, 109–114.
23 Ibid., pp. 107–108, 221, 262.

dialectical materialism insists on the approximate, relative character of every scientific proposition concerning the structure of matter and its properties; in the absence of absolute boundaries in nature; on the transformation of moving matter from one state to another, which from an ordinary standpoint appears evidently irreconcilable, etc.[24]

Lastly, because dialectical materialism acknowledges the inevitable limits of human knowledge, it also accepts the need to act on the basis of incomplete knowledge; that the passage from reflection to action always involves a "salto vitale [vital leap]."[25] With this, Lenin implicates not only idealism and agnosticism, but certain brands of materialism as well, as inherently bound to the preservation of the contemporary social order.

While Lenin's position in the "Report" and in *Materialism and Empirio-Criticism* bears some resemblance, at their core, they are incommensurate. In both texts, Lenin identifies the leap from theory to practice on the grounds of uncertainty. But in the former text, he goes to great lengths to emphasize how the actual crisis of capitalism is an under-determined object, with no clear direction without the struggle between two subjects, i.e., the bourgeoisie and the proletariat.[26] This emphasis on the reciprocal relation of subject and object is largely absent from *Materialism and Empirio-Criticism*, and is due, in no small part, to Lenin's reliance on Friedrich Engels's *Anti-Dühring* (1877) and *Dialectics of Nature* (1883). In these two works, Engels tries to justify the validity of historical materialism by demonstrating the workings of dialectics in nature. With this, however, Engels effectively turns historical materialism into a modified metaphysical or mechanistic materialism. He may defend a new conception of nature, but the subject-object relation remains metaphysical or mechanical; the subject remaining the passive observer of the fixed and immutable laws of nature.[27] Engels fails to recognize that with historical materialism, the emphasis on practice over theory does not simply provide a better way of understanding how the subject approximates knowledge of the object, but rather, provides a new conception of the subject-object relation altogether. In practice, the subject not only grasps the object, but alters it and vice versa. The truth of the object does not consist in its being a thing in-itself beyond the purview of the subject, but rather, a pole of an identical subject-object.[28] This

---

24 Ibid., p. 221.
25 Ibid., p. 156.
26 Slavoj Žižek, "Georg Lukács as the Philosopher of Leninism," in *A Defense of History and Class Consciousness: Tailism and the Dialectic* (New York: Verso, 2002), pp. 164–165.
27 Lukács, *History and Class Consciousness*, p. 4.
28 Ibid., p. 19.

marks Lukács's point of departure in *History and Class Consciousness*, where he writes that Engels

> does not even mention the most vital interaction, namely the *dialectical relation between subject and object in the historical process*, let alone give it the prominence it deserves. Yet without this factor dialectics ceases to be revolutionary, despite attempts (illusory in the last analysis) to retain 'fluid' concepts. For it implies a failure to recognise that in all metaphysics the object remains untouched and unaltered so that thought remains contemplative and fails to become practical; while for the dialectical method the central problem is *to change reality*.[29]

For Lukács, Lenin does not adequately theorize the radical nature of his own strategy and tactics in his philosophical works. Revolutionary theory is not meant to overcome the pacifying elements of mechanistic materialism with a better understanding of the thing in-itself, but with the means of cultivating self-consciousness, or class consciousness, and identifying the object as a moment of itself. With this re-imagination comes a new major obstacle to thinking beyond the thing in-itself, namely, reification.

3   Commodification and Mechanization in *History and Class Consciousness*

In this section, I provide an introduction to Lukács's concept of reification as the obstacle to the proletariat's development of class consciousness. Beyond this, however, I show that Lukács appears to provide two parallel accounts of this phenomenon: one rooted in the commodity-form and the other in the machine analogy. The coalescence of these two forms demands closer attention, insofar as the contours of reification determine the possibility of as well as the means of cultivating class consciousness.

Lukács begins his presentation of reification in the essay entitled "Reification and the Consciousness of the Proletariat." Here, he defines the term as when

> a relation between people takes on the character of a thing and thus acquires a 'phantom objectivity,' an autonomy that seems so strictly rational

---

29   Ibid., p. 3.

and all-embracing as to conceal every trace of its fundamental nature: the relation between people.[30]

In other words, reification occurs when a human practice becomes so deeply habituated and sedimented among its practitioners that the products of that practice appear to have an altogether independent existence. The market is the epitomizing example of this phenomenon, insofar as it is both entirely human-made, at the same time that it appears to function independently and according to fixed and immutable laws.

Reification is not unique to the modern period, as Lukács maintains that it "did play a part in Greek society in its maturity."[31] Its modern incarnation is distinct, however, insofar as it is defined by the commodity-form. He writes that

> at this stage in the history of mankind there is no problem that does not ultimately lead back to that question [of the commodity] and there is no solution that could not be found in the solution to the riddle of commodity-*structure*.... [T]he problem of commodities must not be considered in isolation or ever regarded as the central problem in economics, but as the central, structural problem of capitalist society in all its aspects.[32]

Nor is the commodity-form even specific to the modern period, but it stands apart from its classical counterpart in that it "penetrate[s] society in all its aspects ... remould [ing] it in its own image."[33] In other words, what Marx referred to as "commodity-fetishism" becomes universal, such that the exchange-value of labor and goods takes on the appearance of a natural relation, which is then applied taken to apply to all things.[34]

"Applying to all things" means that no sphere of existence—subjective, objective and intersubjective—goes untouched by reification. This totalization begins when production comes to be organized on the principle of the maximization of exchange-value. From this premise, a quantitative equivalence is established between the work of the laborer and the fruits of his/her labor, as well as among the fruits of labor themselves. The worker receives a wage,

---

30   Ibid., p. 83.
31   Ibid., p. 111.
32   Ibid., p. 83.
33   Ibid., p. 85.
34   Ibid., p. 86. See also Karl Marx, *Capital, Vol. 1*, in *Marx & Engels: Collected Works*, 50 vols., ed. Alexander Chepurenko and trans. Yelena Vashchenko (London: Lawrence & Wishart, 2010), 35: 81–85.

establishing a proportion not only between labor and goods, but between different goods as well. Thus, as Lukács writes,

> [o]bjectively, in so far as the commodity form facilitates the equal exchange of qualitatively different objects, it can only exist if that formal equality is in fact recognized—at any rate in *this* relation, which indeed confers upon them their commodity nature. *Subjectively*, this formal equality of human labour in the abstract is not only the common factor to which the various commodities are reduced; it also becomes the real principle governing the actual production of commodities.[35]

With time, the commodity-form shapes not only production, but society as a whole, as new forms appear to cater to the exigencies of the market. As he writes, "[r]eification requires that a society should learn to satisfy all its needs in terms of commodity exchange."[36] Bureaucracy, the state, the law, etc., emerge from and "harmonise"[37] with production. From this extension, the logic of the commodity-form becomes ubiquitous; at once everywhere and nowhere such that it comes to be taken for granted as entirely natural:

> The divorce of the phenomena of reification from their economic bases and from the vantage point from which alone they can be understood, is facilitated by the fact that the [capitalist] process of transformation must embrace every manifestation of the life of society if the preconditions for the complete self-realisation of capitalist production are to be fulfilled.[38]

With this, the commodity-form characterizes relations of human begins to themselves, to each other and to nature.[39]

At first glance, one might take Lukács to be employing reification as part of a secularized theory of the "Fall of Man," where free and natural human life came to be corrupted by the artifice of institutions. However, Lukács employs the concept as part of his immanent critique of capitalism. It refers not to the break from a primordial origin, but to a fundamental dissonance between the form and the content of life posited within the confines of capitalism. This

---

35 Lukács, *History and Class Consciousness*, p. 87.
36 Ibid., p. 91.
37 Ibid., p. 95.
38 Ibid., p. 95.
39 Ibid., p. 88.

dissonance rears its head during times of capitalist economic crises, ruptures from the day-to-day workings of the market that seem to occur unexpectedly. When people act according to the laws of the market, sooner or later the market fails, signaling a gap between the way that people conceive of the laws of the market and the way that it actually operates, as if two moments of society are superimposed, one upon the other.[40]

This dissonance manifests most acutely in the failure of "bourgeois economics" to properly conceive of these economic crises. This field, according to Lukács, provides an account of the general laws of the market, but in doing so, is incapable of providing any proper theory of economic crises, which it can only account for as mere exceptions to the rule.[41] This not only attests to the limits of bourgeois economics, but of bourgeois science in general, insofar as none are capable of properly conceiving the nature of such crises.[42] And yet, because of the global scale of the market, some kind of totality appears to be implied, yet ever beyond the grasp of human cognition. The task of conceiving this totality falls to a science that can grasp the identical subject-object.[43]

For this, Lukács defends the science of historical materialism. But in grasping crises of capitalism, historical materialism is forced to discard the assumption that capitalism is natural, treating it, rather, as historical; as something which was born, lives and will eventually come to pass. The motor of the historical process itself is the economic base of any society—i.e., the means of production and social relations of production—and its ensuing class conflict.[44] The ability to grasp the totality cannot lie within any one individual, but must reside instead with a particular class. The bourgeoisie, petty-bourgeoisie and peasantry either seek to benefit from capitalism or entertain some ambiguous relation to it, meaning that they bear some interest in obscuring capitalism's historicity. The only class for whom capitalism becomes comprehensible, then, is also the class that is clearly at odds with it, namely the proletariat.[45] From the perspective of the proletariat, however, capitalism appears, on one hand, as a totality because of the world market, but on the other hand, as entirely anarchic because of the lack of any overarching plan for production. This reveals capitalism as such to be at odds with itself, grounded on premises the

---

40   Andrew Feenberg, "Rethinking Reification," in *Georg Lukács: The Fundamental Dissonance of Existence – New Essays on Social, Political and Aesthetic Theory*, ed. Timothy Bewes and Timothy Hall (London/New York: Continuum, 2011), pp. 101–120.
41   Lukács, *History and Class Consciousness*, p. 105.
42   Ibid., p. 107, 243.
43   Ibid., p. 229.
44   Ibid., p. 224.
45   Ibid., p. 39.

functioning of which lead it to its own crises. Comprehending capitalism as a totality, then, requires transcending capitalism altogether and giving rise to a system whose form and content are actually commensurate.[46] Because of the reifying effects of the commodity-form, of course, the impulse to overthrow capitalism is not automatic. The fragmentation of the proletarian worker's inner life and solidarity with other workers, etc., mean that the proletariat must surmount its own "ideological crisis" before it is prepared to take action.[47]

While Lukács's claim that the commodity-form is responsible for this hesitation, he continually refers to analogies to machines in order to describe the, for instance, reified state of subjects, objects and intersubjective relations throughout *History and Class Consciousness*. Like the commodity-form, the mechanization of the subject, object and intersubjective relations plays an important role in pacifying the proletariat and glossing the contemporary social order with a seeming imperviousness to change. The worker, Lukács writes,

> [a]s labour is progressively rationalised and mechanised his [the worker's] lack of will is reinforced by the way in which his activity becomes less and less active and more and more *contemplative*. The contemplative stance adopted towards a process mechanically conforming to fixed laws and enacted independently of man's consciousness and impervious to human intervention, i.e. a perfectly closed system, must likewise transform the basic categories of man's immediate attitude to the world.[48]

This mechanization not only affects the worker's relationship to his/her surroundings, but his/her own psychology as well:

> [w]ith the modern 'psychological' analysis of the work-process (in Taylorism) this rational mechanisation extends right into the worker's 'soul': even his psychological attributes are separated from his total personality and placed in opposition to it so as to facilitate their integration into specialised rational systems and their reduction to statistically viable concepts.[49]

---

46   Ibid., p. 2.
47   Ibid., pp. 305, 310–311.
48   Ibid., p. 89.
49   Ibid., p. 88.

Finally, mechanization comes to be illustrative of society as a whole:

> the mechanical disintegration of the process of production into its components ... destroys those bonds that had bound individuals to a community in the days when production was still 'organic.' In this respect..., mechanisation makes of them isolated abstract atoms whose work no longer brings them together directly and organically; it becomes mediated to an increasing extent exclusively by the abstract laws of the mechanism which imprisons them.[50]

And so, if reification refers not only to the limits of acting and thinking according to the logic of capitalism, but also how that logic corrodes from within, it cannot go without examining the coalescence between the commodity-form and analogies to machines.

To address this coalescence, I argue that it is necessary to provide a Lukácsian account of the emergence of mechanistic philosophy. As previously indicated, mechanistic philosophy denotes all things as quantitative and mechanistic. Moreover, it emerges alongside the bourgeoning world market and the growing predominance of capitalist manufacture, in which machines began to play a more significant role in production. In the two sub-sections of the "Reification" essay, "The Antinomies of Bourgeois Thought" and "The Standpoint of the Proletariat," where Lukács focuses on philosophy, he alludes to, but doesn't fully explore the mechanistic school of thought. He identifies the central theme of modern philosophy as the struggle to know the thing in-itself, epitomized in the work of Immanuel Kant.[51] The thing in-itself is, of course, the manifestation of reification within the context of philosophy; the residue of its incapacity to grapple with the commodity-form as its premise.[52] In wrestling with this problem at its most abstract limits, however, philosophy also bears the possibility of seeing beyond the commodity-form, when transposed to another subject: the proletariat. Philosophy does not spontaneously arise in the consciousness of the proletariat, but rather, through the mediation of a party that transforms philosophy from a theory into practice. Philosophy, as historical materialism, bears the capacity to interpret and generalize the actions of the proletariat in the context of a totality, keeping in mind that the universal and particular contexts are always in flux.[53] But as the founding moments of modern philosophy are traceable to mechanistic philosophy, which Lukács

---

50   Ibid., p. 90.
51   Ibid., pp. 111–112.
52   Ibid., pp. 110–111.
53   Ibid., p. 41.

himself acknowledges, the origins of the problem of the thing in-itself seem no less imbued with analogies to machines. Because of the ambiguous relationship between the commodity-form and analogies to machines, this demands an analysis of the origins of mechanistic philosophy in early capitalist manufacture.

4   Techno-Fetishism in Lukács's "Technology and Social Relations"

As Lukács does not provide any extensive rumination on the origins of mechanistic philosophy in *History and Class Consciousness*, I turn to another of his works that provides, at least, a pathway to addressing this issue, namely, his book review of Nikolai Bukharin's *Historical Materialism* (1921), entitled "Technology and Social Relations" (1925). In this text, Lukács provides some indication of how both the commodity-form and analogies to machines bear responsibility for reification, but that the former should be understood as more fundamental than the latter.

Bukharin's central thesis in *Historical Materialism* is that "the development of technique ... [i]s the 'basic determinacy' of the 'productive forces of society,' etc."[54] He derives his position from his own critique of Heinrich Cunow, who argues that

> [t]he presence of certain raw materials (*das Vorkommen bestimmter Rh-materialien*) determines, for example, whether it is possible for certain forms of technology to develop at all, as well as the direction they will take.[55]

Bukharin challenges Cunow by arguing that technological development cannot be at the mercy of raw materials, because raw materials themselves presuppose some technique/technology according to which they can be appropriated for the fulfillment of human needs. As he writes,

> a certain stage of technology must have been reached before wood, or, fibers, etc., may play the part of raw materials. Coal becomes a raw material only when technology has developed so far as to delve in the bowels

---

54   Georg Lukács, "Technology and Social Relations," trans. unknown, *New Left Review* 1, No. 39 (1966): 29.
55   Heinrich Cunow, "Die Weltwirtrcha/trkrire," *Die Neue Zeit* 39, No. 2 (1921): 350. See also Nikolai Bukharin, *Historical Materialism*, trans. unknown (New York: International Publishers Co., Inc., 1925), p. 120.

of the earth and drag their contents into the light of day. The influence of nature, in the sense of providing materials, etc., is itself a product of the development of technology.[56]

Lukács contends, however, that by treating technique/technology as decisive over raw materials, Bukharin does not overcome fetishism, but simply trades one form of it for another; that is, Cunow and Bukharin treat raw materials and technique/technology, respectively, as though they sprung out of history, independent of human relations:

> [t]echnique is a *part*, a moment, naturally of great importance, of the social productive forces, but it is neither simply identical with them, nor (as some of Bukharin's earlier points would seem to imply) the final or absolute moment of the changes in these forces. This attempt to find the underlying determinants of society and its development in a principle other than that of the social relations between men in the process of production (and thence of distribution, consumption, etc.) —that is in the economic structure of society correctly conceived—leads to fetishism.[57]

To support this claim, Lukács provides numerous examples of historical changes in human relations that were not accompanied by changes in technique/technology. One of the most notable examples that he provides is borrowed from *Capital, Vol. 1*, where Marx points out that the transition from guild handicraft to manufacture involved radical changes in social relations, but almost no change in technique/technology, at least, not in the short term:

> With regard to the mode of production itself, manufacture, in its strict meaning, is hardly to be distinguished, in its earliest stages, from the handicraft trades of the guilds, otherwise than by the greater number of workmen simultaneously employed by one and the same individual capital. The workshop of the mediaeval master handicraftsman is simply enlarged. At first, therefore, the difference is purely quantitative.[58]

And so, while the change of social relations involved in the passage from guild handiwork to manufacture eventually led to widespread mechanization of

---

56 Ibid., 121.
57 Lukács, "Technology and Social Relations," p. 29.
58 Marx, *Capital, Vol. 1*, p. 327. See also Lukács, "Technology and Social Relations," p. 31.

labor, this change was predicated on the change of social relations.[59] That changes in social relations are more fundamental brings to light a further realization, namely, that social relations do not change inevitably, but unfortunately, through the, what Gottl calls, "door of social violence."[60] Changes in social relations do not unfold without struggle, the outcomes of which are often uncertain and so, if social relations do not change without struggle, technological development cannot proceed from immutable laws within technique/technology itself, but upon "the change in labour potentialities and conditions."[61]

By affording primacy to technological development, Bukharin overlooks the main insight of historical materialism, which is that *"all economic or 'sociological' phenomena derive from the social relations of men to one another."*[62] He effectively treats historical materialism as something "suspiciously close to what Marx aptly called bourgeois materialism,"[63] or "bourgeois, natural-scientific materialism [which] derives from his use of 'science' (in the French sense) as a model."[64] In other words, rather than critique the natural sciences with historical materialism, he tries to legitimize the latter by modeling it upon the former; by trying to imbue historical materialism with the capacity to predict social outcomes. For Lukács, this is not only impossible, but misses the point of historical materialism, which is to deconstruct the sense of inertia that underlies all bourgeois sciences.[65] Thus, he writes that

> Bukharin's basic philosophy is completely in harmony with contemplative materialism; that instead of making a historical-materialist critique of the natural sciences and their methods, i.e. revealing them as products of capitalist development, he extends these methods to the study of society without hesitation, uncritically, unhistorically and undialectically.[66]

While Lukács does not specifically use the term "reification" in this review, his critique of Bukharin's fetishism of technology and his critique of commodity-fetishism in *History and Class Consciousness* bear a striking resemblance. However, Lukács also shows that while technological development is, to a certain

---

59 Ibid.
60 Friedrich von Gottl-Ottlilienfeld, *Wirtschaft und Gesellschaft* (Tübingen: Verlag von J.C.B., 1923), pp. 236–239. See also Lukács, "Technology and Social Relations," p. 30.
61 Ibid., p. 30.
62 Ibid., p. 29.
63 Ibid., p. 28.
64 Ibid., p. 29.
65 Ibid., p. 33.
66 Ibid.

degree, plastic, its limits are drawn by the economic system within which it emerges. The fetishism of technology, then, rests upon a more fundamental fetishism of social relations. Analogies to machines, then, become ubiquitous in the context of a system already reified by the commodity-form. How these two forms interact in mechanistic philosophy, however, is not to be found in the works of Lukács, but of Henryk Grossmann.

5 The Sociology of Mechanistic Philosophy according to Grossmann

In his Preface to *History and Class Consciousness* (1967), one of Lukács's various laments over the book was his omission of a robust account of economic crises of capitalism.[67] Rick Kuhn has provided a persuasive argument that this omission can be overcome by Henryk Grossmann's account of economic crises. Grossmann traces the source of this problem to the duality of the concept of value, exchange-value and use-value, which dictates capitalist production.[68] Both Lukács and Grossmann treat mechanistic philosophy as the founding moment of modern philosophy and acknowledge the correlation with early capitalist manufacture. Lukács, however, does not devote considerable attention to mechanistic philosophy, and Grossmann, in his works on mechanistic philosophy, omits references to Marxism, as they were edited for length, making their works ripe for comparison. In this section, I show that Grossmann's understanding of mechanistic philosophy shows analogies to machines to be an effort to conceive the anarchistic nature of capitalist production.

Grossmann's study of early modern, mechanistic philosophy began as a polemic against Franz Borkenau's *Der Übergang vom feudalen zum bürgerlichen Weltbild* [*The Transition from the Feudal to the Bourgeois World-Picture*] (1934).[69] Today, Borkenau (1900 – 1957) is a nearly forgotten figure, but he, like Grossmann, was a member of the Institute for Social Research. He was an active member of the German Communist Party from 1921 to 1929, after which time

---

67 Lukács, *History and Class Consciousness*, p. xvii.
68 Rick Kuhn, "Economic Crisis, Henryk Grossman and the Responsibility of Socialists," *Historical Materialism* 17 (2009): 4. See also Henryk Grossmann, "The Theory of Economic Crisis," trans. Rick Kuhn and Steve Palmer, *Bulletin International de l'Académie Polonaise des Sciences et des Lettres – Classe de Philologie, Classe d'Histoire et de Philosophie* 1 (1922): 285–290; Grossmann, *The Law of the Accumulation of Capital and the Breakdown of the Capitalist System*, Online.
69 Franz Borkenau, *Der Übergang vom feudalen zum bürgerlichen Weltbild* (Paris: Félix Alcan, 1934).

he became disillusioned with the party, but remained a committed socialist.[70] He received funding from the Institute for Social Research to complete "*Der Übergang*," the main argument of which is "that the emergence of an abstract, mechanical philosophy, best exemplified in the work of Descartes, was intimately connected to the rise of abstract labor in the capitalist system of manufacturing."[71] Prior to the book's release, Borkenau published a summary of the main arguments of *Der Übergang* as "The Sociology of the Mechanistic World-Picture," (1932) in the *Journal for Social Research*.[72] Upon reading the article, Max Horkheimer, the head of the Institute for Social Research at the time, panicked as he felt that Borkenau's arguments were "neither Marxist, nor accurate,"[73] spelling potential disaster for the Institute's reputation. *Der Übergang* was eventually published after numerous revisions, but Horkheimer wrote a Preface to the text in which he effectively disowned it.[74] To compensate, Horkheimer commissioned Walter Benjamin to write a response to Borkenau's work, but as he turned down the offer, Grossmann was next in line.[75]

Grossmann rather enthusiastically accepted the offer and what initially began as an attack on Borkenau took on a life of its own. Grossmann almost wrote an entire book on the subject, the title of which would have been *Cartesianism and Manufacture*.[76] He ended up dividing the work into three essays: "The Capitalism of the Renaissance Period," "Manufacture of the 16th–18th Centuries" and "The Beginnings of Capitalism and the New Mass Morality."[77] When he submitted the articles for publication, Horkheimer complained that they were too long and he asked Grossmann to condense them all into a single, 32-page review. Grossmann begrudgingly edited the works, but still ended up submitting something that was three to four times Horkheimer's word limit. Horkheimer, nevertheless, was highly impressed with Grossmann's work and published the piece, omitting the references to Marx for the sake of length and under the assumption that the journal's readership would be familiar with

---

70 Martin Jay, *The Dialectical Imagination: A History of the Frankfurt School and the Institute of Social Research, 1923 – 1950* (Berkeley/Los Angeles/London: University of California Press, 1996), p. 16.
71 Ibid.
72 Franz Borkenau, "The Sociology of the Mechanistic World-Picture," trans. Richard W. Hadden, *Science in Context* 1 (1987): 109–127.
73 Kuhn, Henryk *Grossman and the Recovery of Marxism*, p. 165.
74 Jay, *The Dialectical Imagination*, p. 16.
75 Rick Kuhn, "Henryk Grossman: A Biographical Sketch," in *The Social and Economic Roots of the Scientific Revolution: Texts by Boris Hessen and Henryk Grossmann*, ed. Gideon Freudenthal and Peter McLaughlin (Dordrecht: Springer, 2011), p. 247.
76 Ibid., p. 247.
77 Ibid.

these arguments anyway. The resulting article was "The Social Foundations of the Mechanistic Philosophy and Manufacture."[78] From this same work would later emerge "Descartes and the Social Origins of the Mechanistic Concept of the World," which went unpublished until 2009. Six manuscripts of the Descartes article exist, but none and there is some belief that Grossmann still intended to turn them into a book-length work, but never had the chance to.[79]

In "Social Foundations," Grossmann enumerates thirteen objections to Borkenau's *Der Übergang*, each objection informing Grossmann's overall thesis that the premises of mechanistic philosophy were not founded in the contemplation of the division of artisanal labor, but in the contemplation of actual machines, the exigencies of which arose from the contradictions of early capitalist manufacture and the rising power of large-scale merchants.[80] Citing Marx's *Capital, Vol. 1*, Grossmann defines "manufacture" as the characteristic mode of production from the mid-16th century to the late-18th century "characterized by division of labor in which the labor process is not yet simplified enough that a mechanism can replace the skill of the craftsmen."[81] According to Grossmann, the rise of the division of labor could not possibly have corresponded with the rise of mechanistic philosophy, because nearly a century-and-a-half stands between them. Borkenau mistakes manufacture for being the first mode of capitalist production and thereby, the division of labor, but he entirely overlooks the "decentralized putting-out system," which began as far back as the 14th century.[82] Nor does Borkenau properly date the emergence of mechanistic philosophy, citing figures such as Galileo, Hobbes and Descartes as its founders, when fully realized accounts of mechanistic philosophy date as far back as to the works of Leonardo da Vinci.[83] In other words, if the division of labor had been responsible for the emergence of mechanistic philosophy, the latter still would had to have appeared much earlier.

---

78   Ibid., 248.
79   Freudenthal and McLaughlin, "Classical Marxist Historiography of Science," pp. 39–40. Note that although Freudenthal and McLaughlin draw primarily draw from Mansucript C, "Universal Science versus Science of an Elite: Descartes' New Ideal of Science," they drew from all six manuscripts to compose as complete, though not necessarily definitive, of a text as possible.
80   Henryk Grossmann, "The Social Foundations of the Mechanistic Philosophy and Manufacture," in *The Social and Economic Roots of the Scientific Revolution: Texts by Boris Hessen and Henryk Grossmann*, ed. Gideon Freudenthal and Peter McLaughlin and trans. Gabriella Shalit (Dordrecht: Springer, 2011), p. 107.
81   Ibid., p. 103n. See also Marx, *Capital, Vol. 1*, p. 343.
82   Grossmann, "The Social Foundations of the Mechanistic Philosophy and Manufacture," pp. 112–114.
83   Ibid., pp. 107–112.

Grossmann goes on to argue that Borkenau wrongly assumes that the division of labor is synonymous with the rationalization of labor. Borkenau's conflation of these two notions stems, in part, from his glossing over the dynamic character of manufacture itself. Although manufacture was the dominant regime of production for nearly three centuries, it hardly resisted change, but rather, passed through four distinct sub-phases, which Grossmann identifies as (1) "cooperative," (2) "heterogeneous," (3) "serial," (4) "combination/overall/organic"; the division of labor only being systematically rationalized in the fourth and final phase of manufacture in the 18th century.[84] Until the final phase of manufacture, one thing remained constant; namely, that each moment of the process of production retained the character of artisanal labor.[85] Grossmann goes on to say that the very notion of rationalizing artisanal labor is fallacious as by definition, once labor is rationalized, it ceases to be artisanal.[86] Not to mention that artisans themselves resisted any rationalization of their labor as this precisely would have put them out of work.[87] Thus, the division of labor in manufacture could not have formed the basis of mechanistic philosophy.

Grossmann rightly points out that just as Borkenau oversimplifies more complicated matters, he overcomplicates others. Nowhere in the works of da Vinci, Galileo, Hobbes, Descartes, etc., does one find any reference to the division of labor. Rather than subject their texts to a complex deconstruction to detect innuendo to the division of labor, Grossmann says that one only need only take these thinkers at their word that their method, accounts of human nature and of nature itself follow from the study of actual machines. In fact, throughout the works of these philosophers, one finds an almost overabundance of references to machines.[88] This alone, course, does not settle the question of how mechanics passed into a mechanistic worldview. After all, despite playing a central role in the works of mechanistic philosophers, actual machines played a relatively minimal role in the process of production during the period of manufacture. Handicraft would not begin to lose its footing more extensively until the 18th century. What does manifest, however, is the convergence of the rising merchant class and the crises of manufacture that required the replacement of human labor by machines in specific instances. Human labor had been redundant with machines in certain instances before, but the exigencies of capitalism along with the acuteness of the crisis implied the

---

84 Ibid., p. 121.
85 Ibid.
86 Ibid., p. 120.
87 Ibid., p. 114.
88 Ibid., pp. 130–140.

possibility of a comparison of human labor with machines. Machines played a pivotal role in two areas, where failings in the financial efficacy of manufacture required the replacement of human labor with machines: (1) the use of water power and (2) the extraction of raw materials. In both instances, machines are used as a substitute for human labor, because of their greater efficiency and force.[89] From these cases, Grossmann writes,

> man, in all these technological upheavals, acquired new, important material for observing and contemplating the actions of forces. In the machines, in the turning of the water wheels of a mill or of an iron mine, in the movement of the arms of a bellows, in the lifting of the stamps of an iron works, we see the simplest mechanical operations, those simple quantitative relations between the homogeneous power of water-driven machines and their output, viz. those relations from which modern mechanics derived its basic concepts.[90]

This opened the door to the possibility of conceiving the function of machines as convertible with human labor. The effort to appropriate the machine as an analogy to method, human nature and nature arose from the belief in the greater efficiency and elimination of human toil procured by machines. The study of these machines opened the door to studying machines in general and the possibility of generalizing them onto a more comprehensive worldview.[91]

In the "Descartes" essay, Grossmann turns his attention from Borkenau and mechanistic philosophy in general more pointedly to Descartes. Grossmann's strategy in the "Descartes" essay can, perhaps, be thrown into relief when stood side-by-side with that of Edmund Husserl in *Cartesian Meditations* (1931) and *The Crisis of European Sciences* (1936).[92] Like Husserl, Grossmann affords to Descartes the status of a founding father of modern culture and science. For both, this founding moment can be best characterized as a crossroads, where Descartes, on one hand, sows the seeds that would eventually become the crisis of contemporary culture and science, but on the other hand, highlights possibilities for overcoming that crisis. For Husserl, this overcoming takes the

---

89   Ibid., p. 127.
90   Ibid., p. 128.
91   Ibid., pp. 141–145.
92   See Edmund Husserl, *Cartesian Meditations: An Introduction to Phenomenology*, trans. David Carr (Dordrecht: Martinus Nijhoff Publishers, 1977); Edmund Husserl, *The Crisis of the European Sciences and Transcendental Phenomenology: An Introduction to Phenomenological Philosophy*, trans. David Carr (Evanston: Northwestern University Press, 1970).

form of recognizing Cartesian philosophy as the abortive attempt to found transcendental phenomenology, but for Grossmann, it is the abortive attempt to found proletarian science.

According to Grossmann, Descartes's stature as a thinker is often celebrated, but little understood. Historians often cite the Cartesian algebra, as a new form of mathematics, as Descartes's major contribution. Grossmann asks "[w]hat would have been the consequences for science if Descartes had not written his geometry?"[93] and citing Léon Brunschvicg, he says that "'the evolution of mathematics would not have been profoundly modified by that fact.'"[94] But Descartes did not discover anything that had not already been put forth by other thinkers before him, such as Oresme, Viète and Fermat.[95] Stringing Descartes in line with his predecessors in mathematics may make sense in retrospect, but it makes little sense with respect to the actual historical development. Grossmann contends that

> for the understanding of the character of the Cartesian algebra, the 'internal,' 'logical' reasons for its formation, reasons deriving from the internal development of *mathematics*, are of little use, and must be discarded, for the Cartesian Algebra *as a philosophic method is not connected with the previous development of mathematics* and hence cannot be understood on the basis of this development. Other explanatory factors must be sought. But no attempt to find them has as yet been made.[96]

Rather, Descartes stands out among his peers, because "*as a philosophical method* specially designed to aid in achieving the universal science, the Algebra is Descartes' exclusive, original creation."[97] With his mathematization of method, human nature and the natural world, Descartes sets a task for philosophy that was not designed for "the upper strata of scientists and specialists, but to *the great mass of the unlearned*."[98]

---

93 Henryk Grossmann, "Descartes and the Social Origins of the Mechanistic Concept of the World," in *The Social and Economic Roots of the Scientific Revolution: Texts by Boris Hessen and Henryk Grossmann*, ed. Gideon Freudenthal and Peter McLaughlin and trans. Peter McLaughlin (Dordrecht: Springer, 2011), p. 187.
94 Ibid. See also Léon Brunschvicg, *Les étapes de la philosophie mathématique* (Paris: J. Vrin, 1912), p. 101.
95 Grossmann, "Descartes and the Social Origins of the Mechanistic Concept of the World," p. 187.
96 Ibid., p. 188.
97 Ibid.
98 Ibid., p. 159.

Descartes's decision to apply algebra to philosophy was predicated on "the study of machines, and [his extension of] these principles to physics and finally to the whole universe."[99] This application of the analogy to machines goes all the way to his method, which "is itself an intellectual machine, an intellectual mill, on which one has only to 'turn the handle in order to see the solutions of problems come out of it.'"[100] That Descartes equated machines with this simplifying approach comes from his flourishing during the time of the increased use of machines in manufacture to replace human labor:

> [d]uring the predominance of handicraft and the beginning of manufacture, skilled *specialization* and the individual worker's *virtuosity* in a limited trade set the standard; with the emergence of automatically working machines in industry it became clear that these machines, independently of and without any handicraft training or personal talent of the workers, could perform the work better, in greater quantities and with greater speed; and that this work could be done by *anyone* who knew how to handle the machine by simple manipulations, by women and children, indeed even by idiots and cripples, because the automatism of the machines simplified the operations so drastically.[101]

This diminishing role of specialization in artisanal labor began to be usurped by unspecialized, unskilled labor through the increased use of labor-saving devices in manufacture.[102] This shift is omnipresent in Descartes's work, in his mechanics, natural philosophy and philosophical method, all of which are derived from the analysis of machines.[103] Grossmann argues that Descartes not only saw this approach as appealing to the uneducated, but also took pride in the practical applicability of his notions and how an unskilled laborer could perform the same work better than the artisan, because of his method.[104]

Taken together, Lukács's and Grossmann's writings present the following picture. When the commodity-form becomes the organizing principle of production, production comes to be directed toward the maximization of exchange-value. From this arises a quantitative equivalence between human labor and goods produced. In early capitalist manufacture, though production remains largely in the form of handicraft, the use of machines begins to not

---

99 Ibid., p. 157.
100 Ibid., p. 188.
101 Ibid., p. 163.
102 Ibid.
103 Ibid., pp. 171–174.
104 Ibid., pp. 158–159, 176–179.

only supplement, but to replace human labor in crucial areas, introducing the machine as a mediating agent between human labor and goods produced. As the machine comes to be seen as capable of assuming a greater share of tasks in the process of production, the human perspective comes to grasp only a profile of the moments of production, while the machine unifies them. The machine comes to be seen as paradigmatic of the quantitative equivalence between the human subject and the object. Because the quantitative equivalence is presupposed by the market, analogies to machines can serve as an analogy through which moments beyond production can be understood. Analogies to machines, however, fail to comprehend the totality posited under capitalism, as they try to comprehend the totality of the system posited under capitalism through a singular moment of production. Moreover, analogies to machines attempt to unify a totality that is inherently anarchic and always escapes the grasp of the metaphor. Thus, the mechanistic conception of causality, on one hand, fails to grasp the totality while, on the other hand, conceals its anarchic nature.

6   Conclusion

In this paper, I provided an account of the origins of mechanistic philosophy according to the works of Georg Lukács and Henryk Grossmann. Starting from their common roots in Leninism, I showed that Lukács tries to overcome a basic limitation in Lenin's philosophical theory through his account of class consciousness and reification. I then demonstrated that Lukács's account of reification seems to hover between two paradigmatic forms: the commodity-form and analogies to machines. From there, I showed that for Lukács, the commodity-form is ultimately more fundamental than the machine analogy, but that to complete Lukács's account, Henryk Grossmann's work showed that the machine analogy marks an effort to universalize a particular moment of production that appears in the context of early capitalist manufacture. As new technologies are more and more considered the harbingers of radical social change, Lukács and Grossmann show that technological progress can, in fact, disguise a stasis that can only be overcome through the solidarity among human individuals.

CHAPTER 6

"The Nature of Humanity, or Rather the Nature of Things"—Reification in the Works of Georg Lukács and Walter Benjamin

Andraž Jež

1   **"Ghostly Objectivity" of Alienation, Reification, and Commodity Fetishism**

Marxist theory has provided social and humanist studies with three important concepts about how social relations, in the capitalist mode of production, take the form of relations between things.[1] These concepts are alienation, reification, and commodity fetishism. Though all three roughly denote the disadvantages of capitalist development and they also share a particular theoretical concern for complex relations between praxis and consciousness (as well as a sharp theoretical insight into it), but the concepts are not to be used interchangeably. It is not too hard to distinguish between them, especially alienation and the other two. *Alienation* for Marx deals with the general estrangement as a side effect of the development of capitalist relations of production. While labourer produces a commodity, he does not own it, as it is taken by capitalist, and is thus alienated from the fruits of his own labour. But at the same time, it is also estranged from the capitalist who has to sell it in order to earn profit to perpetuate his business. According to Marx, these are the only two aspects of a general estrangement of humans from their labour and from other humans.[2]

---

1 The quotation in the chapter title is from Walter Benjamin's essay "Calderón's *El Mayor Monstruo, Los Celos* and Hebbel's *Herodes und Mariamne*." (Walter Benjamin, *Selected Writings, Volume 2. 1913–1926*, ed. Marcus Bullock and Michael W. Jennings (Cambridge (MA)/London: The Belknap Press of Harvard University Press, 2002), p. 365.)

2 … And even from human essence, originally *Gattungswesen*; what exactly the latter young Marx's term contains, has been an ongoing debate. The only thing that is sure is that Marx slightly updated his reflection of the "essence" through mid-1840s—namely, it became more unambiguously socially determined and less inviting for the 20th century mystical speculations about "human nature" in his texts—before he thankfully abandoned it (thus already in *The German Ideology* from 1846, Marx and Engels rather wrote of more historically determined *Verkehr[sverhältnisse]* or "interaction"). When reappearing more than a decade later in seminal manuscripts on the critique of political economy, released in 20th century as *Grundrisse*, *Gattungswesen* signified an early historical phase of individualisation of human beings, when a human "appears originally as a species-being [*Gattungswesen*], clan being,

If alienation deals with losing somebody's reflection over his/her conditions of production and activities, then *reification* covers automatization and pragmatisation of relations between people that acquire a form of relations between things. This can only be possible because of a form of consciousness, specifically overdetermined by the capitalist dynamics. This form of consciousness, the so-called *commodity fetishism*, is a general "perverted appearance" of a social relation of production, "characteristic of all social forms of labour positing exchange-value," rather than subjective "imaginary ... mystification."[3] (The quote is from Marx's *Contribution to the Critique of Political Economy* in which it was not yet called "commodity fetishism," respectively.)

A slightly more difficult task would be to distinguish the provisionally described terms with more rigorous demarcations. Firstly, it is important to note that whatever the relation is between them, they do not belong to the same theoretical structure; alienation is derived chiefly from Marx's pre-1848 early scripts that show his theoretical criticism in its foetal form. In contrast, reification, at first glance similar to alienation, is, together with fetishism, an integral part of the well-accomplished Marx's thought that was manifested especially impressively in his critical analyses of bourgeois political economy, such as *Capital* (1867). Likewise, the reification as one of the aspects of commodity fetishism (or as its general manifestation) has only been marginally (if not exceptionally) employed by Marx—and has been canonised as a philosophical term on its own, only later by Georg Lukács.

Due to a format of this short presentational article, I will have to utterly ignore some reliable criticisms of alienation and reification, by some modern authors. Nevertheless, I will briefly bring to light a relatively famous critique, for which I will have to take a digression to French theory. But even so, I will not address it because of its criticism towards the subject, but rather for its contribution to one possible solution of the demarcation between the three concepts—or rather, of their potentially embarrassing *liaison*. The French structural philosopher Louis Althusser did not hesitate to completely disregard early Lukács's (and his followers') attempt to theorise reification. Indirectly put without mentioning the philosopher's name, it was, according to Althusser in his seminal *For Marx* (1965), nothing more than "a projection of the theory of alienation found in the [Karl Marx's] early texts, particularly the *1844 Manuscripts*, on to the [mature Marx's] theory of '[commodity] fetishism' in *Capital*."[4]

---

herd animal—although in no way whatever as a ζῶον πολιτικόν in the political sense." (Karl Marx, *Grundrisse. Introduction to the Critique of Political Economy*, trans. Martin Nicolaus (New York-Toronto: Random House, 1973), p. 496.)

3   Karl Marx, *A Contribution to the Critique of Political Economy*, ed. Maurice Dobb, trans. Salo W. Ryazanskaya (New York: International Publishers, 1970), p. 49.

4   Louis Althusser, *For Marx*, Trans. Ben Brewster (New York: Vintage, 1970), p. 230.

In Althusserian terms, reification "that sees 'things' everywhere in human relations" belongs philosophically to the *young* Marx, the philosopher tainted with Georg Wilhelm Friedrich Hegel's idealist heritage (Althusser is especially suspicious of the young Marx's "humanism"), and is supposed to be of minor importance to the *mature* Marx, the theoretician of *Capital*. Namely, Althusser's typology of Marx's opus strictly follows his notion of the so-called epistemological break—the latter supposedly dividing Marx's works between the early (idealist, Hegelian, essentialist or simply *philosophic*) and the mature, proto-structuralist, or *theoretic*. Marx's work after the alleged epistemological break is considered by Althusser to be the only relevant and theoretically cohesive. Therefore, reification is, in Althusser's view, supposed to owe its main characteristics to the essentialist romantic notion of alienation, but even then Marx rather spoke of "unhumanity," while the notion of "the thing" is, apart from the mature Marx analysis of money form, a category in comparison to which "more foreign to Marx cannot be imagined."[5]

Before we return to reification, it is worth acknowledging a detail often overlooked by philosophers and historians—and Althusser is not an exception here. Whilst it is often claimed that reification (that came to philosophical prominence with early Lukács's *History and Class Consciousness*) is in this or that way connected to the young Marx's alienation,[6] we should bear in mind that Lukács's collection of essays dates to 1923, when two key works by the young Marx (and Engels) that dealt with the topic of alienation, were not yet known to the public. While Marx's *Economic and Philosophic Manuscripts* of

---

5 Ibid.
6 For example, Gajo Petrović's entry in *A Dictionary of Marxist Thought* explains reification as "a 'special' [sic] form of alienation, its most radical and widespread form characteristic of modern capitalist society." ("Reification," in *A Dictionary of Marxist Thought*, ed. Tom Bottomore, Laurence Harris, Victor G. Kiernan, Ralph Miliband (Oxford: Basil Blackwell, 1983), p. 411.) Similarly, Risto Tubić, in another dictionary, designates reification of human relations as "very contiguous to alienation"—it "in fact, only presents one aspect of human alienation …" ("Reifikacija ljudskih odnosa," in *Enciklopedijski riječnik Marksističnih pojmova*, (Sarajevo: Veselin Masleša, 1974), p. 465.) On the other hand, certain authors mention them as two phenomena in the same theoretical system; Stephen Eric Bronner (somewhat superficially) comments on the two "unfreedoms of bourgeois practice": "Alienation was not the only product of the commodity form [sic]: there was also reification …" ("Lukács and the dialectic: contributions to a theory of practice," in *Lukács Reconsidered*, ed. Michael J. Thompson (London-New York: Continuum, 2011), p. 14, 18.) However, his distinction between alienation with its "elusive existential as well as anthropological quality" and reification that "has something more contextually concrete about it" (Bronner, "Lukács and the dialectic," pp. 29–30) is, even despite its rather poetical language, fairly pertinent, especially translated in more definite terms: while alienation could (inherently) manifest in any class society, reification is unambiguously linked to a capitalist mode of production.

1844 (that Althusser explicitly mentions) were only released in 1927, his first major early collaboration with Engels, *The German Ideology*, was released by David Ryazanov's Marx-Engels Institute in Moscow even later, in 1932.

Furthermore, the original German word for *reification* in Lukács's 1923's essay "Reification and the consciousness of the proletariat" (including its title) was *Verdinglichung*, which dislocates reification even further from the domain of the young Marx—with *Verdinglichung*, Lukács explicitly referred to (the mature) Marx's term from *Capital*. This puts in question Althusser's clear stance that a *thing* (*das Ding*) is a category "foreign to Marx" and that in *Capital* "the only social relation that is presented in the form of a *thing*" is money, instead of, as the term reification tends to suggest, "every social relation."[7] Namely, it was in *Capital*—in a section of its first part, entitled "The Fetishism of Commodities and the Secret Thereof"—that Marx famously wrote: "There is a definite social relation between men, that assumes, in their eyes, the fantastic form of a relation between things." The continuation of a passage also helps us to denote the relationship between objectification as seen by (the mature) Marx and his concept of commodity fetishism[8] that—through Lukács—influenced all further development of the theory of reification.

> In order, therefore, to find an analogy, we must have recourse to the mist-enveloped regions of the religious world. In that world the productions of the human brain appear as independent beings endowed with life, and entering into relations both with one another and the human race. So it is in the world of commodities with the products of men's hands. This I call the Fetishism which attaches itself to the products of labour, so soon as they are produced as commodities, and which is therefore inseparable from the production of commodities.[9]

Hence, to understand Lukács's influential use of the concept of reification (which is, warns Michael J. Thompson, not a cultural, but an epistemological

---

7 Althusser, *For Marx*, p. 230.
8 The latter, though being the strongest theoretical concept of all three, will have to be ignored in the continuation of the article. Not only due to space limitations, but also because its further developments in philosophy have not shallowed it to an extent of reification and alienation when these were discovered by behaviourism and popular psychology.
9 Karl Marx, *Capital. A Critique of Political Economy. Volume 1*, in Karl Marx, Frederick Engels, *Collected Works. Volume 35*, ed. Frederick Engels, trans. Samuel Moore and Edward Aveling (London-New York-Moscow: Lawrence & Wishart-International Publishers-Progress Publishing Group, 1996), p. 83.

category[10]), we must trace its direct lineage to the mature Marx of *Grundrisse* and, especially, *Capital*, the latter also being by far the most quoted Marx's title in Lukács's mentioned essay[11] to which I will dedicate the next lines.

This humble, factual update, however, does not rebut Althusser's argumentation in its entirety. Namely, though sparsely using the word "alienation" in the essay, Lukács *did* reference directly to the young Marx and his less remarkable passages about alienation, and—what is more—he relied heavily on Hegel's earlier reflections of alienation from *The Phenomenology of Spirit*. The latter were recruited in Lukács's essay merely to be refuted by Marx's materialist update, but in a way that constantly (at least in retrospect) self-critical Lukács much later mocked as "an attempt to out-Hegel Hegel,"[12] meaning simply that by his tentative disposition of the working class as "the identical subject-object of the real history of mankind" early Lukács did not successfully overcome idealist limitations in his Marxist interpretation of Hegel's philosophy, but rather provided the latter with a fairly Hegelian solution that Hegel himself had avoided.[13] From Lukács's essay on reification, however, this point is far less palpable to a non-philosopher than Lukács's favourable attitude towards Marx's own update of Hegel in his early works.

Looking at the essay "Reification and the consciousness of the proletariat" more closely, Lukács does not point out any particular ruptures in Marx's opus; notions from *Capital* were supported by several lines from Marx's early writings, and vice versa. Thus, Althusser was not wrong in pointing out that in general, Lukács did not distinguish strictly between the young and the mature Marx's conceptions. (The dilemma, to what extent Marx's earliest works are compatible with his seminal works such as *Capital*, is still being seriously discussed.) And, to confirm the French philosopher's mid-1960s perspective even more, even Lukács himself—though philosophically very distant from

---

10 Michael J. Thompson, "Introduction," *Lukács Reconsidered*, ed. Michael J. Thompson (London-New York: Continuum, 2011), p. 6.
11 Also a title of the present chapter begins with a phrase from *Capital* (Marx, *Capital*, p. 48; orig. *gespenstige Gegenständlichkeit*; in the translation I used for this article, *unsubstantial reality*; other translations include *spectral* and *phantom[-like, -atic] objectivity*) that, in passing, Lukács adopted in his essay "Reification and the consciousness of the proletariat," and Benjamin in *Arcades Project*.
12 Georg Lukács, *History and Class Consciousness. Studies in Marxist Dialectics*, trans. Rodney Livingstone (Cambridge (MA): Merlin Press, 1971), p. xxiii.
13 Moreover (or rather on the contrary) Slavoj Žižek in defence of Hegel from common and persisting idealist (mis)readings accuses early Lukács—due to his proposal of "simply replacing Hegelian Spirit with the proletariat as the Subject-Object of History"—of being "not really Hegelian, but a pre-Hegelian Marxist." (*Living in the End Times* (London-Brooklin: Verso, 2011), p. 226.)

Althusser—charged his own early investigations of reification in 1967 of being "based on the supposed equation of objectification [i.e., reification] and alienation."[14] Moreover, he admitted that "the phenomenon of reification is closely related to that of alienation but is neither socially nor conceptually identical with it; here the two words were used synonymously."[15] This retrospectively conceived strong ties between the young Marx's alienation and his mature work helped popularise early Lukács's own concept of reification with time—but before I briefly explain how, let me explain what is reification to early Georg Lukács.

2   "A Relation between People Takes on the Character of a Thing": Reification via Lukács

Lukács wrote "Reification and the consciousness of the proletariat" in 1923. It is necessary to underline that the essay, a pioneering critique of the capitalist systematic and determining formation of an individual's consciousness, had appeared even before Edward L. Bernays' books on propaganda techniques that were successfully used by emerging advertising industries and by Joseph Goebbels (not to mention Peter F. Drucker's and similar ideologues' deliberate applications of the capitalist market laws to the last consciously critical group that henceforth became recognised as "knowledge workers"). Originally, Lukács's account on "the power of consumer society to vitiate and even displace revolutionary politics"[16] was written primarily to explain why large sections of the proletariat in the most industrially advanced societies, suffering an enormous exploitation, "were 'seduced' or overcome by the prevailing system even as they fought, through their unions, for higher wages and improved working conditions."[17] His stark formulations were, however, accurate and advanced enough in analysing the main tendencies of capitalist society to gain relevance with time—and with development of the capitalist mode of production.

At the beginning of his famous essay, Lukács explained "the problem of commodity" as "the central, structural problem of capitalist society in all its aspects," and not only its economics.[18] Proceeding from Marx's critical analysis

---

14   Lukács, *History and Class Consciousness*, p. xxxv.
15   Lukács, History and Class Consciousness, pp. xxiv–xxv.
16   Stanley Aronowitz, "Georg Lukács's Destruction of Reason," Lukács Reconsidered, ed. Michael J. Thompson (London-New York: Continuum, 2011), p. 52.
17   Lukács, *History and Class Consciousness*, p. 52.
18   Ibid., p. 83.

of the bourgeois economy, Lukács switched "to a discussion of the problems growing out of the fetish character of commodities, both as an objective form and also as a subjective stance corresponding to it."[19] According to him, even the duality between the objective development and its subjective answer is merely one of the numerous dualities in which the commodity exchange manifested socially. Regularly referring to Marx, he emphasised that the reification of society did not appear immediately with the historical occurrence of a (specifically capitalist) commodity exchange, but only with the advent of *modern*, universalised capitalism. Or:

> The commodity can only be understood in its undistorted essence when it becomes the universal category of society as a whole. Only in this context does the reification produced by commodity relations assume decisive importance both for the objective evolution of society and for the [subjective] stance adopted by men towards it ... Reification requires that a society should learn to satisfy all its needs in terms of commodity exchange.[20]

Even more precisely—reification only appeared at a point in the historical development of the process of labour, where the latter was established systematically as "abstract, equal, comparable labour, measurable with increasing precision according to the time socially necessary for its accomplishment."[21] The philosopher noted that the development from the handicraft to machine industry showed "a continuous trend towards greater rationalisation, the progressive elimination of the qualitative, human and individual attributes of the worker," while the process of labour was, through the same development, gradually "broken down into abstract, rational, specialised operations so that the worker loses contact with the finished product and his work is reduced to the mechanical repetition of a specialised set of actions." The decisive factor of such mechanisation of work was the time necessary for the work to be accomplished[22]—from "a merely empirical average figure" of the early capitalist formation to "an objectively calculable work-stint that confronts the

---

19 Ibid., p. 84.
20 Ibid., pp. 86–91.
21 Ibid., p. 88.
22 "Above all, as far as labour-time is concerned, it becomes abundantly clear that quantification is a reified and reifying cloak spread over the true essence of the objects and can only be regarded as an objective form of reality inasmuch as the subject is uninterested in the essence of the object to which it stands in a contemplative or (seemingly) practical relationship." (Ibid., pp. 166–167.)

worker as a fixed and established reality."[23] Each part of a working process for which the capitalist rationalisation found a way to *be calculated*, was one step further from previously "irrational and qualitatively determined unity of the product."[24]

> Rationalisation in the sense of being able to predict with ever greater precision all the results to be achieved is only to be acquired by the exact breakdown of every complex into its elements and by the study of the special laws governing production. Accordingly it must declare war on the organic manufacture of whole products based on the *traditional amalgam of empirical experiences of work*: rationalisation is unthinkable without specialisation.[25]

This is extremely important for the topic of the present article as, henceforth, the acquired object was ceasing to be "the object of the work-process," but was instead gradually turned into "the objective synthesis" of rationalised processes of the division of labour, of which unity as a commodity could less and less coincide with the unity as use-value—moreover, the former unity would become "determined by a pure calculation."[26]

Such rational segmentation of the production of use-value in time and space—and here we move from conditions of reification to the reification itself—"necessarily entails the fragmentation of its subject."[27] Lukács's description of processes of the objectification of human consciousness and their relations from the early 1920s appears strikingly valid today—even the most superficial repercussions of the extreme liberalisation of the world economy after 1989 make Lukács's reflection sound like a prediction, and not solely a description of a diachronic capitalist trend: "In consequence of the rationalisation of the work-process the human qualities and idiosyncrasies of the worker appear increasingly as *mere sources of error* when contrasted with these abstract special laws functioning according to rational predictions."[28] Neither objectively nor subjectively does the worker now act as a master of the process—instead,

---

23 Ibid., p. 88.
24 Ibid., p. 89.
25 Ibid.
26 Ibid., pp. 89–90.
27 Ibid., p. 89.
28 Ibid.

> he is a mechanical part incorporated into a mechanical system. He finds it already pre-existing and self-sufficient, it functions independently of him and he has to conform to its laws whether he likes it or not. As labour is progressively rationalised and mechanised his lack of will is reinforced by the way in which his activity becomes less and less active and more and more *contemplative*. The contemplative stance adopted towards a process mechanically conforming to fixed laws and enacted independently of man's consciousness and impervious to human intervention ... must likewise transform the basic categories of man's immediate attitude to the world: it reduces space and time to a common denominator and degrades time to the dimension of space ... In this environment where time is transformed into abstract, exactly measurable, physical space, an environment at once the cause and effect of the scientifically and mechanically fragmented and specialised production of the object of labour, the subjects of labour must likewise be rationally fragmented.[29]

Henceforth, since the systematisation of the capitalist mode of production was total, "the personality" could not but "look on helplessly" while its existence was no more than an anonymous particle of an alien and inconceivable system. This was especially salient since the historical disintegration of a previously organic process of production into its components tore apart bonds of the medieval community fundamentally. Mechanisation minimised the social aspect of work for the community. "The internal organisation of a factory could not possibly have such an effect—even within the factory itself—were it not for the fact that it contained in concentrated form the whole structure of capitalist society." Lukács juxtaposed the capitalist society to Ancient Rome and its slaves—oppression and exploitation had been present since long ago, he wrote, but "mass projects of this type could never be rationally mechanised; they remained isolated phenomena within a community that organised its production on a different ... basis and which therefore lived a different life."[30] This changed radically and qualitatively with the universalisation of commodity exchange: "The fate of the worker becomes the fate of society as a whole; indeed, this fate must become universal as otherwise industrialisation could not develop in this direction. For it depends on the emergence of the 'free' worker who is freely able to take his labour-power to market and offer it for sale as a commodity 'belonging' to him..."[31]

---

29   Ibid., pp. 89–90.
30   Ibid., p. 90.
31   Ibid., p. 91.

This obviously implied a universal application of rational mechanisation and calculability to all aspects of life. Consumer articles ceased to appear as products of processes in a community, but increasingly occurred as "abstract members of species," whose (non-)possession depended on rational calculations. Only in the aftermath of society's total fragmentation into isolated acts of commodity exchange could the "free" worker as an isolated atom appear, and simultaneously "his fate becomes the typical fate of the whole society."[32] But Lukács audaciously dug even deeper; namely, as he pointed out, the isolation and fragmentation of the society is only apparent when:

> The movement of commodities on the market, the birth of their value, in a word, the real framework of every rational calculation is not merely subject to strict laws but also presupposes the strict ordering of all that happens. The atomisation of the individual is, then, only the reflex in consciousness of the fact that the 'natural laws' of capitalist production have been extended to cover every manifestation of life in society; that for the first time in history the whole of society is subjected, or tends to be subjected, to a unified economic process, and that the fate of every member of society is determined by unified laws. (By contrast, the organic unities of pre-capitalist societies organised their metabolism largely in independence of each other).[33]

But even if the atomisation is just an illusion, it is for Lukács a necessary one for the reproduction of (relations of production of) a capitalist formation; universalised market with its "obedience to 'natural laws' ... in a [seemingly] finished form, as something immutably given" can *only* reproduce itself "in the form of rational and isolated acts of exchange between isolated commodity owners," whose faith is typical for society as a whole.[34] But apart from this general capitalist characteristic, the modern age intensified commodification beyond the previously imagined borders: "It also integrates into its own system those forms of primitive capitalism that led an isolated existence in pre-capitalist times, divorced from production."[35] However subordinated in their entirety to actual capitalist's extraction of surplus value via production, these forms are generally perceived in the bourgeois society as "the true representatives of [somebody's] societal existence." The reified mind necessarily accepts

---

32   Ibid.
33   Ibid., pp. 91–92.
34   Ibid., p. 92.
35   Ibid., p. 93.

the "commodity character of commodity" as "the form in which its own authentic immediacy becomes manifest and—as reified consciousness—does not even attempt to transcend it ... Just as the capitalist system continuously produces and reproduces itself economically on higher and higher levels, the structure of reification progressively sinks more deeply, more fatefully and more definitively into the consciousness of man."[36]

Lukács's theoretical suspicion towards the immediate perception as a methodological tool, especially in the wake of the rationalised and reified society, remains as another strong point contributing to the essay's eminent relevance for a critical revision of today's social processes. Against a major stream in today's popular (as well as academic) disputes of transgressing impoverished human relations through immediate, authentic, or direct experiences (that is supposed to de-reify them), Lukács insisted on surpassing the "immediate" by converting its logic with the Hegelian notion of "second nature,"[37] the latter evolving in a reified bourgeois society "with exactly the same inexorable necessity as was the case earlier on with irrational forces of nature (more exactly: the social relations which appear in this form)."[38] To a reified consciousness, perceived as the immediate experience of a commodified world can in fact merely reproduce the reified structural forms of the contemporary society.

The structural forms of the society are visible directly neither to people who experience them nor to a historian[39]—instead, they have to be searched for using the materialist analysis. In subsequent chapters of the essay, Lukács meticulously investigated how the reified second nature functioned, especially in the interaction with a theoretically consistent idea "of a total social situation caught up in the process of historical change."[40] Some formulations are thrilling, especially if we bear in mind that they were written in the early 1920s:

> At first sight—and anyone who insists upon immediacy may never go beyond this 'first sight' his whole life long—it may look as if the next stages implied a purely intellectual exercise, a mere process of abstraction. But this is an illusion which is itself the product of the habits of thought and feeling of mere immediacy where the immediately given

---

36   Ibid.
37   When use-values historically appeared universally as commodities, they gained "a new objectivity" which they could not yet have attained in centuries of sporadic exchange. (Ibid., p. 92.) This "self-created immediacy" then affected not only the self-complacent capitalist economy, but also bourgeois philosophers that correctly sensed the reifying process of the modern age, but ascribed it to ahistorical factors. (Ibid., p. 95.)
38   Ibid., p. 128.
39   Ibid., p. 153.
40   Ibid., p. 162.

> form of the objects, the fact of their existing here and now and in this particular way appears to be primary, real and objective, whereas their 'relations' seem to be secondary and subjective. For anyone who sees things in such immediacy every true change must seem incomprehensible. The undeniable fact of change must then appear to be a catastrophe, a sudden, unexpected turn of events that comes from outside and eliminates all mediations.[41]

The change, with which the ossified relations of exploitation should be surpassed, must be thought of in terms as far from the immediate experience as possible.

> If change is to be understood at all it is necessary to abandon the view that objects are rigidly opposed to each other, it is necessary to elevate their interrelatedness and the interaction between these 'relations' and the 'objects' to the same plane of reality. The greater the distance from pure immediacy the larger the net encompassing the 'relations,' and the more complete the integration of the 'objects' within the system of relations, the sooner change will cease to be impenetrable and catastrophic, the sooner it will become comprehensible.[42]

This change was for Lukács, following the young Marx's *Theses on Feuerbach* (and tracing the idea in its rudimentary form back to Johann Gottlieb Fichte[43]), only realisable through praxis, but due to its complex stratification a larger and larger part of human activity had become instrumentalised by a commodity fetishism. An individual in a capitalist society confronts reality, itself constructed via class relations, as "a natural phenomenon alien to himself," and thus all his activity (especially if leaning on the immediacy) is limited "to the exploitation of the inexorable fulfilment of certain individual laws for his own (egoistic) interests."[44]

Even in such an "activity," the individual remains an object—and not a subject—of his actions, which smoothly contribute to the reproduction of capitalism. In his investigation on how to overcome this chain of circumstances, Lukács moved from the reified individual action to a class action of the whole proletariat, or from the virtual subject of modern history (i.e. an *individual*)

---

41   Ibid., pp. 153–154.
42   Ibid., p. 154.
43   Ibid., pp. 39, 123–124.
44   Ibid., p. 135.

to the actual one (i.e. the oppressed *class*).⁴⁵ It is only through the *conscious* action of the proletariat—the action of which underlying materialist and historically aware conceptualisation will be able to encompass all concrete manifestations of the dialectical totality and recognise them as reified—that the reification can be dissolved. This is in Lukács's view a decisive step to the dissolution of subject-object duality that Fichte as well as Hegel sought to postulate, albeit in an idealistic manner. However, "this will only be true if the road beyond immediacy leads in the direction of a greater concreteness, if the system of mediating concepts so constructed represents the 'totality of the empirical'—to employ Lassalle's felicitous description of the philosophy of Hegel."⁴⁶

It was precisely Lukács's deep and permanent appreciation of Hegel throughout various and often contradictory periods of his philosophical development, as well as his pioneering analyses of the early, "Hegelian" Marx in mid-1930s, that guaranteed him a special place in a specific stream emerging in the western academic sphere between late 1920s and 50s that focused mostly on—if we use Althusser's distinction—*humanist* aspects of Marx's philosophy. The trend of the research on the young Marx and topics such as alienation, triggered by Lukács in 1930s, had a greater or lesser impact on—for instance—the Frankfurt School, Sartrian existentialism (especially Sartre and Maurice Merleau-Ponty until the latter's political conversion), or on the philosophy of such independent thinkers as Henri Lefebvre, Alexandre Kojève, or Walter Benjamin—the latter's adoption of the term will be discussed in the next chapter—, to mention only those that remained inside a frame of a Marxist thought. Namely, if Lucien Goldmann and Pierre Bourdieu were correct, Martin Heidegger's *Time and Being* (1929) had not only been strongly influenced by Lukács's *History and Class Consciousness*, especially in the German philosopher's reflections of alienation,⁴⁷ but had, in many senses, been a direct

---

45 Ibid., p. 165.
46 Ibid., p. 154.
47 The thesis is provocative, but let me repeat Heidegger's lines (also included in a longer passage that Lukács himself quoted in his analysis of Heidegger in his heavily underrated *Destruction of Reason*): "The 'who' is not this one, not that one, not oneself [*man selbst*], not some people [*einige*], and not the sum of them all. The 'who' is the neuter, the 'they' [*das Man*]. We have shown earlier how in the environment which lies closest to us, the public 'environment' already is ready-to-hand and is also a matter of concern [*mitbesorgt*]. In utilizing public means of transport and in making use of information services such as the newspaper, every Other is like the next. ... [T]he Others, as distinguishable and explicit, vanish more and more. In this inconspicuousness and unascertainability, the real dictatorship of the 'they' is unfolded. We take pleasure and enjoy ourselves as they [*man*] take pleasure; we read, see, and judge about literature and art as they see and judge; likewise we shrink back from the 'great mass' as they shrink back; we find 'shocking'

polemic[48] against it/him despite Lukács's name never being mentioned. Thus, even though Lukács as reification's main theoretical proponent essentially relied on the Marx's mature work in his referential essay, the concept of reification would perhaps gradually come to (somewhat self-evident) proximity to the young Marx's alienation even if Lukács himself would never have implied their reciprocity.

3   "Self-estranged Human Being … with Armor against the Reified World":[49] Walter Benjamin's Reification between *Erlebnis* and *Erfahrung*

To the young Walter Benjamin, Lukács's concept of reification provided the "first Marxist theoretical tool"[50] with which he could conceptualise his notions

---

what they find shocking. The 'they,' which is nothing definite, and which all are, though not as the sum, prescribes the kind of Being of everydayness." (Martin Heidegger, *Being and Time*, trans. John Macquarrie and Edward Robinson (Oxford-Cambridge: Blackwell, 2001), p. 164, orig. pag. 126–127. With a different English translation, see also Georg Lukács, *Destruction of Reason*, trans. Peter Palmer (Atlantic Highlights, New Jersey: Humanities Press, 1981), p. 499.)

48   For instance: "If world-time thus belongs to the temporalizing of temporality, then it can neither be volatilized 'subjectivistically' nor 'reified' by a vicious 'Objectification.' These two possibilities can be avoided with a clear insight …" (Heidegger, *Being and Time*, p. 472, orig. pag. 420.) In fact, on the last page in the German original of Heidegger's seminal work, at its endmost conclusion, lies the clearest reference of all; however, nor Lukács nor the title of his essay are mentioned—instead, the problematic is effectively ahistoricised: "It has long been known that ancient ontology works with 'Thing-concepts' and that there is a danger of 'reifying consciousness.' But what does this 'reifying' signify? … Why does this reifying always keep coming back to exercise its dominion? What positive structure does the Being of 'consciousness' have, if reification remains inappropriate to it? Is the 'distinction' between 'consciousness' and 'Thing' sufficient for tackling the ontological problematic in a primordial manner? Do the answers to these questions lie along our way?" (Heidegger, *Being and Time*, p. 487, orig. pag. 437.) Lukács in his own analysis of Heidegger's "unauthenticity" of the everyday existence—as if answering the pompous paragraph—wrote: "Heidegger, as we have noted, did not explicitly contest the economic doctrines of Marxism-Leninism or the political consequences they entailed—neither he nor the caste he represented was capable of it. He attempted rather to avoid the necessity of drawing social conclusions by 'ontologically' branding all man's public activity as 'unauthentic.'" (Georg Lukács, *Destruction of Reason*, trans. Peter Palmer (Atlantic Highlights, New Jersey: Humanities Press, 1981), p. 503.)

49   Walter Benjamin, *The Arcades Project*, ed. Rolf Tiedemann, trans. Howard Eiland and Kevin McLaughlin (Cambridge (MA)/London: The Belknap Press of Harvard University Press, 1999), p. 322. The quotation depicts Charles Baudelaire.

50   Esther Leslie, *Walter Benjamin. Overpowering Conformism* (London-Sterling: Pluto Press, 2000), p. 9. See also Margaret Cohen, "Benjamin's phantasmagoria: the Arcades Project,"

of an empty and apathetic society, especially in his reflection of cultural forms as its products, as well as of a phenomenon of melancholy.[51] Before that time, he had shown neo-Kantian affinities, sporadically tempted by his keenness towards romantic aesthetics of Schlegel and Novalis, while his general philosophical-theological frame had been (and remained) the traditional Jewish mysticism. In contrast to many other leftist Jewish thinkers of—more or less—his generation who had previously embraced mysticism but abandoned it until the end of World War I through their philosophical development (including Lukács!), Benjamin remained faithful to his theological roots for his whole life. Although his materialism was gradually becoming more coherent throughout 1920s and 30s, his later texts often referred to his own material from the idealistic period without the slightest revision.[52]

Benjamin, as a prolific and well-informed thinker, was familiar with Lukács even before the period of *History and Class Consciousness*, as reveal Benjamin's letters to his close friend and life-long correspondent, mystical philosopher Gershom Scholem.[53] Due to his ambivalent philosophical insights,[54] Benjamin's path to Lukács's theses was not straight; it is perfectly safe to assume that numerous ambiguities, occurring as he was trying to incorporate Lukács's theses into his own romantic and mystical, philosophical framework, helped to articulate his specific view on reification. In June 1924 he wrote to the above-mentioned correspondent about Ernst Bloch's review of *History and Class*

---

in *The Cambridge Companion to Walter Benjamin*, ed. David S. Ferris (Cambridge: Cambridge University Press, 2004), p. 201.

51 Susan Sontag, "Introduction," in *Walter Benjamin. One-Way Street and Other Writings*, trans. Edmund Jephcott and Kingsley Shorter (London: NLB, 1979), pp. 15–16, 20, 22–23.

52 NLB, "Publisher's note," in Walter Benjamin, *One-Way Street and Other Writings*, trans. Edmund Jephcott and Kingsley Shorter (London: NLB, 1979), pp. 29–31. See also Beatrice Hanssen, "Language and mimesis in Walter Benjamin's work," in *The Cambridge Companion to Walter Benjamin*, ed. David S. Ferris (Cambridge: Cambridge University Press, 2004), p. 64; Cohen, "Benjamin's phantasmagoria," p. 210.

53 Walter Benjamin, *The Correspondence of Walter Benjamin 1910–1940*, ed. Gershom Scholem and Theodor W. Adorno, trans. Manfred R. Jacobson and Evelyn M. Jacobson (Chicago-London: The University of Chicago Press, 1994), p. 180, 204.

54 The list of his closest friends and associates in 1920s and 30s, all of whom made a strong and lasting remark on Benjamin's thought and most of whom despised or at least refused each other ideologically, is very telling. Apart from the solemn Scholem, who was close to Jewish spirituality and feared Benjamin's Marxist excursions, also philosopher Theodor W. Adorno and Bertolt Brecht, an eccentric communist poet and playwright, was particularly misprized by the other two. (Rainer Nägele, "Body politics: Benjamin's dialectical materialism between Brecht and the Frankfurt School," *The Cambridge Companion to Walter Benjamin*, ed. David S. Ferris (Cambridge: Cambridge University Press, 2004), p. 153, 166.)

Consciousness, obviously already aware of a certain affiliation between his and Lukács's central topics: "The review seems to be by far the best thing [Bloch] has done in a long time and [Lukács's] book itself is very important, *especially for me* ... I am unable to read it now."[55]

It is no surprise that Benjamin became ambivalent towards some of the author's theses very early—in fact even before actually reading the book. In September of the same year, he wrote:

> While proceeding from political considerations, Lukács arrives at principles that are, at least in part, epistemological and perhaps not entirely as far-reaching as I first assumed. The book astonished me because these principles resonate for me or validate my own thinking ... I want to study Lukács's book as soon as possible and I would be surprised if the foundations of my nihilism were not to manifest themselves against communism [to which Benjamin at the time had reservations while Lukács defended it] in an antagonistic confrontation with the concepts and assertions of Hegelian dialectics.[56]

Benjamin, however, was well acquainted with Lukács's book by 1925. He read the seminal chapter on reification together with Bloch and Asja Lācis,[57] a Lithuanian communist and Benjamin's fatal lover at the time, during holiday on Capri in 1924.[58] Next year, while writing about "the jubilee anniversary number of one thousand" books that he had read,[59] he mentioned among the last entries "*History and Class Consciousness*, an extraordinary collection of Lukács's political writings."[60] A little later, he was also interested in Soviet philosopher

---

55 Benjamin, *The Correspondence*, p. 244. See also Nägele, "Body politics," p. 154.
56 Benjamin, *The Correspondence*, p. 248.
57 Very possibly it was exactly Lācis' influence that motivated thoroughly fascinated Benjamin enough to read Lukács. (NLB, "Publisher's note," pp. 32–33.)
58 Cohen, "Benjamin's phantasmagoria," p. 201. This was also the year when Benjamin met Adorno, another lifelong friend and associate. (Nägele, "Body politics," p. 154.)
59 Nevertheless, interestingly a Marxist thinker "who read virtually everything and had spent fifteen years sympathizing with revolutionary communism, had barely looked into Marx until the late 1930s." (Sontag, "Introduction," p. 18.) ... And even then possibly only due to Adorno's direct appeal: "[T]his is where I speak so brutally because of the enormous seriousness of the matter. As was probably your intention, the fetish conception of the commodity must be documented with the appropriate passages from the man who discovered it." (Theodor W. Adorno, "Letters to Walter Benjamin," in Ernst Bloch et al., *Aesthetics and Politics*, ed. Ronald Taylor (London: Verso, 1980), p. 117.)
60 Benjamin, *The Correspondence*, p. 268.

Abram Deborin's relentless critique of Lukács's book.[61] But how was Benjamin's thinking of things affected by Lukács's?

To answer adequately, it is worth noting that Benjamin's philosophical development was not smooth, and even the philosopher's texts from the same period were often mutually ambiguous if not controversial—which is already a key difference to Lukács's concise and systematic conceptualisation of reification. But there is another notable difference that should be clear at the beginning of the present examination; if Lukács was fundamentally *concerned* with the objectified relations and consciousness, Benjamin was also avidly interested in objects themselves, in (an indeed very broad span of) *things* that he also collected throughout his lifetime.[62] In a sense just like Lukács, Benjamin sought to take the concrete world of things as a possible starting point of reflection that would fathom and surmount mystifications of a commodifying process. But while Lukács's analysis produced a theory, of which an integral part was a prediction of a system that could methodologically grasp *any* particular thing, Benjamin usually introduced his aspects of reification via concrete topics, and only subsequently developed them into more abstract argumentations.

Besides—and in connection to the concreteness of his analyses—, Benjamin, compared to Lukács and most other materialist philosophers, did not systematically refute the "experience" of the immediate in a (reified) society as necessarily futile; and things appeared to him as traces, as well as tools, of human experiences. He embraced them as not just unavoidable manifestations of a reified society (or rather, "its rejects"[63]) but as theoretically productive due to their inherent ontological ambiguity. The double essence of "things" as a consequence to capitalist reification and, at the same time, an irreducible residue of what is reified and thus a key to overcome it, could have been derived from Benjamin's mystical notions or, on the other hand, from his earliest attempts at dialectical philosophical streams. I will return to this specific duality later when I touch on Benjamin's problematic of *Erlebnis* and *Erfahrung*, but first I must introduce a broader perspective on Benjamin's specific view of reified relations of production.

In the most developed (and yet protean) form, Benjamin's notions of reification (and of "things" in general) are scattered over his vast and asymmetrical

---

61   Ibid., 279.
62   Less known is that Benjamin in his love for used things followed his close friend Brecht. (Peter Buse, Ken Hirschkop, Scott McCracken and Bertrand Taithe, *Benjamin's Arcades: An UnGuided Tour* (Manchester-New York: Manchester University Press, 2006), p. 50.)
63   NLB, "Publisher's note," p. 35.

opus magnum, the so-called *Arcades Project* that was only released in full (and yet incomplete) form in 1983, containing more than one thousand pages. *Arcades* began their life in mid-1920s as an accompanying essay to his travel diary enriched by his reflective observations entitled "One-Way Street"[64] from 1928,[65] but developed into an ambitious life project. Benjamin's thoughts were constantly being reworked correspondingly to "objective" political and economic tensions that first brought a financial crisis of the capitalist world in 1929 and later culminated in the rise of the European fascism and a world war. Benjamin's constant reminiscences and reflections as well as discussions with his closest friends all affected his subtle and elusive work.

Lukács's views on reification encouraged Benjamin to bear some provocative conceptual consequences of Marx's critique of political economy over the late 1920s. Namely, the semi-metaphorical explanation of commodity fetishism in the first book of *Capital*, that he found elaborated in Lukács's text, implied to Benjamin a fundamental irrationality of the capitalist society that the Enlightenment did not surmount—and that he, due to his mystical inclinations and, moreover, his strong influence by (post)romantic irrationalists such as Kierkegaard or Nietzsche, was ready to adopt even in his Marxist vision. Benjamin stressed the irrational or "transcendental"[66] foundations of capitalism to focus on the general mystifying process of modernity.

With somewhat expected reservations towards Hegelian (and thus, indirectly, also Lukács's) totality as being too abstract,[67] he was prepared to find a way for conjoining, as he put it, "a heightened perceptibility [or *graphicness*; orig. *Anschaulichkeit*] to the realization of the Marxist method" by posing a semi-rhetorical question of whether Marxist understanding of history must "necessarily be acquired at the expense of the perceptibility of history."[68] As I will try to show later on, Marxist insight prevented Benjamin's theory to fall

---

64 Describing his current "One-Way Street," Benjamin wrote: "For the rest of the book owes much to Paris, and represents my first confrontation with it. I continue it in a second work, entitled 'Parisian Arcades'..." (Ibid.)

65 Ibid.

66 Benjamin, *Selected Writings, Volume 2*, p. 290.

67 For better orientation about the approximate sequence of his main influences throughout 1920s: "When Benjamin works his way from a radical dualism, doubly affirmed by his immersion in Kantian philosophy and by what he considers the center of his Jewish experience (*Erfahrung*, in contrast to *Erlebnis* ...), toward his *Dialektik im Stillstand* (dialectic at a standstill) and the dialectical image, it is more through Hölderlin's concept of the caesura than through Hegel's dialectic." (Nägele, "Body politics," p. 156.)

68 Benjamin, *The Arcades Project*, p. 461. See also Cohen, "Benjamin's phantasmagoria," p. 202.

under the influence of contemporary phenomenology[69] that as well tended to displace things from their context—but with different motivations and, particularly, different consequences. Rather, his method anticipated Foucauldian discourse analysis, as its first presumed stage was "to carry over the principle of montage into history. That is, to assemble large-scale constructions out of the smallest and most precisely cut components. Indeed, to discover in the analysis of the small individual moment the crystal of the total event."[70]

By merging Freud's account of dreams, as used by the Surrealists with his own reflections on Marx's somewhat oneiric rhetoric about commodity fetishism, he came to a provocative, yet undialectical and socially naïve hypothesis. Benjamin claimed that the irrational dimensions of modern life could be merely manifestations of a big collective sleep that covered Europe with the rise of capitalism; if so, the philosophy should awaken Europeans from the dreams of the previous century.[71] By intertwining his own Marxist account of superstructure being an "expression" of base[72] with psychoanalytical notion of dreaming as an expression of unconscious (in an "optimist" Surrealist rendition rather than Sigmund Freud's original concept), his specific vision of analysing totality via reflection of montaged reified particularities would finally become clearer. When rethinking his idea of perceptibility that a presentation of history should possess, he concluded that it should be "neither the cheap and easy perceptibility of bourgeois history books nor the insufficient perceptibility of Marxist histories. What it has to fix perceptually are the [dialectical] images deriving from the collective unconscious."[73] Though taking as a basis two complex theoretical conceptions, namely Marxist and Freudian, Benjamin's specific tendency toward perceptibility also owes a lot to other philosophical and theological streams that he was concerned with and that also distinctively shaped eclectic passages of which *Arcades Project* consists—sometimes not too productively.

Namely, on certain points, Benjamin came close to bourgeois vitalist philosophers who at the beginning of the century, in contrast to Lukács's

---

[69] Benjamin admitted that he felt more in common with "crude and rudimentary analyses of Franz Mehring than with the most profound periphrases from the ambit of the ideas produced by school of Heidegger today." (NLB, "Publisher's note," p. 38.) I will focus on his nevertheless complex philosophical relation to the contemporary philosophical currents in the next chapter.

[70] Benjamin, *The Arcades Project*, p. 461.

[71] Cohen, "Benjamin's phantasmagoria," p. 205.

[72] Cohen, "Benjamin's phantasmagoria," pp. 205–206.

[73] Benjamin, *The Arcades Project*, p. 911. See also Cohen, "Benjamin's phantasmagoria," p. 206.

contemporary essay, fetishized experience and were in great majority far from the progressive in the political sense. One such case is a (proto-)fascist philosopher Ernst Jünger with whom Benjamin shared, as Esther Leslie puts it, the idea of an "expanded experience."[74] Throughout *Arcades*, there are several passages that show his contempt for systematic and rational approach of a theory in favour of experience.[75] In a certain formative period, Benjamin started to distance himself from a theoretical justification in general, simply because he saw the theories as too dependent upon the intentions of theorists. He enthusiastically believed that the "historical truth" of his authentic fragments of the 19th century was manifested objectively, while any theoretical superstructure would contaminate this authentic objectivity. He went even further (most certainly away from Lukács's positions, as well as those of his colleagues of the Frankfurt School) in claiming that historical truth is not available to a theory at any possible time; instead, it becomes "legible" or "recognisable" only at specific moments[76] which he likened to a "prophetic gaze that catches fire from the summits of the past."[77] In resemblance to the weaker moments of the contemporary *Lebensphilosophie*, he wrote: "The dialectical image is an image that emerges suddenly, in a flash."[78]

4   "The Commodity Is ... an Alien Survivor that Outlives Its Own Immediacy":[79] Adorno's Critique of Benjamin

These are but a few examples of Benjamin's general inclinations towards mysticism on the one hand and his sporadic adoption of the contemporary (crypto-)irrationalist aversion towards theory on the other that were—perhaps rightfully—attacked by Adorno[80] in a famous letter written in August 1935 known as the Hornberg letter, that Benjamin described as "great and memorable"—, as well as in forthcoming correspondence.[81] Adorno considered

---

74   Leslie, *Walter Benjamin*, p. 26.
75   This is, again, rather unusual for a major name of the interwar critical theory.
76   Max Pensky, "Method and time: Benjamin's dialectical images," *The Cambridge Companion to Walter Benjamin*, ed. David S. Ferris (Cambridge: Cambridge University Press, 2004), p. 180.
77   Walter Benjamin, *The Arcades Project*, p. 473.
78   Ibid.
79   "Letters to Walter Benjamin," p. 113. The quotation is taken from Adorno's famous August 1935 letter.
80   See also Cohen, "Benjamin's phantasmagoria," p. 207.
81   David Frisby, *Fragments of Modernity (Routledge Revivals): Theories of Modernity in the Work of Simmel, Kracauer and Benjamin* (New York: Routledge, 2013), pp. 204–205.

the entire first draft of *Arcades* to be highly pre-theoretical or, with his words from November 1938, "a wide-eyed presentation of mere facts ... at the crossroads of magic and positivism."[82] Adorno's critique that Benjamin took very seriously and that influenced his concept of *Arcades* during the last years before his death, was a request for Benjamin to use more concise, theoretical language instead of ahistorical terms and reflections that "overvalue the archaic" and mystify the specificity of the modern capitalist alienation that arose with the "industrial production of commodities."[83] In other words, Adorno suggested him engaging more critical and politically conscious aspects.

Probably—but not necessarily—it was due to Adorno's critique that Benjamin's specific notion of experience, at least in its later, developed form, the inventive updates of Lukács's materialist concept of the reification could be observed. Let us take his special distinction between two fundamental types of experience, namely a distinction between *Erlebnis* and *Erfahrung* (translated respectively as "isolated" or "immediate experience" and "long experience") explained in his 1940's essay "On some motifs in Baudelaire," well after Adorno's most distinctive criticism. Like many of Benjamin's concepts, the distinction verges on poetical metaphor—yet, it remains productive in a theoretical sense. I hope it is not too farfetched for me to claim that even Benjamin's principal division between the two types of experiences could—but could as well not—be traced back to Lukács's conceptualisation of praxis (and, indeed, further to the problematics connected to the German idealism), particularly in connection to numerous dualities that, according to Lukács, capitalism generates in a social totality. Videlicet, these experiences represent two opposite, or rather complementary, ways of dealing with the reified world; whilst *Erlebnis*—a concept that Benjamin could have found in social as well as aesthetic theory[84]—is merely an expression of the reification, the other type of experience, *Erfahrung*, deals with a necessarily reflected praxis with which the *Erlebnis* should be surpassed.

A more nuanced look on the opposition between reified *Erlebnis* and reflected and subversive *Erfahrung* draws argumentation even closer to Lukács's

---

82   Adorno, "Letters to Walter Benjamin," p. 129. "That spot [i.e. intersection between magic and positivism] is bewitched. Only theory could break the spell—your own resolute, salutary speculative theory. It is the claim of this theory alone that I am bringing against you." (Ibid., pp. 129–130.)

83   Adorno, "Letters to Walter Benjamin," p. 114. See also Howard Eiland and Michael W. Jennings, "Chronology, 1935–1938," in Walter Benjamin, *Selected Writings, Volume 3. 1935–1938*, ed. Howard Eiland and Michael W. Jennings (Cambridge (MA)/London: The Belknap Press of Harvard University Press, 2002), p. 423.

84   Buse et al., *Benjamin's Arcades*, p. 51.

"Reification" essay. Let us remember the latter's words about a potential change that must necessarily appear alien and incomprehensible to a reified consciousness that "sees things in ... immediacy": Lukács, as mentioned, wrote that "[t]he greater the distance from pure immediacy ... the sooner change will cease to be impenetrable and catastrophic, the sooner it will become comprehensible."[85] Benjamin's notes on function of shock in Baudelaire's poetry as if would take these words as their starting point; there, it is stated: "The greater the shock factor in particular impressions, the more vigilant consciousness has to be in screening against stimuli; the more efficiently it does so, the less these impressions enter long experience [*Erfahrung*] and the more they correspond to the concept of isolated experience [*Erlebnis*]."[86] Benjamin wrote these words in the context of a modern urban *Erfahrung* in which he put much aspiration: spontaneously, life in the city tends towards a more general modern alienated experience, or *Erlebnis*. But also the reflection, accordingly to Benjamin needed to transcend the reified immediacy, could more easily emerge in quickly developing cities as their inhabitants were increasingly exposed to the shocking aspects of modernity which diminished their inherent shock and provided a tool for a vigilant "screening against stimuli."

A critical addition is required when Benjamin's reflection is put in a historiographical perspective—constant shocks aside, urban environment was, historically speaking, only likely to transform *Erlebnis* into *Erfahrung* after the pre-established division of labour that had, because of its gradual specification, also given rise to schools of different kinds, and finally, the public school system. Before that important fact, i.e. in the times of burgeoning *urbanisation* itself, Benjamin's theses would have proven far less fitting. We only need to take a look at the primitive accumulation of capital in England with its villages liberalised, i.e. brutally turning into privatised areas of a mass exploitation via

---

85   Lukács, *History and Class Consciousness*, p. 154.
86   Walter Benjamin, "On some motifs in Baudelaire," in *Selected Writings, Volume 4. 1938–40*, ed. Michael W. Jennings (Cambridge (MA)/London: The Belknap Press of Harvard University Press, 2003), p. 319. See also Walter Benjamin, *Charles Baudelaire: a Lyric Poet in the Era of High Capitalism*, trans. Harry Zohn (London: Verso, 1997), p. 117. Authors of a newer book about Benjamin's crucial work locate his notions of long and isolated experience directly into *Arcades*' earliest genesis, when he was stunned by Louis Aragon's *La Paysan de Paris*. Shocked by the text's recapitulation of modernity (reportedly Benjamin could only read a few pages before his heartbeat was too intense to continue) he needed years to "reconfigure the shock of the text as *Erfahrung*. Only through relating the shock defence—the conditioned and habitual response to modernity—to reflective experience can the experience of modernity be properly understood." (Buse et al., *Benjamin's Arcades* 52.)

enclosure of the commons, manufactures etc. especially after the European "discovery" of Americas, and its consequent development until (and including) the first Industrial Revolution in the 18th century. Apart from those murdered, a large number of dispelled peasants of all ages was forced to leave their farms and settle in urban(ised) areas where they had to work under murderous conditions or perish—while begging was severely punished, even a harmless theft induced a capital punishment up to 1832. While (the surviving) subjects to these activities were exposed to permanent shock to which today's bourgeois city life is barely comparable (and which bears more similarities to slums and sweatshops in the most exploited countries of today), there was hardly any sign of a distant reflection or "screening against stimuli" which Benjamin idealistically attributed to urban experience, until lonely critical voices appeared in mid-18th century. The criticism grew constantly with the development of the public school system before it could arguably be understood as a general urban reaction to constant dramatic circumstances. Thus, Benjamin was partly correct to locate this phenomenon in a modern city experience, but was not accurate enough in determining its material causes.

If this only owed to an inconsistency, then clear traces of anti-theoretical sentiment can also be seen in mature Benjamin's essay on Baudelaire, sometimes outweighing the essay's theoretical conceptions. For instance, a dialectical *Erfahrung* must, after Benjamin in the abovementioned essay, include "memory [*Gedächtnis*] with material from the collective past."[87] A wish "in the strict sense of the word" likewise, Benjamin loosely stated, "appertains to an order of experience." Furthermore: "[A] wish fulfilled is the crowning of experience."[88] If such formulations, as well as the sole fact that Benjamin insisted on a pre-theoretical notion of experience for his critical philosophical achievements, still contained an uncanny echo of the abovementioned Jünger and similar authors, the most concise points of his essay on Baudelaire—in a Lukácsian manner—displayed the immediate experience of shock as essentially unproductive until actively reflected: "Without reflection, there would be nothing but the sudden start, occasionally pleasant but usually distasteful..."[89]

Finally, to understand Benjamin's seemingly intuitive approach to reification, it should nevertheless be stressed that his ideas such as "collective

---

87 Walter Benjamin, "On some motifs in Baudelaire," p. 316.
88 Ibid., 331.
89 Ibid., p. 319.

consciousness,"[90] "myth"[91] or "experience"[92]—even in spite of his curiosity for the spiritual and supernatural—never or very seldom reached an unambiguous proximity to socially conservative thinkers such as Carl Gustav Jung, Ludwig Klages, Oswald Spengler, the above noted Ernst Jünger or, for that matter, Alfred Rosenberg. Adorno's demanding critique aside, it seems that this is predominantly true even if Benjamin's earlier phases, i.e. his writings prior to Adorno's dramatic intervention, are in question. But then, how to distinguish between the young Benjamin and the abovementioned philosophers? Were they *actually* that different? Certainly Benjamin and Jünger converged philosophically from the viewpoint of present-day cultural studies that often neglect the social and political dimensions of their content. Benjamin of the 1920s bestowed the militant essayist's notions about an atrophy of the ability to experience in a world dominated by technocratic rationality and mass media projections. Consequently, they both saw modern society as a disenchanted realm of automatized actions that should essentially be revived by a—to the present moment—suppressed experience.[93] Paradoxically, apart from the consistency-lacking cultural studies of today, there is a certain justification with which even a theoretically concise critique could dismiss Benjamin's idea of "expanded experience" and his temporary aversion towards theory as naïve, uncritical, and grounded in the apologetic bourgeois ideology of the imperialist era—which would, again, put Benjamin in an uncanny proximity of an inciting anti-theoretical reactionary Jünger. In fact, it was only due to their different broader philosophical frameworks that the two authors' intentions functioned noticeably differently—but this is enough to radically switch the perspective of their relation.

Accordingly, both thinkers' (interpretations of their own) notions of "experience" that modern society had suppressed could hardly have been more

---

90   From Adorno's famous letter: "The notion of collective consciousness was invented [by Jung] only to divert attention from true objectivity and its correlate, alienated subjectivity. It is up to us to polarize and dissolve this 'consciousness' dialectically, and not to galvanize it as an imagistic correlate of the commodity character." ("Letters to Walter Benjamin," p. 113.)
91   From Adorno's Hornberg letter: "Lastly, moreover, the mythic-archaic category of the 'Golden Age'—and this is what seems socially decisive to me—has had fateful consequences for the commodity category itself ... Thus disenchantment of the dialectical image leads directly to purely mythical thinking, and here Klages appears as danger, as Jung did earlier." Exactly in this context Adorno explicitly speaks about (Lukácsian) class-consciousness. ("Letters to Walter Benjamin," p. 113.)
92   Again from Adorno: "The term *Lebensgefühl* (attitude to life), used in cultural and intellectual history, is highly objectionable." ("Letters to Walter Benjamin," p. 116.)
93   Leslie, *Walter Benjamin*, p. 26.

dissimilar, even despite a notion that both originally proposed an "aesthetic" solution to it. Benjamin coherently articulated a reflexive aesthetic experience of the reified society that could, in connection to Marxist political praxis, de-reify it (through renewed consideration of things). Conversely, anti-Marxist Jünger, volunteer in the World War I, throughout his life praised the military—particularly battlefield—experience and amazing new technologies[94] as the ultimate tools to overcome the mechanical rationality of the modern decadent society. Namely, the intensification of experience as the "aesthetic consciousness," proposed by Jünger and similar philosophers,[95] involves a viewpoint of *désinvolture*; aesthetic consciousness thus provides armour of apathy of the killing machines, or as Leslie states: "[Jünger's so called 'soldier-critic'] is anaesthetized, as he aestheticizes."[96]

Hence, in terms of the present article, it is obvious that in such ideologies there is no place whatsoever for the analytical concept of reification, especially in connection to class dynamics. The seemingly critical notions of banal modernity by Ernst Jünger and numerous other bourgeois philosophers were in fact deeply conformist and perfectly attuned to the political-economic interests of the European ruling classes that during 1920s and 30s perpetually *provoked* banalisation and automatization. Hence, such philosophers—as a matter of reified and commodified social relations, could be added—*criticised* the banalization and automatization from exactly the same, i.e. elitist, conservative and militant, positions that caused it, and therefore they constantly helped intensifying it without proper reflection. Such an irresolvable loop of argumentation (and consequent actions) of the interwar bourgeoisie could only culminate in crises of capitalist economy and resulting imperialist wars—no wonder that most of the conservative thinkers relying on "experience" greeted

---

94 "An over-valuation of machine technology and machines as such has always been peculiar to bourgeois theories in retrospection ..." (Adorno, "Letters to Walter Benjamin," p. 116.)

95 Jünger was a self-understood heroic veteran that sold his unrecovered experiences from the WW I battlefields over and over again and thus vocally promoted war. From the wider historical perspective, he undoubtedly belonged to what Eric Hobsbawm called "a relatively small, but absolutely numerous, minority for whom the experience of fighting, even under the conditions of 1914—1918, was central and inspirational; for whom uniform and discipline, sacrifice—of self and others—and blood, arms and power were what made masculine life worth living ... These Rambos of their time were natural recruits for the radical Right." (*Age of Extremes. The Short Twentieth Century 1914–1991* (London: Abacus, 1994), p. 125.)

96 Leslie, *Walter Benjamin*, p. 27.

the war gladly.[97] Benjamin severely criticised these positions from the beginning, immediately recognizing a "class myopia" (to use Leslie's term) of such writing. His harsh critique of Jünger from 1926—almost ten years before Adorno's famous letter—presents one of the earliest occasions for him to implement his tentative Marxist analysis.[98] As illustrated above, Benjamin nonetheless never abandoned the notion of "experience,"[99] so frequently used by the abovementioned philosophers of the extreme Right. Why did he insist, with such persuasion, on using a philosophical notion that most other materialist philosophers largely avoided?

The paper at its conclusion does not intend to provide a perfect answer, but rather hints to a peculiar historical coincidence that might be in favour for the theoretical aspect of Benjamin's writings; whilst his bourgeois and theologically founded upbringing somewhat obviously allowed him to quickly embrace the anti-theoretical and (at least usually) socially conservative ideology of the "experience" (but, importantly, also theologian's discipline of thought that prevented him from adopting the contemporary *Lebensphilosophie*),[100] his own subsequent "experiences" developed in a specific direction (very different from the likes of Jünger) due to numerous convoluted and hardly surprising factors. As a Jewish Marxist intellectual trying hard to make ends meet and relying existentially on his entrepreneur father until the latter's death in 1926, he struggled with loathsome economic circumstances and political persecution especially in the 1930s, while letters and polemics with his critical associates also shaped his abstract notion of the "experience" that he then did not attribute to its usual, socially conservative philosophical consequences.

It is hardly surprising that, according to the socially conservative hegemonic streams that relied on an unreflected experience of the most conservative stratum of a German society, he was an obvious outcast—Marxist Jewish

---

97 It should also not surprise us that Jünger, who never refused his extreme positions, and Heidegger (of whom could be said the same: see his unconvincing minimisation of his Nazi past, as well as his elitist mythologizing about the supposed inner kinship between German and Greek language and thought against other world languages, in famous *Der Spiegel* interview from September 1966) mutually respected each other's work and became regular correspondents after ww II.

98 Leslie, *Walter Benjamin*, pp. 27–28.

99 Rather, he accused Jünger's tendency to technologisation of everyday life of "banalizing of experience." (Leslie, *Walter Benjamin*, p. 27.)

100 In his Hornberg letter to Benjamin, Adorno explicitly—and favourably—juxtaposes Benjamin's rather rational or consistent theological kernel against his more intuitivist moments that brought him too close to the contemporary militant bourgeois milieu. (Nägele, "Body politics," p. 163; Adorno, "Letters to Walter Benjamin," p. 114.)

intellectual with unsecure employment status (but seemingly competing with German white-collars) provided not a natural protagonist of the burgeoning extreme Right, but rather its to-be-expelled antipode. Thus, Benjamin could easily reject the crypto-fascist philosophical leanings of his less critical contemporaries (such as Jünger) already *in statu nascendi*. His link to mysticism, however, diverted him from abandoning the reflection of experience as such that was already becoming an insignia of the conservative thinkers. Thus, Benjamin was (and remained)—just like the conservative bourgeois philosophers—keen on the philosophical tradition of experience, but—just like his critical associates of the Frankfurt School—he resisted any conservative conclusions inherent to the majority of the contemporaneous philosophy that fetishized it.

It is far from surprising then that not only did he observe the category of experience in a perfectly unique way, hardly comparable to any of his socially conservative compatriots, but also his experiences alone were rather complementary to theirs. Or, with Benjamin: "Well. Experience has taught me that the shallowest of communist platitudes contains more of a [theological] hierarchy of meaning than contemporary bourgeois profundity, which is always no more than apologetic."[101] In other words, Benjamin's personal experience (as well as its theoretical consequences) was a far cry from the usual socially conservative determinations of the immediacy, the latter becoming constitutive for a huge majority of German bourgeois thinkers gradually leaning closer and closer to fascism in their fetishization of experience during the 1920s and 1930s. Only via this theoretically lucky historical chance it is possible to explain the soundest, unparalleled correspondence between Benjamin's most spiritual meditations and most theoretical insights that were finally, as I have tried to show, synchronised in his notion of experience. This unique correspondence did not exclude his mystical aspects either; again with Benjamin: "It is absolutely necessary … to be clear that the [Communist] movement has its own mystical elements, even if they are of a quite different type. Of course, it is even more important not to confuse these mystical elements, which belong to corporeality, with religious ones."[102]

From this necessary digression that led us to explain Benjamin's unique materialist notion of experience with selected emphases from his biography, I will return to the integral theoretical problematic that the paper is trying to illustrate. In a nutshell, Lukács's important upgrade of Marx's concept of the commodity fetishism in his own analysis of consciousness in the globalised capitalism triggered various theoretical and philosophical reflections that

---

101   NLB, "Publisher's note," p. 38.
102   Leslie, *Walter Benjamin*, p. 23.

reached the zenith in the 1940s and 50s. Among the first and arguably the most innovative responses to Lukács's theory of how relations between humans take the shape of relations between things—or how they reify—due to the universalised commodity fetishism, was Walter Benjamin's multifaceted thought. The latter, whilst leaning on Lukács's conceptions, was notwithstanding rooted in an (albeit materialistically reconditioned) orthodox Jewish mysticism, and occasionally enticed by contemporary bourgeois thought. Therefore, Benjamin developed a specific theoretical frame centred on the individual experience that led him cogitate the corporeal and the concrete with distinct conclusions, different from the contemporaneous bourgeois philosophers (praising experience of the corporeal and concrete, but lacking a critical distance from its ideologically overdetermined immediacy), as well as from his fellow materialist acquaintances (who developed a strong critical apparatus, but—in Benjamin's view—majorly ignored experience and perceptibility).

His peculiar notion of things as not sole remnants of reification of human relations but also the potential inception to de-reify them via reflection, perhaps also helped to shape his style of writing; while most materialist philosophers—including Lukács and Adorno—developed wider theoretical frameworks, and only subsequently applied it to actual examples, Benjamin usually displayed his theoretical conceptions only after certain particular detail from the "perceptible" world—from arcades via work of art in the age of reproduction to Baudelaire's urban attitude—had been introduced. Though initially influenced by Brecht, Benjamin's lifelong avid collecting and meditating objects manifested his peculiar distinct meticulous endeavour to save things from their immediacy, namely their service to commodity exchange as their ultimate scope, and to use them as aims to cultivate a richer consciousness, aware of the broader conditions needed to be surpassed. Or, as Lukács put it at the end of his brief praising text about Benjamin: "Where the world of objects is no longer taken seriously, the seriousness of the world of subject must vanish with it."[103]

---

103 Georg Lukács, "On Walter Benjamin," in *Walter Benjamin: Critical Evaluations in Cultural Theory Vol. III. Appropriations*, ed. Peter Osborne (London-New York: Routledge, 2005), p. 6.

CHAPTER 7

Lukács on Reification and Epistemic Constructivism

Tom Rockmore

Classical Marxism was invented by Engels after Marx died, and Hegelian Marxism was simultaneously invented in the early 1920s by Lukács and Korsch. In *History and Class Consciousness*, Lukács, in inventing Hegelian Marxism, simultaneously forges a theory of reification. In the eleventh of the "Theses on Feuerbach," Marx suggests the need not only to interpret but also transform society. In *History and Class Consciousness*, Lukács links this aim to what he calls "reification." Writing soon after the end of the First World War, he claims that any and all problems now lead back to commodities. This is the central problem of economics, the central problem of modern industrial society, and at least potentially the solution of all problems of contemporary capitalism. "For at this stage in the history of mankind there is no problem that does not ultimately lead back to that question and there is no solution tht could not be found in the riddle of commodity-structure … That is to say, the problem of commodities must not be considered in isolation or even regarded as the central problem in economics, but as the central structural problem of capitalist society in all its aspects."[1]

This paper will study three related themes: reification and proletarian consciousness, Marx and classical German philosophy, and Marx's relation to Marxism and philosophy. I will be arguing two points. First, reification is an important contribution to our grasp of Marx that, however, conflates objectification and alienation. Second, Lukács does not and cannot show that at this stage in the history of mankind all problems lead up to and can be solved through reification.

1 On Understanding Lukács Today

Important figures are often not understood in their own time and understood differently in later periods. Lukács is an important figure, a many-sided

---

[1] Georg Lukács, *History and Class Consciousness*, translated by Rodney Livingstone, Cambridge: MIT Press, 1971, p. 83.

intellectual giant with important contributions to literary theory, aesthetics, philosophy and Marxism. His best philosophical writings bear comparison with anything written in the twentieth century. He is arguably by a number of criteria the single most important Marxist intellectual, but someone who is also often misunderstood.

One reason is above all his great originality within the Marxist debate due to his quasi-Hegelian grasp of German idealism or in his terminology classical German philosophy. Lukács, who was mainly trained in Germany, was thoroughly familiar with classical German philosophy before he converted to Marxism in 1918 at the end of the First World War. At the time of his conversion, he brought with him a philosophical baggage that was sometimes equaled by non-Marxist colleagues, but arguably unequalled by even the most philosophically qualified Marxists, such as Ernst Bloch.

Second, there is a profound dualism due to the concerted effort running throughout his long Marxist period to serve two masters simultaneously. This dualistic effort arose from Lukács's orthodox philosophical background. Lukács's grasp of classical German philosophy, which was not unusual before he became a Marxist, was very unusual after his conversion.

This dualism shows itself in different ways in Lukács's writings and actions during his long Marxist period. It includes Lukács's non- or anti-Marxist conception of Marx, correctly in my opinion, as building on rather than breaking with Hegel and classical German philosophy. Marxism tends to insist on continuity between Marx and Marxism and equally strongly on a break between Marx and philosophy, perhaps most radically in Althusser. In his long Marxist period, Lukács has an equivocal attitude with respect to Marx and Marxism, which he separates philosophically, but conflates politically. Since Engels' invention of classical Marxism, Marxists tend to treat Marx and Marxism as continuous and Marx as if he were a Marxist. Lukács breaks with the Marxist view of Hegel in criticizing Engels as philosophically incompetent and as proposing merely another reading of Marx. Yet he has no hesitation about subordinating his philosophical views to Marxist politics. An instance is his servile praise of Lenin when, after the publication of *History and Class Consciousness*, he came under politically-dangerous criticism.

2 On "Reification"

It will be useful to start with some remarks on "reification" (Verdinglichung). The publication of the *Paris Manuscripts* with their important account of alienation only became widely available in English after the Second World War. The availability of the *Manuscripts* led to an important debate about so-called humanist Marxism. This term is an obvious misnomer. It conflates Marxian theory, which may or may not be "humanist," depending on how that term is understood. Yet it is unlike Marxist practice that, however understood, has never been humanist.

As part of the debate around Marxist humanism, efforts were made to determine whether Marx's conception of alienation, which is important in the *Paris Manuscripts*, still has a role to play in his later writings. Istvan Mészáros, Lukács's former assistant, argued strongly and convincingly, based on careful study of the text, that Marx does not abandon but continues in various way to rely on alienation in his later writings, including *Capital*.[2] The effort to show the importance of concept of alienation in Marx's later writings, when the relevant texts were unavailable, was obviously much more difficult. Lukács's inference, on the basis of the later Marxian writings, to what he in *History and Class Consciousness*, that is before the appearance of the *Paris Manuscripts*, calls "reification," is an enormous hermeneutical feat.

Reification always was and remains a controversial concept. Objectification, which was not invented by Lukács, is anticipated in different ways by Fichte and Hegel, and possibly others. According to Hegel, we objectify or "concretize" ourselves in what we do, including economic products, such as commodities, social contexts, and finally world history.

Alienation is a more controversial concept. In China after Deng Xiaoping came to power, is was regarded as mistaken to discuss Marx's conception of alienation since this problem supposedly could not exist in a socialist country. Alienation, which is understood in many different ways, is anticipated by Fichte, Hegel and perhaps even the Bible.

In the *Paris Manuscripts*, Marx describes an elaborate series of four kinds of alienation that supervene within the framework of modern industrial capitalism. Under the heading of "reification" Lukács famously conflates, as he later acknowledged – and blamed on overly closely following Hegel – "objectification" and "alienation." The subsequent debate has focused on getting clear about the relation of "reification," "alienation," and – since fetishism is related to, but not the same as reification" – (commodity) fetishism.

According to Petrovic, though reification is implicit in such early writings as the *Paris Manuscripts*, the two most important accounts of reification in Marx's writings occur in *Capital I*, Chapter 1.4 in the account of fetishism, where there are indications toward a theory of reification but no definition, and in *Capital III*, Chapter 48.[3]

---

2 See István Mészáros, *Marx's Theory of Alienation*, London: Merlin, 1970.
3 See Gajo Petrovic, "Reification," in *A Dictionary of Marxist Thought*, edited by Tom Bottomore, Cambridge: Harvard University Press, 1983, 411–413.

In the first passage, Marx calls attention to the distinction between the self-objectification of workers in the process of production and either the physical properties of the commodity or its material relations. He goes on to say that, in virtue of the subordination of human beings to commodities, social relations, which are inverted, take on the ontological form of relations between things that he calls the fetishism of commodities. He points out that from the point of view of human development, producers are ruled over or depend on their products and not conversely.

Marx writes:[4]

> The mystery of the commodity form, therefore, consists in the fact that in it the social character of men's labor appears to them as an objective characteristic, a social natural quality of the labor product itself ... the commodity form, and the value relation between the products of labor which stamps them as commodities, have absolutely no connection with their physical properties and with the material relations arising therefrom. It is simply a definite social relation between men, that assumes, in their eyes, the fantastic form of a relation between things... This I call the fetishism which attaches itself to the products of labor, so soon as they are produced as commodities, and which is therefore inseparable from the production of commodities ... To the producers the social relations connecting the labors of one individual with that of the rest appear, not as direct social relations between individuals at work, but as what they really are, thing-like relations between persons and social relations between things ... To them their own social action takes the form of the action of things, which rule the producers instead of being ruled by them.

Engels' « Umrisse zu einer Kritik der Nationalökonomie », an early article published in the "Deutsch-Französischen Jahrbüchern" (1844), influenced the young Marx at a crucial time as he was beginning to work out his alternative conception of modern industrial society. Marx later returns to this theme in Chapter 48, titled the "Trinity Formula" in the third volume of *Capital* quarried from his *Nachlass*. Marx here discusses the outlines of political economy through the Engelsian categories of capital- profit or -interest, land-ground rent and labor-wages. According to Marx, though capitalism is mysterious, through these three categories the so-called mystification provides, that is leads to or again brings about, in a word causes the so-called mystification of capitalism. This economic model includes the reification of social relations, by inference the objectified and alienated social relations, including their

---

4 *A Dictionary of Marxist Thought*, p. 411.

material, social and historical determinations. In and through economic reification, capital (Monsieur le Capital) and the social world (Madame la Terre) take the double form of social characters, or men and women, as well as commodities or things.

Marx writes:[5]

> In capital-profit, or still better capital-interest, land-ground-rent, labor-wages, in this economic trinity represented as the connection between the component parts of value and wealth in general and its sources, we have the complete mystification of the capitalist mode of production, the reification [Verdinglichung] of social relations and immediate coalescence of the material production relations with their historical and social determination. It is an enchanted, perverted, topsy-turvy world, in which Monsieur le Capital and Madame la Terre do their ghost-walking as social characters and at the same time directly as things.

3 Class Consciousness and Reification

In the seminal account of "Reification and the Consciousness of the Proletariat," reification plays at least three roles. They include, as the title suggests, class consciousness, then the Marxian solution to the unsolved problems of classical German philosophy, and finally the relation of Marx to philosophy and science.

Lukács's theory of class consciousness is an original contribution to the problem of the transition from capitalism to communism. It is well known that Marx rejects theory that leaves everything in place. He is famously concerned with theory that goes beyond mere interpretation to change the world. His view of changing the world turns on the transition from modern industrial capitalism, the present stage of the development of society, to a postmodern phase including the transition from capitalism to communism or, if there is a difference, to socialism.

The transition from capitalism to communism is both central to the Marxian position as well as unclear. An example is the aim in view. According to Marx, communism, which is a later stage in the evolution of human society, is neither the final phase nor an end in itself. It is rather a means to an end, that is, a meaningful or at the very least more meaningful form of human freedom in the modern world.

---

5 *A Dictionary of Marxist Thought*, pp. 411–412.

So far so good. Now there are two main problems with this view. They concern what Marx means or conceivably could mean by the idea of freedom in modern industrial society and how to obtain it. On the one hand, and though his corpus is immense, Marx himself published very little during his lifetime. Many, in fact most of the texts that have come down to us reflect Marx's frequent attempts at self-clarification, often in terms of the main but ever-expanding project of the description and transformation of modern industrial society in theory as well as in practice.

Unquestionably, Marx is interested in human freedom in modern industrial society. This general concern, which is on the agenda at least since early Greek philosophy, runs through the entire later tradition. The problem changes in the modern tradition as a result in the period between Hobbes and Rousseau of the onset of the Industrial Revolution. At the time of Hobbes, the problem of human freedom could still be addressed through a social contract. The Industrial Revolution brought about a change in the situation that beginning with Rousseau takes the form of human freedom in the context of different instantiations of modern capitalism. This theme interests not only Rousseau, but also later thinkers such as Kant, Hegel and Marx.

A glance at Marx's writings shows that, though he floated various suggestions at different times, and though there is a certain resemblance between some of the passages, he seems never to have settled on a view of human freedom in capitalism, hence on a goal for a type of theory intended as useful in both theory as well as practice.

Here are four among the many suggestions of Marx's conception of human freedom to be realized after the end of capitalism in a future communist society. They include Marx's comments on James Mill's *Elements of Political Economy*, a passage from the *German Ideology*, another from the *Grundrisse*, and a final passage quarried from the third volume of *Capital* in his Nachlass. In the comments on Mill, Marx suggests that in production each of us affirms others.[6] In a widely cited passage from the *German Ideology* someone, perhaps neither Marx nor Engels, suggests a person can function as a hunter, a fisherman or a critic without being any of them.[7] Though this passage is often cited, its lack of economic realism as well as the fact that the Feuerbach chapter was not written by Marx and Engels renders it dubious as a source of either of their views at best. In a third passage in the *Grundrisse* Marx rejects division of labor.[8] And

---

[6] See *Marx-Engels Collected Works*, London: Lawrence and Wishart, 2010, Vol. III, pp. 227–228.
[7] See *Marx-Engels Collected Works*, Volume V, p. 47.
[8] See Karl Marx, *Grundrisse: Foundations of Political Economy*, trans. Martin Nicolaus, Marmondsworth: Penguin, 1973, p. 488.

finally in a fourth passage from the third volume of *Capital* Marx, who in the meantime seems to have turned from revolution to reform, insists on the shortening of the working day.[9]

The other main difficulty lies in the problem, to whose solution Lukács contributes, of the transition from capitalism to communism. At least in theory there seem to be four ways to carry out this transition. These ways are identified with the revolutionary proletariat, an unmanageable economic crisis, the party as the vanguard of the revolution and critical social theory.

It has already been noted that critical social theory only arose later in reaction to the views of Lukács and Korsch. Thus, when he wrote this chapter, Lukács had only three choices at his disposal. Now Lukács rejects both an unmanageable economic crisis as well as the party as the vanguard of the revolution is extremely interesting. Both rejections are related to his preference, when he wrote *History and Class Consciousness,* for Luxemburg over Lenin. This preference is even more interesting since it was quickly reversed when Lukács's study came under sharp criticism after Lenin's *Materialism and Empiriocriticism* was translated into Western languages.

Luxemburg was important for a number of reasons at the time. On the one hand, she favored an economic alternative to the Marxian view of the inevitability of an unmanageable economic crisis. More precisely, she thinks that the unavailability of further markets would eventually undermine capitalism. In rejecting an economic approach to the transition from capitalism to communism, Lukács rejects both Marx's view of the significance of the falling rate of profit, his main economic solution, as well as Luxemburg's alternative suggestion of the eventual restriction of available markets.

The reason why he rejects a political solution is that he, like Luxemburg, is opposed to dictatorship and perhaps, though this is not clear, even committed to democracy. His rejection of an economic solution is more complex. He seems to reject the idea of economic crisis, perhaps in favoring Luxemburg's view of the increasing restriction of the market, or even perhaps since he thinks that, as he stresses, reification contradiction is not merely economic but rather spread throughout society.

Luxemburg was a prophetic critic of Bolshevism. Lenin, who initially favored democracy, by the time of the Russian Revolution overtly favored dictatorship. Luxemburg, perhaps the only adversary that he treated as roughly equal, famously foresaw that the dictatorship of the proletariat that Lenin recommended would lead to the dictatorship of the party over the proletariat and finally of one man over the party. Writing in the wake of the October Revolution,

---

9 *Marx-Engels Collected Works,* Vol. XXVIII, pp. 411–412.

it is possible that, if for no other reason, Lukács turns away from an economic outcome to the transition from capitalism to communism because he agreed in the need to favor democracy over dictatorship. Yet, since we simply do not know, anything is possible.

Since Lukács rejects both economic and political solutions to the transition from capitalism to communism, the only remaining possibility is the revolutionary proletariat. Marx expounds a theory of the revolutionary proletariat in his early article titled "Critique of Hegel's Elements of the Philosophy of Right: Introduction." In the *Republic*, Plato describes a society organized along hierarchical lines with respect to intrinsic abilities. In his text, Marx advances a Platonic view of the then emerging proletariat that, since it was supposedly incapable of guiding itself, will be guided down the revolutionary path by philosophers. Since, when Marx wrote his article the proletariat, the proletariat, as he indicates, was only in the process of emerging, and since Marx's view is not based on empirical study of any kind, it is at best speculative. There is no reason to think that the proletariat that Marx envisioned in the early 1840s ever existed. And in the meantime, through the evolution of society at least in the so-called first world countries the proletariat has largely been replaced through so-called white-collar jobs. Marx, who mentions the proletariat from time to time, never later returned to the proletarian solution to the transition from capitalism to communism.

Lukács replaces Marx's Platonic vision of the revolutionary proletariat by a romantic Hegelian vision. In the *Phenomenology of Spirit*, Hegel famously discusses the relation of masters and slaves in suggesting that in the long run the slave is the master of the master and the master is the slave of the slave. Lukács suggests that, when the proletariat becomes consciousness of itself, this will lead to the revolutionary transformation of society. This romantic view suggests that the proletariat will free itself in by inference unrealistically depicting capitalism as existing only because workers are not aware of the situation. One strategy might be the dream of a mass strike elaborated by Sorel and others. Yet, since capitalism is not about to go away or otherwise disappear merely because the proletariat becomes aware of their role within it, the dream of the mass strike is finally only a dream.

4   Marx, Classical German Philosophy and the Thing in Itself

I have so far suggested that Lukács seeks, through his account of reification, to transform Marx's view of the transition from capitalism to communism in practice. In pointing to the link between classical German philosophy and

Marx's position, Lukács further suggests Marx solves or resolves the problems left over from classical German philosophy. This suggestion rests on two presuppositions, including descriptions of classical German philosophy in the context of the philosophical tradition as well as of Marx's position.

The idea of the end of philosophy is persistent in the modern tradition. Kant, for instance, insists that in the critical philosophy he both begins and ends philosophy worthy of the name. According to Kant nothing in the critical philosophy can be modified without destroying reason.

In his brochure on Feuerbach, Engels, who was not philosophically trained, shares the young Hegelian view, popular at the time, that philosophy comes to a high point and an end in Hegel. This view was famously formulated by Heinrich Heine, the German romantic poet. According to Heine, Hegel brings to an end everything undertaken since Kant and even philosophy itself, since his position is the end of all philosophy in the accepted sense of the word. If, as Engels and other Young Hegelians think, in Hegel philosophy comes to a high point and an end, then it obviously cannot, as Heine also thinks, be carried further by any of the post-Hegelian thinkers. Heine spoke for many others when in the context of the enormous void left by Hegel's departure from the scene he wrote: "Our philosophical revolution is concluded; Hegel has closed its great circle."[10] Feuerbach's role lies in the transition from Hegelian idealism to materialism supposedly lying beyond philosophy. Feuerbach simply breaks with what goes before, or, in a different formulation, finally breaks completely with Hegel.

Engels applies the young Hegelian view of Hegel to Marx, whom he depicts as a post-philosophical figure. This interpretation is based on the relation of Marx to Feuerbach. In the period when he wrote the *Paris Manuscripts*, the young Marx was strongly influenced by Feuerbach before rapidly turning against him in the "Theses on Feuerbach." Feuerbach was a minor Hegelian critic as well as an important Protestant theologian. In his brochure on Feuerbach, Engels seems unaware of Kierkegaard, Nietzsche, Marx and others. He depicts Feuerbach as the only contemporary philosophical genius. According to Engels, Marx followed Feuerbach away from Hegel, whom he simply threw aside, hence away from classical German idealism, and toward materialism, or post-philosophical science.

Marx's view of Hegel is infinitely more positive than Engels' view. Marx takes himself to be Hegel's disciple, but Engels regards the German thinker as in effect a "dead dog." Marx took a doctorate in philosophy at a time when

---

10   Heinrich Heine, *Religion and Philosophy in Germany*, John Snodgrass, trans., Albany: SUNY Press, 1986, p. 156.

Hegel, who had only recently left the scene, was still the dominant philosophical figure. When Engels was active, positivism was in the air. In his classical elaboration of positivism, Comte insists on the discontinuity between religion, philosophy and science. Engels's effort to depict Marx as a post-philosophical figure presupposes a series of supposed discontinuities, above all between philosophy and science. Engels often suggests that Marx is responsible for the extra-philosophical, scientific component of Marxism. Though he suggests that Marxism is proud of its sources in Kant, Fichte and Hegel, he typically distinguishes between utopian and Marxist, or supposedly scientific socialism. In his speech at Marx's graveside, Engels generously compares Marx to Darwin. He claims that Marx "discovered the law of development of human history," which, if this is a reference to political economy, presumably means that economics is prior to every other explanatory factor in its capacity as "the special law of motion governing the present-day capitalist mode of production and bourgeois society that this mode of production has created."[11]

The term "science" (Wissenschaft) functions in classical German philosophy as a claim to rigor. Engels, who is interested in recent science, overlooks the distinction between science and rigorous or non-rigorous forms of philosophy. His suggestion that Marx discovered the law of the development of human history comparable to the Darwinian law of evolution is based on a series of misunderstandings. If "law" refers to a causal relation, then, since there is no biological law, Darwin did not discover a law of the evolution of species. Similarly, Marx did not discover the law of the development of human history, since history has no laws. Engels apparently conflates the view that science is not philosophy, and philosophy has in the meantime come to an end, with the very different view that rigorous philosophy that is not science is, however, scientific.

Hegel discovers the history of philosophy through his view of later philosophical positions as building on what is still valid in earlier positions. Lukács, who stresses Hegelian Marxism, not surprisingly formulates a Hegelian view of the relation of Marx to classical German philosophy in displacing the supposed completion of philosophy from Hegel to Marx. He breaks with classical Marxism, in depicting Marx as not turning away from, but as rather building on and carrying forward, German classical German philosophy that reaches a high point and an end in Marx's post-Hegelian theory culminating in the concept of reification.

Early in the Greek tradition, the pre-Socratic Parmenides influentially suggests the unity of thought and being. With his Greek predecessor in mind,

---

11   *Marx-Engels Collected Works*, Vol. XXIV, p. 107.

Hegel claims that the Western philosophical tradition consists in an ongoing effort to demonstrate the unity of thought and being. According to Lukács, claims to know are never aperspectival, or what is sometimes called a view from nowhere, but always perspectival, always the view of a particular segment of the population. From Lukács's Marxist point of view, Marx is a turning point in the philosophical tradition. The tradition is divided into what can be called pre-Marxian irrationalism and Marxian rationalism.[12] The divide between irrationalism and rationalism runs between capitalism and Marx. From the Marxian angle of vision, "irrationalism" refers to any theory that, in reflecting the bourgeois perspective, fails to grasp modern industrial society. The bourgeois point of view is irrational, hence incapable of knowing capitalism. Rationalism, on the contrary, reflects the perspective of the proletariat that alone is capable of knowing modern industrial society.

Lukács links the solution to the problem of knowledge, more specifically knowledge of modern industrial society, to Kant's Copernican revolution in philosophy. Kant distinguishes two general approaches to knowledge. On the one hand, there is the traditional approach popular since Parmenides that to know means to grasp the mind-independent world or, in Kantian terminology, the thing in itself. According to Kant, there has never been any progress toward knowing an independent object. On the other hand, there is the view that we only know what we can in some sense construct. Epistemic constructivism, the Kantian alternative, consists in suggesting we will have greater success in inverting the relation between subject and object in seeking not to know the mind-independent but rather to know the mind-dependent object.

Lukács refers to Kant's Copernican revolution in correctly pointing out that the latter did not invent the constructivist approach. He links Kant to Marx, who suggests, following Vico, that human beings who do not make nature, but rather make human history. According to Lukács, this theme runs throughout modern philosophy. "From systematic doubt and the *Cogito ergo sum* of Descartes, to Hobbes, Spinoza and Leibniz there is a direct line of development whose central strand, rich in variations, is the idea that the object of cognition can be known by us for the reason that, and to the degree in which, it has been created by ourselves."[13]

Instead of dismissing classical German philosophy, Lukács provides a quasi-Hegelian account of Marx as building on the philosophical tradition. The young Hegelians think that philosophy ends in Hegel, who never says that

---

12   See, for this argument, Tom Rockmore, *Irrationalism: Lukács and the Marxist View of Reason*, Philadelphia: Temple University Press, 1992.
13   Lukács, *History and Class Consciousness*, p.112.

philosophy comes to an end in his position. Lukács applies this young Hegelian view to his interpretation of Marx's relation to the philosophical tradition. In refuting classical Marxism, Lukács holds that Marx builds on Hegel and classical German philosophy. It would go beyond the scope of this paper to discuss epistemic constructivism. Suffice it to say that Kant's a priori version of the constructivist approach to knowledge that becomes a posteriori in the writings of Fichte and Hegel. We owe to Fichte a post-Kantian exposition of the view that the object depends on the subject.[14] Hegel follows Fichte in claiming that the subject, who does not know reality, knows only the human world, including its social surroundings and human history that it constructs. According to Lukács, the problem of knowledge does not reach a high point and an end in Hegel but rather in Marx's position.

The epistemic debate in modern philosophy is literally transformed, for Lukács as well, through the post-Kantian development of the constructivist approach to knowledge. The transformation includes the turn from the unavailing effort to know a mind-independent object to the by implication bourgeois approach to knowledge of modern society. This approach reaches its high point in the end of philosophy that arrives in Marx's version of the post-Kantian constructivist approach to knowledge from the proletarian perspective. Kant still describes reality as the uncognizable thing in itself. This approach, presumably from the bourgeois angle of vision, is further developed before Kant by Vico, whom Lukács names, as well as Francis Bacon, Hobbes and others before him, and Fichte, Hegel and other bourgeois thinkers after him.

According to Lukács, Marx's decisive contribution to the philosophical tradition is two-fold. On the one hand, he abandons the bourgeois perspective that reflects the interests of a small social segment in turning for the first time to the point of view of the proletariat. Since it is universal, at least in theory as well as practice, the proletarian perspective represents the interests of all mankind. On the other hand, Marx formulates a theory of reification that lies at the heart of modern industrial society. Reification belongs to an economic theory whose interest does not only lie in its economic function. In Marxian language, reification concerns both the cultural superstructure as well as the economic base, in enabling us to know as well as to transform modern industrial society. In other words, the Kantian problem of the unknowable thing in itself that echoes through post-Kantian classical German philosophy is finally solved in Marx's theory of modern industrial society.

---

14   See "First Introduction to the Science of Knowledge" in *Fichte: Science of Knowledge*, Peter Heath and John Lachs, trans., New York: Cambridge University Press, 1982, p. 4.

5 Lukács on Reification and Epistemic Constructivism

I come now to my conclusion. Many things could be said about Lukács's brilliant rereading of Marx's concept of reification as the solution to the central problem of classical German philosophy. I will limit myself to three brief comments.

According to Lukács Marx brings philosophy to a high point and an end. But philosophy does not and cannot come to an end in any ordinary sense. Philosophy defeats any effort to bring it to an end. A glance at the philosophical tradition shows that any argument will be more or less rapidly met by a counter argument. If philosophy does not come to an end but continues, then Marx does not and could not bring it to an end.

Further, the end cannot and could not lie in Marx's concept of reification that is not the most basic but rather a derivative concept in Marx's position. When Lukács composed the central chapter of *History and Class Consciousness*, the relevant texts were not yet available. Lukács, who inferred the view of the early Marx under the heading of reification from Marx's later texts, conflated objectification and alienation. Objectification is the precondition for alienation. To put the same point in Marxian economic language, surplus value requires the production of value through the self-objectification of human beings in commodity-form.

The final point concerns the relation of Marx to classical German philosophy, hence to philosophy. Lukács surpasses the Marxist view of Marx as conceptually-isolated, sui generis, incomparable, and unrelated to others. In this way he makes it possible to understand Marx as carrying forward the constructivist moment of modern philosophy. For when all is said and done, Marx is clearly an original thinker with a foot in classical German philosophy and another foot in economics. In building on the concept of reification, Marx does not invent but carries further a constructivist approach to knowledge of the world, above all of modern industrial society. I conclude that Lukács is incorrect in inferring that either through reification or in any other way Marx brings philosophy to an end, but correct in suggesting that in this and other ways he contributes to classical German philosophy.

PART 3

Reification and the Idea of Socialism: Lukács's Contributions to the Renewal of Radical Politics and Their Limitations

∴

CHAPTER 8

The Project of Renewing the Idea of Socialism and the Theory of Reification

Rüdiger Dannemann

To simply reject the great 19th century idea of socialism[1] is – as Axel Honneth has pointed out[2] – lacking good sense. He provides several reasons for his view. Firstly, he explains that, "very likely there have never been so many people outraged at the same time about the social and political consequences that accompany the globally unrestrained market economy since the end of Word War II."[3] He continues to list the consequences of eliminating any "idea of socialism": "It would be the dominance of a fetishizing notion of social conditions that would have to be held responsible for the fact that the mass outrage about the scandalous distribution of wealth and power has currently lost any sense of being an achievable goal."[4] Taking this into account, he aims to question "the causes for the apparent loss of the *decisive, reification-destroying effectiveness* of all the classic, formerly influential ideals."[5]

As in other contexts, the theoretical intervention of today's most influential representative of Critical Theory is valuable and should not be subjected to crude polemics. Many critics fail to recognize that his aim is not to rediscover a long-dead ideal as they do not recognize the profound and widespread

---

1 An earlier version of my reflections was published by the Contours Journal (Issue 8: Spring 2017 (Translator: Andreas Kahre) (http://www.sfu.ca/humanities-institute/contours/issue8/theory/3.html)) under the title "Georg Lukács's Theory of Reification and the Idea of Socialism." For suggestions, hints and criticism, I would like to thank Michael J. Thompson, Hans Ernst Schiller, Georg Lohmann, Konstantinos Kavoulakos, Andreas Kahre, Johan Hartle, Erich Hahn, Samir Gandesha, Frank Engster, Dirk Braunstein and Sarah and Anna Dannemann.
2 Axel Honneth, *Die Idee des Sozialismus. Versuch einer Aktualisierung* (Frankfurt/ Main: Suhrkamp, 2015).
3 Ibid., p. 15. Similarly, Robert Castel notes as early as 2009: "The financial, economic and social crisis which is threatening to strangle millions of people in the entire world, makes apparent the inanity of the liberal constructs which are based on the hegemony of a self-regulating market. The possibility of averting this catastrophe depends on the will to draw boundaries, to enact legislation in order to tame this hubris of capital." (quoted from Peter V. Zima, *Entfremdung. Pathologien der postmodernen Gesellschaft* (Tübingen: A. Francke, 2014), p. 135).
4 Honneth, *Idee des Sozialismus*, p. 19.
5 Ibid., p. 20 (emphasis mine).

antipathy towards the global capitalist economic system, and the post-democratic conditions closely connected to it. That is why today's objective literally needs to be securing the legacy of the socialist (and the "communist"[6]) idea. It needs to be further developed in order to foster and spark alternatives to the dominant socio-political and economical conditions, which are condemned by countless positions and, therefore represent more than just a few representatives of some leftist subcultures.

However, one might voice various misgivings about the influence of Honneth's attempted reconstruction. He believes that reclaiming socialism's appeal needs to go hand in hand with a dismissal of Marx's philosophical positions. Honneth sets out three main reasons for this "unavoidable" renunciation. Firstly, he criticises Marx's *Critique of Political Economy* due to its model of "progress." According to him, it establishes an unacceptable determinism of a historic philosophy. Secondly, – even though Honneth at times admits that it has become challenging to demonstrate that any modern institution, any social subsystem, perseveres a sphere unaffected by the logic of economic exploitation – he maintains that there are several social subsystems which have to be examined separately and which follow their own, distinct logics.[7] This applies in particular to the domains of politics, law, and family.[8] He claims that anyone who insists on emphasizing the relevance and ultimate dominance of the economic, even in non-economic realms of society, unmasks himself as prone to confuse modernity with the social conditions during Marx's lifetime. According to Honneth, Marx's emphasis on the proletariat constitutes the most obvious proof of his attachment to the social conditions of the time of the industrial society, thus, to the antiquated conditions of the 19th century.[9] Honneth therefore proposes to break with Marxist tradition as a precondition

---

[6] As in the case of socialism, and even more thoroughly with communism, we have to probe critically and self-critically, which forms fit for continuation and which are to be rejected as pernicious and inimical to enlightenment and emancipation, and even to be combatted practically. Just as the generalized identification of communism and fascism under the category of "totalitarianism" is of little use, there must be a clear and distinct distancing from forms of socialism and communism that are inimical to democratization.

[7] Cf. Honneth's critique of the Hegel-Marx concept of "totality," Honneth, *Idee des Sozialismus*, p. 92 et seq. and p. 127 et seq.

[8] For consistency's sake, he would have to add art as another sub-system with its own, autonomous logic.

[9] Cf. Robert Lanning, *Georg Lukács und die Organisierung von Klassenbewusstsein* (Hamburg: Laika 2016). Lanning's examples from North Africa can be accompanied by counterparts in Europe and hereabouts. Guido Speckmann, for example, was not altogether wrong when he wrote in a review of Honneth: "The eminent Frankfurt professor overlooks that institutional achievements don't just drop from the sky but that they have social carriers who attain them by engaging in social struggles. The right of co-determination is inconceivable without the class compromise following Word War II, any more than the institutionalization of minimum

for a successful revitalizing of the "actual idea of socialism" and the irreversible legacy of the French revolution by taking its ideals seriously. At the core of Honneth's interpretation lays the emphasis on the aspect of freedom, or, in the author's words, "the unconstrained interplay of all social freedoms in the difference of their respective functions."[10] Consequently, any society is to be called "social" "when every member of society can satisfy their requirements which they share with every other member, for physical and emotional intimacy, for economic independence and political self-determination, in such a way that they can rely on the empathy and support of their partners in any interaction."[11] Traditional forms of class struggles do not constitute a way to reach this goal. A mode of discourse has to be employed among differential social subsystems, in initiatives of all stripes that proceed experimentally.[12]

Georg Lukács followed a very different path of lived thought. He argues for a renaissance of Marx in order to re-actualize the idea of socialism. Axel Honneth not only holds him in high regard[13] but has also attempted in 2005 to contemporize his ideas – albeit in a very idiosyncratic form, namely by means of recognition theory. On the following pages I attempt to outline Lukács's theory as an alternative path and consider the question whether Honneth's approach of rejecting Marx, or Lukács's emphasis on a necessary renaissance of Marx hold greater plausibility at the present time.[14] In my analysis I will focus on the conceptual development of Lukács theory of reification, rather than every single theoretical twist of his late works,[15] although these also are relevant in this context.

---

wage by the struggles of trade unions." ("Nebulös und unverbindlich. Der Sozialphilosoph Axel Honneth möchte die Idee des Sozialismus aktualisieren – und lässt kaum etwas von ihr übrig," Neues Deutschland (October 28, 2015): 13).

10   Honneth, *Idee des Sozialismus*, p. 166.
11   Ibid.
12   Honneth refers to Dewey, in order to reach "an experimental understanding of historical processes of transformation"(ibid., p. 96 and p. 96 et seq., as well as p. 150 et seq.).
13   He is not alone in this, as he great international resonance to the closing of the Lukács archives in Budapest demonstrated. Information about the scandal of the closing of the archive can be found on the facebook page of the International Georg-Lukács-Society (http://www.facebook.com/Lukácsgesellschaft.htm).
14   But a renewing of Marxism will only be possible if the limitations and aberrations of the historical forms of Marxism – and there are too many of them – are critically reviewed and an enlightened "Integrative Marxism" (Thomas Metscher) open to theoretical innovations is developed.
15   I wish to distance myself as clearly as possible from the interpreters of Lukács who honour his work selectively, i.e. with a focus on his early work. From my point of view, for example, we have to re-examine whether labour, taking the term in the meaning of Lukács's late work *Zur Ontologie des gesellschaftlichen Seins* (cf. Georg Lukács, *Zur Ontologie des gesellschaftlichen Seins*, 2 vols. Georg Lukács Werke (GLW) Vol. 14 (Darmstadt/ Neu-

1 Lukács's Theory of Reification and his Project of a Renaissance of Marx

In various autobiographical sketches, the esteemed Hungarian philosopher repeatedly recollected that his own theoretical trajectory would follow the leitmotif of "My path toward Marx" – a path that began in 1918, and did not end until Georg Lukács's death in 1971. The fact that this process took so long and never truly reached a conclusion (except through the biological fact of his death), calls for an explanation. How is it possible, asks the contemporary scholar who is used to trading paradigms in order to avoid any kind of fixation, stagnation, stigmatization and ultimately loss of relevance so to remain present in the public market of academia, for a thinker to remain so singularly focused?

Four reasons may serve towards an explanation:

(1) Lukács's intellectual life is complex and his appropriation of Marx is not free of predispositions informed by the kind of theoretical premise characteristic of the pre-Marxist Lukács.

(2) What constitutes Marxism and Marx's theory is of course in itself a subject of controversy. As early as 1918 (the year at the end of which Lukács joins the Hungarian KP), interpretations deviate, e.g. Karl Kautsky's orthodoxy, that of the revisionist Eduard Bernstein (to whom Honneth makes positive reference[16]), of the Austro-Marxists, of the syndicalists and –increasingly significant – that of the Leninists. The question of what constitutes Marx's "actual" teaching requires then and now clarification.

(3) Even more important is another aspect: For Lukács, Marxism is practical philosophy, that is to say primarily a theory that is able to explain reality better than any other approach, and one that has to make certain of its connection to real socio-political movements. This also means that Lukács, in his approach to Marx's theory, is continually challenging the understanding of the ever-changing social world, and demonstrating accordingly the adequacy of the tradition of Marxist thought. Thus his analysis of Marx is always inseparably connected with an effort to diagnose contemporary development and to render plausible the assertion that

---

wied: Luchterhand 1986), 2:67–117), has lost its constitutive significance in modern society and the chapter on alienation in the Ontology contains valuable impulses for contemporary analysis.

16 Honneth, *Idee des Sozialismus*, p. 63 et seq.

the pathologies of modern society can be explained from a Marxist vantage point.

(4) The appropriate reconstruction of Marx's approach is exceedingly difficult. Even his closest co-combatants and co-authors were not always able to comprehend Marx's theoretical revolution without truncating it. Lukács, in his central text of *History and Class Consciousness*, and "Reification and the Consciousness of the Proletariat," points out Engels' tendency to equate natural and human history, laws of nature and human historical development.[17]

2 A Case for a Socialism in the Tradition of Lukács's Marx

2.1 *Some Remarks on the History and the Problems of Reception and Access*

It is often forgotten that by 1923 Lukács was neither a Marx-philologist nor a novice theorist, but a philosopher whose work is marked by personal experiences, intuitions, and thematic obsessions. In March 1967, Lukács thought it important to highlight that he had "never slipped into the error, which I have been frequently able to observe in workers, (and) petit-bourgeois intellectuals, that they were ultimately impressed (...) by the capitalist world." And he adds: "My contemptuous hatred, conceived during my boyhood, against life in capitalism saved me from this."[18]

Lukács's first philosophical steps could perhaps be described as a personal rebellion by a banker's son, a reaction against the unbearable experience of his environment and cultural frustration, which is also found in the context of the Fin de Siècle movement and the associated "transcendental homelessness" of the intellectual. This protest, which was, at first, articulated more intuitively against the spread of the bourgeois form of socialization institutes the biographical underpinnings of the reification theory that was to emerge later. Even in his early "History of the Development of Modern Drama", the young aesthete and aestheticist[19] reflects the problematic position of art in modernity,

---

17 Georg Lukács, *Die Verdinglichung und das Bewußtsein des Proletariats* (Bielefeld: Aisthesis 2015), p. 121 et seq. and 164 et seq.
18 Georg Lukács, "Preface" (1967) to the new edition of *Geschichte und Klassenbewußtsein*, in: GLW Vol. 2 (Neuwied/ Berlin: Luchterhand, 1968), p. 13.
19 Cf. Konstantinos Kavoulakos's illuminating study *Ästhetizistische Kulturkritik und ethische Utopie. Georg Lukács's neukantianisches Frühwerk* (Berlin: de Gruyter 2014). On Kavoulakos's discoveries cf. Rüdiger Dannemann, "Muss Georg Lukács's Frühwerk neu gelesen werden?," Deutsche Zeitschrift für Philosophie 63, No. 6 (2015): 1158–1168.

a modernity characterized by a cumulative factualization of life – what Max Weber refers to as the disenchantment of the world. While Lukács, in *Soul and Form* sets form in contrast to a life devoid of contours, and presents aesthetic form as an opportunity for an exodus from the banality of the quotidian life, he first attempts in his *Theory of The Novel* a historical-philosophical analysis of the emanations of objective reason (the novel) as an expression of the world's devastating condition. It is not difficult to recognize the widely diverse theoretical approaches Lukács borrows from along the way to formulating his reification theory. The apt pupil from the centre of Europe makes reference to Georg Simmel's Lebensphilosophie (life-philosophy), in particular his *Philosophy of Money*, to Max Weber's theory of modern rationality, but also to Marx and Hegel. Furthermore it is important to note that Neo-Kantianism, notably through Heinrich Rickert and Emil Lask, left a lasting impression on him. During the process of his political radicalization, triggered by his experiences during Word War I, Lukács who, unlike Simmel and Weber, had always opposed the war, encountered other theoretical traditions in Russian authors such as Solovjov, Ropschin and particularly Dostojewski. In his Dostojewski-fragments – that were written during the war, but published only posthumously – Lukács develops the framework of an anti-formalist and anti-institutionalist ethic.[20]

Lukács's complex intellectual path, his early work on aesthetics, his borrowing from Lebensphilosophie, but also from Slawic tradition, developed his sensibility early on for questions that later come to be treated under the category "everyday life" (Alltagsleben), and which focused on the relationship between the most abstract theoretical configurations with everyday "forms of life" (Lebensformen) – a term that already appears in *History and Class Consciousness* and not only represents the relationship between cultural and socio-economic developments, but also the problematic moral situation of modernity.[21] It

---

20 This is not an exhaustive list of the sources that found their way into the discourse of *Geschichte und Klassenbewußtsein*. Other formative elements are classical German philosophy (especially Kant, as read in the Neo-Kantian variant, Fichte, especially in the interpretation of Emil Lask, increasingly Hegel, who needed to be re-discovered at the time), alongside the life philosophy of Bergson and Simmel, Husserl's Phenomenology (Lucien Goldmann has identified *Die Seele und die Formen* as an early existentialist work), legal theoreticians like Kelsen and Jellinek (we must remember that Lukács had also studied law and obtained a doctorate in political science (rer. oec.)), the Weimar classics (in particular Goethe and Schiller's critique of Kant), but also romantic philosophy (cf. M. Löwy, *From Romanticism to Bolshevism* (London: New Left Books, 1979)); in addition to the increasingly dominant influence of Marx and Lenin, that of Rosa Luxemburg and of syndicalism.

21 The critical reception of Lukács has not infrequently taken the aforementioned theoretical melange/melee/mashup as a cause for criticism – giving rise to accusations of eclecticism, of being equivocal; later on of revisionism, of an improper synthesis of incompatible

shows that Lukács's difficulty in embracing Marx's theory is also formed by his intellectual progress. One important consequence of this early theoretical history[22] is that there has always been, and continues to be, conflicting approaches to his idiosyncratic attempts at synthesizing different theories. The nearly one hundred years of the reception of *History and Class Consciousness* demonstrates that there are many, quite divergent modes by which one can approach this classic and erratic work.[23]

The diversity of approaches to *History and Class Consciousness* is no accident. It is a manifestation of the nonlinear intellectual biography of its author and the many sources from which his thinking grew, as well as a product of contemporary academic life with its peculiar rules. Another aspect that needs to be mentioned is that *History and Class Consciousness* is by no means a singular work, conceived as a unified whole, but a collection of essays, created in different contexts, that document their authors ceaseless process of learning – at an exceptionally high level. A main aspect of Lucács's theoretical conduct during the 1920s is self-critical reflection. As an example, Lukács admitted several times that in some essays his arguments were influenced by an overly optimistic revolutionary euphoria and not free of illusions.[24] While Lenin plays no significant role in the reification essay, the main argument in "Towards a Methodology of the Problem of Organization" relates very heavily to the Bolshevik pioneer. Qualities such as these demonstrate that *History and Class Consciousness* is a mirror image of the rapid changes during the years between 1919 and 1922. Not least of all, it is an experimental attempt to address the increasingly critical situation of Marxism and the revolution by means of a theoretical approach.

---

theoretical approaches. The Neo-Kantians object to Lukács's Hegelianism, the self-appointed orthodox Marxists to the Fichte-inspired historical philosopher, the 68 generation to the bourgeois–son–turned–revolutionary's reading of Weber and Simmel, or his allegedly unreserved conversion to "orthodox" Marxism etc. Other readers, less concerned with orthodoxy (of whatever stripe) on the other hand, have pointed to the wealth, and the scope of his perspective: Even in the 1930s or 50s, Lukács's singular intellectual position in the context of the Marxist school of philosophy was remarked on by his contemporaries.

22 On the evolution of Lukács's thinking, cf. the relevant works of Apitzsch (1977), Arato/Breines (1979), Congdon (1983), Dannemann (1987 and 1997), Feenberg (2014), Grauer (1985), Hermann (1985), Jung (1989 and 2001), Kadarkay (1991), Kammler (1974), Löwy (1979).

23 At least nine different modes of access can be observed, which can of course also be combined or may intersect. Cf. Rüdiger Dannemann, "Nachwort" to Georg Lukács, *Die Verdinglichung und das Bewußtsein des Proletariats*, pp. 182–186.

24 Cf. Georg Lukács, *Geschichte und Klassenbewußtsein*, p. 5.

2.2 The Project of Reification Theory

The goal of the following analysis is not to provide a comprehensive analysis of Lukács's reification theory, but to give an outline of the theory project proposed in *History and Class Consciousness,* in order to project shortened forms of reception and critique. At this point it is important to note that Lukács opposes a simplified understanding of Marx's doctrine that was catching on during the time of the 2nd International, as well as the Comintern, construing it as a positivist science along the lines of Karl Kautsky or Bukharin. Both understood Marx as a kind of Darwin of history, or society, without sufficient consideration of the methodological premise of his critique of political economy. Lukács attempts to reconstruct Marx's dialectic theory as a coherent philosophical concept and consequently he (together with Karl Korsch) starts the discourse about the relationship between Marxism and philosophy that continues until the present,[25] He chooses Marx's doctrine of "Wertform" (value form) developed in Volume I of *Das Kapital* as a systematical point of reconstruction. Furthermore he demonstrates that the chapter on fetish basically contains Marx's critical philosophy in a concise way. This, in Lukács's view, should be understood not just as an economic theory limited in its claims to the framework of a disciplinary specialty, but to contain several dimensions:
- a philosophy of contemporary society,
- a theory of ideology (which may also be drawn on for an explanation of scientific and philosophical theories),
- a theory of history,
- a political philosophy of revolutionary kairos,
- in short: the theoretical offering of a view of the totality of social being.

Lukács attempts to "systematically explain the connection between the various forms of experience of reification."[26] Therefore he is very much aware of the risky and experimental character of his project. He considers his studies in dialectics and their practical intentions about reification as a fresh impulse

---

25 In Ernst Bloch, Lukács found a collaborator for a philosophical understanding of Marx's thinking, both of them develop in relevant late works theoretical principles of an ontology of social being or ontology of not-being-not-yet. I agree with Doris Zeilinger's assessment that "the ontological issue has accompanied both Bloch and Lukács to the end of their lives and they have considered ontology indispensable as a condition of the possibility of thinking of the overall context (Gesamtzusammenhang). Both lifework culminates in works dedicated to this subject." Doris Zeilinger, Ontologie bei Bloch und Lukács. Einleitende Vorbemerkungen. (Lecture at the conference Bloch und Lukács: Die Russische Revolution als philosophisches Schlüsselereignis, which took place on March 11, 2017 in Berlin, Man., p. 8).

26 Titus Stahl, "Verdinglichung als Pathologie zweiter Ordnung," Deutsche Zeitschrift für Philosophie 59, No. 5 (2011): 734.

and a major research project. His diagnostic texts on time are similarly sketches, fragments of ideas that were intended to be extended and filled with concrete content (i.e. more philosophical and interdisciplinary studies). For his outline of modern philosophy since Descartes, whose – often latent – effect on the 1968 generation of scholars Peter Bürger has recently testified to,[27] similar intentions apply. In it, he already formulates the beginning of a critique of a concept of rationality that is dominant to this day.

2.3 Cornerstones of the Reification Theory

From my point of view and tailored to our contemporary context, Lukács reification theory can be outlined using six cornerstones or essential elements.

(1) Lukács reads Marx's critique of political economy of the fetish chapter in *Das Kapital* as a theory of commodity production, in which exchange value is no longer a peripheral phenomenon, but becomes the dominant factor in the framework of capitalist production of commodities. This development includes a process of abstraction and reduction to quantities, which affects not only the products of labour in society, but also its agents, the workers, respectively the proletariat. Reification thus becomes social reality, and a form of life. This situation gains special volatility against the background that in capitalism, Vico's description of history as having being "created" by humanity has found its first, but extremely problematic instance of realization: the producers of the modern social world, the social subject of the socialization of humanity is a subject only in the form of a commodity, which is compelled to take on all the characteristics of de-subjectivization und self-objectification. Autonomy takes place here only in the form of heteronomy.[28]

(2) In this process, social relations are increasingly anonymized and fetishized. They present as relationships between objects. An ideological inversion of social relationships takes place. To put it pointedly, capital appears to be "money generating money" seemingly able to generate surplus value. The relationship between wage, labor and capital appears no longer as an exploitative relationship but a legally regulated, appropriately fair exchange of resources.

---

27 Peter Bürger, "Lukács-Lektüren. Autobiographische Fragmente," in: Rüdiger Dannemann (ed.), *Lukács und 1968. Eine Spurensuche* (Bielefeld: Aisthesis 2009), p. 19 et seq.
28 This applies primarily to the proletariat, but also to the beneficiaries of the economic system of modernity.

(3) The capitalist production of commodities exhibits totalitarian qualities.[29] Following Max Weber one might interpret the abstract-quantifying logic of capitalist economy as a process of rationalization or a demonstration that this type of formal rationality appropriates and transforms all aspects of modern life. That is to say: The capitalist economy creates a social environment, a legal system and a conforming state system suited to its needs. Especially in domains that are removed from clear economic imperatives such as art, the totalitarian strain of capitalism becomes evident. The trend to utilise works of art as objects of market activity continues well into our time. This analysis of the cultural industry as part of the Critical Theory has concretized and contemporized Lukács's relevant approaches in this area from the 1920.

(4) The process, we are describing, has not even spared the remits of thought. Modern philosophy, from Descartes to Kant, has developed dualist subject-object models that are elevated to the state of unresolvable antinomies: Antinomies of the actual and the prescribed, of being and appearance, of freedom and necessity. In order to avoid such a restrictive form of rationality, it seems necessary to refocus the type of dialetic thinking that, for Lukács, can be identified as process and totality. He refers positively to Hegel's dictum: "The truth is the whole" (Das Ganze ist das Wahre) as well as to Marx's thesis formulated in *The Poverty of Philosophy*: "The conditions of production of any society constitute a totality."[30] In Marx's concept of a concrete totality, Hegel's ingenious suggestions written in *The Phenomenology of Spirit* find their full expression. It is important to note: For Lukács, Marx's theory is a philosophical approach, the – up to that point – most highly developed methodically conceived apprehension of reality. That is why he puts the greatest emphasis on uncovering the methodological foundations of Marx's discourse.

(5) Lukács – unlike Critical Theory later on – does not emphasize a submissive acceptance of the universe of reification. After all, he considers his

---

29 Even in his philosophical testament, his *Ontology*, Lukács reaffirms this aspect: "from language to the motives of their actions, the process of reification suffuses all the utterances of contemporary humans." (Georg Lukács, *Zur Ontologie des gesellschaftlichen Seins*, Vol. 2, p. 598).

30 Karl Marx, *Das Elend der Philosophie. Antwort auf Proudhons "Philosophie des Elends,"* Marx-Engels-Werke (MEW), Vol. 4, p. 130. Even in his Bloch-critique in the context of the expressionism debate of the 1930s, Jahre Lukács refers at a central point of his argument to this Marx-quote, in order to legitimize his notion of totality (cf. Lukács, "Es geht um Realismus" (1938), in: GLW Vol. 4 (Neuwied/ Berlin: Luchterhand 1971, p. 316)).

present as kairos, as a potential moment of transformation from the barbaric epoch of reification to the potential domain of autonomy, of a more than formal freedom. As is well known, he considers the proletariat to be the most prominent victim of the process of capitalist rationalization. Although in practical terms all humans have by now become victims of reification, the social condition, according to Lukács, prevents non-proletarian segments of society from the necessary (certainly painful) process of realisation.

(6) The difficulty of this process is evident in the ideological crisis of the potential revolutionary subject, which is virulent as early as 1918. It can be explained precisely because the historical process for Lukács is not subject to the laws of nature. Instead, it is valid to say: the revolution requires its protagonists to make a conscious, unconstrained decision.[31]

3 More Recent Adaptions and Transformations of Reification Theory

External and internal problems[32] as well as the dominance of other scientific paradigms removed from Marxism, have caused Lukács's reification theory to be either ignored or revisited irregularly at best. Many critical approaches have influenced the dominant understanding of the theory: In the field of Marxist

---

31 Thus ends the famous reification essay in *Geschichte und Klassenbewußtsein* (Lukács, Verdinglichung und Bewußtsein des Proletariats, p. 176). In his late writings, Lukács distanced himself equally clearly from a deterministic interpretation of historical processes; he emphasizes that economic development merely produces a "margin of possibility [Möglichkeitsspielraum]," "whose realization can only be enacted by humans themselves" (Lukács, *Ontologie des gesellschaftlichen Seins, Vol. 2*, p. 629). – This is not the place for a detailed discussion of the important 7th pillar of reification theory, that of its organizational theory, respectively its concept of "imputed" [zugerechnetes] class consciousness, since we are primarily concerned with the aspect of how realizable reification theory is.

32 The further development and continuation of his reification project took an entirely different form than its author had imagined. It did not take place among the circle of recipients he had intended, that of politically engaged and even organized practical philosophers – with the aforementioned exceptions – but among theorists, who would later come to be renowned as Frankfurt School (respectively as Critical Theory). The more than difficult relationship between Lukács and Adorno is a lesson in the kind of problems in communication and discourse typical of left intelligentia of the 20th century. Cf. the dossiers "Georg Lukács und Theodor W. Adorno" (1. und 2. Teil) in: F. Benseler, W. Jung (eds.), *Lukács 2004. Jahrbuch der Internationalen Georg-Lukács-Gesellschaft* (Bielefeld: Aisthesis, 2004), pp. 65–180; *Lukács 2005, Jahrbuch der Internationalen Georg-Lukács-Gesellschaft* (Bielefeld: Aisthesis, 2005), pp. 55–189.

discourse, a critique in the tradition of Backhaus, based mainly in a philology of Marx, which purposes the progress in the development of the theory of forms of value, the structuralist deviation of a Marxist historicism, in particular the anti-humanism of Althusser, Bloch's meta–critique of Lukács's rejection of an utopian–speculative understanding of philosophy, Adorno's supposition of Lukács's "positive" understanding of dialectics as a legitimizing ideology, and, not least, Lukács's own self-critique, which appears to confirm, at its core, allegations of excessive proximity to Hegel and a deficient, insufficiently "materialist" ontology.[33] Outside of the Marxism discussion, Lukács's approach is frequently interpreted as an emanation of theoretical extremism, or is categorized in the history of philosophy in the context of 20th century Neo-Hegelianism.[34]

All the same, most remarkable developments have taken place in the field of Critical Theory, notably with Jürgen Habermas and Axel Honneth. For the newer representatives of Critical Theory it seemed clear –since Habermas's turning away from his early "Theory and Practice" phase– that the fundamental assumptions of Marx's radical anti-capitalist critique could no longer be accepted. Despite the fact that Habermas –unlike Benjamin– did not admire the "philosopher of the revolution," his respect was the result of Lukács's synthesis of Marx and Weber: "that he was able to consider the separation of the sphere of social labor from the context of the living world [Lebenswelten] from both aspects simultaneously; that of reification and that of rationalization."[35] For Habermas, Lukács became paradigmatic by recognizing the philosophical stature and value of Marx's value-form analysis and by founding an entire area of Critical Theory. He undertook the encouraging project of describing both economic and non-economic processes of modernization as an increase in rationality and as a passion story at the same time, respectively "dialectically."

---

33   Cf. the contributions of Robert Fechner und Fabian Kettner in: Markus Bitterolf, Denis Meier (eds.), *Verdinglichung, Marxismus, Geschichte* (Freiburg: ça ira, 2012); Louis Althusser, Etienne Balibar, *Das Kapital lesen* (Hamburg: Rowohlt, 1972); the essays by Hans-Ernst Schiller, Ivan Boldyref, Werner Jung, Wolfgang Fritz Haug, Hans-Heinz Holz in: Beat Dietschy, Doris Zeilinger, Rainer E. Zimmermann (eds.), Bloch-Wörterbuch (Berlin/Boston: de Gruyter, 2012); Dirk Braunstein, Simon Duckheim, "Adornos Lukács. Ein Lektürebericht," in: Rüdiger Dannemann (ed.), *Jahrbuch der Internationalen Georg-Lukács-Gesellschaft 2014/ 2015* (Bielefeld: Aisthesis, 2015), pp. 55–189; Georg Lukács, "Preface."

34   Cf. Norbert Bolz, *Auszug aus der entzauberten Welt. Philosophischer Extremismus zwischen den Weltkriegen* (München: Fink, 1991); George Lichtheim, *Georg Lukács* (München: dtv, 1971); Wolfgang Röd, *Der Weg der Philosophie*, 2 vols. (München: C.H. Beck, 1996), 2:417 et seq.

35   Jürgen Habermas, *Theorie des kommunikativen Handelns*, 2 vols. (Frankfurt/ Main: Suhrkamp, 1981), 1:479.

Nevertheless, Habermas considers the philosophical foundation of Western Marxism to be unfashionable. He doesn't want to become a member, like Lukács, of a circle of materialist dialecticians plumbing the innovations in methodology by the critics of political economy; Habermas has left the domain of so-called consciousness philosophy altogether und wants to clear the way for what he calls the interactionist–communicative turn in philosophy.

Fairness demands that we point out that Habermas does not simply reject the reification paradigm; he makes an attempt to reformulate it. It is no coincidence that Habermas's project of creating a new foundation for Critical Theory "merges into a reconstruction of the reification theorem."[36] At the core of this project lies the thesis of uncoupling the system and the living world in the processes of modernization. The process of objectification [Versachlichung] (the term used by Simmel and the early Lukács) takes on the character of colonization. The high degree of de-radicalization in the approach of *History and Class Consciousness,* if one no longer shares its capitalism-theoretical and revolutionary premises, becomes apparent, when one observes Habermas as he describes the social pathologies of our present time. In particular he pins his hopes on the constitutional state, in order to limit the colonialist tendencies of market (money) and power, and to curtail the total mediatization of the living world, along with the tools of an enlightened public and communicative reason. At the same time, Habermas does not believe that a revision, let alone a revolutionizing of the economic sphere, is necessary to defend it. His primary concern is the protection of rules of law and civil rights. Axel Honneth, in relation to this, notes that little has remained of the early Habermas's radicalism. Along with "his turn toward the Kantian-dominated tradition, Habermas is in danger of losing essential insights, which his early works (more oriented toward his understanding of Hegel) had contained. There seems to be no longer any mention of a pathology of capitalist societies, nor as bold an idea as a systematically distorted interaction in his recent writings."[37] The critique quoted here leaves one curious how Honneth is hoping to regain the valuable insights he mentions.

The Frankfurt philosopher begins by clarifying that the notion of reification is part of the incompletely processed intellectual legacy of Critical Theory. The phenomenon of reification, long ignored, returns while masquerading in widely varying forms of fictional as well as theoretical texts and contexts. Crass

---

36   Rahel Jaeggi, *Entfremdung. Zur Aktualität eines sozialphilosophischen Problems* (Frankfurt/ Main: Campus, 2005), p. 28.
37   Axel Honneth, "Unser Kritiker. Jürgen Habermas wird siebzig: eine Ideenbiographie," Die Zeit (June 17, 1999).

forms of reification (surrogate motherhood, the marketization of romantic relationships, the explosive growth of the sex industry,[38] as well as the observable trend toward emotional management, the pervasive social atmosphere of a cold practicality) have induced many writers including Martha Nussbaum to use the term reification. The term is also used for critical reflection on scientific trends; an example is brain research: we can speak of reification, for example, when we observe the attempt to explain emotions and actions by a mere analysis of neuronal networks in the human brain. For Honneth however there is no doubt that the term can only be reintegrated into contemporary scientific discourse if a definition of reification that rejects Lukács's Fichtean extravagance of subject-object-identification, and correspondingly his concept of a (very idealistically interpreted) "true" praxis is used. Honneth considers as transferable, and more modest in scope, a definition of reification as "the habit or custom of a merely observant behaviour, whose perspective recognizes the natural environment, the social collective and one's own personality's potential without empathy and neutral in emotional affect, as a mere object."[39] Honneth finds the following description, cleansed of revolutionary radicalism, of Lukács "true praxis": it possesses "those qualities of participation and interest which have been destroyed by the expansion of commodity exchange; not the creation of the object by a subject expanded to form a collective, but another, inter-subjective attitude of the subject constitutes the pattern here, which serves as a contrasting foil for the definition of a reified practice."[40]

If one were to completely avoid (deviating from Lukács) the totalizing critique of commodity production which in highly differentiated cultures is thought to have become obsolete for reasons of efficiency, and if one were to uphold that there are spheres in which observant, detached behaviour plays a legitimate role, one could by means of reformulating Lukács's reification concept from an action-theoretical approach gain a perspective that provides a cause for illuminating speculation.[41] Obviously, Honneth hopes to pave the way toward a positive reception of Lukács, which allows for a link to the current debate on theory, especially the theory of recognition based on a disconnection from the tradition of Marxist theory. Only then could the weaknesses in Lukács's conception be eliminated, since Lukács's aggressively asserted

---

38   Cf. Eva Illouz (ed.), Wa(h)re Gefühle: Authentizität im Konsumkapitalismus (Frankfurt/Main: Suhrkamp, 2018).
39   Axel Honneth, Verdinglichung. Eine anerkennungstheoretische Studie (Frankfurt/ Main: Suhrkamp, 2005), p. 24.
40   Ibid., p. 27.
41   Ibid., p. 28.

orthodox Marxism resulted in factual and thematic prejudices, which did not do justice to the complex differentiations of modern societies. By this he means primarily that the preoccupation with a "through-capitalization of society" caused domains removed from economy to be relegated to the background.[42]

Honneth's recognition-theoretical reframing renders two main points: the critique of self-reifying attitudes, and a form of inter-subjective reification, which becomes noticeable in cases "where persuasion systems with explicit typecasting of other groups of people are deployed."[43] Examples of this include contemporary forms of job interviews or dating services, as well as racist or similar ideologies. Honneth is convinced – and in this he proves to be a loyal student of Habermas after all – that one can elude the reifying power of commodity production that the Marxist Lukács has posited, provided one adopts the principles of the constitutional rule of law. In Honneth's eyes, the economic actants are protected in at least an elementary form by the (however rudimentary) legal character of their economic relationship. At least they guarantee to recognize each other's status as persons.

Honneth also refers to concepts from Heidegger and Dewey that are not entirely dissimilar to Lukács's theory, and demonstrates that he is quite open to new attempts to formulate a contemporary phenomenology of reification. However much one might applaud this openness, there remains dissent with respect to the question of how one reacts theoretically to the fundamental impulse of *History and Class Consciousness*, which consists in protesting against the totalizing of the commodity and exploitation principle as it produces reifying effects. It is becoming increasingly difficult to protect domains of life against the logic of commodity production. Lukács insisted, not without good reason, throughout his entire life that such problems can't be solved without a radical change in the system.[44]

---

42   Honneth notes the absence of proof from the 1920s author, that there is in the family, in the political public sphere, in the relationship between parents and children, in the culture of recreation, an actual process of "colonisation" by the principles of the capitalist market, of the exchange principle. The privileging of the economic sphere is claimed to have bizarre consequences. Unchecked forms of dehumanizing reification express themselves in racism or in human trafficking, especially of women. Ibid., p. 90.

43   Ibid., p. 102.

44   Honneth views this quite differently, without doubt: In his reflections on the international debate that his essay has triggered, he steps back even further (cf. Axel Honneth, "Nachbetrachtung zu 'Verdinglichung,'" in: Frank Benseler/ Rüdiger Dannemann (eds.), *Lukács 2012/ 2013. Jahrbuch der Internationalen Georg-Lukács-Gesellschaft* (Bielefeld: Aisthesis, 2012), pp. 67–79): Now Honneth wants to define the circle of reification phenomena even more narrowly, and limit the term to the, in his opinion unlikely, cases where the

It is remarkable that Honneth's attempt, despite its anti-Marxist impetus, has triggered astonishingly harsh reactions between the conservative as well as the "liberal" camp (unlike Rahel Jaeggi's study of alienation). There is talk of a "regression to the yearned-for authenticity of contemporary 'social romanticism'" believed to ontologically eclipse even Rousseau's hypothetical return to nature.[45] The anger of these authors, especially the decidedly conservative ones, is understandable, since Honneth with his study is opening the path to a potentially, truly contemporary debate about reification by offering evidence and material for discussion as to what a contemporary reification theory might look like. He connects the discourse of alienation and reification, anchored as it is in contemporary living and contemporary scientific discourses, with contemporary lives caught in the tension between personhood, role identity, the striving for self-actualization, and the requirement of self-marketing. The international attention that Honneth's brief study *Verdinglichung* (reification) has commanded shows that we have an attentive observer of social pathologies who has hit a nerve.

Nevertheless, the left's critique of Honneth's study remains strong. Honneth's appropriation seeks to re-articulate Lukács's concept in such a way that it becomes compatible with social-philosophical approaches that are recognized today. In favour of this compatibility, however, Honneth sacrifices essential aspects of the theory: Following the spirit of the Habermas school, he wants to suspend Lukács's Hegelianism, his methodical grasp and of course his – however it may be defined – orthodox Marxism. Following the communication–theoretical turn, there is no room left for a materialist dialectic, however sophisticated. The critique of capitalism, as the critique of a system of (naturally capitalist) commodity production is replaced by a critique of pathological states of emergency, which claims that these aberrations can be compensated for, or in part eradicated, by a democratization of the family, a moralization of the economy, and of course a democratized public sphere.[46]

---

ontological difference between a person and a thing is consigned to permanent institutional oblivion.

45   Cf. Ralf Konersmann, "Anerkennungsvergessenheit. Für Sozialromantiker: Axel Honneth über Verdinglichung." Süddeutsche Zeitung 17 (21./22. Januar 2006) p. 14. Ähnlich Wolfgang Kersting in der Frankfurter Allgemeinen Zeitung vom 7.11.2005, anders Michael Schifzyk in der Neuen Zürcher Zeitung vom 18.10.2005. Judith Butler in her quite critical discussion of Honneth's essay also points to a link between his idea of a genuine praxis and Rousseau (cf. Judith Butler, "Taking Another's View: Ambivalent Implications," in: Axel Honneth, *Reification. A New Look at an Old Idea* (Oxford: Oxford University Press, 2008), pp. 97–119).

46   In the tradition of the Frankfurt School, there is a tendency to think of critical theory merely as a branch of moral philosophy that is concerned solely with questions of social

Even more naive than Honneth's appropriation is the transformation, by avowed Aristotelian philosopher Martha Nussbaum, of reification theory.[47] She investigates practices of "objectification" by using examples from sexist and pornographic attitudes and depictions. And she arrives at seven attributes of reification, which she understands to mean any form of subjects turning themselves into mere objects. These attributes are:

- Instrumentalization (subjects are made into a tool for satisfying the requirements of other subjects);
- Denial/deprivation of a subject's autonomy;
- Subjects are deprived of their ability to act, condemned to passivity (this demonstrates the proximity to Lukács's notion of contemplative subject's behaviour);
- Functionalization, i.e. subjects are accorded value only on account of their function (and thus can be exchanged for other carriers of the same function);
- Violence (subjects are denied their physical integrity, their bodies can be manipulated, and under certain circumstances even destroyed);
- Appropriation (subjects are commodities that can be traded and sold);
- Denial of subjectivity (subjects are not regarded as subjects with their own experiences/emotions, or these are deemed irrelevant).

Nussbaum's attributions are illuminating, and can certainly be used as guidelines for an analysis of certain reification phenomena, such as demonstrating the problematic consequences of reification tendencies for a "proper life," or to capture the emotional culture of capitalist modernity (including its digital variant) – a project indispensable to the comprehension of modern subjectivity. But their grasp is limited when the goal is to comprehend reified social conditions

---

equity. The original approach remains relevant precisely because Lukács does not interpret reification morally, or reduces it like Honneth to a "set of *individual* attitudes" (Timothy Hall, "Returning to Lukács: Honneth's Critical Reconstruction of Lukács's Concepts of Reification and Praxis," in: Michael J. Thompson (ed.), Georg Lukács Reconsidered. Critical Essays in Politics, Philosophy and Aesthetics (London/ New York: Continuum, 2011), p. 197). Recent Anglo-American authors (like Hall) identify the search for the "good life" under the conditions of modernity as the core of reification critique. A search that, in Lukács's eyes, could not be undertaken in a singular act but only "by a concrete relationship to the concretely manifesting contradictions in the total development." Therefore it has to be concerned "with the contextually specific suspending of pathological obstacles to aquisition (Aneignungshindernisse) of every individual case." (Titus Stahl, Verdinglichung als Pathologie zweiter Ordnung, p. 743).

47   Martha C. Nussbaum, "Verdinglichung," in: Nussbaum, Konstruktion der Liebe, des Begehrens und der Fürsorge. Drei philosophische Aufsätze (Stuttgart: Reclam, 2002), pp. 90–162.

that elude the awareness, respectively the control, of individual subjects. Quite rightly, Markus Wolf writes: "She misses the phenomenon of reification because it refers to structures that are not available to individual actants, and that a moral critique cannot claim as its subject."[48] Despite the justified and necessary critique it must be noted that Nussbaum, like the previously mentioned representatives of Critical Theory, has sharpened our gaze to the fact that reification critique does not exhaust itself in mere philological Marxism, and that it aims at more than to a decoding of ideological consciousness structures. Reification critique is, at its a core, a radical critique of a form of life which can be described as bourgeois-capitalist socialisation, in the meaning of Hegel and Marx.[49]

4 The Current Relevance of Reification Theory and the "Idea of Socialism"

Even if there are good reasons to criticize the lack of radicalism in the attempted rearticulations by Habermas and Honneth, or the moralizing narrowing of Nussbaum's view of the phenomenon of reification,[50] the question remains how we might treat Lukács's critique of reification in our "post-communist" era, with its absence of a revolutionary subject. Three indicators might help to demonstrate that the relevance of the theorem remains undiminished – even if one considers teleological historical metaphysics and the historical messianism of Lukács in the 1920 to be unacceptable Fichtean-Hegelian relics:

1. Humans continue to be habitually treated *in everyday life* not as persons but as objects; i.e. they are being treated as something that may be intrumentalized, sold, used, destroyed (to paraphrase Kant's reflections in his *Metaphysics of Morals/Metaphysik der Sitten*). It must be noted very clearly that reification is not normal, not a social-ontological fate (fatum). That the act of turning–oneself–into–an–object, that Lukács has described, nowadays takes place in a sometimes consciously-playful form, frequently consumption-oriented and cynical, pretend-authentic,

---

48 Markus Wolf, "Verdinglichung kritisieren. Was, warum und Wie?," in: Hans Friesen, Christian Lotz, Jakob Meier, Markus Wolf (eds.), *Ding und Verdinglichung. Technik- und Sozialphilosophie nach Heidegger und der Kritischen Theorie* (München: Fink, 2012), p. 285.

49 Nussbaum is also critical of the term reification because of its lack of focus, and even finds positive aspects in certain "natural" forms of reification.

50 Cf. Christoph Henning, "Von der Kritik warenförmiger Arbeit zur Apotheose der Marktgesellschaft. Verdinglichung in Marxismus und Anerkennungstheorie," in: Friesen, *Ding und Verdinglichung*, pp. 243–272.

always masked, and impregnated by self-deception, may complicate the matter, but does not alter the fact that it constitutes self-alienation.[51] How quickly the cheerful cynicism of a playful, allegedly controlled "self-reification of humans"[52] turns into pathological catastrophes is only too well known to anyone employed in social work, in hospitals or schools. The field of working life remains a domain where reification does not appear to be diminishing, and that holds true not only for less developed regions of the global village. While we may currently enjoy the status of a legal subject in working life,[53] we are far removed from living autonomous subjectivity in the context of labor.[54] Even if some people prefer to draw a picture of a new culture of work, allegedly marked by shallow hierarchies, creative autonomy, there certainly are social realities that lead one to expect the opposite development: as soon as we enter the working world, we adopt the internalized attitude of image production[55] and self

---

51 In his *Ontology*, Lukács emphasizes the currently observable changes in capitalism as due to the "expansion of large capital production to the entire domain of consumption and service, which causes them to influence the everyday lives of most humans in a completely different, direct, active, and directly intervening sense than was ever possible in earlier economic models." (Lukács, *Ontologie des gesellschaftlichen Seins*, Vol. 2, p. 682).

52 Ibid., p. 587.

53 Both Habermas and Honneth fervently insist on this. Opinions divide perceptibly when it comes to the assessment of bourgeois law: Lukács insists even in Sozialismus und Demokratisierung, his political legacy, and in the *Ontology* on his critique of formal civil/bourgeois law (human rights [die Rechte des homme] "offer humanity the full freedom to reify themselves socially and naturally also ideologically to their hearts content," according to his pointedly phrased diagnosis [Lukács, *Ontologie des gesellschaftlichen Seins*], Vol. 2, p. 561), whereas Honneth accuses the (early) socialists and their successors of "their persistent blindness to the law" (Honneth, *Idee des Sozialismus*, p. 127). In the framework of contemporary Marxism, the great problematic field of human rights is new and differentiated to think through, since these are "among the most important political-theoretical inheritance of the bourgeois Enlightenment" (Thomas Metscher, *Integrativer Marxismus, Dialektische Studien. Grundlegung* (Kassel: Mangroven, 2017), p. 163).

54 In the *Ontology* Lukács puts it, not without a hint of pessimism, like this: "Reification and alienation may have a greater actual power now than ever before." (Lukács, *Ontologie des gesellschaftlichen Seins*, Vol. 2, p. 656).

55 In his *Ontology*, the late Lukács emphasized this aspect: "In that humanity subordinates its actions in everyday life to the enlarging of its 'image,' clearly such an elevation of the standards of living must give rise to a new form of alienation, an alienation in and of itself." (Ibid., p. 683, c.f. p. 627). On the contradictory-paradoxical forms of modern individuation cf. Hans Ernst Schiller, *Das Individuum im Widerspruch. Zur Theoriegeschichte des modernen Individualismus.* (Berlin: Frank & Timme, 2006), esp. chap. 9: "Der entkernte Selbstverkäufer. Erich Fromms kritische Sozialpsychologie").

marketing,[56] never to relinquish it again in the decades that follow, regardless of whether we earn our living as dependent employees or whether we are moving around as modern nomads.[57] And the modern manager, whom we address on a first name basis, and who may be barely distinguishable externally from his "co-workers" will, in a conflict situation and especially when it comes to the bottom line, prove to be someone who exercises power after all, even if they pose as charitable benefactors. The digital revolution, on which some have placed great hopes for gains in autonomy, has not been able to prevent itself from being colonized by the logic of commodity production. The rapid development of technology and biological sciences is likely to increase the probability that we are approaching, as Günter Anders argues, the final level of reification: In *The Obsolescence of Humanity* (*Die Antiquiertheit des Menschen*) Anders distinguishes three levels of reification. On the final level, now increasingly in the process of becoming reality, where the difference between cyborg, clone and person is blurred, humans tend to become a "device among devices," an appendix (more politely: an interface) of computer-based social interaction.[58]

2. There is still a *reification of social (especially political) practices* in the sense that participation in them is no longer being regulated socially, but appears as an objective constraint (in the meaning of objective causal relationships) that the participants are confronted with in a position of powerlessness, in the sense of Lukács's use of the term "contemplative"; the "contemplative" attitude, which they have to adopt toward these relationships "prevents a reflective assurance of their social mutability, and thus undermines the autonomy of subjects."[59] It is no secret that the more recent debate about our *post-democratic* society provides more than enough material for contemporary forms of political reification. Despite ubiquitous social networks we are still far from the formation of a type of public sphere in which individuals who are habituated to reifiying

---

56 It would be worth investigating, to what extent the forms of self-marketing in working life find their "voluntary" continuation in the rampant cult of beauty and physique. Ansätze zu einer Phänomenologie der Quantifizierung des Sozialen finden sich bei Steffen Mau (*Das metrische Wir: Über die Quantifizierung des Sozialen.* (Berlin: Suhrkamp, 2017)).

57 Naturally there are significant differences between employees as to how they experience instances of freedom/autonomy, but that changes nothing about the self-objectification demanded by the system's rationality.

58 Thomas Zoglauer, "Zur Ontologie der Artefakte," in: Friesen, *Ding und Verdinglichung*, pp. 26–27.

59 Titus Stahl, *Verdinglichung als Pathologie zweiter Ordnung*, p. 741.

structures can transform their heteronomy into self-determined processes of communicative reason.

In the post-democratic condition, the citizen appears to become a marginalized political object, whose participation is limited to taking part in formal democratic procedures and in the public debate about symbolic actions (Ersatzhandlungen) on the political stage.[60] One of the consequences of this development, lamented volubly but hardly believably by the representatives of the political class, is the fading interest in democratic elections,[61] which is in no small measure a symptom of the daily experience of disenfranchisement. Lukács's lifelong sympathy for the forms of council democracy [Rätedemokratie] sets its hopes against this undermining of democratic procedures in a social model in which the social actants are actually given an opportunity, in a social environment not designed to create obscurity and overcomplexity, to freely make decisions aimed at practicing solidarity.[62]

3. Not only is the time-diagnostic potential of the theorem practically unbroken, however, as the first two points indicate, but the *reification theorem's aspects of a theory of science and a critique of ideology* find a wide field of applicability. Take the debate about the death of the (philosophical term of the) subject. To the extent that the ideological character of many concepts of the end of subjectivity is becoming apparent, it is possible to regain access to Lukács's fundamental philosophical concept. Consider further, for example, the lack of articulation and inability to communicate between representatives of different scientific disciplines, who can no longer find a shared language – with disastrous consequences for a comprehensive, integrated view of reality and the emancipatory value of their research.[63] Not least among preconditions for improving this situation is that the Marxist school of philosophy is allowed to reclaim its rightful place in scientific culture. The self-deceptions of the currently dominant directions in philosophy as well as the social and cultural sciences include the belief that they are able to do without the legacy of this school in their attempt to overcome the poor abstractions of modern rationality, which, in the 20th century, have been most effectively

---

60 The late Lukács, despite the protests of a counter-public, is convinced of the poor state of the public in our "age of manipulation [Manipulationszeitalter]"(Lukács, *Ontologie des gesellschaftlichen Seins, Vol. 2*, p. 635).

61 If once in a while voter turnout should increase and lead to undesirable consequences, the ruling political class likes to complain about populist trends, which are to be kept outside the political arena.

62 Cf. Georg Lukács, *Sozialismus und Demokratisierung* (Frankfurt/ Main: Sendler, 1987).

63 Cf. Lukács, *Ontologie des gesellschaftlichen Seins, Vol. 2*, p. 598.

described by Lukács und Heidegger.[64] It is not difficult to prove that contemporary forms of scientific rationality (in Lukács's meaning) are particularized and insufficient. The science of economy, for example, is still unable to eliminate economic crises (we all know that in our time the opposite is the case), the number and intensity of military conflicts, which Lukács would undoubtedly have understood in the context of a theory of imperialism, has increased alarmingly. The mainstream of traditional-academic philosophy shows itself to be even less prepared than contemporary art and literature[65] to react both theoretically and practically to the global-intercultural challenges, in line with Marx's last thesis on Feuerbach (assuming it takes any note of it all). Scientific praxis in our time appears to be aiming to confirm Wittgenstein's dictum "that even when all *possible* scientific questions have been answered, our living problems will not have been touched at all":[66] In his *Ontology,* the late Lukács remarks, not without justification, in his assessment of "the most influential directions of bourgeois philosophy"[67] that in both philosophy and science "the principle of manipulation" has come to be dominant: "For if science is not orientated towards an as adequate as possible knowledge of reality-in-itself, if it does not strive to discover these new realities by its ever more perfected methods, which are by necessity founded ontologically as well, and which deepen and increase ontological insights, its activities reduce themselves in the final analysis to supporting praxis in its immediate sense. If it cannot or will not rise above this level, then its activity transforms into a manipulation of facts which are of practical interest to humanity."[68]

If the evidence so far demonstrated is correct, or at least partly correct, then the obvious conclusion seems to be that the pathological tendencies of our

---

64   Despite all ist deficits, among the strengths of the "Marburg School" formed around Wolfgang Abendroth and Werner Hofmann, unlike the Frankfurt school's protagonists, counts its insistence, on the indispensable role of Marx's theory to gain adequate insights and to be able to address practical-political problems in contemporary society. Cf. Lothar Peter, *Marx an die Uni. Die "Marburger Schule" – Geschichte, Probleme,* Akteure (Köln: Papyrossa, 2014).
65   While in bourgeois art "the revolt against the alienations (...) has remained unextermineable" Lukács detects more tendencies towards adaptation for bourgeois philosophy – "despite mock opposition." (Lukács, *Ontologie des gesellschaftlichen Seins, Vol.* 2, p. 678).
66   Ludwig Wittgenstein, *Tractatus logico-philosophicus* (London: Routledge & Kegan, 1955), p. 186 (quoted in: Lukács, *Ontologie des gesellschaftlichen Seins, Vol.* 2, p. 374).
67   Lukács includes especially Neo-positivism, the philosophy of language succeeding Wittgenstein and Existentialism.
68   Ibid., p. 344 et seq.

present time, described temporarily as the post-industrial, knowledge-, risk-, adventure- or digital-society, require an updating of Lukács's phenomenology of reification, which would logically have to take into account the legitimate points of criticism that have been discussed in the decades since it was first made public.[69]

In closing, I would like to return to my opening remarks once more. The experiences of our contemporary crises – according to our initial thesis – provoke the question whether it is feasible to simply renounce the great tradition of socialist and revolutionary thought. The "idea of socialism," and here one can agree with Axel Honneth, has not become obsolete with the collapse of the traditional proletarian movements.[70] It requires without doubt, however, new theoretical efforts and reticulations.[71]

5 Perspectives of a New Reification Theory and a New Integrative Marxism[72]

No one can simply advocate for a renaissance of the practical philosophy of the 1920s. It was an ambitious attempt to respond to a revolutionary situation

---

69 In more recent, as yet to be seriously investigated mass phenomena of everyday culture [*Alltagskultur*] similar reification phenomena can be found. As the above examples demonstrate, reification critique did not concern itself with "marginal practices" but with the central practices of a form of life in which entire bundles of practices are systematically intertwined. (Stahl, *Verdinglichung als Pathologie zweiter Ordnung*, p. 742).

70 The great media resonance to Honneth's essay indicates, that the author's assessment is correct. That professional recipients frequently respond to his work, similarly to his study of reification, with a mixture of sympathy and (harsh) criticism, confirms that his thoughts are inciting a relevant discussion, which is awaiting continuation.

71 It is not correct, however, that the original reification theory is unable in principle to perform a critique of the many concrete forms of reification such as racism, repression of women etc. On the contrary, it is an approach that places the concrete forms of reification in the context of a social totality, and can thus explain them adequately. That is at the core of the radical quality of this approach, which links the critique of individual phenomena with the question of the system as a whole. To put it pointedly: The struggle against racism and xenophobia is always justified, but it becomes comprehensive, i.e. "radical" in Marx's meaning of the word, in the context of a praxis that brings about radical changes.

72 Thomas Metscher's term "Integrative Marxism" is similar to Haug's concept of "plural Marxism," however, the goal is to dissolve the constrictions of Haug's Marx reception in the line Luxembourg-Gramsci-Brecht-Haug (ibid., p. 71, fn. 28). Characteristics of "Integrative Marxism" are radical openness to scientific innovations, the renunciation of a hybrid concept of absolute knowledge, the emphasis on the role of art and culture in the conscious appropriation of reality by humans, whose lives and thinkings according to the Feuerbach theses of Marx are primarily characterized by their practice and their changes.

in theoretical terms. It is completely uncertain whether the utopian elevation of the political, which we could observe especially in Lukács's theory of contemporary life and of the party, can be re-integrated into philosophical discourse. Indisputable as well is that many of our contemporaries will reject, with some outrage, the thought that they live in an age of reification, or respectively that they are subject to patterns of self-reification.[73] But even if in the "developed," "democratic" societies some forms of reification like direct violence (i.e. subjects are denied their physical integrity, their bodies may be manipulated or destroyed) and appropriation (i.e. subjects are sold like slaves as commodities) are not widely practiced and are not considered normal,[74] instrumentalization, functionalization and denial of subjectivity continue to be present in the "age of manipulation"[75] at the core of social life.[76] They appear, however, in *entirely new forms* that did not yet exist during the times of the Taylorization of the work process, or the classic cultural industry. During the final years of his life, Lukács lamented that Marxist theory, with regard to the analysis of modern capitalist theory, was still in its infancy. "Thirty years of theoretical stagnation of Marxism have created the disgraceful situation that today, nearly a century after its coming into effect, Marxists are still unable to offer an at least somewhat adequate economic analysis of contemporary capitalism."[77] Something similar can be said of a contemporary "integrative" reification theory: the new, "reifying forms of life and living situations"[78] in our brave new digital world need to be theoretically worked through in their peculiar rationality and irrationality, their technical magnitude and human particularity at last. It is a truly ambitious project waiting to be undertaken.[79]

To discuss would be Metscher's proposal to understand metaphysical-religious questions as assurances in the field of questions of meaning (Sinnfrage) and no longer to reject a limine or in an ideology-critical manner.

73   There is a new culture, a new form of life, unfortunately hardly analyzed from a Marxist perspective until now, of unapologetic narcissistic egotism, which ignores the dimensions of politics and human history and completely prevents the memory of possible experiences of alienation and reification.

74   Recent customs in the treatment of the current streams of refugees give us reasons to fear that such forms of an immensely violent, reifying treatment of humans.

75   Lukács, *Ontologie des gesellschaftlichen Seins*, Vol. 2, p. 635.

76   Similarly, the diagnosis of the late Lukács, who speaks of the disappearance of "man-eating overabundance" ("menschenfresserischen Überabeit") and the fading "obvious brutality"("sinnfällige[r] Brutalität,") "but only to leave a 'voluntary' affirmative place" ("jedoch nur um einer 'freiwillig' bejahten den Platz zu überlassen") (ibid.).

77   Ibid., p. 706.

78   Ibid., p. 736.

79   The first attempts to capture the changes in the lifeworld through the digitization of the social have been found in the work of Weizenbaum since the 1970s and more recently in the descriptions of "digital subject formatting", cf. W. Seppmann, *Kritik des Computers*.

But this self-critical assessment does not mean that one should dispense with the advantages of Marx's approach in rearticulating a contemporary socialist theory, as Honneth is proposing: Unlike the Marxists, he wants to base his hopes for a contemporary socialism on modern institutions, respectively institutional regulations, as "carriers of normative requirements."[80] He views institutionalized progress such as co-determination and minimum wage as the "foreshadowing of the future" ["Vorschein des Zukünftigen"] or, following Kant, as "historical symbols," while he believes that orientating oneself by social movement gives rise to problems, "because that would lend far too much weight to what is fleeting and contingent among the ever more rapid transformations."[81] Honneth places his bet on functional differentiation. Against a fixation on economics, he wants to see law and politics considered as following their own logics and thus as spheres to be treated separately. In concrete terms, this means he wants to take the realm of the democratic formation of decisions much more seriously than has been the case in socialist traditions, especially of Marxist persuasions, to date. By this he wants to emphasize the normative foundations of a socialist alternative to existing society, instead of obscuring them in a philosophy of history.

Indeed it cannot be denied that in the history of the workers' movement – certainly not least the one based on Marx and others, by their own avocation Marxists, theoreticians and politicians – there have been strong anti-democratic tendencies, which produced new forms of alienation.[82] Traditions such as these, which have to be assessed as "relapses into totalitarianism and primitivism,"[83] are rightly met with increasing skepticism. Lukács's emphasis must be worked through and replaced by an understanding of politics that recognizes democratization as an indispensable characteristic of socialist politics. A modern socialist understanding of politics, however, must not ignore the fact that, in a reified world, people existing in reified forms of life are confronted with a difficulty of forming a political will, recognizing their own requirements and interests, shaping and articulating these in ways that

---

        Der Kapitalismus und die Digitalisierung des Sozialen (Kassel: Mangroven, 2017), p. 253 et seq.

80   Honneth, *Idee des Sozialismus*, p. 117. – Despite all the criticism of Honneth, his impetus to overcome the pure, history-philosophical negativity of Adorno is appropriate to the facts and productive for the further development of modern critical theory. Lukács always opposed the hyperradical gesturing of the negativity of the *Minima Moralia*, since he views – with Marx and Aristotle – humans as "responding beings" (Lukács, *Ontologie des gesellschaftlichen Seins*, 2: 524, 2: 573).

81   Honneth, *Idee des Sozialismus*, p. 116.

82   Cf. Lukács, *Ontologie des gesellschaftlichen Seins*, 2: 551.

83   Peter V. Zima, *Entfremdung*, p. 134.

are informed by solidarity. The phenomenon of the ideological crisis of the proletariat is not a Leninist invention, but a result of the inherent obscurity of the capitalist system, and of the profound reification of thinking and living.

Lukács's path to Marx is accompanied and characterized by reflections on culture[84] and ethics. As late as 1918, he rejects the Bolshevik revolution from a Kantian perspective – on the grounds of moral considerations. And even after turning toward Marxism, his moral impulse, that humans must not be degraded to serve as means, robbed of their autonomy and reduced to a "troll" (in the words of Ibsen).[85] Since *History and Class Consciousness*, however, the lifelong admirer of St. Francis of Assisi,[86] the Hungarian philosopher has been convinced that the loss of autonomy is not an individual-moral phenomenon, but a structural characteristic of capitalist commodity production. Revolutionizing the latter is a possible product of the historical process, and, having become realizable in this context, is the moral postulate of the struggle against the diverse forms of reification. This struggle is always susceptible to relapses, an insight that Lukács, who ever since his notes on Dostojewski had little faith in institutions and the conformist, law-abiding behavior they demanded, never let go off. The de-reification, de-commodification of social relationships is substantially a matter of everyday living, a form of life for which it holds true "that the active alienating of another person necessarily entails one's own alienation."[87]

---

84 Metscher's emphasis on the cultural as an essential momentum of the future society is fully in keeping with the tradition of the Lukács School of Marx Interpretation. For the specific use of the term "Lukács School" cf. Dannemann, Rüdiger und Michael Löwy. "Lukács-Schule," in: Wolfgang Fritz Haug, Frigga Haug, Peter Jehle, Wolfgang Küttler (eds.), *Historisch-kritisches Wörterbuch des Marxismus*, Vol. 8/II, (Hamburg: Argument, 2005), columns 1354–1371.

85 Cf. Georg Lukács, "Lob des neunzehnten Jahrhunderts," in: *Essays über Realismus*, GLW Vol. 4 (Neuwied/ Berlin, 1971), p. 662: "(...) man becomes man, by wanting to become self; the troll rejects this should [Sollen], any should [Sollen]; it sufficient unto itself [in its particular immediacy [Unmittelbarkeit], R.D.]."

86 As the Hungarian Lukács scholar Istvan Hermann reports, he became interested in St. Francis early, and insisted throughout his life that in humanity's memory there were actually three figures whose human behavior had been completely homogeneous, and in this sense, they became universal symbolic figures: Jesus Christ, Socrates and St. Francis of Assisi. (Istvan Hermann, *Georg Lukács. Sein Leben und Wirken* (Wien/ Köln/ Graz: Böhlau, 1986), p. 35)

87 Lukács, *Ontologie des gesellschaftlichen Seins*, Vol. 2, p. 519. Cf. The brief but exemplary abstract of a history of the relationship between the sexes (Ibid., 517 et seq.) – Incidentally: Mere recourse to "the remaining critical intellectuals (such as the ones highlighted e.g. by Zima, R.D.)," who are supposed to continue to mount resistance in the areas that remain

A critique of economics [Ökonomismus] must not overlook the realism that is characteristic of the Marx-Lukács assessment of the political: even non-Marxist authors are recognizing that the present is marked by a "dominance of the economic system."[88] The economic system is – as we have emphasized above – totalitarian in tendency, it leaves its mark on politics and private life and "will perhaps precisely because of that (because of its ubiquity) rarely be recognized";[89] through the medium of money it secures the "social cohesion," precisely by invading as exchange value every social domain (of a functionally differentiated modern society)."[90] Only if a change in system is initiated that offers hope of social control of the economic domain and provides space for modes of praxis that serve their own purposes,[91] can a functional differentiation, in the sense that Honneth desires, have a hope of succeeding. In the process of transcending the *hic et nunc*, a true democratic formation of collective can take place, and culture and private life can find configurations that are appropriate to their domains. Honneth's reflexions on the "democratic forms of life," which will at that point be on the agenda, can provide valuable suggestions for this socialist future.[92] As a set of instructions for our capitalist reality they are less useful. Despite this criticism, it is important to recognize that the renewal of the idea of socialism and the theory of reification should be understood as related projects. Without the overdue elaboration of a contemporary unmasking of our reified forms of life and thought, the impetus of a recovery of the potential of the idea of socialism enlightened by the bitter experiences of the twentieth century remains fragmented.

---

open to them, "Science, Education, Art and – Politics" (Zima, *Entfremdung*, p. 92) is not a convincing option.

88   Ibid., p. 101.
89   Ibid., p. VII.
90   Ibid., p. 101.
91   In the terminology of the Ontology these constitute forms of praxis of the species-for-itself [Gattungsmäßigkeit-für-sich].
92   When human history ceases to function as if grown out of nature, spaces for individual autonomously defined forms of law, politics and love are created – in a new quality (cf. Georg Lukács, "Der Funktionswechsel des historischen Materialismus," *GLW* Vol. 2, pp. 398–431).

CHAPTER 9

Georg Lukács's Archimedean Socialism

Joseph Grim Feinberg

1   A Standpoint without the Proletariat?

The years have not been kind to "the standpoint of the proletariat." Although this notion is central to Lukács's best-known essay, "Reification and the Consciousness of the Proletariat," probably no other aspect of Lukács's work has suffered more at the hands of critics—among whom we must count Lukács himself.[1] Lukács's "Reification" essay is still celebrated for its diagnosis of modernity's malaise, but the general consensus is that the diagnosis—and any possible cure—can be undertaken without standing in the position of the working class. Yes: a world that is made by people appears to them as an agglomeration of things beyond their control. Thinking subjects are separated from knowable objects, leaving us frustrated by the impossibility of truly knowing. And this state of affairs, Lukács showed, is not the eternal condition of fallen humanity, but the historical result of market capitalism, which transformed the products of human labor into commodities that could be alienated from the people who made them and bought and sold as if they had never been made. Lukács offered a social basis to anchor and explain the existential angst that prevailed in his day and which seems bound to return and return. Yet when Lukács, in the course of his essay, tries to trace a path out of this condition by appealing to the proletariat and its unique ability to achieve non-reified consciousness, many readers turn away. After all: even if the abolition or significant curtailment of reification is possible at all, can the working class really be taken as its sole standard-bearer? Rather than asking the working class to rescue humanity from reification, wouldn't it be easier to rescue the theory of reification from the working class?

No doubt it would be, and it has been. But in abandoning the "standpoint of the proletariat," contemporary readers of Lukács may be overlooking significant conceptual moves made by Lukács when he chose to this point on which to stand. It may be true that in tying the history of reification to the fate of the

[1] Georg Lukács, *History and Class Consciousness: Studies in Marxist Dialectics*, trans. Rodney Livingstone (Cambridge, MA.: MIT Press, 1971), xxii–xxiii.

proletariat, Lukács placed an apparently universal human phenomenon on the particular ground of a single social class. But in the process he pointed to a new understanding of that class and a new grounding for its claims to universality. It may be true that Lukács himself, like so many of his readers, eventually stopped insisting on the exceptional nature of proletarian consciousness. But I would like to return to just this exceptional quality. I would like to return to the way Lukács conceptualized the proletariat as a class that is an exception from the system of bourgeois society, a class whose specific epistemological position derives not from the privileged position it enjoys within the social order, but from its peculiar exclusion from the order as a whole. It is a class that is able to grasp the social totality not because it stands at the top *or* bottom of society, but because it stands, somehow, outside.

Lukács did not extensively develop the notion of the proletariat with which he was working. His depiction of the proletariat contains several ambiguities, and he did not draw out all the consequences of his most innovative conceptual moves. It is not surprising, then, that he has often been understood in the terms developed by other Marxists before him, which he took up and reworked. Within these terms, a privileged position ascribed to the proletariat might be problematic indeed. If the proletariat were one class among others within the social order, if it were a concrete group of numerable individuals, then any attempt to ascribe it exclusive access to knowledge or to transformative power would mean excluding other groups. And if the most relevant quality of the proletariat were the positive, empirical fact that its members work for wages, or that its members conform to some stereotype of working-class identity, then there would be no reason to expect that the proletariat's coming to consciousness would necessarily reveal and confront other dimensions of social existence and domination. The standpoint of the proletariat would await supplementation by other standpoints, and the proletarian struggle to overcome its particular condition of domination would be supplemented by other, parallel struggles.

From this perspective it is quite understandable that feminist standpoint theory, perhaps the most intellectually potent attempt in recent decades to revive Lukács's notion of the standpoint, has been rather unconcerned with the "proletarian" side of the notion. It has focused attention instead on the basic structure of the standpoint as a socially situated perspective on knowledge, and it has pointed to the multiplicity of possible standpoints that might be added to the standpoint of the worker. The standpoint of the proletariat serves as a model for understanding other standpoints, but it does not appear as a structure that might itself mediate the formation of those other standpoints. Standpoint theory begins with the observation (drawn as much from figures such as Alfred Sohn-Rethel[2] as it is from Lukács) that capitalism generates the proletariat and the bourgeoisie as differing social positions, each with its own access to social understanding. From there it proceeds to identify an *additional* opposition between the socially structured consciousness of men and women (or, more precisely, of male domination and feminism, understood as socially constructed standpoints made possible by the bifurcation of social experience). Capitalism generates multiple, parallel positions from which it can be viewed. From the standpoint of standpoint theory, oppressed groups occupy a privileged epistemological position—not relative to one another, but relative to their oppressors. Their position offers them a view of oppression that is otherwise hidden, absent from dominant ideologies. The standpoint of the oppressed thus provides an opportunity to fill out the picture of a society founded on oppression. When the lower part of society—lower in prestige, but also deeper and more essential—comes to light, it reveals the upper part of society—the oppressive institutions and their ideological appearances—as "perverse inversions of more humane social relations."[3]

For Lukács in the "Reification" essay, however, the standpoint of the proletariat does not represent one standpoint among many, but a unique point of access to social totality. This Lukács says quite clearly. What he implies less clearly is that the unique quality of the proletariat is not its position *below* the ruling class, but its ability to position itself *outside* the prevailing structures that it itself has built. In order to see how Lukács's political-epistemological claims might outlast the context in which they were written, when they entered a revolutionary movement for which working-class power was still an article of faith, we should return to his suggestive yet undeveloped reconceptualization of the proletariat. In the notion of the proletariat to which he pointed—and which we can today reconstruct, invoking Fredric Jameson's call for us to "finish" Lukács's project[4]—the proletariat's claim to universality is not exclusive. Rather, it is *exceptional*, in one specific sense: It is not grounded in the privilege of a one partial perspective over others, but in the perspective of exclusion from all privileged perspectives. It may well be true, as standpoint theorists remind us, that all consciousness is localized.[5] But some locations

---

2 Alfred Sohn-Rethel, *Intellectual and Manual Labour: A Critique of Epistemology* (Atlantic Highlands, N.J.: Humanities Press, 1978).

3 Nancy Hartsock, "The Feminist Standpoint: Developing the Ground for a Specifically Feminist Historical Materialism," in *The Feminist Standpoint Theory Reader: Intellectual & Political Controversies*, ed. Sandra Harding (New York and London: Routledge, 2004), 36.

4 Fredric Jameson, "History and Class Consciousness as an 'Unfinished Project,'" *Rethinking Marxism* 1, No. 1 (1988): 72.

5 See e.g. Donna Haraway, "Situated Knowledges: The Science Question in Feminism and the Privilege of Partial Perspective," in *The Feminist Standpoint Theory Reader: Intellectual & Political Controversies*, ed. Sandra Harding (New York and London: Routledge, 2004), 81–101.

might also de-localize. There may well be multiple standpoints worth taking, but I am concerned here with one whose significance still remains to be clarified: an epistemology of *dislocation*.

In order to clarify the specific character of this dislocation, let's look closely at the problem that, in Lukács's account, the proletariat was meant to solve.

2 In and Out of Reification

Lukács's conception of the proletariat in the "Reification" essay is marked by contradiction. This contradictory character complicated Lukács's attempt to present the proletariat as a clear and consistent answer to the problem posed by bourgeois society. If the proletariat offers an answer, it is no *simple* answer. It is an answer that does not immediately dissolve the problems it faces, but rather contains these problems within itself. Yet Lukács emphasizes that there is a difference between the contradictory character of proletarian consciousness and the contradictory character of bourgeois thought: whereas the contradictions of bourgeois society set the limits of bourgeois thought, they push proletarian consciousness forward, toward their overcoming. This overcoming is possible to imagine because the proletariat, though a constituent part of bourgeois society, does not share the bourgeoisie's privileged position in that society, nor the bourgeoisie's stake in keeping that society in existence.

"The proletariat," Lukács writes, "shares with the bourgeoisie the reification of every aspect of its life."[6] Insofar as capitalist relations "penetrate society in all its aspects,"[7] the proletariat faces the same limitations to consciousness that are faced by the bourgeoisie. As Lukács writes especially clearly in the "Class Consciousness" essay that immediately precedes the essay on "Reification," the bourgeoisie is trapped in a situation where economic activity is driven by individual interests and the bourgeoisie experiences society through the eyes of isolated, individual actors; the collective, social result of these individuals' activity appears uncontrollable, like the outcome of natural laws.[8] Insofar as workers also are buyers and sellers of commodities, their consciousness too is fragmented, structured by the separation of the products of their labor into units that can be individually bought and sold. And insofar as workers produce commodities, their consciousness is structured by the division of their labor process into units whose value can be rationally calculated, taken apart, and

---

6 Lukács, *History and Class Consciousness*, 149.
7 Lukács, 85.
8 Lukács, 62–63.

reassembled in rationalized form.[9] They sell the units of their labor power as commodities. They work beside others who have sold their labor power, but for the length of the working day they renounce their claim to free association with one another, and at the end of the day the commodities they produce are taken from them, only to confront them again, on the market, as objects alien to them. Workers, like all people who interact with one another at least partly and at crucial moments through the medium of commodities, experience the world immediately as an accumulation of things beyond their control. The social structure that gives shape to this process of accumulation lies beyond the scope of immediate human experience.

Yet there is something about the proletariat, Lukács tells us, that points beyond the consciousness that capitalist relations impose. Lukács presents a number of parallel arguments, whose mutual compatibility is not at all moments clear, in order to support this claim. He says, for example, that, "For the bourgeoisie, method arises directly from its social existence and this means that mere immediacy adheres to its thought, constituting its outermost barrier, one that cannot be crossed. In contrast to this the proletariat is confronted by the need to break through this barrier, to overcome it inwardly from the very start by adopting its own point of view."[10] As Marx puts in a passage from *The Holy Family* quoted by Lukács, "The propertied class and the class of the proletariat present the same human self-alienation. But the former class finds in this self-alienation its confirmation and its good, its own power: it has in it a semblance of human existence. The class of the proletariat feels annihilated in its self-alienation; it sees in it its own powerlessness and the reality of an inhuman existence."[11] This suggests that although the bourgeoisie experiences reification as a *problem*, it is compelled in the final instance to accept reification, because reification is the very basis of the social order that guarantees the existence and dominance of the bourgeoisie. The great bourgeois philosophical systems have thus been developed as attempts to come to terms with reification, understanding it without questioning the social conditions that ground it. But because the proletariat is not compelled to accept the conditions of reification, it is also able to point beyond the limitations that reification places on thought.

---

9   Ibid., pp. 88–90.
10 Ibid., p. 164.
11 Karl Marx and Friedrich Engels, *The Holy Family or Critique of Critical Critique* (Moscow: Foreign Language Publishing House, 1956), 51 Cited in Lukács, *History and Class Consciousness*, p. 149.

In capitalist society, Lukács explains further, "reality is—immediately—the same for both the bourgeoisie and the proletariat," but "this same reality employs the motor of class interests to keep the bourgeoisie imprisoned within this immediacy while forcing the proletariat to go beyond it."[12] Because bourgeois interests are only the interests of a *particular* class, bourgeois consciousness must remain on the subjective level and cannot become the consciousness of the social whole. Bourgeois thought—consciousness of the world as experienced from the bourgeois standpoint—is unable to grasp the conditions that generate reification or to imagine them changing—because to imagine them changing would also mean imagining the end of the conditions that allow the bourgeoisie to prosper. So the objective world continues to appear to bourgeois consciousness as immutable and natural, beyond the grasp of subjective knowledge. But the "interest" of the proletariat—or, as Lukács puts it elsewhere, the class's "goal"[13] or "aim"[14]—compels it to *practically* undermine the social conditions of reification, because these are the conditions of the proletariat's experience of domination and misfortune. Then, in undermining the conditions of reification, the proletariat can achieve a *theoretical* standpoint that enables it to resolve the problems that appeared to bourgeois consciousness as irresolvable. And since reification is a problem facing all of society, "When the proletariat furthers its own class-aims it simultaneously achieves the conscious realization of the—objective—aims of society"[15]—it is able to emancipate not only itself, but society as a whole. And because the proletariat has made the world that it seeks to know and change, its knowledge of this world is also self-knowledge, and its particular, subjective interest is also a universal, objective interest. In the process of overcoming reification and taking control of the means of social creation, the proletariat plays the role of the "identical subject-object" of history, capable of knowing the objective world that collective human subjectivity itself has created.

3 A Class Apart

But if the proletariat's claim to objectivity is justified by its interest in changing objective reality, how do we know that these are its interests? What is it about

---

12 Lukács, *History and Class Consciousness*, 164.
13 Ibid., p. 163.
14 Ibid., p. 149.
15 Ibid.

the proletariat's character that gives it these interests? In other words: What exactly *is* the proletariat?

In the "Reification" essay, Lukács's answer is ambiguous. He seems to move freely between two different conceptions without consistently distinguishing between them. At times the proletariat appears as a set of specific people who could be sociologically distinguished from other people based on their status as waged laborers. This was the conception that Lukács inherited from the Social Democratic theory of the Second International. Lukács and other Left Communists outdid the Social Democrats in pushing for a radical break between proletarian and bourgeois elements of life—they called for proletarian consciousness, proletarian culture, and proletarian political power, purified of what they perceived to be bourgeois—but this workerism generally took for granted the Social Democratic conception of the proletariat itself. The proletariat appeared in their thinking as a class analogous to other classes but superior to other classes. Their conception was essentially a *positive* one: the proletariat was characterized by a set of basic attributes (wage labor—or, in some cases, unspecified "labor" as such—and its empirical opposition to the bourgeoisie). To these basic attributes others could be successively added (revolutionary consciousness, proletarian culture) until the class came to power and established its positive attributes as the attributes of society as a whole.

Nevertheless, several characteristics of the proletariat tended to undermine this conception and pushed Lukács (along with some of his Left Communist contemporaries) toward a reconceptualization. The bulk of Social Democratic theory had been worked out in conditions when proletarian revolution appeared to be a matter of an abstract future. Although it was known that in principle the proletariat would abolish itself in a future classless society, that eventual aim was overshadowed by the short-term concerns of the actually existing working class in the process of developing its own ideas and political organization. But for Lukács in 1919–22, when he was working on *History and Class Consciousness*, proletarian revolution was a problem of the concrete present, and so was the proletariat's task of abolishing class society and, with it, abolishing itself as a class. Whereas other classes could lead revolutions that placed them at the top of a new social order, there was no stable social order atop which the proletariat could sit. As soon as the proletariat ceased to be exploited, it would cease to be a proletariat; but if it continued to be exploited, it could hardly be considered to sit atop the society that exploited it. The only kind of rule to which it could aspire was a provisional "dictatorship" that enabled it to wield political power until its exploitation—and its class existence— ended. And when the proletariat ceased to exist as a class, the bourgeoisie that depended on it would necessarily cease to exist as well, and the new society would have no place for any class at all. In this regard, the proletariat was not just a class among other classes, but a class against all classes, including its own. And so there emerges a negative conception of the proletariat as a force of negating classes.

This is the first respect in which the proletariat takes on negative form in the "Reification" essay: it possesses a determinate *political* aim that cannot be derived from any positive content contained within its current existence; the proletariat, Lukács writes, "has no ideals to realize."[16] At the same time the proletariat's immediate *economic* experience characterizes its existence negatively in a second respect. While other classes also experience reification, their daily activity itself is not a commodity. But the proletariat experiences the foremost feature of its social experience as an object (a sequence of valorized units of time) that can be bought and sold ("His work as he experiences it directly possess the naked and abstract form of the commodity."[17]) In the commodity, then, "the worker recognises himself"[18] in objectified form. The worker's consciousness is "the *self-consciousness of the commodity*," and because the commodity, in Lukács's analysis, is the central mediating structure of capitalism, this self-consciousness is also the "self-knowledge" and "self-revelation" of capitalist society as a whole.[19]

At this point, however, Lukács's argument seems to be missing a crucial piece. He tells us that *when* the proletariat becomes conscious of its own condition, *then* its consciousness must be the consciousness of capitalist society as a totality. He does not tell us how the proletariat is actually able to achieve this consciousness. He suggests at numerous points that the achievement of proletarian consciousness corresponds to the political process of class struggle; this enables practice to unite with theory, transforming the conditions of reification and revealing the reified moments of capitalist production as parts of a total social process, in which workers are not only a commodified object but also a self-commodifying subject capable of ending its self-commodification. But Lukács writes further that "This process *begins* when the proletariat becomes conscious of its own class point of view,"[20] which suggests that class consciousness is a pre-condition for the very political transformation that makes class consciousness possible. The circularity of this argument would seem to require some additional factor that catalyzes the simultaneous and

---

16 Ibid., p. 178.
17 Ibid., p. 172.
18 Ibid., p. 168.
19 Ibid.
20 Ibid., p. 189.

mutually reinforcing development of class consciousness and political transformation, of theory and practice. What could this factor be, which occupies the standpoint of the proletariat and yet is somehow external to the proletariat as it actually exists, and thus is capable of provoking the proletariat's movement from a pre-theoretical to a theoretical plane? As many interpreters have noted, the Leninist vanguard party provides a ready answer: it can *actually* see what the proletariat *potentially* sees and *must* see if it is to fulfill its class aim. The party appears as the link between the objectified proletariat and the revolutionary proletarian activity that is a precondition for the proletariat's self-consciousness, which is itself a precondition for revolutionary activity.

Nevertheless, it should be taken into consideration that although Lukács discusses the role of the party in several of the essays in *History and Class Consciousness*, and although in his 1967 preface he would assert that in the "Class Consciousness" essay he understood class consciousness as something that must be "implanted in the workers 'from outside,'"[21] in the "Reification" essay the party does not directly appear. One reason for its absence may be that it does not really solve the problems that Lukács, in this essay, has set up. The party, as Lukács characterizes it in these essays from 1919–1922—in contrast to the attitude taken in the 1967 preface—can hardly do anything that the class itself is not able to do. Although in Lukács does present the party in "The Marxism of Rosa Luxemburg" as "the bearer of the class consciousness of the proletariat,"[22] he in the same essay he also writes that the party must be "fed by the trust of the *spontaneously* revolutionary masses."[23] The party must be "nourished by the feeling that [it] is the objectification of [the masses'] own will."[24] It is "the visible and organized incarnation of their own class consciousness."[25] The party may be the "form taken by the class consciousness of the proletariat,"[26] but it would seem that the form is determined by the content—class consciousness—rather than the other way around. And class consciousness itself is determined by the class's "spontaneous" activity—insofar as this activity is revolutionary and does not merely reflect the "actual, psychological state of consciousness of proletarians," which, as Lukács emphasizes in the "Class Consciousness" essay, may not correspond to the proletariat's *potential* consciousness of its historical mission.[27] The party is depicted in

---

21   Ibid., p. xviii.
22   Ibid., p. 41.
23   Ibid., p. 42, my emphasis.
24   Ibid.
25   Ibid.
26   Ibid., p. 41.
27   Ibid., p. 72.

these essays not as the unconditionally genuine bearer of proletarian consciousness, but as a *contingent* factor that is "more likely to be the effect than the cause of the revolutionary process."[28] *If* class consciousness embodies itself, *then* its embodiment is the party. And if what goes by the party name ceases to be the objectification of the class's will, then it is only logical that it will cease to be the party. Although it is known that Lukács continued to accept the Communist Party's self-identification longer than many observers might think was warranted, this later development need not change the meaning of his earlier definition.

It would seem that we are back where we began. The proletariat needs something outside itself that might enable it to achieve its class consciousness. But the party only exists outside the class as an objectification of that very class consciousness that it might (for example, in Lenin's view) instill in the class. What's more, it is not enough for this something to be located outside the class. The subject that is able to observe society as a totality in historical motion must be located outside this society as a whole. In this respect Lukács's Left Communist workerism may have more consistent with his philosophical approach than was the more orthodox Leninist vanguardism that Lukács would attribute to himself retrospectively in 1967: A vanguardist insistence on instilling revolutionary consciousness would not have solved the problem of how the proletariat could grasp the social totality. If the party was distinct from the class and instilled consciousness from an indefinite position outside, as Lenin suggested, then it would still be necessary to explain how the party's position offered it a view of society that was not available to the proletariat, and the problem of the standpoint of the proletariat would simply be transposed onto the problem of the standpoint of the party. But if the party's standpoint was the same as the class's, as Lukács suggested, then the search for a solution would take us back to the specific character of the proletariat. In order to uncover the element of the proletariat that enables it to accomplish the task Lukács set for it—in order to further develop the "negative" conception of the proletariat to which I referred above—we might turn from Lenin to another of Lukács's chief sources of inspiration: Marx. In particular, to Marx's "Introduction" to his *Contribution to the Critique of Hegel's* Philosophy of Right, a text from which Lukács drew heavily throughout *History and Class Consciousness*, and which provided the "Reification" essay with its epigraph.

In this text Marx for the first time turned his attentions resolutely toward the proletariat, and perhaps for just this reason he *justified* this turn rather than taking it for granted. Marx asks here whether any existing social class,

---

28 Ibid., p. 41.

proceeding from its particular situation, is capable of undertaking the *general* emancipation. He answers that although historical circumstances might press any class to claim that it acts on behalf of society as a whole, there is only one class that is *forced* to work toward general emancipation by the very condition of its material existence—by its "*radical chains.*"[29] This class, Marx says cryptically, is "in" bourgeois society but is not "of" it. It is a class that is "the dissolution of all classes"; it "has a universal character because its sufferings are universal"; it "does not claim a *particular redress* because the wrong which is done to it is not a *particular wrong* but *wrong in general*"; it is, "in short, a *total loss* of humanity," and it "can only redeem itself by a *total redemption of humanity*. This dissolution of society, as a particular class, is the *proletariat.*"[30]

Marx here explains what Lukács left unspecified: that the proletariat's claim to universality is based not only on the proletariat's structural presence in the heart of capitalism, as the living embodiment of the commodity form, but also on its structural *absence* from the human side of that very society that exists by dehumanizing those who sell their labor power. This is how we can understand Marx's peculiar assertion that the proletariat is "in" bourgeois society but not "of" it. No ordinary class, no class that is firmly and exclusively located within bourgeois society, is pushed to transcend that society and emancipate all classes in the course of its own self-emancipation. Yet there is one class that can never be fully a part of bourgeois society, but exists necessarily both outside and inside. And its divided character reflects the divided character of bourgeois society as a whole. Only, other classes are unable to see this division, because in their own existence they do not straddle the divide—bifurcation is not the defining structural character of their class and, thus, is not the central factor that structures their class consciousness. But whereas Marx emphasizes the proletariat's bifurcated inclusion and exclusion from bourgeois society, Lukács contributes an analysis of how this bifurcation appears in the worker's immediate consciousness. The worker's "compulsion to objectify himself as a commodity" induces a "split between subjectivity and objectivity"[31] as "a man's achievement is split off from his total personality and becomes a commodity."[32] The objectified labor of the proletariat piles up to form bourgeois society and its human values, but the proletariat's subjective existence—what it does not sell or cannot buy—remains outside this society. Its subjectivity consists in

---

29 Karl Marx, "Contribution to the Critique of Hegel's Philosophy of Right: Introduction," in *The Marx-Engels Reader*, ed. Robert C. Tucker, 2nd ed. (New York: Norton, 1978), p. 64.
30 Ibid., p. 64.
31 Lukács, *History and Class Consciousness*, p. 168.
32 Ibid., p. 171.

observing its own achievement taken from it and made into the objective building blocks of society. Bourgeois society, dependent on proletarian labor, generates humanistic ideals; but, as Lukács writes, the "transformation of labour into a commodity removes every 'human' element from the immediate existence of the proletariat."[33] The proletariat can only observe humanity, including its own humanity, as an object existing outside itself. It is a loss of the very humanity that its labor makes possible. The proletariat is, in effect, *outside itself*.

This is the crucial point toward which Lukács's account seems to gesture, but which it leaves out: the proletariat is able to find the "Archimedean point from which the whole of reality can be overthrown"[34] because the point where the proletariat stands—its particular, socially situated standpoint—places it outside the world. As long as the proletariat is understood as a particular set of people who can "claim a *particular redress*," such as the alleviation of *their* exploitation and the improvement of *their* lives, there will be little basis for identifying their claims with the claims of humanity. But if the proletariat is defined by the principle of inclusive exclusion, then this very exclusion offers the basis for claims of generality. If the proletariat is defined by its lack of the positive privileges and social content that define other classes—if the proletariat is, in other words, classified as that which is outside the established order of classes—then its aim appears not as the improvement or empowerment of one class, but as the elimination of the principle that defines it. Its aim is *general declassification*. The fact of exclusion, once recognized, provides the missing link between the experience of objectification and the ability to recognize objectified reality as a socially malleable whole. This wholeness is cognizable because the proletariat not only stands at the center of bourgeois society but also sees the structure of bourgeois society as an arrangement of objects that distance themselves from their makers as they pile up, pushing the proletariat to that point from which it can reach under the whole of society from afar, brace itself, and push.

4   Toward an Archimedean Socialism

But on what basis can we presume that such a class exists? Lukács himself, in his 1967 preface to *History and Class Consciousness*, would suggest that the notion of the proletariat as the identical subject-object of history was nothing

---

33   Ibid., p. 176.
34   Ibid., p. 193.

more than a "metaphysical construct," "an edifice boldly erected over every possible reality."[35] If the claim were that a distinct proletarian substance exists, and that the world is only its self-alienation (as Lukács understood his argument in retrospect), then the criticism might hold true. But if the proletariat is understood as a part of its reality that is generated by the reality that is in turn regenerated by it, and if the proletariat's separation from that society is explained as a social characteristic of that society itself (as Lukács suggested but did not definitively assert in *History and Class Consciousness*), then the question can be differently posed. It is not a matter of metaphysics but of social structure and of the conditions of possibility of that structure's movement and transformation. Bourgeois society came into being through a historical process of classifying reality, and reality, thus divided, generated both limitations on consciousness and the possibility of transgressing those limits (because limits imply the possibility of transgression, while transgression is only possible in the context of limits). Whereas a wholly independent metaphysical substance might simply bypass these limits, existing beyond their reach, the process of consciously transforming the established system of classification requires that the system be perceived and confronted. This process requires a this-worldly consciousness that can only rise out of the consciousness that precedes it in the world. The young Marx, after all, had already presented the peculiar subjectivity of the proletariat as a thoroughly negative subjectivity, not grounded in any positive substance but developing from the recognition of its debased condition. Lukács, in spite of his workerist exaltation of the class's potential and goal, never departed from Marx on the question of the class's lowly point of departure, a point located entirely within the society that generated the class in the process of debasing it.

Lukács's notion of the identical subject-object can be understood not as metaphysical but as *conditional*. *If* the conditions that generate the proletariat are present, *then* the social structure of cognition makes it possible for the proletariat, but not other classes, to come to consciousness of these conditions. *If* a standpoint can be found from which this consciousness is attainable, *then* it will be the standpoint of the proletariat. But that consciousness is not equal to any "actual, psychological state of proletarians."[36] It is a state of consciousness that *can* arise when consciousness follows and pushes against particular limits that are set by the bourgeois system of classification, which has placed proletarian experience both inside and outside the socially legitimated sphere of psychological being. Any given proletarian may remain within one or the other

---

35   Ibid., p. xxiii.
36   Ibid., p. 74.

sphere of experience on either side of this divide, either adopting the ready-made discourse of the legitimate bourgeois public sphere, or affirming the experience of proletarian life that has been historically excluded from legitimate public expression. Any given proletarian may thus ignore the mutual interdependence of these spheres of bifurcated experience, but the potential for recognizing the whole remains. The proletariat, then, is not a substance that exists prior to any social process. Nor is it a group of people who empirically predates the class's historical achievements and historical goals. The proletariat is better understood as an aspect of the structure of reality and, in a derivative sense, as a possibility of development contained within one part of this structure. As Lukács writes, the dialectical evolution of proletarian consciousness is the process of "how the proletariat becomes a class."[37] Or elsewhere (in "The Marxism of Rosa Luxemburg"): "The proletariat can constitute itself as a class only in and through revolution."[38] There is no proletariat before its consciousness. So when Lukács writes at other moments of the proletariat as a subject that thinks certain things or does certain things, such statements must presuppose that the process of the proletariat's self-constitution has already begun. Bourgeois society only creates a principle of classification—it does "no more than create the *position* of the proletariat in the production process"[39]—it does not provide a method for becoming aware of this principle nor a collective actor that stands in this position. That is the work of "revolution."

By understanding the proletariat in the first place as a principle of classification and only in the second place as a group of people who may come into existence and may collectively act, we can reframe the perennial question of whether the proletariat should be granted priority in movements for social change. From the fact that bourgeois society generates a proletariat that is both inside and outside it, it does not follow that the actually existing aggregate of workers, defined according to any accidental, positive characteristics (factory labor, working-class manners or culture, regular wages) must be the leaders of any given struggle. What does follow is that the principle of proletarian classification creates a point from which the social totality can be observed simultaneously from inside and outside. Nothing in this conception predetermines the type of proletarian who can stand at this point. The possibility is open to anyone whose being is struck through by the principle of proletarian classification. In the context of late capitalism, large groups of workers (for example, under the banner of "the white working class" or various other

---

[37] Ibid., p. 205.
[38] Ibid., p. 41.
[39] Ibid., p. 209, my emphasis.

nativist and national-chauvinist emblems) may choose to step away from this point, ignoring the excluded proletarian aspect of their existence and affirming their participation in bourgeois society, asserting their privilege relative to others who remain excluded. Other people whose proletarian position has been historically ignored (women workers, new immigrants, factory workers in the global south, the unpaid laborers of social reproduction) may come to occupy the proletarian standpoint. Their entire being is not proletarian. It is necessarily bifurcated. Not all waged workers are proletarian in every aspect of their lives. But the vast majority of people are proletarian in some aspect of their lives. They may have different complaints and demands, but they all—all people who contribute to the production and reproduction of society without possessing power over what they have made—can occupy this same point. It can become a point of intersection and articulation of many struggles, a position from which particular claims can become universal. The proletariat, in this conception, is not privileged *instead* of other political actors. Its sole advantage lies in its ability to represent the principle of inclusive exclusion and, thus, in negative form, to represent the principle of these actors' potential unity in struggling against this principle.

This conditional understanding of the proletariat implies a considerable degree of contingency in the process of constituting a conscious proletariat. Lukács, especially in the "Class Consciousness" essay, seemed to find the answer to this contingency in the party. It could ensure that the working class achieved consciousness of the social totality, rather than affirming separation and exclusion. It could act as the receptacle of consciousness that individual workers, left to themselves, without organization, hardly had the means to develop. But what happens when we recognize that the party, this apparently crucial node in Lukács's political epistemology, has hardly any definition of its own, other than that is the bearer of proletarian consciousness? When its claim to act as this bearer is as contingent as the process of constituting proletarian consciousness? Nothing in the party's structure justifies its claim. Its claim is justified only by its adherence to the principles attributed to the proletariat. Either the party is merely an "effect" of the revolutionary process and an expression of spontaneous proletarian activity (in which case its role as a mediator of consciousness disappears, and class consciousness appears to be immediate), or it "implants" its consciousness onto the proletariat from outside (in which case nothing explains where this consciousness came from and how one can know that the party's consciousness is proletarian). Neither of these two notions of the party, between which Lukács seems to oscillate, specifies an organizational form that can lessen the contingency in the process of achieving proletarian consciousness and transforming the social totality that is grounded on exclusion. The organizational basis for the proletariat's claim to inclusive universality remains unspecified.

Lukács is very careful in the "Reification" essay to distinguish the standpoint of the proletariat from the standpoint of the bourgeois subject whose claim to universality rests on an abstract notion of the individual.[40] The abstract individual treats a historically specific social experience as if it were general and eternal, and the bourgeois claim to see the entire (relevant) world depends on a blindness toward the historical conditions that enable and set limits to bourgeois thought. The universalized bourgeois individual cannot explain how it is able to stand outside the world upon which it looks down. It must derive its universal values from universal principles that are only derived from one another. The bourgeois universalist stands without a body, without ground on which to stand. But the proletarian claim to universality is historically and socially situated. It is not possible at all times and in all places, but it might become possible. The proletariat's universalism is not absolute but relative, derived from its peculiar exclusionary inclusion in a particular historical form. It is not the result of immediate experience. It must be mediated. But what can be the mediator, if the party appears at some moments to dissolve into the position of the proletariat, while at other moments it appears as a disembodied subject floating over the world, like the projection of the absolute, universal individual in the mind of the bourgeoisie? Whereas the proletariat's claim to knowledge is carefully situated, the party appears to take the form of what Lukács calls "mythology": the attempt to bridge between two points when it has become impossible to "discover any concrete mediation between them."[41] The myth of the party covers over the absence of a concrete conception of mediation.

If there is to be a non-mythological social form that structures proletarian activity as a movement toward self-consciousness and structures proletarian consciousness as a movement toward the practical overcoming of reification, then this form has yet to be characterized. The mediator of proletarian consciousness should be a structure that lies both inside and outside the proletariat, taking as its organizing principle the proletariat's exclusionary inclusion in bourgeois society, pushing against this principle of social division that is heart of capitalism, of reification, and of the dehumanized proletariat itself. And it should be a point of mediation between multiple social forms that intersect at capitalism's point of inclusive exclusion. What emerges may be an international of the excluded, wherever and whenever they may be, in the

---

40 See, e.g., ibid., pp. 193–194.
41 Ibid., p. 194.

interstices of everyday bourgeois life and at the unseen margins of bourgeois society. As these multiple points are uncovered and brought together through intersecting political action, they constitute the shared standpoint around which to organize.

Capitalism generates the proletariat as a lever. It is the uncompleted task of proletarian organization to find the point at which to fix the lever, so that we might move the world.

CHAPTER 10

Lukács's Idea of Communism and Its Blind Spot: Money

Frank Engster

The three main concepts of Lukács's famous book *History and Class Consciousness* are already contained in the title: History, Class and Consciousness.[1] These three concepts are especially developed in the longest and most important essay of the book, "Reification and the Consciousness of the Proletariat."[2] I will bring these three concepts "Class–Consciousness–History" together into a single thesis, which is that Lukács's reification essay combines these concepts in an *existentialist way*. More precisely, he unites them into the *first great existential blueprint of communist revolution*.[3] My aim is to radicalize with this "existential" the common interpretations of Lukács which claim that, in his critique of alienation and reification, he brought questions of subjectivity, consciousness and praxis into the Marxism of his time, and that his "Praxisphilosophie" transformed traditional Marxism into what would later be called "Western Marxism." My thesis instead claims that Lukács's existentialist critique of capitalism accomplished the same kind of radicalization that Kierkegaard had done for religion long before him, and that Heidegger did for ontology shortly after him.

The first question of course is why we should consider Lukács to have formulated an "existential critique" at all, since we usually think of the connection between Marxism and Existentialism with French philosophers like Jean-Paul Sartre, Lucien Goldmann or Simone de Beauvoir. Moreover, Lukács never described himself as an existentialist. On the contrary, he vehement criticized it in the early 1950s.

One way to answer this is by situating Lukács's essay in the social, philosophical, and political situation of his time. In the historical context of *History and Class Consciousness*, there was an existential crisis in all three areas, social,

---

1 Georg Lukács, *History and Class Consciousness. Studies in Marxist Dialectics* (Cambridge, Mass: Merlin Press, 1971, in the following HCC).
2 Lukács, HCC, pp. 83–222.
3 To the connection of the three terms see the preface from Agnes Heller in: Hanno Plass (Ed.), *Klasse. Geschichte. Bewusstsein* (Hamburg: Verbrecherverlag 2015), p. 25.

philosophical, and political, and Lukács's reification essay is indisputably a reaction to all of them – something he himself would surely admit.

The three crises are:

1. The social crisis: The experience of the First World War triggered the most powerful crisis of bourgeois society and bourgeois self-understanding as yet.
2. The philosophical crisis: In philosophy, bourgeois self-understanding was given its highest self-assurance and dignity, and consequently social changes and crises, such as those brought on by the First World War, were also reflected in a philosophical way and should provide, if not solutions, at least answers. But these answers were lacking in those days when the bourgeois self-understanding was so radically unsettled by the war.
3. The political crisis of Marxism: Marxism was, in fact, supposed to provide these answers to the philosophical self-assurance of the bourgeoisie, offering an alternative to bourgeois society in general. The profound uncertainty and crisis that triggered the First World War in bourgeois society and its philosophical self-understanding should have been the high point of Marxism. However, Marxism was itself in a deep crisis, especially by the failure of the Second International before the First World War and the failure of a socialist revolution in Germany and in countries of central Europe at the end of the war, but ironically also because of the success of the Russian Revolution which contradicted the historical development as it was expected by Marxism.

Immediately after the First World War, all three crises were relevant to Lukács, who was still quite young at that time, as he was writing the essays for *History and Class Consciousness*: the general social crisis triggered by the First World War, the crisis of Marxism, but also the crisis of bourgeois philosophy. This bourgeois philosophy was already relevant to the young Lukács since he himself belonged to it immediately after the First World War. We can attribute to him the then prevailing currents in philosophy, Phenomenology and Neo-Kantianism. This lasted precisely up to the moment when Lukács underwent a highly existential personal experience, namely, until he encountered Marxism. That was, to be precise, in December 1918. For him, Marxism was really something like an "existential awakening," as Marxism seemed to offer answers to the open questions and problems of Phenomenology and Neo-Kantianism.[4]

---

4   The same goes for his interpretations in Aesthetics and Literature. One has just to think of the word "transcendental homelessness" in Lukács's *Theory of the Novel*, which became the signum of a whole epoch. Further, the entry into the Communist Party of Hungary in 1918 was an "existential step" for him. From then on, Lukács in his own personal existence was divided

Or, rather, "the existential" for him was that this answer seemed to lead *beyond* Phenomenology and Neo-Kantianism. Moreover, the answer seemed to go beyond bourgeois philosophy as a whole, and this meant an overcoming of philosophy *as* philosophy. Lukács's profound insight that he at that time found in Marx was that philosophy could indeed reflect society and bring it to conceptualization; philosophy could therefore develop the contradictions and problems of society. But it can do so only in a philosophical way. It can give answers and solution only immanently, in the content and the concepts of philosophy and in the form of philosophy itself. Philosophy remains as much immanent to capitalist society as it remains contemplative towards it. By contrast, the solution in Lukács's reading of Marx lies beyond philosophy in the realm of *social practice*. And this practice for Lukács seems to offer a solution also to the two other existential crises, that of bourgeois society after the First World War, but also to the crisis of Marxism itself.

This idea of overcoming philosophy as such leads to the actual existentialist aspect, because the existential does not only lie in the critical situation at that time, but in Lukács's reaction to these that he develops in his reification essay. The essay is an overlapping and culmination point of various strands: the philosophical situation in phenomenology, Neo-Kantianism and vitalism (*Lebensphilosophie*), Lukács attempt to connect Ontology, Ethics and Epistemology, his personal commitment in both the party and non-dogmatic thinking. All this comes together, as it will be shown below, in his attempt to not only reformulate, but to practically overcome, with Marx's critique of the commodity form, the unsolved problems of German idealism, especially the necessity of antinomies.

The situation at that time almost seemed to ask for such an overcoming, especially in the philosophical situation of Phenomenology, but also in Neo-Kantianism. In phenomenology, hints of existentialism seemed to lie within the logic of the concepts of consciousness, experience and vitalism. But an existential "overcoming" of Phenomenology was not only tried by Lukács with

---

between his loyalty to official party politics and his commitment as a radical thinker in Marxism, Literature and Aesthetics, see Eric-John Russell, "Georg Lukács: An Actually Existing Antinomy," in *Handbook of Frankfurt School Critical Theory*, Vol. 1, eds. Beverley Best, Werner Bonefeld, Neil Larsen, Chris O'Kane (Sage: forthcoming 2018). And finally, there are direct connections to the existentialism of Kirkegaard to whom Lukács in one writing also explicitly referred. More explicit are the crucial terms of existentialism he uses in the essays in *HCC* such as will, decision, faith and so on. The last proof maybe is Lukács himself, who in his preface to the new edition of *HCC* from 1967 attested himself a "messianic utopianism" in his early years, see Lukács, *HCC*, p. xxv.

Marxism; it also happened, almost without any recourse to Marx, in the sphere of bourgeois philosophy itself, namely in Martin Heidegger.

1 The Three Formulas of a Revolution: the Objectivism in Classical Marxism and the Subjective Factors in Lenin and Luxemburg

So, the question is: How does Lukács attempt an existential overcoming with Marx of bourgeois society in general and its philosophical self-understanding in particular? The answer lies in the inner connection of the three terms "class," "history" and "consciousness" that Lukács puts into a kind of existential formula. To show how Lukács put these three terms into a specific formula, there are to be developed, however, first three *different versions* of this class-consciousness-history formula. There were hence already three other, non-existential versions. The first version came from classical or traditional Marxism that is from the first generations of social democratic parties, the labor movement and the Second International; the second formula came from Lenin, who introduced a "subjective factor" into it; and to Lenin we can thirdly oppose Luxemburg's version of such a subjective factor. Only the last version is Lukács's formula, in which the three terms form an existential connection in the "identical subject-object of history."

With these formulas of the concepts of class, history, and consciousness, the Marxist discussion in the time of the young Lukács encompassed the whole field of revolutionary theory. Lukács was, so to speak, only the last to design such a theory of revolution in a strong sense in his reification essay. His theory of revolution in its existential version was also a kind of conclusion and final version, precisely by drawing the consequences from the problems of the preceding formulas. Lukács's existential formula was in a sense the last way possible to positively justify the necessity of revolution. This should also justify Lukács's theory of revolution in its actuality today. Lukács is, so to speak, the last prophet of communist revolution, and the last prophet is, in the religious order, not the final one with the ultimate message, but the one closest to us. But there is also an important, decisive blind spot not only in Lukács, but in the critique of capitalism and the idea of communism in general, and to situate the blind spot, Lukács existential formula is a perfect prototype.

But before we get to Lukács himself and its blind spot, we have to start with the "class-history-consciousness" formula of traditional Marxism, that is, with the classical formula of Marxism from Marx's time up to the Second International and to Lenin and Luxemburg. Here the three terms were brought together in a way that was claimed to be "economistic" and "objectivist-determinist," following a "philosophy of history." These terms are certainly well known, as well as the harsh criticism that traditional Marxism received in the name of these concepts. Nevertheless, we have to look briefly at what "economist," "objectivist-determinist" and "history of philosophy" actually mean.

In the formula of classical Marxism, the first connection is between class and consciousness, that is, short and simple, *class consciousness*. The idea is that the contradiction between labor and capital should come to full consciousness within the working-class. That the contradiction "should come to full consciousness" means that, on the one hand, the social determination of labor and its productive power should become conscious in the working class. On the other hand, it implies that the domination and exploitation of the same labor by capitalist property relations and by the bourgeois class, should also become conscious, but also the power and the possibilities of resistance and of overcoming capitalism that in the working class, at least possibly, exists.

The *logic* of the connection between class and consciousness is decisive: the social *objectivity* of the contradiction between labor and capital must *subjectively* come to consciousness in the class in an entirely forced, quasi-automatic way. And with this automatism between objectivity and subjectivity, the third term now comes into play, history. More precisely, the famous notorious historical *determinism* comes into play, for class achieves revolutionary consciousness precisely with the necessity of a quasi-automatic, natural development; class consciousness is characterized thus by recognizing the necessity which is objectively present in the contradiction between labor and capital, and which forces itself into subjective consciousness.

So, it seems to be a historical necessity that the working class becomes aware of the contradiction between labor and capital and wants to overcome this contradiction.Therefore, the social-democratic or socialist party must only take on what is objectively determined in society anyway. By politically only *representing* labor and class, the party can appeal to a supra-historical necessity, a necessity that invokes a party to represent it and organize it without really adding anything to it. That is what can be called the "traditional formula" history, class, and consciousness.

Lenin brought the three terms together in a new formula. He recognized a problem in the Marxism of his time precisely in the question of historical necessity. Although Lenin's starting point was also the contradiction between labor and capital, and although he also claimed the necessity of its revolutionary overcoming, he intervened against the objectivism and historical determinism of the "traditional formula." He stated that the proletariat "spontaneously" produces "only trade-unionist consciousness,"[5] that is, a reformist consciousness,

---

5 "The history of all countries shows that the working class, exclusively by its own effort, is able to develop only trade union consciousness (...)." Vladimir Ilyich Lenin, "What is to be done,"

but not a revolutionary one. Thus, history does *not* produce with necessity a revolutionary class consciousness; history does not create by itself a revolutionary situation and a corresponding consciousness. On the contrary, according to Lenin, without an "external addition," the consciousness of the working class remains "trapped" in capitalist conditions and in immediate economic class interests. History therefore takes at best an evolutionary and reformist path – without revolution.

The addition that must come from outside is, of course, the notorious *party*. But we have to be aware that Lenin brought the party in a new position. For Lenin, the party must fill in for what is *lacking* in objectivity and necessity: the party must stand in for the lack of revolutionary awareness. The party must therefore *replace* historical determinism, which in the Marxism of his time would almost certainly provide a revolutionary consciousness. "Replace" means that the party has to jump in for a *missing* determinism and act *in its place*. Lenin conceived this as the duty of a party of a "new type." A "new type" of party means one that must literally take on the consciousness of the working class, since the party must lead and guide them as a "vanguard,"[6] a vanguard that leads consciousness out of immediacy and beyond reformist and economist immanence. Although the vanguard party cannot remove the revolutionary consciousness from the working class and take it up on its own (this is was later happened under state-socialism and Stalinism[7]), the party nevertheless has to jump in for a lack of revolutionary consciousness to provide for its revolutionary awareness.

---

in *Lenin's Collected Works*, Vol. 5 (Moscow: Foreign Languages Publishing House, 1961), pp. 347–530, quote p. 375.

6   "(…) it is not every revolutionary situation that gives rise to a revolution; revolution arises only out of a situation in which the above-mentioned objective changes are accompanied by a subjective change, namely, the ability of the revolutionary class to take revolutionary mass action strong enough to break (or dislocate) the old government, which never, not even in a period of crisis, 'falls,' if it is not toppled over." V.I. Lenin, "The Collapse of the Second International," in *Collected Works*, Vol. 21 (Moscow: Progress Publisher, 1974), pp. 205–259, quote p. 214. The necessity of a vanguard he developed already between 1901 and 1902 in "What is to be done." For Lenin's critique of on the one hand the social-democratic parties of his time and on the other hand spontaneism and radical leftist politics see V.I. Lenin, "Two Tactics of Social-Democracy in the Democratic Revolution," in *Lenin's Collected Works*, Vol. 9 (Moscow: Progress Publishers 1962), pp. 15–140, and "'Left-Wing' Communism: an Infantile Disorder," in *Lenin's Collected Works*, Vol. 31, (Moscow: Progress Publishers, 1964) pp. 17–118.

7   This "friendly takeover" by the party was indeed decisive for the dynamism after the Russian Revolution, that is, for the development of the party to the omnipotent and omnipresent state-party and the disempowerment of the class. It is this "gap" between revolution and disempowerment by Stalinism where Trotskyism and later Maoism came in with the demand of a "permanent," and respectively, a "cultural" revolution.

This external addition, which Lenin introduced into the formula of class-consciousness-history, included a very prominent concept, that of the "subjective factor." It is often forgotten that is was Lenin who introduced a subjective factor into the economism and determinism of Marxism. But there was another important version of the subjective factor, namely Rosa Luxemburg's version. Luxemburg too criticized objectivism and historical determinism in the Marxism of her time, and she too saw the necessity to organize the revolutionary consciousness. But in contrast to Lenin, this factor does not come from the outside in the form of a vanguard party of professional revolutionaries. Luxemburg rather emphasises a revolutionary development that must come from *inside*, from inner learning-processes, self-organization and from the spontaneity of the masses.[8]

These references to objectivism in classical Marxism and to the two different versions of a subjective factor in Lenin and in Luxemburg are important because we will now see that both the objectivism and the subjective factor receive in Lukács a turn, namely the announced "existential" turn.

2   Lukács's Existential Turn of Objectivism *and* of the Subjective Factor

Lukács in his reification essay somersaults beyond Lenin's and Luxemburg's criticism, but not without taking the great insight of Lenin and Luxemburg: the necessity of revolutionizing consciousness by a subjective factor. But the addition required by Lenin for this revolutionizing, the external ingredient of the party, and the addition required by Luxemburg, the processes inside the masses and its struggles, both the external and the internal subjective factor are immediately taken back into the consciousness of the working class, just as in classical Marxism. So Lukács comes back to the starting point, to the objective necessity of a revolution in classical Marxism, but without its historical determinism. In a simplified summary, Lukács cuts both the historical objectivism-determinism *and* Lenin's and Luxemburg's subjective factor from the formula.

This abbreviated revolutionary formula provides a kind of short circuit to "the existential." The existential exists, more precisely, in an existential *situation*, and this existential situation is simply the existence of the worker in

---

[8] See in particular two writings, together published in Rosa Luxemburg, "The mass strike: The political party and the trade unions," and "The Junius Pamphlet" (New York: Harper torch books, 1971). On Lukács's discussion of the difference of Lenin and Luxemburg see "Critical Observations on Rosa Luxemburg's a 'Critique of the Russian Revolution'" in Lukács, HCC, pp. 271–294.

capitalist society. At first sight, it seems that with the existence of the worker, social objectivity itself creates revolutionary consciousness, just as in classical Marxism. The crucial difference, however, is that Lukács does not proceed from the objective social character of labor which contradicts its capitalist use for profit and the private property of the means of production, as in traditional Marxism. Instead, he proceeds directly from the "reification" and "alienation" of the labor by the *commodity form* – and here Lukács's existential version of a subjective factor comes in.[9]

It is this reification and alienation of the social determination and productive power of labor that determines human beings' social existence in capitalist modernity in total, that is, *all* individuals of that society. Alienation and reification thus determine both the existence of the working class and the bourgeoisie; in this respect, both classes share the same existence. More precisely, according to Lukács all individuals and both classes share the same *epistemological problem*, namely that social objectivity appears only through its reification by the commodity form. It is thus disseminated into the variety of single commodities in an incoherent appearance. Labor, therefore, cannot be seen as the essence of the social totality. On the contrary, this essence appears as always already reified and alienated.

But on the other hand, it is always *labor* that appears in a reified and alienated manner in all commodities. Thus, the same commodity form which reifies and alienates labor, the same commodity form makes labor an object that precisely *because* of its alienation and thanks *through* its reification can be reflected upon like an external thing and thereby becomes transparent as the essence of society and the identical quality in all the different reified and commodified external appearances.

Therefore, the social determination and the productive power of labor can come to consciousness as the essence of the social totality. But labor becomes transparent as the being of a social totality whose existence falls into a history that remains external to its subject. It is as if the essence of social totality itself is alienated, alienated from the subject that produces in the society its own being and becoming. However, history reveals its own existential void and meaninglessness if the subject of labor sees in its own negation by the commodity form – and at once sees itself as the only subject that could give history meaning by producing history *as such*.

---

[9] "It is no accident that Marx should have begun with an analysis of commodities when, in the two great works of his mature period, he set out to portray capitalist society in its totality and to lay bare its fundamental nature." Lukács, HCC, p. 83.

This ambivalent, contradictory status of the commodity form and hence of reification and alienation is decisive for the existential turn. It is important to note that Lukács does not develop alienation and reification as a negative fate, as it is later interpreted in Critical Theory, especially with Adorno. Neither does he refer to labor as the essence of a social totality that only must overcome its status of reification and alienation.[10] The commodity form has an epistemological status, it is the "condition of possibility" (Kant) for its own overcoming, as it themselves ensures that the very essence of society can be reflected as an external object and become recognizable.

However, within this contradictory status of reification and alienation, the actual existential point is still not yet found. The existential idea is that in capitalism not only labor becomes commodified in its results, but that *labor power itself* becomes a commodity – and here the position of the proletariat differs from the bourgeois point of view. While the bourgeois standpoint can reflect on labor, and with labor the essence of the social totality, only from an external and contemplative standpoint (and this, according to Lukács, expresses philosophy as philosophy, particularly German Idealism), the dramatic insight for the proletariat is that its own labor power, that is, its own subjectivity and life, becomes an object and commodity for use by capital. Through the self-consciousness of the particular commodity labor power, nothing less than the productive force of society as a whole comes to consciousness and becomes, to bring it to the point, *reflexive*.

This dramatic insight offers a kind of existential self-knowledge only for the proletariat. The insight is existential because such self-knowledge can no longer remain external to labor, it can no longer stand contemplative and passive towards the world as in the case of the bourgeois point of view. Rather, the standpoint of the proletariat requires a leap into a practical self-conquest, just like the leap or jump that is characteristic of existentialism in general since

---

10 It is a strange misreading when Postone relates Lukács to an essentialist and ahistorical understanding of labor like the one in traditional Marxism precisely where Lukács introduced the rupture and referred in an epistemological and categorial way (the same "categorial" way Postone claimes for himself) to the form of social mediation instead of an pre-reflexive human substance or essence; see Moishe Postone, "Lukács and the Dialectical Critique of Capitalism," in: *New Dialectics and Political Economy*, ed. R. Albritton and J. Simoulidis (Basingstoke and New York: Palgrave Macmillan, Houndmills, 2003), –. 88–100. What Postone criticized, however, can rather be found in Humanist Marxism and Philosophy of Praxis which for their part miss that crucial point in Lukács. Lukács's critique is not concerned to re-configure a self-alienated or fragmented totality but a pre-reflexive one, and this pre-reflexivness is what in his view is reflected in Kant's Antinomies and solved in Hegel only negatively in an ideal supra-individual Spirit.

Søren Kierkegaard.[11] In Lukács's own words: "He [the worker] is therefore forced into becoming the object of the process by which he is turned into a commodity and reduced to a mere quantity. But this very fact forces him to surpass the immediacy of his condition."[12] Thus, the commodity form provides the particular commodity labor power with a form of self-consciousness and self-knowledge that allows it for a leap to practically overcome its own social existence.[13]

Only the proletariat has this possibility "to jump" because only they can make their own subjectivity an object of their self-consciousness as a commodity. And such self-consciousness is already more than a mere act of knowledge and consciousness, more than an external and passive reflection. On the contrary, in the self-knowledge of its reification and alienation, the worker is already going beyond himself and herself and leaping over into *practice*. The self-knowledge of the commodity labor power is a leap of theory into practice by which it revolutionizes itself. The revolutionary leap is the moment when the *empirical* working-class becomes aware of what it can address or "impute" itself, as Lukács puts it,[14] and jumps over into the revolutionary status of a proletariat that is aware of its own social form and its implications for both a critique of the existing society and its overcoming by a communist one.

No Communist Party can relieve commodity labor power from this necessity of self-reflection and self-realisation. On the contrary, the proletariat, first of all and in the last instance, has to take part for itself that means it has to acknowledge the form of social mediation of its own productive power for capitalist society and take over the potency to overcome it. This is because to the proletariat, its own self-knowledge is not only a leap into practice. More than that, through its self-knowledge, it realizes nothing less than the *idea of communism*, that is, the idea of its practical self-realization, or self-realization *by* practice. Lukács's idea of communism is that the constitution of social objectivity and the productive power of history becomes reflexive by the commodity form in the particular commodity labor power. This communist self-realization would be possible for the proletariat if its labor, and with labor the productive power of society and history, were not alienated and reified. This alienated existence

---

11 In fact also the bourgeoisie from its standpoint can reflect labor as the essence of social being – as Adam Smith and David Ricardo already did. Up to this point, their class share the same epistemological status. But the bourgeois class, as will be shown, cannot "jump," that is it can not overcome its standpoint in a practical manner.
12 Lukács, HCC, p. 166.
13 Marxist-Leninist critics of Lukács saw this as pure idealism, but to be precise, it was not idealism, but existentialism.
14 Lukács, HCC, p. 323.

must instead be overcome by a self-empowerment that grounds a new collective existence in the self-realization of the proletariat. This leap is possible only for the commodity labor power, for only this particular commodity can turn the productive power to produce all common commodities, and hence to produce society as a totality, into a theoretical self-consciousness *and* a practical self-application in a communist self-realization.

That is Lukács's great idea, that in capitalism, labor can become reflexive through the commodity form. The fascination and attraction of Lukács's reification essay – first on Western Marxism and Critical Theory, and then again on the '68 movements – lies in this existential leap: the *theoretical criticism* of capitalism turns into its *practical overcoming* by the self-reflection of the commodity labor power, and in the same self-reflection already lies the *idea* of the self-realization of the proletariat in a communist society. He puts the terms class-history-consciousness into a formula that can best be interpreted existentially, namely the formula of the "identical subject-object of history."[15] This formula is undoubtedly the culmination of the whole essay; here the radicalization of the objectivism of classical Marxism, but also the radicalization of the subjective factor in Lenin and Luxemburg come together in a striking way. For Lukács, the situation is only objectively ready for revolution if the proletariat not only by its self-consciousness adds its own subjectivity to the objective conditions. This *subjectivity* consists in the ability to *objectify itself in society's future history*. And the revolution is precisely the existential jump, namely the moment when the *empirical* working class by its self-knowledge imputes its *pure logical status* to itself and overcomes its own empirical being as working class. It also overcomes a social situation that from an empirical point of view might be not revolutionary at all. The revolutionizing of capitalism that in classical Marxism is existent in the contradiction of labor and capital so that the party only must execute an objective necessity, while Lenin and Luxemburg saw the necessity to add a subjective factor in form of a vanguard and inner processes of learning – the revolutionizing of capitalism in Lukács is done "only" by the social form of capitalist mediation.

Perhaps this is the existential idea of subject-object *par excellence*: the productive power of society comes to consciousness in a proletariat that calculates with nothing other than – itself. The proletariat can acquire for itself the production of a social totality in which it can speculatively calculate with its own productive power, similar to Hegel's idea of the speculative identity between substance and subject in the *Phenomenology of Spirit* and of subject and object in the *Science of Logic*, which however in Lukács's view gets realized

---

15   Lukács, *HCC*, p. 149ff.

only by an as well ideal as negative reason which Hegel claims for – bringing alienation and reification to its last form – phenomenologically a supra-individual Spirit and pure logically for the mediation of being and thinking by the concept.[16]

3 Lukács's Actuality: Western Marxism, Critical Theory, and Post-Marxism

It is of course true that the traditional image of the Party can also be found in Lukács, perhaps even in most of his work. In fact, the existential relation between class, consciousness, and history as shown here is only present in the essay on reification.[17] But it is also true that in this single essay, Lukács does not simply repeat the conventional arguments for the party, nor does he present the traditional concepts of class, consciousness, and history. The attraction of this essay is in how it overcomes both Lenin's concept of the party as well as the objectivist historical determinism of Marxism before Lenin. Usually, however, only a "Praxisphilosophie" is developed out of all this, which is really just the opposite pole to the authoritarian concept of the party. This antithesis was particularly relevant for all those who in capitalist western and in socialist eastern societies sought a counterpart to the traditional party form. Although some Marxists and philosophers have perceived this existential radicalization, especially Lucien Goldman, it has not been seen precisely where it is most effective. Namely, that because of the commodity form of labor, the productive power of society for the first time in history can be reflexive and recognize itself through the self-consciousness of the proletariat.

However, Lukács brought three shifts into the critique of capitalist society which became influential in Western Marxism and Critical Theory:
- The contradiction of labor and capital is not immediately given, neither in the objectively social being nor in consciousness? It is always already mediated by commodity form, and so is knowledge and consciousness. Lukács

---

16   According to Hegel the logic of the notion is to identify object and subject by both their separation and mediation; this is developed in his *Science of Logic*. The phenomenological identification of consciousness with the experience of both objectivity and its own subjectivity by self-consciousness is developed in the *Phenomenology of Spirit*. Lukács, like most Marxists, is more oriented to the *Phenomenology*, to which, in the reification essay, he explicitly refers.

17   He in HCC constantly states that, "the Communist Party is the organised form of class consciousness" (e.g. p. 75).

understood labor, class and consciousness from the totality of a social mediation by commodity form, and this form has an as practical as epistemological status and constitutes both social objectivity and subjectivity.
- The consciousness is not revolutionized by the party or by a subjective factor, it must come by the form of capitalist mediation itself.
- By this form of social mediation, also the rupture between, on the one hand, the empirical situation with an at best reformist consciousness of working class, and on the other hand, the necessity of a revolution, can be overcome. Lukács was the last who brought together an already fissured theory and praxis before in particular Critical Theory used the critique of the commodity form to explain why the unity of theory and praxis seems irretrievably broken. After Lukács, in Western Marxism and Critical Theory a critique of the commodity form, of reification and alienation began without such a revolutionary leap by an identical subject-object.

But more important than these shifts: Lukács gave to the theory of revolution a final radicalization, and with that radicalization revolutionary theory attained a climax, but also a kind of last exit and conclusion. "Conclusion" does not mean that Lukács formulated a definitive revolutionary theory. Rather, he discovered the only formula capable for combining class, consciousness, and history in a way that still seemed possible and open after the time of historical determinism and after Lenin and Luxemburg added a subjective factor to it. Since then, there has been no comparable effort to develop a consistent theory of revolution around the Proletariat, and perhaps this is not possible any more. In any case, social critique has refrained from such efforts across the board.

But perhaps precisely because of the impossibility of a logically consistent revolutionary theory, there is an astonishingly great temptation to map out the critique of capitalism, the possibility of revolution, and the idea of communism in an if not existential, at least ontological way. These attempts have become popular above all in the context of academic and philosophical Marxism, and primarily in what has now been called "post-Marxism":
- Derrida's "weak Messianism" and negative theology in the legacy of Benjamin,
- Badiou's concept of "the event" (here we maybe have the most consistent formula or formalization of a revolution theory in the strong sense),
- the "coming insurrection," as it is foreseen by the *Invisible Committee* and Tiqqun,
- considerations from Agamben or Jean-Luc Nancy on the "coming community" or "inoperative community,"
- and, with reservation, also the post-operaist idea of the self-organization of the Multitude and its constitutive power, as represented in Antonio Negri,

Paolo Virno, Michael Hardt and others (here we have a return to the formula of classical Marxism, whilst surpassing the critique it had by operaism). All these versions attempt to escape the determinism and economism of classical Marxism, but they also want to make due without a Leninist party and without invoking a vanguard. They also do not rely, like Luxemburg, on the self-organization and the spontaneity of the class or the masses. Rather, they aim for an open situation or a decision, for the Kairos or for the event, for the coming insurrection or coming community – and they all try to bring in something else between the objective conditions and necessities on the one hand and the subjective factor on the other. Lukács's idea of an "identical subject-object of history" should not only be included in these attempts, but it should be put at the beginning – and the beginning is always what remains.

However, Lukács marks also a kind of endpoint. It lies in his attempt to overcome what Hegel brought to an end in his dialectical Logic and in his idea of an absolute Spirit. Here Lukács stands in line with Kierkegaard and Heidegger.

4 The Three Universal Existentials: the Faith, the Being, and the Social

Lukács with his formula accomplished for capitalist existence what Kierkegaard accomplished for religious existence and Heidegger for ontological existence. When the religious world became radically unsettled by the emergence of an enlightened and secular society, Kierkegaard sought to establish an individual religious existence without an intermediary, that is, without the church. Without this mediation, however, the individual has to take refuge in faith: the ultimate justification for God's existence is groundless, and precisely this groundlessness provides the reason for the necessity of a practical leap into faith. In the enlightened world, individual existence is thrown back onto itself. The individual is placed on his or her own, and there is no space for a belief in the existence of God. Only with a leap can the individual enter into a direct, existential relationship with God – only with a leap of faith is there an immediate experience of God's existence.[18]

---

18 Like Lukács, Kierkegaard, in his personal existence, also lived an antinomic life. While Lukács in an "as well as" tried to serve two masters, the party as well as philosophy and literature, Kierkegaard was divided between ethic und aesthetic, lived an "either-or." Both furthermore where interested in the antinomies of modern society on a supra-individual scale, both saw these antinomies as a form of specific modern – religious or social – life,

Heidegger formulated the same mode of existence for an ultimately godless world in which however religious existence can only be experienced *ontologically*. The bourgeois subject is no longer confronted with an uncertain existence of God. Rather, in anticipation of death, the subject is exposed to its own being and must base its existence in the finitude of one's own being. But this being is as such as unexperiencable as one's own death. More over, being, according to Heidegger, is not only not adequately experiencable, also this withdrawn of being is not even known and "forgotten." Instead, the "essent" is taken for the being. Meanwhile although being withdraws itself, this withdraw *is* being insofar as being is, as Heidegger states in his main work, *temporal*.

In Lukács we have both "existentials." What first regards Kierkegaard, the existence of the individual labor commodity is also directly confronted with God. But it is confronted with a God in the sense of "absolute Spirit," a Spirit that received its "socialization" in Marx's critique of capitalist society as well as in the idea of communism. In Lukács's confrontation with this "God," communism occurs through the self-consciousness of this particular commodity, in which the totality and essence of capitalist society and the power of history itself comes into being. Consequently, the labor commodity can, like a worldly God or a materialist Spirit, reflect on its own existence as the essence of the social totality. More than this, it can leap *into* praxis and fulfill history with its own power; history from now on receives its meaning from a collective subject that objectifies itself as the essence of the social totality. The labor commodity can thus reflect the idea of communism directly through its existence, without intermediary, that is, without the church of the working class: the Communist Party. As in Kierkegaard, the proletariat can immediately leap into communism without being represented by a mediator, and as in Kierkegaard's leap of faith, this is no longer a leap of knowledge, but of a practice that is beyond knowledge, namely, a leap into the practice of self-realization that is at the same time the realization of a communist society.

And as in Heidegger's Ontology, this practical self-realization is based on a being that exists primarily as *temporal*. The commodity labor-power is a temporal power as it produces more value in commodities than it needs for its own reproduction and gets as wage, and this difference gets exploited, becomes a quantitative existence in profit, and leads to the self-extension of capitalist reproduction. In short, the commodity labor power can go beyond its own presence. Labor power thus transcends society, and thereby establishes the historical dimension of time; labor-power "ex-ists," a word Heidegger writes with a

---

and for both the solution of this antinomies could only be a practical leap: Kierkegaard into faith, Lukács into communism.

dash to mark the salient and excessive in existence. As the productive power of the social totality and the productive essence of history, labor-power with its self-consciousness could, like a communist God or spirit, calculate with the temporality of its own social being, with its own identity in the finitude of society's existence; through this self-calculation, it can create the (socialist) history into which it would practically enter.

This revolutionizing is possible at any time, independently of empirical social conditions and historical maturity. The revolution occurs solely through the act of self-knowledge of the commodity labor-power. It leaps abruptly into practice, and this practice is transformed into the logic of a self-realization, becoming historical. Or rather it becomes the logic of history itself: with its self-consciousness, the proletariat collectively produces in a reflexive use of time the same history into which it simultaneously is thrown.

That is precisely the connection that Lukács sought for: the connection between epistemology, ontology, and ethics.[19] It can also be added to what first Hegel and then existentialism has been searching for: to overcome the standpoint of the reflecting individual mind by coming already back to it from an absolute Spirit (Hegel), from the faith in God (Kierkegaard), from being (Heidegger), and, in Lukács case, from the identical of subject-object.[20]

5   The Identical Subject–Object of the Capitalist Mode of Production: Capitalist Money

As big as Lukács's idea is, so is its problem. There is a problem with the existential idea of revolutionizing the capitalist existence that regards the critic of society in general and the critic of its mediation through the commodity form in particular, but also the idea of communism. It concerns not only Lukács, but the whole tradition of Western Marxism and Critical Theory right up to the new Marx-readings that started in the 1960s. All share the same blind spot: the

---

19   While the young Lukács brought the three terms epistemology, ontology, and ethics in an existential way together in the three terms history, class, and consciousness, the late Lukács in his ontological writings set them a part in an encyclopaedic, divided way. That is the exciting in the young and the boredom in the late Lukács.

20   The biggest difference between Lukács's existentialism and that of Kierkegaard and – at least the young – Heidegger is that Lukács has to go beyond the individual. The individual commodity labor power has to be brought up to the level of the collective proletariat, and here the argument comes in that finally the party must jump in to take on the form of a supra-individual, collective self-consciousness.

mediatedness by commodity form is a necessary but false semblance produced by the social mediation Lukács bases his idea on.

5.1 Money as the Unconscious Self-consciousness of Social Mediation

The problem of "the ascension" of labor-power as a commodity in Lukács and its "resurrection" in the idea of an almost divine self-realization is that in capitalism, the commodity *already has a kind of self-consciousness*. The society hence already has a place where it gets reflexive. It has a self-consciousness that Lukács does not consider at all, although it is a self-consciousness that puts both the commodity and labor into a relationship of social totality. This self-consciousness is *money*, more precisely, capitalist money.

Marx develops already in the beginning of *Capital* Vol. 1 that money unites the commodity as "form of value" and labor as "substance of value" into one and the same "purely social" relation, the "value relation."[21] Money does this through its three main functions which Marx then in the course of *Capital* Vol. 1 develops as (1) measure of value, (2) means of realization of value and (3) form of capitalist valorization of value. The development turns out that through these functions, money already realizes the social totality and the productive power that lies in the valorization of the labor commodity. Moreover, the capitalist functions of money already provide capitalism with a reflective treatment of this social totality and this productive power. Therefore, in money, society not only has a supra-individual self-consciousness, the society also has the power of an encompassing, total social reflection; just as Hegel developed it for the supra-individual Spirit.

Therefore Lukács's great idea that the productive power of our society becomes aware of itself in the self-consciousness of the labor commodity, and leaps into the praxis of a communist self-realization – this idea is, as it were, withheld in money. This "withholding" has the "ghostly" status of the absolute Spirit in Hegel that Lukács tries to socialize, for the idea of communism in money is present and absent at the same time: the productive power of the valorization of labor and capital is given through the technique of money, but this technique is responsible both for the objective quantitative realization of this productive power *and* its withdrawal.

---

21 See beginning of *Capital*: Karl Marx, *Capital Vol. 1* (Harmondsworth: Penguin, 1978), pp. 125ff. That money sets labor and commodity as form and as substance of value is the outcome of especially the new reading of *Capital* in Germany, meanwhile also called New Marx Reading, which has contributed a critique of all pre-monetary value-theories and of a pre-monetary commodity.

5.2 *Money as the Reflection of the Productive Power by Its Quantification*

To understand how money gives the productive power existence *through* its withdrawal would require a development on the one hand of money's functions and on the other the valorization of labor and capital.[22] Here it must be sufficient to state that money with its functions realizes the productive power of labor and capital by their quantification. Together, these functions of money are the *technique* of how it gives the productive power the formless form of purely quantitative values, thus a purely *negative* being.[23] But money turns this negative being into the *positivity* of decisive magnitudes, and thereby the negativity becomes the productive essence of the capitalist valorization process.[24] So, the valorization of labor and capital on the one hand receive in money an objectively determined quantitative existence. But this existence on the other hand vanishes in the pure validity of money and in the finite values it presents on the side of the relation of commodities.

But still the crucial point is not reached, as in the course of its capital-form, money *itself* is converted into the forms of this valorization. Money is thus not only present in the forms of labor and capital in a speculative way, it also converts the realized magnitudes back into the process they resulted from; Marx formalizes this movement as Money-Commodity-Money with profit (M-C-M').[25] Money thus becomes the technique to measure the productive power of a valorisation in which money itself constantly has to be converted; and through this, money becomes the self-reflection and self-relation of an "automatic subjectivity" (Marx).[26] In short, the whole relation between money and the social relation it quantifies and sets in power should be developed as a *self-measuring process*, starting with the first function of money as measure and ending with its capital-form and the valorisation process of labour and capital

---

22 For the whole development see Frank Engster, *Das Geld als Maß, Mittel und Methode. Das Rechnen mit der Identität der Zeit* (Berlin: Neofelis, 2014).

23 For money, self-consciousness and concept as the same techniques to constitute both objectivity and a reflecting subject see Frank Engster, „Geist, Logik, Kapital und die Technik des Maßes", in *Revista Opinião Filosófica*, Porto Alegre, v. 07; n°. 01 (2016), pp. 136–205.

24 By realising the products of the valorisation process, money like in a reflection and an encompassing social measurement determines and is itself determined by the two elements of commodity production: labour and capital, namely by determining the crucial (average) magnitudes for their further valorisation (for the "socially necessary labour time" Marx, *Capital*, pp. 201, 340ff., for "surplus-value" ibid., p. 339ff., for the "average profit" ibid., pp. 320ff.).

25 Marx, *Capital*, pp. 247ff.

26 Ibid., p. 255.

it realises by the values of its results, i.e. the commodities – realising the results of a valorisation money itself constantly gets converted into.

Therefore, if there exists a subject that has to reflect social relations as properties of commodities and that have to realize in their relation a social objectivity that it itself realizes, then this subject is not, at least not at first, the particular commodity labor power, but the universal commodity money. Lukács's aim to bring the labor power to the standpoint of an "identical subject-object of history" is an attempt to bring the "particular commodity" labor power to the standpoint that the universal and at once unique commodity money in capitalist society already takes on, namely the standpoint of an ideal unit that becomes the measure of value, the means of its realization and the form of its valorization. To realize Lukács's idea of a communist revolution: the total social self-realization of the proletariat, the commodity labor-power would have to internalize the social technique that money does so that the proletariat can mediate and valorize immediately itself.

5.3 *Quantifying Time: Money as the Identical Subject-Object of History*

But as much as money gives quantitative form to productive power and constitutes social objectivity, and as much as it transforms itself into these two forms of productive valorization, the productive power in money is literally *unavailable*. The productive power of the capitalist mode of production and the encompassing, overarching character of its social totality is only given by money's functions, it is present only in quantitative magnitudes, and it remains in power only in money's capital movement. The same money that gives productive power and social totality a form, withdraws this power and this totality in the formless form of pure quantitative validity. The productive power and totality of capitalist society passes over in money purely quantitatively, just like the negative essence of a supra-individual, ideal Spirit.

With the quantitative presence that money gives, we also finally have the identical subject-object or the identity as such. Money, by constituting social objectivity in quantifying social relations, transferring these quanta and by converting them again and again in the forms of their valorization – money becomes the identical of capitalist society, but this identical is neither subjective nor objective. It has no substance at all, as it is *temporal*: time. Time is "the identical" – or the identity as such – because by exposing labor and capital to a quantification money sets free an "economy of time" (Marx), and this economy of time enters always already in determined quanta, making these quanta the identical quality or the quality of identity itself. To show this economy of time, Marx explicitly translates labor and capital into two time relations. The first is past and present labor-time, embodied in labor and capital, and this relation between the past and the present of our society sets in power a second relation, that between "necessary" and "surplus labor-time."[27] Or rather it is not Marx who converts quantitative relations in these two time relations. He rather shows that money's functions do so; yet, money *is* this conversion or translation.[28] It not only translates time relations in quantitative relations, with that it also allows to calculate with the identity of time. It not only translates time relations in quantitative relations, with that it also allows to calculate with the identity of time. This calculation is on the side of the values money realizes, mediates and converts with quantitative precision, like in mathematics. But on the other hand, the calculation has a speculative character, as all subjects in capitalist society have to calculate in, so to speak, second order with a calculation that money does for them, for their social totality – the calculation with the identity of time again is a withdrawal which at once seems to withhold the idea of communism.

By this conversion of time relations into quantitative relations and vice versa, the time money quantifies and stands for becomes *history*, making money the identical subject-object of *history*. This is because money, by quantifying social relations, not only realizes time as the identical quality of capitalist society in its totality, it also converts what seems to be a natural-physical, ahistorical time into historical time. It is as if time enters into its own historical being: What seems to be a natural time which by money becomes the measure for the valorisation and its productivity enters always already quantified as a *socialized* time into society, becoming its historical time. And precisely this passage between an ahistorical time which is the universal measure of the productive power of the capitalist society in its totality and the historical time of this social totality is what money stands for. Money stands as a measure of value for an ahistorical, "timeless" time, but this time gets by the measured valorisation presented as a socialised time. Money not only presents this socialised time, it also holds it in time identical. The productive power of labor and capital, hence of the relation of past and present and of necessary and surplus labor-time time, remains in power because money, by realizing the results of these

---

27 Marx, *Capital*, pp. 448ff.
28 There have been not only several attempts to connect the Spirit in Hegel with capital in Marx, but also to decipher the connection between capital and time and cause the famous term "time is money," e.g. Jacques Derrida, Moishe Postone, Daniel Bensaid, Stavros Tombazos, Peter Osborne, David Harvey, Massimiliano Tomba, Hartmut Rosa, Jonathan Martineau and others. However, the connection was mostly determined in an "exoteric" way, while the "esoteric" connection between money and time in my view has to be searched in quantification and measurement, see Engster, *Das Geld als Maß, Mittel und Methode*, pp. 647ff.

time-relations, holds its power in specific quanta in time and space identical and timeless. Moreover, money in its capital-form also converts time-relations which are stored by values back into the forms of labor and capital and temporalizes these time-relations it holds quantitatively identical.

Money thereby becomes the passage between past and future, being their presence and presentation. The same quantification that converts physical-natural time into socialized time and vice versa, the same quantifaction also actualizes and presents the productive power of the *past* valorisation and converts them into the elements of the *future* valorisation. Moreover, money thereby determines from the past valorization of labor and capital, the average magnitudes that become decisive for their further productive valorization, hence for the reproduction of labor and capital itself, just as if the turn into quantitative existence is an overarching social (self-) reflection by a (self-) measurement of the valorization process.

If there exists something like a self-consciousness for the productive power of the particular commodity labor power, a self-consciosness that realizes this power in all its alienation and in all its reificated forms of capital and commodities, then this self-consiousness is money. And if there exists in capitalism a fissured subject of social totality, an "identical subject-object of history" that is alienated from its own social determination and productive power, one that exists only through its reification in the forms of labor and capital and alienation in history, then this subject-object is money in its capital-form. Only in money we have a subject that by the ideal value unit it stands for and with the magnitudes it realizes calculates with its own social identity, opening with this identity an economy of time that becomes social history. It is therefore, on the one hand, too quick to trace the idea of communism to the social determination and productive power of labor, thus to the subject of labor, *without* taking into account that the productive power and the social determination of labor can only be achieved through their mediation and valorization by the technique of money. On the other hand, Lukács's idea of communism itself depends on the reification that money produces when it makes the productive power appear as if it is a property of labor. However, only in money in its capitalist form does the labor commodity have its own self-consciousness and the form of its self-reflection. The identical subject-object of history should be sought here, in the capital-form of money rather then in the commodity form of labor – and with it the blind spot in Lukács's idea of communism.

PART 4

Social and Political Interventions in the Idea of Reification: Gender, Race, Neoliberalism, and Populism

∴

CHAPTER 11

The Revolutionary Subject in Lukács and Feminist Standpoint Theory: Dilaceration and Emancipatory Interest

Mariana Teixeira

> ...and the totality, in its highest vitality, is only possible through a reconstitution out of the highest separation.
> G.W.F. Hegel, *Differenzschrift*, in *Werke*, 20 vols. (Frankfurt am Main: Suhrkamp, 1970), 2:21–22.

Georg Lukács's theory of reification, with its original combination of Weberian and Simmelian themes within a Hegelian-Marxist framework, has had an incredibly fertile influence on 20th century social philosophy[1] – including numerous renowned philosophers, literature scholars, and social theorists, as well as collective theoretical enterprises such as the Praxis and Budapest Schools, the Situationist International, and Critical Theory. Yet, in his essay on "*History and Class Consciousness* as an 'Unfinished Project,'" Fredric Jameson provocatively suggests that "the most authentic descendency of Lukács's thinking is to be found, not among the Marxists, but within a certain feminism, where the unique conceptual move of *History and Class Consciousness* has been appropriated for a whole program, now renamed (after Lukács's own usage) standpoint theory."[2] Jameson makes reference to the groundbreaking works of Nancy Hartsock, Sandra Harding, and Alison Jaggar – and Dorothy

---

1 This chapter is a revised and expanded version of papers presented at the conference "The Legacy of Georg Lukács" (Budapest, April 2017) and the "11th International Critical Theory Conference" (Rome, May 2018). I would like to thank Michael Thompson and János Kelemen for organizing the conference in Budapest and Richard Westermann for putting the panel on Lukács together at the Rome conference, as well as the participants of both events who discussed the ideas presented here. This chapter has also benefited from many years of instructive exchanges with Marcos Nobre and from the discussions held by the Women's Research Group of the Brazilian Center for Analysis and Planning. Finally, my thanks to Greg Zucker for the invitation to contribute to this volume and for the patience during the production of the manuscript.

2 Fredric Jameson, "*History and Class Consciousness* as an 'Unfinished Project,'" *Rethinking Marxism: A Journal of Economics, Culture & Society* 1, No. 1 (1988): 63–64.

Smith could very well be added to this list.[3] Regardless of the adequacy of Jameson's unreserved claim about "authentic descendency," the affinity of this ongoing project to Lukács's Marxism is remarkable: the idea that the proletariat might achieve a distinctive, and potentially privileged, standpoint that allows (and even compels) it to grasp capitalist society in its totality has a parallel in the affirmation made by feminist standpoint theorists that women might also attain a privileged perspective on the dynamics of patriarchal societies.

Although the Lukácsian and Marxian lineage of feminist standpoint theory is usually alluded to, this relationship is often taken for granted and not further problematized. Indeed, some of the proponents of this paradigm themselves do not give a detailed account of their (certainly not seamless) connection to Marxism in general, and Lukács in particular.[4] In this chapter, I address two prominent early versions of feminist standpoint theory, namely, those of Nancy Hartsock and Dorothy Smith, with the aim of exploring both the connections and the contrasts to Lukács's theory regarding their accounts of the experiences of "the revolutionary subject" – the proletariat, women. By addressing the affinities between feminist standpoint theory and Lukács's Marxism, the purpose of this chapter is not to legitimate the former based on its relatedness to the latter, but rather, in a sense, the opposite: to argue that Lukács's theory of reification is still relevant not least because it provides a theoretical framework that is fruitful for contemporary debates within feminism and critical thought more generally.

It might seem odd to address, in order to discuss Lukács's importance for the present, texts that were first published more than thirty years ago – feminist standpoint theories have their origins in debates within academia and women's social movements which date back to the 1970s and 1980s. Its current

3   Cf. Nancy Hartsock, *Money, Sex and Power* (New York: Longman, 1983), Sandra Harding, *The Science Question in Feminism* (Ithaca, NY: Cornell University Press, 1986), Alison M. Jaggar, *Feminist Politics and Human Nature* (Totowa, NJ: Rowman and Allanheld, 1983), and Dorothy Smith, *The Everyday World as Problematic: A Feminist Sociology* (Boston: Northeastern University Press, 1987).

4   Jameson equally refrains from further exploring this connection in his essay. Two tentative exceptions, which nonetheless put more emphasis on the divergences between Lukács and feminist standpoint theories, are: W. Scott Cameron "The Genesis and Justification of Feminist Standpoint Theory in Hegel and Lukács," *Dialogue and Universalism*, No. 3–4 (2005): 19–41, and Bob Ellis and Rodney Fopp, "The Origins of Standpoint Epistemologies: Feminism, Marx and Lukács," *TASA 2001 Conference*, The University of Sydney, 13–15 December 2001. Andrew Feenberg presents a brief, most interesting analysis – but focusing on the specific case of Sandra Harding's discussion of the politics of science – in "On Bridging the Gap between Science and Technology Studies: Sandra Harding's *Is Science Multicultural?*," *Science, Technology, & Human Values* 24, No. 4 (1999): 483–494.

relevance is attested, however, by the role played by its central concern – i.e., the material conditioning of knowledge and the cognitive potentiality of socially subjugated standpoints – in contemporary scholarly discussions on epistemic injustice and ignorance[5] as well as in the articulation of collective action against oppression.[6] It should be noted, moreover, that such debates have surpassed the limits of academia and organized social movements, reaching the broader public sphere.[7]

What could Lukács's contribution to such debates be? It is noteworthy that feminist standpoint theory (especially in the academic setting) has gradually been focusing less on women's subjugation and struggles and more on the discussion about the validity of truth claims, which is often connected to embracing a postmodern view to the detriment of the dialectical tradition that has its origins in Hegel, Marx, and Lukács.[8] By discussing the works of Hartsock and Smith and their connection to Lukács's theory of reification, this paper aims at countering the tendency to reduce standpoint theory to a purely epistemological debate centered on discourse. Finally, a further reason to discuss these founding texts of feminist standpoint theory is an effort to shift the discussion back to the (politically and epistemologically) *enabling* features of subjugated

---

5   Cf., among many others, Boaventura Sousa Santos, *Epistemologies of the South: Justice against Epistemicide* (New York: Routledge, 2016), José Medina, *The Epistemology of Resistance: Gender and Racial Oppression, Epistemic Injustice, and Resistant Imaginations* (Oxford: Oxford University Press, 2012), Shannon Sullivan and Nancy Tuana, eds., *Race and Epistemologies of Ignorance* (New York: SUNY Press, 2007), and Ian James Kidd, José Medina, and Gaile Pohlhaus, eds., *The Routledge Handbook of Epistemic Injustice* (New York: Routledge, 2017), with contributions by Linda Martín Alcoff, Charles W. Mills, Miranda Fricker, Patricia Hill Collins, Amy Allen, Sally Haslanger et al.
6   Consider, for example, the controversies within social movements around the possibility of allyship between deprived and privileged subjects, or the question of empowerment (as opposed to representation) of victims of sexism, racism, homophobia, and other forms of oppression.
7   This can be seen, for example, in the dissemination bolstered by social media of neologisms such as *mansplaining*, *manterrupting* and *bropriation*, all of which allude to the necessity of legitimating women's voice as conveyors of knowledge.
8   Cf. Cynthia Cockburn, "Standpoint Theory," in *Marxism and Feminism*, ed. Shahrzad Mojab (London: Zed Books, 2015), 342–343. A key figure in this movement is Donna Haraway and her influential essay "Situated Knowledges: The Science Question in Feminism and the Privilege of Partial Perspective," *Feminist Studies* 14, No. 3 (1988): 575–599. For a favorable account of the transition from (dialectical) standpoint theory to (postmodern) situated knowledge, cf. Fernando Garcia J. Selgas, "Feminist Epistemologies for Critical Social Theory: From Standpoint Theory to Situated Knowledge," in *The Feminist Standpoint Theory Reader: Intellectual and Political Controversies*, ed. Sandra Harding (New York and London: Routledge, 2004), 293–308.

standpoints, in contrast to contemporary studies in epistemic injustice that see only the *disabling* consequences of oppression.[9]

I begin in Section 1 by presenting Nancy Hartsock's conception of standpoint theory and discussing some problematic features of her proposal, especially the idealization of women's standpoint as free from dichotomies. In Section 2, I argue that looking back at Lukács's theory of reification and his phenomenology of the dilacerated subject might contribute to addressing such difficulties. I turn then in Section 3 to Dorothy Smith and argue that her seminal essay on women's experience of disjunction and bifurcated consciousness as the starting point of a critical sociology shares with Lukács the key feature that enables her to avoid the complications identified in Hartsock's work: the connection between dilaceration and emancipatory interest.

1   Hartsock: the Feminist Standpoint as Free from Dichotomies

In a famous essay proposing a specifically feminist historical materialism, Hartsock systematizes five claims that characterize, for her, both Marxist and feminist standpoint theories.[10] The *first claim* asserts that material life both structures and sets limits on the understanding of social relations, echoing Lukács's view that forms of knowledge and scientific methods are always conditioned by the social being of a class. Hence, Hartsock sets off from the idea she draws from Marx and Lukács that "epistemology grows in a complex and contradictory way from material life,"[11] so that "each division of labor, whether by gender or class, can be expected to have consequences for knowledge."[12] *Secondly*, Hartsock claims that the vision of groups whose material life is structured in fundamentally opposing ways will represent an inversion of one another, and in systems of domination the vision available to the rulers will be both partial and perverse. Among the consequences that the division of labor has for knowledge, therefore, Hartsock stresses that, "there are some perspectives on society from which, however well-intentioned one may be, the real relations of humans with each other and with the natural world are not

---

9   Cf. Miranda Fricker, *Epistemic Injustice: Power and the Ethics of Knowing* (Oxford: Oxford University Press, 2007).
10 Nancy Hartsock, "The Feminist Standpoint: Developing the Ground for a Specifically Feminist Historical Materialism," in *Discovering Reality*, ed. Sandra Harding and Merrill B. Hintikka (Dordrecht: D. Reidel, 1983), p. 285.
11 Ibid.
12 Ibid., p. 286.

visible."[13] Like the position of the proletariat in the production process grants it a structurally distinct experience when compared to that of the capitalist, women's experiences differ structurally from those of men, and thus "like the lives of proletarians according to Marxian theory, women's lives make available a particular and privileged vantage point on male supremacy, a vantage point which can ground a powerful critique of the phallocratic institutions and ideology which constitute the capitalist form of patriarchy."[14] Just as the standpoint of the proletariat enables the access "beneath bourgeois ideology, so a feminist standpoint can allow us to understand patriarchal institutions and ideologies as perverse inversions of more humane social relations."[15] *Thirdly*, the vision of the rulers structures the material relations in which all parties take part, and therefore cannot be dismissed as merely false. Like Lukács, Hartsock does not take the dominant – be it bourgeois or masculinist – mode of thought as merely ideology, in the sense of false, illusory consciousness with no real connection to the concrete social relations at the basis of capitalist and patriarchal societies. The dominant vision of the world is an effective force that shapes the world in which everyone – capitalists and proletarians, men and women – must participate. *Fourthly*, and in consequence, the vision available to the oppressed group must be struggled for and represents an achievement which requires both theoretical and political activity. Again in a way similar to Lukács, who talks about the standpoint of the *proletariat* and not about the sum of the perspectives of the individual proletarians,[16] Hartsock argues that the actual vision of women should not be taken at face value. The properly *feminist* standpoint is not a given, but rather a result of a laborious effort to overcome the dominant vision in which women are socialized and compelled to live, work, and understand the world. Finally, the *fifth claim* states that the engaged vision from the standpoint of the oppressed exposes the real relations among human beings as inhuman, and thus points to a liberation beyond the status quo.

Echoing Lukács's argument about Orthodox Marxism,[17] Hartsock states that these meta-theoretical claims are more helpful to feminists than Marx's actual

---

13   Ibid., p. 285.
14   Ibid., p. 284.
15   Ibid.
16   Cf. the differentiation between imputed (*zugerechnet*) and empirical class consciousness in Georg Lukács, "Class Consciousness," in *History and Class Consciousness: Studies in Marxist Dialectics*, trans. Rodney Livingstone (Cambridge, Mass.: The MIT Press, 1971 [1923]), 46–82.
17   Lukács, "What is Orthodox Marxism?," in *History and Class Consciousness*, 1–26.

critique of capitalism.[18] In spite of setting off from Marx's theory, then, Hartsock goes on to characterize women's position in patriarchal societies in a way that is absent from Marx's own account and its Lukácsian version.[19]

From this brief reconstruction, it appears that Hartsock's argument for the epistemic priority of the standpoint of women – or, as she puts it in accordance with the fourth claim just mentioned, the *feminist* standpoint – rests on the idea that any socially dominated group is in a potentially advantaged position to come to grasp the relations of domination within unequal societies. That is how Jameson understands the project of standpoint theory as a whole: "The presupposition is that, owing to its structural situation in the social order and to the specific forms of oppression and exploitation unique to that situation, each group lives the world in a phenomenologically specific way that allows it to see, or better still, that makes it unavoidable for that group to see and to know, features of the world that remain obscure, invisible, or merely occasional and secondary for other groups."[20]

If that is the case, that is, if we take into account solely those five claims in their abstract formulation, it might be possible to defend Hartsock against the objections of *essentialization and exclusion* often directed to feminist standpoint theory. Hartsock's claims can be said to escape the objection of essentialization of identities insofar as they are general enough not to hypostasize any concrete characteristics of particular groups. Rather than positively, the oppressed groups whose standpoint might allow for a more penetrating insight

---

18   Cf. the following passage of Lukács's essay: "Let us assume for the sake of argument that recent research had disproved once and for all every one of Marx's individual theses. Even if this were to be proved, every serious 'orthodox' Marxist would still be able to accept all such modern findings without reservation and hence dismiss all of Marx's theses *in toto* – without having to renounce his orthodoxy for a single moment. Orthodox Marxism, therefore, does not imply the uncritical acceptance of the results of Marx's investigations. It is not the 'belief' in this or that thesis, nor the exegesis of a 'sacred' book. On the contrary, orthodoxy refers exclusively to *method*" – namely, dialectical materialism (ibid., p. 1). The centrality of the method is stressed by Hartsock in other places as well, for example: "At bottom feminism is a mode of analysis, a method of approaching life and politics, rather than a set of political conclusions about the oppression of women," Nancy Hartsock, "Fundamental Feminism: Prospect and Perspective," in *Building Feminist Theory*, ed. Charlotte Bunch (New York: Longman, 1981), p. 35.

19   Hartsock goes so far as to claim that "capitalism is an outgrowth of male dominance, rather than vice versa" (Hartsock, "The Feminist Standpoint," p. 290). The discussion about the ultimate priority of class or other kinds of social relations – what Jameson rightly calls "an essentially metaphysical polemic" (Jameson, "*History and Class Consciousness* as an 'Unfinished Project,'" p. 71) – does not take us very far in our purposes and will not be addressed here.

20   Jameson, "*History and Class Consciousness* as an 'Unfinished Project,'" p. 65.

into the exercise of power and social domination are negatively defined, precisely as those who are somehow in the disadvantaged side of a given set of unequal social relations. To the extent that it does not positively and essentially posit any social identity as its bearer, moreover, standpoint theory as presented in Hartsock's five claims cannot be considered exclusionary. If we interpret it as suggested by Jameson, hence, standpoint theory can be appropriated by differently excluded and oppressed social groups – besides (white, middle-class, heterosexual, able-bodied, cis-) women.

In the remainder of her essay, however, Hartsock does not actually endorse this more general take on standpoint theory, for she does not favor the experience of any oppressed, explored or degraded social group. She gives priority, rather, only to a specific set of activities and experiences associated (biologically or historically) with women, especially those connected to childbearing and childrearing. The feminist standpoint that arises from such experiences is, for her, "an important epistemological tool for understanding and opposing *all forms of domination*,"[21] not just patriarchy. What, then, can be said to give this position its special standing?

Women have, according to Hartsock, a double contribution to subsistence in capitalism: they produce both commodities *and* human beings: "Whether or not all of us do both, women as a sex are institutionally responsible for producing both goods and human beings and all women are forced to become the kinds of people who can do both."[22] As a consequence, the feminist take on the world is similar to the class consciousness of the proletariat because both are, for Hartsock, more closely connected to the materiality or the concreteness of the natural and social worlds than the position of the male and the capitalist. This materiality allows for a perspective we can call, even though Hartsock does not invoke Lukács's terminology at this point, *non-reified*: "Women and workers inhabit a world in which the emphasis is on change rather than stasis, a world characterized by interaction with natural substances rather than separation from nature, a world in which quality is more important than quantity."[23] In producing socially defined goods, both women and workers experience a sort of unification of mind and body.[24] The similarities to Lukács's critique of reification are visible: like Lukács, Hartsock criticizes the quantification of things and people, the abstraction of their concrete qualities, and the over-instrumentalization in one's relationships to objects and other subjects.

---

21 Hartsock, "The Feminist Standpoint," p. 283 (my emphasis).
22 Ibid., p. 291.
23 Ibid., p. 290.
24 Ibid., p. 292.

Hartsock's characterization of "abstract masculinity" echoes Lukács's critique of the antinomies of bourgeois thought: abstract masculinity and phallocentric social theory are marked by dualisms like "abstract/concrete, mind/body, culture/nature, ideal/real, stasis/change [...] along with the dominance of one side of the dichotomy over the other."[25]

Yet, however close the experience of workers and women might be, there are, for Hartsock, important differences. She claims that the feminist standpoint is related to the proletarian standpoint, but deeper going[26] – and the main reason for that can be traced back to the fact that "a larger proportion of women's labor time is devoted to the production of use-values than men's. Only some of the goods women produce are commodities (however much they live in a society structured by commodity production and exchange)."[27] For Hartsock, "the female experience in bearing and rearing children involves a unity of mind and body more profound than is possible in the worker's instrumental activity."[28] Relying on the idea, drawn from Marx's *1844 Manuscripts*, that sensuous activity is the very fabric of life itself, Hartsock considers that "the vantage point available to women on the basis of their contribution to subsistence represents an intensification and deepening of the materialist world view and consciousness available to the producers of commodities in capitalism, an intensification of class consciousness."[29]

Differently from Lukács, hence, for whom reification penetrates the consciousness of every member of capitalist societies, Hartsock's argument seems to be precisely that women's consciousness and experience are *not* reified. These are taken as "dialectical" and thus as avoiding the antinomies of masculinist thought:

> The female construction of self in relation to others leads in an opposite direction – toward opposition to dualisms of any sort, valuation of concrete, everyday life, sense of a variety of connectednesses and continuities both with other persons and with the natural world. If material life structures consciousness, women's relationally defined existence, bodily

---

25   Ibid., p. 297.
26   Ibid., p. 290.
27   Ibid., p. 292. Her explanation of the differences in the lived experience of men and women relies not only on an account of the sexual division of labor but also, on a prior level, on the distinct impact on boys and girls of their being socialized by their mothers, as was argued by authors in the psychoanalytic strand of object-relations theory (Jane Flax and Nancy Chodorow).
28   Ibid., p. 294.
29   Ibid., p. 292.

experience of boundary challenges, and activity of transforming both physical objects and human beings must be expected to result in a world view to which dichotomies are foreign.[30]

Thus, while Hartsock's five claims for a feminist standpoint theory seem able to escape the criticisms of essentialism and exclusion, her ontological account of the priority of women's activities in the household, childbearing, and childrearing proves less able to do so. To the extent that she equates care and subsistence work with women's activities, and these activities with a non-reified, quasi emancipated sensuous praxis, Hartsock indeed (1) ascribes a series of positively formulated, a-historical characteristics to women, defining this group in an essentializing fashion; and in so doing she (2) excludes from the feminist standpoint all those who, regardless of whether they consider themselves as women or not, do not perform the specific activities of the mother and/or the housewife. These important points have been convincingly made by other authors,[31] and specially by third wave feminists,[32] so I will now focus on a less discussed but also problematic aspect of Hartsock's early proposal of standpoint theory.

In Hartsock's view, because women's consciousness is not reified, emancipation would be a matter of redefining and restructuring the whole of society on the basis of women's material activity. The feminist standpoint would only need to be generalized to the social system as a whole in order to allow for the creation of "a fully human community, a community structured by connection rather than separation and opposition."[33] But if women's material activity is a

---

30 Ibid., p. 298.
31 Nadine Changfoot, for example, highlights not only the exclusionary essentialization of the feminine identity in Hartsock's work, whereby a woman is seen as "an able-bodied, nurturing, heterosexual, and Euro-influenced wife and mother," but the essentialization of men's identity as well, whereby men are the bearers of "abstract masculinity." Cf. Nadine Changfoot, "Feminist Standpoint Theory, Hegel and the Dialectical Self: Shifting the Foundations," *Philosophy & Social Criticism* 30, No. 4 (2004): 477–502.
32 Third wave feminists often point out the need to account for the intersectionality of different kinds of oppression, criticizing the second wave tendency to generalize the experience of privileged women and thereby to obscure the specificity of working class women, women of color, etc. Hartsock herself later acknowledges the exclusionary aspect of her original proposal: "[...] I committed an error similar to that of Marx. While he made no theoretical space for any oppression other than class, by following his lead I failed to allow for the importance of differences among women and differences among other various groups – power differences all." Nancy Hartsock, "Comment on Hekman's 'Truth and Method: Feminist Standpoint Theory Revisited:' Truth or Justice?" *Signs* 22, No. 2 (1997): 368.
33 Hartsock, "The Feminist Standpoint," p. 305.

model on which to build an emancipated, non-reified society, Hartsock argues not for overcoming (in the sense of *aufheben*) patriarchal capitalism, but rather negating it somewhat abstractly, from the outside. Instead of dissolving the dichotomies between abstract and concrete, ideal and real, stasis and change, etc., Hartsock limits herself to shifting the balance by means of ascribing to the second element of each pair an emancipatory potential, thus leaving the dichotomies themselves untouched. She therefore recreates precisely what she had been criticizing in abstract masculinity: a dichotomy with no mediation between the poles.

Hartsock's characterization of women's experience is problematic, thus, not only because it excludes groups of people from her analysis, but also because it places women outside history, and significantly outside capitalism, so that their activities are conceived as a sort of pre-capitalist remainder within a capitalist society.[34] Her emphasis on natural, organic processes bears resemblance to a sort of anti-capitalism with romantic undertones and potentially reactionary implications, something Marx and Lukács had been very cautious about – both favor an immanent critique or a determinate negation of capitalist society over an external (either utopian or nostalgic) critique.[35] This has important consequences for Hartsock's fourth claim for a standpoint theory, i.e., that the vision available to the oppressed group is not a given and must rather be struggled for. For Lukács, on the one hand, the achievement of standpoint of the proletariat would transform capitalist social relations – and eventually lead to a classless society, the abolition of the proletariat and of the reified labor it carries out in capitalism. For Hartsock, by contrast, as we can now see, the struggle for the feminist standpoint does not mean for women much more than acknowledging the emancipatory potential of the activities they already carry out in the home. This would not lead to an essential transformation in their practice, but only its universalization for every member of society.

The third claim also assumes a different meaning once Hartsock develops her concrete analysis of women's lived experience. This claim stated that the vision of the rulers structures the material relations in which all parties take part, and therefore cannot be dismissed as merely false. But Hartsock now seems to take the masculinist mode of thought, with its dichotomies and

---

34 This tendency can also be found in other strands of the women's movement. Cf., for example, the claim for a *subsistence perspective* in Maria Mies and Vandana Shiva, *Ecofeminism* (London: Zed Books, 1993).

35 Lukács does draw on the romantic critique of capitalism and modern society present in German classical sociology; instead of mourning a lost unity, however, Lukács articulates this critique in such a way as to open a space, within the present, for the possibility of a new, differentiated unity.

abstractness, as an ideology in a rather straightforward sense, as a false take on the world that should be dispensed with. It is hard to envision, in Hartsock's text, how the dominant ideology could have a truth content – in the sense that "the 'false' is at the same time as 'false' and 'non-false' a moment of the 'true.'"[36]

Furthermore, taking women's everyday experience as non-reified in character makes it difficult for Hartsock to explain why women rebel against their situation in patriarchal society, or why they should do so. Whereas Lukács considers that the proletarian is torn apart by reification and, thus, for him "to become aware of the dialectical nature of its existence is a matter of life and death,"[37] Hartsock does not address the kind of negative experiences constitutive of women's practices that compel them to grasp their own situation and to struggle against it. In a nutshell: there is no account of the genesis of women's emancipatory interest in overthrowing patriarchy. With regard to these issues, looking back at Lukács's account of reification and class consciousness can offer some valuable insights.

2   Lukács: Dilaceration and the Standpoint of the Proletariat

Lukács divides the central essay of *History and Class Consciousness* in three parts: "The phenomenon of reification," "The antinomies of bourgeois thought," and "The standpoint of the proletariat." In the first part, he argues for the effectiveness of reification in the immediate reality of proletarians and capitalists. Following Marx, however, Lukács also argues that each class experiences reification in a specific way. Thus, in the second part, he explores how bourgeois thought has proven unable to raise reification to consciousness without crystallizing and eternalizing it; and in the last part he indicates the proletariat's possibility (and necessity) of both grasping reification in theory and overcoming it in practice.

(1) As a historical phenomenon, reification appears for Lukács with modern capitalism, when the exchange of commodities becomes the form par excellence of the metabolism between human beings; when objects are produced primarily to be exchanged, not consumed. The general pre-eminence of exchange-value, to the detriment of the use-value of objects, manifests itself in the pre-eminence of the abstract-formal aspect of things to the detriment of their concrete-qualitative content. The abstraction of *human labor* is vital in

---

36   Lukács, *History and Class Consciousness*, p. xlvii (translation amended).
37   Lukács, "Reification and the Consciousness of the Proletariat," in *History and Class Consciousness*, p. 164.

this process: the commodity-form equates and exchanges qualitatively different things, which can only occur by means of the abstraction of their qualities and particular content, and the concrete particular content of objects produced as commodities is the concrete, particular, qualitative human labor that creates them. In this way, abstract, comparable, calculable labor prevails over concrete, empirical, unique human labor.

This description is strongly indebted to the classical Marxian characterization of commodity fetishism. But since "Marx's chief work breaks off just as he is about to embark on the definition of class,"[38] one of Lukács's specific contributions consists precisely in exploring the subjective consequences of the fact that human labor also enters the market as a commodity to be owned, bought and sold – like any other. For Lukács, the worker who objectifies his labor-power into something opposed to his total personhood appears as "a mechanical part incorporated into a mechanical system."[39] This phenomenon is intensified with the increasing rationalization of the division of labor, which obeys the principle of calculability; and it affects both the subject and object of the production of commodities, because the tearing apart of the object of production means necessarily the tearing apart of the producer.[40]

On the side of the *object*, the calculability of work activities implies that the rational-calculatory breakdown of the work process "destroys the organic necessity with which inter-related special operations are unified in the end-product,"[41] so that the work process and its object are torn apart into independent calculable units. On the side of the *subject*, Lukács shows how the worker is torn apart not only from the product of his work and from his own work activities, but also from the community of social relations he belongs to and, ultimately, from and within himself: "With the modern 'psychological' breaking down of the work-process (in Taylorism) this rational mechanization extends right into the worker's 'soul': even his psychological attributes are separated from his total personality and placed in opposition to it."[42]

---

38   Ibid., p. 46.
39   Ibid., p. 89.
40   An observation should be made about the translation of *zerreißen* and similar terms employed by Lukács, such as *zerstückeln, zersetzen, zerfallen, zerspalten,* and *auseinanderreißen*. In several occasions, the English translation underplays the negative, detrimental, and often violent character present in these and other German terms. The clearest example of this is the common translation of *Zerrissenheit* or *Zerreißen* into "fragmentation," which conceals the destructive tearing apart at work in Lukács's concept of reification. For this reason, I use the terms "dilaceration," "tearing apart" or "split" instead of "fragmentation."
41   Ibid.
42   Ibid., p. 88 (translation amended).

It should be noted that, according to Lukács's approach, reification is a phenomenon that affects society as a whole: just as the commodity-form transforms every object destined to the satisfaction of human needs into objects to be exchanged, "there is no natural form in which human relations can be cast, no way in which man can bring his physical and psychic 'qualities' into play without their being subjected increasingly to this reifying process."[43] No class nor individual can escape it, and no social sphere is immune to it.

Reification encompasses, therefore, the production of knowledge. Lukács addresses the cases of Political Economy, Law, and Philosophy to show how science, divided into specialized systems that are formally closed and governed by partial laws, cannot grasp the material substratum of its own object, creating methodological barriers that it cannot overcome. Philosophy, for example, in the context of a reified and reifying society where every image of the totality is lost, is unable to articulate the other sciences organically, thus limiting itself to justifying the existence and validity of each of them separately.

(2) In the second part of his essay, Lukács examines modern rationalism, culminating in classical German philosophy, and argues that the antinomies of bourgeois thought are expressed in the clearest, most refined, and sincere way in the philosophy of Kant, Lukács's main interlocutor in this second part. Instead of trying to conceal the antinomies that necessarily arose from his critical philosophy, Kant radically exposed their insolubility. The oppositions between subject and object, freedom and necessity, individual and society, form and content, is and ought, phenomenon and thing-in-itself, etc., are hence brought to consciousness, but not so that they can be overcome – on the contrary, they are crystallized into rigid dichotomies. Without the appropriate mediations, this mode of thought cannot explain transformation and change.

(3) Up to this point, only the seemingly unlimited pervasiveness of reification has been stressed. Had Lukács finished his essay at this point, his analysis would hardly differ from the analyses carried out by "bourgeois" thinkers who were also concerned with the negative effects of the phenomenon of reification in modern capitalist societies, like (to use Lukács's own examples) Carlyle and Sismondi. But Lukács's critical perspective impels him to go beyond a mere diagnosis of the present situation, to look for the emancipatory breaches and counter-tendencies immanent to his own diagnosis – and that is when the standpoint of the proletariat comes into view.

Although reification affects everyone in modern capitalist societies, members of the working class experience it in a much more acute way: "The forms in which it [the proletariat] exists are – as we demonstrated in Section I – the

---

43   Ibid., p. 100.

repositories of reification in its acutest and direst form and they issue in the most extreme dehumanisation."[44] Lukács then quotes the following excerpt from Marx's *The Holy Family*:

> "The property-owning class and the class of the proletariat represent the same human self-alienation. But the former feels at home in this self-alienation and feels itself confirmed by it; it recognizes alienation as its own instrument and in it it possesses the semblance of a human existence. The latter feels itself destroyed by this alienation and sees in it its own impotence and the reality of an inhuman existence."[45]

Members of the capitalist class do not experience this dilaceration within themselves: their reified situation appears not as passivity, but as activity; they seem to be the active embodiments and agents of the reified reality of capitalism.[46] The position of the bourgeois is unproblematic and materially comfortable, which makes it unlikely for him to view the established social conditions as questionable in any way, so that "[t]his illusion blinds him to the true state of affairs."[47] Unveiling the mediations immanent to reification would reveal tendencies towards the abolition of capitalism "and so for the bourgeoisie to become conscious of them would be tantamount to suicide."[48]

The proletarian, on the other hand, does not have this option: "the worker, who is denied the scope for such illusory activity, perceives the split in his being preserved in the brutal form of what is, in its whole tendency, a slavery without limits."[49] Workers experience themselves as objects in spite of the fact that they are actually the ones transforming the world through their work, and as a consequence they are split or torn apart in the innermost layers of their physical and psychic being.[50] Hence, the proletarian has in himself both sides, he is a subject and an object at the same time. The standpoint of the proletariat is the standpoint of the dilacerated subject, one that has a part of himself as an other within – and this other is not a mere object, as opposed to subject, but a *commodified* object, an object to be sold according to its exchange-value, rather than its concrete, particular qualities.

---

44 Ibid., p. 149.
45 Marx quoted in ibid.
46 Ibid., p. 181.
47 Ibid., p. 166.
48 Ibid., p. 181.
49 Ibid., p. 166.
50 Ibid., p. 110.

But this very dilaceration contains, for Lukács, the potential to unveil reification: "because of the split between subjectivity and objectivity that arises in the man that objectifies himself as a commodity, the situation becomes one that can be made conscious."[51] This situation, says Lukács, "forces upon him" the knowledge that the fulfillment of his needs is always a moment of the production and the reproduction of capital, which, in turn, "forces him to surpass the immediacy of his condition."[52] Hence, this is not only a possibility, but also a tendency: "the proletariat is confronted by the need to break through this barrier, to overcome it inwardly from the very start by adopting its own point of view."[53] The proletariat experiences this like it is a matter of life and death – here lie the limits of reification, the possibility of resistance, and the genesis of the proletariat's emancipatory interest in overthrowing capitalism.

Dilaceration, therefore, according to Lukács's approach, is not something to be avoided or even reversed, but rather a stage in the path to a possible new, mediated unity: "The reconstitution of the unity of the subject [...] has consciously to take its path through the realm of dilaceration and tearing apart. The different forms of dilaceration are so many necessary stages on the road towards a reconstituted man and they dissolve into nothing when they come into a true relation with a grasped totality, i.e. when they become dialectical."[54] The task, thus, is not to deduce the totality from a given reality, but rather "to deduce the unity – which is not given – of this disintegrating creation and to prove that it is the product of a creating subject. In the final analysis then: to create the subject of the 'creator.'"[55] The proletariat, as revolutionary subject, is yet to be created out of its present dilaceration.

**

If one considers Hartsock's critique of reified thought, it is remarkable that, albeit focusing on the antinomies typical of abstract masculinity, it displays a strong affinity with Lukács's characterization of the antinomies of bourgeois thought. Both Hartsock and Lukács stress the necessity of unveiling the

---

51   Ibid., p. 168.
52   Ibid., p. 165 and 166.
53   Ibid., p. 164.
54   Ibid., p. 141 (translation amended). The Hegelian tone of Lukács's theory is confirmed by his quotation of Hegel's *Differenzschrift*: "the necessary diremption [*Entzweiung*] is a factor of life which advances by opposites: and the totality, in its highest vitality, is only possible through a reconstitution out of the highest separation." Hegel quoted in ibid. (translation amended).
55   Ibid., p. 140.

processual, historical character of reality – which is only possible from the feminist viewpoint or the perspective of the proletariat, respectively. The most significant difference between Hartsock and Lukács does not lie, however, in the *subject* (either women or workers) who would be in a privileged position to bring about the unveiling of reification – it lies, rather, on *why* their position is considered to be a distinctive (and in a sense privileged) one. For Hartsock, as we have seen, the feminist standpoint is privileged because women's material practices are more connected with organic, natural processes than men's, resulting in a worldview free from dichotomies. For Lukács, by contrast, the reason for the distinctive standpoint of the proletariat is precisely the fact that those reified dichotomies are constitutive of the workers' experience under capitalism.

This means that, for Lukács, the rupture with reified reality cannot rely on an external critique: it must be based on the limits and contradictions inherent in the reified process of reality itself. In this sense, Hartsock's approach, in so far as it goes beyond her general claims for standpoint theory and hypostasizes women's experience as non-reified, can be the object of a critique similar to Lukács's objection regarding Feuerbach's humanism. As Lukács argues, although Feuerbach contributes to overcoming Hegel's idealism by considering man – instead of Spirit – as the measure of all things (*der Mensch als Maß aller Dinge*), he nonetheless turns man into a fixed objectivity; his anthropological materialism does not apply the measure to itself, does not make the conception of *man himself* dialectical, and so ends up absolutizing it.[56] Similarly, Hartsock can be said to absolutize her conception of woman. For Lukács, on the other hand, there is no template of non-reified praxis to be followed. The proletariat does not present itself as a model: "The proletariat only perfects itself by annihilating and transcending itself [...]."[57] The struggle for the creation of a classless society "is not just a battle waged against an external enemy, the bourgeoisie. It is equally the struggle of the proletariat against itself, against the devastating and degrading effects of the capitalist system upon its class consciousness. The proletariat will only have won the real victory when it has overcome these effects within itself."[58]

The point in bringing this divergence between Hartsock and Lukács to the foreground is not to accuse her of any kind of heterodoxy. Unfaithfulness to the cannon is not *per se* a deficiency, and there are many other stances of divergence between them where Hartsock's position can be considered more

---

56   Ibid., p. 189.
57   Ibid., p. 80.
58   Ibid.

adequate. Lukács's dialectical conception of the revolutionary subject can, nevertheless, offer resources to overcome the absolutized vision of women which is one important deficiency of Hartsock's proposal. In the next section, I argue that Dorothy Smith's version of feminist standpoint theory avoids this deficiency by ascribing a central stand to the dichotomies experienced by women in their daily lives.

3 Smith: Disjunction and the Perspective of Women

In her 1987 book *The Everyday World as Problematic*,[59] Dorothy Smith reflects on how a paper she had presented in 1972 in the meetings of the American Academy for the Advancement of Science reached a much larger audience than she had expected even before it was published by the journal *Sociological Inquiry* two years later.[60] Smith's widely shared proposal of a radical critique of sociology from women's perspective can be considered one of the first works on feminist standpoint theory. In her seminal essay, Smith asks "how a sociology might look if it began from the point of view of women's traditional place in it and what happens to a sociology which attempts to deal seriously with that."[61] In her view, it would not suffice to supplement the already existing sociological frameworks with studies on previously overlooked topics related with women's activities, which "merely extends the authority of the existing sociological procedures and makes of a women's sociology an addendum,"[62] obscuring the tension or separation between the worlds of men and women. Because of this separation, and since sociology has been established in a male dominated world, women sociologists often feel a *disjunction* between their experiences and the conceptual frameworks available for them to think about such experiences. Moreover, since that tension entails not only a separation, but also an authority of one pole (men's) over the other (women's), women learn to discard their lived experience "as a source of reliable information or suggestions about the character of the world."[63]

---

59 Smith, *The Everyday World as Problematic*, pp. 45–46.
60 Dorothy Smith, "Women's perspective as a Radical Critique of Sociology," *Sociological Inquiry* 44, No. 1 (1974): 7–13.
61 Smith, "Women's perspective," p. 7.
62 Ibid. Instead of a shift in the subject matter, Smith proposes "a different conception of how it is or might become relevant as a means to understand our experience and the conditions of our experience (both women's and men's) in corporate capitalist society" (ibid., p. 8).
63 Ibid.

Smith describes this process as a *conceptual imperialism* whereby the requirement of objectivity "lifts the actor out of the immediate local and particular place in which he is in the body."[64] A distinction is thus posited between the transcendental realm of the concepts and the concrete experience of the body. There arises, for Smith, a *bifurcation of consciousness* that affects everyone who engages in theoretical, conceptual activities: "It establishes two modes of knowing and experiencing and doing, one located in the body and in the space which it occupies and moves into, the other which passes beyond it. Sociology is written in and aims at this second mode."[65] Women's lives, however, are anchored in the former.

In addition to that, women take care of the entire logistics of men's bodily existence so that men can work, produce theory, take part in professional and managerial circles: "If he is to participate fully in the abstract mode of action, then he must be liberated also from having to attend to his needs, etc. in the concrete and particular."[66] Women therefore "mediate for men the relation between the conceptual mode of action and the actual concrete forms in which it is and must be realized, and the actual material conditions upon which it depends."[67] The better women perform this mediation, the more they become subjected to the authority of men's abstract activities, the greater the dichotomy and estrangement between both worlds, and the less men have to engage and become conscious of their own bodily existence – which also makes *men* alienated with regard to the material conditions of their own activities.

It is important to note that Smith argues, in a Lukácsian vein, that whereas the bifurcation of consciousness is present for everyone, women "stand at the center of a contradiction;" women sociologists, in particular, stand at the center of a contradiction "in the relation of our discipline to our experience of the world."[68] This contradiction, the structure of the bifurcated consciousness is continually visible to women because of the basic organization of their experience. It then "becomes for us a daily chasm which is to be crossed, on the one side of which is this special conceptual activity of thought, research, teaching, administration and on the other the world of concrete practical activities [...] in which the particularities of persons in their full organic immediacy [...] are inescapable."[69]

---

64   Ibid., p. 9.
65   Ibid.
66   Ibid.
67   Ibid., p. 10.
68   Ibid.
69   Ibid.

An alternative approach must, for Smith, *transcend* the contradiction, rather than simply invert the power balance between the poles. It must recognize that sociology is not an objective knowledge independent of the sociologist's situation, being instead deeply rooted in a determinate position in society: the unavoidable situatedness of sociology should be taken as its beginning, as an integral part of its methodological and theoretical strategies. This means that the sociologist must make "her direct experience of the everyday world the primary ground of her knowledge,"[70] for this original and immediate knowledge allows the social character of everyday experience to become not only observable, but also problematic: "Women's direct experience places her a step back where we can recognize the uneasiness that comes in sociology from its claim to be about the world we live in and its failure to account for or even describe its actual features as we find them in living them."[71] Women are in a particularly adequate position because they are, in Smith's words, "native speakers"[72] of their situation, a situation in which social contradictions make themselves felt with great acuteness. Therefore, "[t]hough such a sociology would not be exclusively for or done by women it does begin from the analysis and critique originating in their situation."[73] It is necessary, however, that women overcome the deep-seated tendency brought about by their training as sociologists to "ignore the uneasiness at the junctures where transitional work is done [...]."[74]

Smith argues that, as it exists today, sociology deals with phenomena that "are objectified and presented as external to and independent of the observer,"[75] it is a *view from the top* in which "[i]ssues are formulated as issues which have become administratively relevant not as they are significant first in the experience of those who live them."[76] But Smith does not suggest that women try to *stand outside* sociology, since one can only know a socially constructed world and a set of socially constructed practices *from within*. Only from within the male dominated world can women experience the dissonance that might make that world problematic: "Even to be a stranger is to enter a world constituted from within as strange. The strangeness itself is the mode in which it is experienced."[77]

---

70 Ibid., p. 11.
71 Ibid., p. 13.
72 Ibid.
73 Ibid.
74 Ibid., p. 12.
75 Ibid., p. 11.
76 Ibid., p. 8.
77 Ibid., p. 11.

Even from the standpoint of women, the standpoint of contradiction, however, "[t]here are human activities, intentions, and relations which are not apparent as such in the actual material conditions of our work. The social organization of the setting is not wholly available to us in its appearance."[78] We cannot pass beyond "our essential ignorance" of the social constitution of everyday life simply by means of observation and analysis of commonsense knowledge: "Our direct experience of it constitutes it (if we will) as a problem, but it does not offer any answers. The matrix of direct experience as that from which sociology might begin discloses that beginning as an 'appearance' the determinations of which lie beyond it."[79]

Thus direct, bodily located experience should be the starting point of theoretical endeavors, and also work "as a constraint or 'test' of the adequacy of a systematic knowledge [...]"[80] – but such direct experience cannot be an endpoint. In order to understand one's directly experienced world (and how it relates to the worlds directly experienced by those "who are differently placed"[81]) one cannot remain within the boundaries of one's own immediate experience. The sociologist "aims not at a reiteration of what she already (tacitly) knows, but at an exploration through that of what passes beyond it and is deeply implicated in how it is."[82] For Smith, accounting for the reified world in which we live and make theory "leads us back into an analysis of the total socio-economic order of which it is part."[83]

***

Although writing independently from one another, Smith and Hartsock share a number of affinities in their proposals for, respectively, a critique of sociology from women's perspective and a feminist historical materialism. Remarkably, Smith's work is in accordance with those five claims Hartsock outlines, some years later, at the beginning of her article, i.e.:
1) the material conditioning of knowledge;
2) the difference in the vision from materially opposed groups;
3) the effectivity of the dominant's view;
4) the view of the oppressed as an achievement instead of a given; and

---

78 Ibid., p. 13.
79 Ibid.
80 Ibid., p. 11.
81 Ibid., p. 12.
82 Ibid., pp. 11–2.
83 Ibid., p. 12.

5) the emancipatory power of the knowledge that takes the experience of the oppressed as its starting point.

But whereas Hartsock tends to deviate from her own fourth claim when applying these methodological premises to women's concrete realities, Smith offers, with the notions of *disjunction* and *bifurcated consciousness*, a more complex account of women's standpoint. Women's experiences are seen in a less romanticized way – not as relating mainly to organic processes purified from dichotomies, but quite the contrary, as permeated by acute contradictions. Such contradictions are precisely what allows and compels those who experience them to *see them* and, more than that, to *see them as problematic*. For Smith, the direct everyday experience of women is only the starting point that might lead us to problematize the total socio-economic order. In this sense, the feminist standpoint would be a result in a proper sense, a mediated knowledge, rather than an immediate perspective to be universalized as it is. Smith makes this clear, for example, when she differentiates *concrete experience* from *subjective perspective*, the latter echoing the immediacy present in Lukács's concept of empirical class consciousness.[84]

Smith's proposal also has an advantage concerning the criticism of exclusionary essentialization often directed to standpoint theorists. To some extent, Smith shares with Hartsock a valuing (and essentializing) of women's material practices in certain care activities which is typical of second wave feminism and tends to neglect (and exclude) the experience of differently situated women. But Smith's approach – like Hartsock's five metatheoretical claims taken separately from her portrayal of women's material activities – does not necessarily exclude difference. In a later text, Smith explains how her proposal to start from the social actors' everyday experience can be a tool for precisely taking differences into account:

> In this political context, the category 'women' is peculiarly non-exclusive since it was then and has remained open-ended, such that boundaries established at any one point are subject to the disruption of women who enter speaking from a different experience as well as an experience of difference. It is a commitment to the privileges of women to speak *from*

---

[84] Cf. the following passage: "Let me make it clear that when I speak of 'experience' I do not use the term as a synonym for 'perspective.' Nor in proposing a sociology grounded in the sociologist's actual experience, am I recommending the self-indulgence of inner exploration or any other enterprise with self as sole focus and object. Such subjectivist interpretations of 'experience' are themselves an aspect of that organization of consciousness which bifurcates it and transports us into mind country while stashing away the concrete conditions and practices upon which it depends." Ibid., p. 11.

experience that opens the women's movement to the critique of white and/or heterosexist hegemony from those it marginalizes and silences.[85]

Thus conceived, feminist standpoint theory is closer to the unfinished project Fredric Jameson identified in *History and Class Consciousness*.

4   Concluding Remarks

Hartsock makes an invaluable contribution to the articulation of feminism and Marxism by insisting that not only activities of social production but also those connected to social reproduction have a material basis, even though the latter are repeatedly relegated to a subordinate role within many strands of traditional historical materialism. At the same time, however, the emancipatory potential of Hartsock's feminist standpoint is somewhat static: it depends solely on women – and possibly men – becoming aware of, valuing, and generalizing women's material activities *as they exist today*. Hartsock ascribes a kind of wholeness to women's experiences in social reproduction so as to purify them from dichotomies and contradictions – and this, among other problems, makes it hard for her to explain women's motivation to become a "revolutionary subject," i.e., to strive to overcome the structure of patriarchal capitalism. The standpoint of the proletariat as proposed by Lukács's, by contrast, has an inherent transformative moment: when the worker becomes aware of his subject-object status, he comes to a position from where it is possible to unveil and transform the reifying dynamic of capitalism. Emancipation, for Lukács, does not mean taking the experience of the proletariat as a model for the whole of society, but quite the contrary: it means abolishing this reified situation altogether, which only becomes a possibility because reification contains within itself the seed of its overcoming. This seed, so to speak, lies in the dilaceration experienced by the worker in his daily existence in the process of production of capital, which creates in him an emancipatory interest with political and epistemological consequences. Smith, by contrast to Hartsock and closer to Lukács, places contradiction at the heart of women's experience in late capitalism, which is expressed in the notions of disjunction and bifurcated consciousness. Like Lukács, Smith regards this contradiction as the very requirement to being able to see the world as problematic, to inquire into the social-economic structure of the world beyond the immediate, dominant

---

85   Dorothy Smith, "Comment on Hekman's 'Truth and Method: Feminist Standpoint Theory Revisited,'" *Signs* 22, No. 2 (1997): 394.

perspective.[86] It provides the motivational potential for the emancipatory standpoint to be theoretically and politically achieved.[87]

To conclude, it is important to point out that feminist standpoint theory has faced different criticisms since its first formulations in the 1970s and 1980s. On an epistemic level, it has received the (opposite) accusations of both relativism and foundationalism. The idea that knowledge is produced from a standpoint has led, on the one hand, to an identification of standpoint theory with a perspectivism that argues that there is no universal truth or objective knowledge. Each possible standpoint would provide an equally justified validity claim and,

---

[86] A similar argument, but one focused on the experience of Black women in the USA, can be found in Patricia Hill Collins, "Learning from the Outsider Within: The Sociological Significance of Black Feminist Thought," *Social Problems* 33, No. 6 (1986): S14–S32.

[87] Without doubt, although I have been stressing the affinities between Lukács and Smith, a few differences come into view on a closer inspection of how each of them conceives of the contradictions experienced by workers and women in their everyday life. The theoretical and political consequences of such differences would need to be further examined, but such an analysis cannot be carried out within the purview of this chapter and I will limit myself to pointing out two of them. (1) The Lukácsian notion of dilaceration is much more forceful than Smith's account of disjunction: whereas women experience an *uneasiness* (Smith, "Women's perspective," p. 12) that suggests a possible problematization of the world, workers feel that overcoming reification is *a matter of life and death* (Lukács, *History and Class Consciousness*, p. 164). (2) There is also the contrast between the kind of domination experienced by each group (reification and gender oppression). For Lukács, the dilaceration of the worker stems from his objectification, from the fact that he is transformed into a thing, that his labor power turns into a commodity. The proletarian is split between subject and object within the realm of work itself. For Smith, on the other hand, the disjunction experienced by women seems to emerge in the transitional juncture between wage labor and unwaged (mostly care) activities. While some argue that this discrepancy puts Lukács and feminist standpoint theorists at odds with each other (cf. Bob Ellis, Rodney Fopp, "The Origins of Standpoint Epistemologies"), others do not think that this sets them apart in a significant way. Jameson, for example, uses "constraint" or "privation" to account in a relatively neutral manner for such different situations "which are often monolithically subsumed under single-shot political concepts such as 'domination' or 'power;' economic concepts such as 'exploitation;' social concepts such as 'oppression;' or philosophical concepts such as 'alienation.'" Instead of discussing which experience of privation has an ontological or explanatory priority over the others, however, for Jameson "[w]hat seems more productive is to dissolve this conceptuality once again back into the concrete situations from which it emerged: to make an inventory of the variable structures of 'constraint' lived by the various marginal, oppressed or dominated groups – the so-called 'new social movements' fully as much as the working classes – with this difference, that each form of privation is acknowledged as producing its own specific 'epistemology,' its own specific view from below, and its own specific and distinctive truth claim" (Jameson, "*History and Class Consciousness* as an 'Unfinished Project,'" pp. 70–71). Such theorization from multiple standpoints differs from a total relativism, for Jameson, in that there is a common object of analysis: late capitalism.

hence, it would be impossible to discriminate between true and false depictions of reality. On the other hand, however, some have criticized standpoint theory for granting one specific perspective a more objective, or less distorted, access to reality, so that the correctness of knowledge would be warranted by the subject that carries it out. Neither of these criticisms, however, seems to apply properly to standpoint theory in its dialectical (either Lukácsian or feminist) formulations. Whereas it recognizes the important role social and historical circumstances play on the production of knowledge, standpoint theory as proposed by the three authors discussed here is not relativist in the sense of seeing every cognitive practice as having an equal status with regard to its validity claim: there are true and false claims that can be distinguished from one another. Furthermore, the truth does not depend on the perspective of the subject of knowledge: the standpoint of an oppressed group is not the immediate (in Lukács's terms: empirical) perspective of the members of such group at some given time and space, but rather a standpoint one can *arrive at* by means of disentangling the appearance of objectivity of the dominant view. It does not suffice to *be* a woman, for example, to make theory from a feminist standpoint – just like, for Lukács, it does not suffice to *be* a worker to have direct access the class consciousness of the proletariat. The truth of feminist standpoint theory does not lies in its subject, in its simply being made by women, even though the material conditions of women's lives make it easier for them to be in a position to grasp the merely immediate efficacy of the dominant, patriarchal perspective.[88]

In the face of these and other criticisms, moreover, it is important to take the following into consideration: feminist standpoint theory is often taken as a homogeneous school of thought (both by its critics and its supporters[89]), but, as I have tried to indicate, although authors usually identified with this strand do have some shared concerns – above all, the distinct and potentially

---

[88] In addition to that, most of the authors in the feminist standpoint tradition argue at least for the *communicability* of the experiences of domination; as Dana Cloud puts it: "And because a standpoint is not an essence, it does not 'belong' only to the least privileged among us. Intellectuals, too often employed to create and disseminate rationales for the system (idealist philosophy, 'great man' theories of history, utilitarian scientific agendas, or capitalist economics), may be taught the rudiments of working class politics in order to hear, and operate in solidarity with, the exploited and oppressed." Dana Cloud, "Review of *History and Class Consciousness* and *A Defense of History and Class Consciousness: Tailism and the Dialectic*," Quarterly Journal of Speech 101, No. 1 (2015): 288.

[89] Cf. Susan Hekman's critique in "Truth and Method: Feminist Standpoint Theory Revisited," Signs 22, No. 2 (1997): 341–365. Jameson is one example among the supporters.

emancipatory character of knowledge produced from the standpoint of women –, they differ in many other respects, e.g.: *how* to characterize such standpoint, *why* it is distinctive, and *what* makes it (potentially) emancipatory. By evidencing the differences between two of its "founding mothers," the aim of this chapter has also been to present feminist standpoint theory as multifaceted, to challenge its reduction to a monolithic endeavor, and thus to suggest that it cannot be so easily dismissed at a single blow. In this sense, feminist standpoint theory as proposed by Hartsock and Smith can and should be taken as important moments in continuing critical thought – as experiments within the unfinished project of critical theory (and practice) that stimulated, together with the work of Alison Jaggar, Sandra Harding, and others, a renewed debate on knowledge production and social struggles in late capitalism.

CHAPTER 12

Linking Racism and Reification in the Thought of Georg Lukács

Gregory R. Smulewicz-Zucker

An influential tradition of African-American and Africana thought,[1] often referred to as the Black Radical Tradition, has brought the questions and concerns of Marxism to bear on the analysis race and racism. Scholars have explored issues including the relation of class exploitation to racial oppression, the intersection of race and class, and the roles of colonialism and slavery in the capitalist system.[2] While these works have engaged large swaths of Marx and Marxist theory, surprisingly absent from this dialogue has been a sustained engagement with the application of the work of Hungarian Marxist philosopher Georg Lukács.[3] This essay delves into Lukács's work on racism, how it might fit into Lukács's broader philosophical concerns, and what it might contribute to Africana and African-American philosophy dealing with racism.

There are good reasons for reconsidering Lukács's thought as a potential contributor to discussions of racism. Lukács explicitly dealt with the topic in his, often underappreciated, monumental work *The Destruction of Reason*. There, Lukács analyzed the significance of the race pseudo-sciences of the nineteenth century as an important feature of irrational strains of thought

---

1 Frank M. Kirkland and Linda Martín Alcoff provided critical comments on earlier drafts of this essay. Though they may disagree with the final result, their incisive criticisms made this a far better piece than it was in its initial form. It goes without saying that any errors are my own.
2 Some of the major texts I have in mind include: C.L.R. James, *The Black Jacobins: Toussaint L'Ouverture and the San Domingo Revolution* (New York: Vintage Books, 1989); W.E.B. Du Bois, *Black Reconstruction in America* (Oxford: Oxford University Press, 2007); Angela Y. Davis, *Women, Race, and Class* (New York: Vintage Books, 1983); and, Cedric J. Robinson, *Black Marxism: The Making of the Black Radical Tradition* (Chapel Hill: The University of North Carolina Press, 2000).
3 Two noteworthy exceptions include Léopold Sédar Senghor and Cornel West. For Senghor's discussion of Lukács, see: Léopold Sédar Senghor, "Nationhood: Report on the Doctrine and Program of the Party of African Federation" in *On African Socialism*, Trans. Mercer Cook (New York: Frederick A. Praeger Publishers, 1965), 35–37. For West's, see: Cornel West, "The Indispensability Yet Insufficiency of Marxist Theory" in *The Cornel West Reader* (New York: Basic *Civitas* Books, 1999).

that laid the foundation for fascist ideology and practice. Further, in the early 1960s, the French-Hungarian sociologist, Joseph Gabel, insightfully employed Lukács's concept of reification from Lukács's earlier *History and Class Consciousness* to argue that racism can be understood as a form of reification. Since Gabel, however, little has been said on the topic of Lukács and racism.

This essay contributes to a reevaluation of Lukács in three ways. In the first section, I revisit Lukács's analysis of racism in *Destruction of Reason* and its relation to irrationalism. *Destruction of Reason* has been neglected by scholars for purportedly being an exemplar of a more dogmatic phase in Lukács's career.[4] Scholars have privileged the earlier *History and Class Consciousness*, in part, because it represents a Lukács more willing to challenge Marxist orthodoxies. Yet, in the second section, I show how Lukács's concern with racism in *Destruction of Reason* reveals continuities between the earlier Lukács who developed the influential concept of reification and the work of the later Lukács. Here, I draw on Gabel, but diverge from him in significant ways. Further, I point to affinities between Lukács's thought and that of his contemporary, W.E.B. Du Bois.[5] I argue that a consideration of Du Bois' insights, particularly the notion of double consciousness as developed in *The Souls of Black Folk*, is necessary to make Lukács's concept of reification applicable to the analysis of racism. I conclude with some broader considerations on how Lukács, framed as a thinker with something significant to say about racism, might add to the discourse advanced by more recent philosophers and social theorists dealing with race and racism.

1   Lukács's Destruction of Reason and Racism

Beginning with F.W.J. Schelling and concluding with fascist ideology, Lukács's *Destruction of Reason* provides a philosophical history of irrationalism. Yet, as János Kelemen has noted, an immediate difficulty in assessing the contemporary philosophical salience of Lukács's book is that Lukács "has no brief and

---

[4] For a discussion of the criticisms of *Destruction of Reason*, see: Stanly Aronowitz, "Georg Lukács's *Destruction of Reason*" in *Georg Lukács Reconsidered: Critical Essays in Politics, Philosophy, and Aesthetics*, Ed. Michael J. Thompson (London: Continuum International Publishing, 2011).

[5] Whether Du Bois was aware of Lukács and his work is unknown. It is interesting to note that Lukács expressed admiration for Du Bois, sending him birthday wishes. Lukács's note is quoted in W.E.B. Du Bois, *In Battle for Peace: The Story of My 83rd Birthday* (Oxford: Oxford University Press, 2007), 132.

general definition neither of rationalism, nor of irrationalism."[6] Rather, Lukács offers his readers a series of characteristics of irrationalism: "The disparagement of understanding and reason, an uncritical glorification of intuition, an aristocratic epistemology, the rejection of socio-historical progress, the creating of myths and so on are motives we can find in virtually any irrationalist."[7] It is important, therefore, with respect to Lukács's discussion of racism, to first see how racist thought meets these characteristics and, second, whether or not, more broadly, Lukács is correct to define racist thought as irrational. Kelemen's interpretation provides useful guidance in addressing these issues.

In an effort to arrive at a clearer account of Lukács's conception of irrationalism, Kelemen begins, rightly in my view, by stressing that Lukács approaches the problem of irrationalism "from the history of thinking." Irrationalism "is a reaction to the questions and problems brought up and left unresolved by science and philosophy."[8] This first definition of irrationalism as reaction to the progress of science and philosophy and the problems they leave unresolved fits with Lukács's account of the development of racial theories. As Lukács puts it, "the various stages of irrationalism came about as reactionary answers to do with the class struggle. Thus the content, form, method, tone, etc., of its reaction to progress in society are dictated not by an intrinsic, inner dialectic of this kind, but rather by the adversary, by the fighting conditions imposed on the reactionary bourgeoisie."[9] Here, Lukács includes the historical struggles for democratization and for human equality under the banner of the class struggle.

From this standpoint, Lukács's argument, when applied to racism, shows a marked similarity to the argument recently put forward by the historian Ibram X. Kendi. Kendi argues, "Racially discriminatory policies have usually sprung from economic, political, and cultural self-interests, self-interests that are constantly changing."[10] He adds, "The principal function of racist ideas in American history has been the suppression of resistance to racial discrimination and its resulting racial disparities… We have a hard time recognizing that racial discrimination is the sole cause of racial disparities in this country [the United

---

6 János Kelemen, "Lukács's Rationalism: In Defence of *The Destruction of Reason*" in *The Rationalism of Georg Lukács* (New York: Palgrave Macmillan, 2014), 73.
7 Georg Lukács, *The Destruction of Reason*, trans. Peter Palmer (London: Merlin Press, 1980), 10.
8 Kelemen, 76.
9 Lukács, *Destruction of Reason*, 10.
10 Ibram X. Kendi, *Stamped from the Beginning: The Definitive History of Racist Ideas in America* (New York: Bold Type Books, 2016), 9–10.

States] and in the world at large."[11] Kendi challenges what he sees as the common misconception that racist ideas come first and shape racially discriminatory policies. Instead, for Kendi, it is the interest in preserving a racially discriminatory order for those who benefit from it that leads to the creation of racist ideas to legitimate that order. This more materialist reversal, which places the interests of the powerful first, has much in common with Lukács's argument that nineteenth and early twentieth century race theorists developed their ideas to stymie the spread of movements on behalf of equality and democracy. This perspective guides Lukács's interpretation of the rise of racist thought.

Lukács's history of racist thought begins with Arthur de Gobineau's influential *The Inequality of the Human Races* in the mid-nineteenth century. It is important to note that Lukács begins with Gobineau not because Gobineau was the first racist thinker – the history of ideas is full of racists and racist ideas. Rather, Lukács begins with Gobineau because he is the first significant thinker to assert the inequality of races against the spread of the first major historical movement premised on the notion of human equality, the French Revolution (and, we might add to this, the Haitian Revolution as an effort to extend those revolutionary ideals to their logical conclusion). For Lukács, the ideal of equality established itself on the historical scene as a powerful political force with the Revolution. Irrationalism only has meaning to the extent that it seeks to uphold what historical progress has already shown to be outmoded forms of thought. In this vein, Lukács argues that Gobineau's racism is an effort to sustain inequality in the face of the progress of the ideal of equality: "Gobineau's starting-point and principal bias was the struggle against democracy, against the 'unscientific' and 'unnatural' idea of the equality of men."[12] Gobineau's thought constitutes a reaction against the emerging tendencies of the age.

In order to stave off the progress of equality and democracy, Gobineau, Lukács argues, attacked the notion of the historical progress of humanity writ large: "The dogmatic insistence on the inequality of men implied a rejection of the concept of mankind, and with this there vanished one of the finest achievements of modern science: the idea of the uniform and regular development of men."[13] The denial of equality entailed the rejection of humans as historically developing beings in favor of an alternative notion of historically fixed races:

11   Ibid., 10. My brackets.
12   Lukács, *The Destruction of Reason*, 671.
13   Ibid., 680.

This view of history now yielded a unique 'theory' of primitive history which was to remain a part of racial theory. For the racial theories, the differences in the stages of culture no longer signified phases of development that were completed by one and the same people, one and the same society. Instead, each stage was equated with specified races and placed in an eternal, metaphysical context.[14]

This argument paves the way for a conception of racial essences that could legitimate the colonial project to which the ideal of equality posed a threat: "So we see that in Gobineau the destruction of historical science was already far advanced. His view reflects not only the feudal traditions of the European colonizers but also their racial arrogance toward the 'coloured people,' whom they regarded as 'lacking a history' and uncivilizable."[15]

It is worth noting that Lukács's line of argumentation shows much in common with that of one of Gobineau's earlier critics, the Haitian intellectual, Anténor Firmin. Lukács would only recognize what Firmin had already explicitly laid out over a half century before, i.e., the role of race theory in legitimating the colonial project. As Firmin explains:

> One does not easily renounce the age-old practice of exploiting one's fellow human beings, which is the main objective of colonization, an enterprise fostered by the need of major industrialized nations for constantly expanding spheres of activity and markets. Thus economists, philosophers, and anthropologists become adept at constructing lies, misusing both nature and science for purposes of propaganda. In fact, in so doing they are merely pursuing in the intellectual and moral sphere the same abominable results achieved by former colonizers who succeeded so well in rendering Yellow and Black slaves mindless through sheer exhaustion.[16]

But this is one of the rare sections in his work where Firmin is explicit about the political motives underlying the pseudoscientific claims of race theorists. An important difference between Lukács and Firmin lies in the fact that Firmin primarily focuses his attack on debunking the pseudoscientific claims of race theorists by using the tools of natural science. Lukács, in contrast, attacks

---

14   Ibid., 681.
15   Ibid.
16   Anténor Firmin, *The Equality of the Human Races*, trans. Asselin Charles (Urbana: University of Illinois Press, 2002), 384.

racism by demonstrating that race theorists deny the histories and social bases of racial oppression in order to advance the claim that unchanging racial essences exist and inhere in individuals.

With Gobineau, according to Lukács, the capacity for historical progress is recognized in some races and denied to others. In order for race theorists to sustain their arguments, they required a method that could explain the fixity of races with reference to the natural sciences, particularly because of the progress the natural sciences made as a result of Darwin's theory. It is with the social Darwinist turn to natural science that Lukács's critique evidences a bit more in common with Firmin's assault on pseudoscience. Yet, Lukács still insists that this strategy is primarily tied to an effort to reject the significance of history (and, as a result, historical systems of oppression) and represent seeming racial differences as natural. "By means of this supposedly natural-scientific method," Lukács writes, "Social Darwinism revoked history. Man, it claimed had not changed in the course of history... Thus sociology in its Darwinist garb expelled from the observation of society not only all economics, but also all social elements. That was methodologically necessary. For if sociology is founded on biology or anthropology, then it cannot permit of any essential change, let alone progress."[17] In this respect, social Darwinism moves beyond Gobineau's historical argument for racial inequality and gives it a naturalistic basis through the blurring of the lines between the natural and social sciences.

At this point, an important question emerges. While Lukács's history of the development of race theory is consistent with the claim that irrationalism is reactionary, we only see two of Lukács's characteristics of irrationalism exemplified by the theories of Gobineau and social Darwinism: aristocratism (Gobineau) and the rejection of socio-historical progress (social Darwinism). Even if the reasons that justify the racism of Gobineau or the social Darwinists can be (and have been) disproven, they are reasons nonetheless. Racism only appears to become fully irrational, on Lukács's reading, with the work of Houston Stewart Chamberlain. To the previous arguments on behalf of race theory, Chamberlain adds the appeal to intuition. Lukács explains, "This 'argument' was of great import for the future of racialism. For here Chamberlain was reversing the issue: intuition was not intended to judge the truth or falsity of an objective set of facts, but itself determined the racial standing of the inquirer, and anyone who did not have this intuition would be proved a cross-bred, a bastard, by dint of that very fact."[18] While Gobineau's and the social Darwinian arguments on behalf of racism could be challenged on the basis of appeal to

---

17   Lukács, *The Destruction of Reason*, 688.
18   Ibid., 702.

stronger historical or scientific arguments, which was notably the strategy adopted by Firmin, Chamberlain's appeal to intuition evades all rational challenges. It was Chamberlain's move that, according to Lukács, lay the foundation for the irrationalism of Nazism.

What are we to make of Lukács's narrative of the development of racist thought for the purposes of gaining a broader understanding of racism today? Certainly, racists of various stripes continue to justify their racism via appeals to arguments very similar to those of Gobineau, social Darwinists, and Chamberlain. Lukács is correct to highlight the distinctiveness of Chamberlain insofar as the arguments of his predecessors are open to falsification through recourse to historical and scientific research while his intuitionism cannot be. In that case, what unifies these thinkers given that Lukács's account takes the form of an historical development? Kelemen's interpretation of *The Destruction of Reason* becomes instructive once again.

The definition of irrationalist thought as reactionary speaks to the historically situated causes of its emergence. To this, Kelemen adds a second, more substantive, definition of irrationalism as a form of "evasion." Evasion, Kelemen explains, "states that irrationalist philosophers refuse to answer the real problems, and from the very existence of these problems they infer that there is and there cannot be a rational answer for them. This Lukács considers the 'decisive hallmark' from which he deduces further constitutive elements of irrationalism – intuitionism, aristocratism, agnosticism, and historicism."[19] Kelemen adds a second definition of evasion, writing, "In Lukács's portrayal, big irrationalist thinkers do not evade problems. They do sense the answers but evade accepting them because of their interest, social role and other reasons."[20] In which of these two senses are the race theorists Lukács reviews evasive?

In Lukács's account, there seems to be some overlap between the two types of evasion on the part of race theorists. Yet, these figures, in general, seem to tend toward the second type of evasion. We might suggest that the problem (what they saw as a problem) with which race theorists were confronted – the one they were evading – was that the notion of inequality was increasingly being shown to be without either normative or scientific merit. They evaded the answer that equality had merit because of their interests and social roles.

Recently, Justin E.H. Smith has proposed his own argument that racism is a form of irrationality because racists succumb to a confirmation bias. While he offers less of an explanation for the causes of and motives for this confirmation

---

19 Kelemen, 77.
20 Ibid., 79.

bias than Lukács, Lukács would agree with Smith when he writes, "not only does correct information sent their way about the science of human diversity not have the desired effect, but it is shot down, before it can be processed, by the various half-truths and errors that the racist has weaponized in his defense."[21] This would explain why the strategy of, say, a figure like Firmin who marshals numerous historical and scientific examples against the claims of Gobineau and social Darwinism does little to persuade racists that they are wrong. The same can be said of the approach of K. Anthony Appiah, which rests on the fact that race has no biological basis.[22] Even if race is biologically non-existent, racists are invested in its existence and, if need be, they will resort to making intuitive cases for its existence reminiscent of Chamberlain.

Increasingly, it seems that what Lukács was talking about is what, today, is more aptly referred to as an ideology of white supremacy. If we take seriously Kelemen's characterization of Lukács's account of irrationalism as a form of evasion, it looks far more like the end result of this brand of irrationality is an ideology. The problem, however, with respect to Lukács's own corpus is that it displays a relatively weak engagement with the Marxist conception of ideology.[23] If we are to assess the value of Lukács's work to a discussion of racism, it would seem that moving into the terrain of the analysis of racism as an ideology renders Lukács's contributions questionable. Indeed, there are better sources in both the works of Marx and of other Marxist thinkers that take the notion of ideology far more seriously than does Lukács.

There is an alternative route for exploring the significance of Lukács's insights in *The Destruction of Reason* about racism and applying them to the discourse on racism. Specifically, there are relevant commonalities between the way Lukács characterizes racism and the phenomenon of reification, which Lukács famously articulated decades earlier in *History and Class Consciousness*. While their particular strategies differ, Gobineau, the social Darwinists,

---

21 Justin E.H. Smith, *Irrationality: A History of the Dark Side of Reason* (Princeton: Princeton University Press, 2019), 69.

22 See: K. Anthony Appiah, "Race, Culture, Identity: Misunderstood Connections" in K. Anthony Appiah and Amy Gutmann, *Color Conscious: The Political Morality of Race* (Princeton: Princeton University Press, 1996), 67–74.

23 The issue is that, at the time Lukács began his engagement with Marx, Marx's writings on ideology had not yet been made publicly available. Still, Jorge Larrain is largely correct when he notes that Lukács's use of the term "ideology" does not have the negative meaning it would later acquire for Marxists after works like *The German Ideology* became available. See: Jorge Larrain, "Lukács's Concept of Ideology" in *Lukács Today: Essays in Marxist Philosophy*, ed. Tom Rockmore (Dordrecht: D. Reidel Publishing Company, 1988). Readers should also consult Andrew Feenberg's essay in this volume, which offers observations on the connection between reification and ideology.

Chamberlain, and other racists, ultimately, share the claim that there are unchanging essences associated with particular races. Existent social relations of inequality are justified by appeal to these essences.

The socio-historical factors, particularly the rise of systems of domination and oppression, which actually explain the differences in the status of supposedly racially differentiated groups, are expelled from consideration. Put in Kendi's terms, "Consumers of these racist ideas have been led to believe there is something wrong with Black people, and not the policies that have enslaved, oppressed, and confined so many Black people."[24] If we consider this point through the lens of Lukács's analysis of reification in *History and Class Consciousness*, then racism, on Lukács's terms, ought to constitute a form of reification. That is, much as the capitalist system operates by objectifying, and consequently dehumanizing, the worker, the system of white supremacy attempts to objectify and dehumanize individuals by attributing racial essences to them. In both cases, however, it is the material conditions of oppression that come first. Reification is a consequence of and perpetuates the oppression.

2 Reification and Racism

An immediate difficulty confronts any effort to link the work of the old Lukács to that of the young Lukács. Lukács, under pressure from the Comintern, infamously recanted his argument in *History and Class Consciousness*. Many of Lukács's admirers (particularly when *History and Class Consciousness* was rediscovered by radical theorists in the 1960s and 1970s) condemned him for this. If Lukács had surrendered to the Comintern, it followed that all his subsequent work, including *Destruction of Reason*, was little better than orthodox screeds in the service of Soviet propaganda.[25] More recent discoveries and scholarship have shown that the story of Lukács's kowtowing to Soviet orthodoxy is not so simple.[26] Nevertheless, even for many of Lukács's sympathetic critics, it remains questionable whether the attempt to identify continuities in Lukács's thought

---

24 Kendi, 10.
25 For example, in his otherwise excellent study of Lukács's work, George Lichtheim is dismissive of works produced during Stalin's reign. He writes, "Lukács adopts the manner of the party propagandist who can see his opponents only as conscious or unconscious tools of 'reaction.'" George Lichtheim, *Lukács* (London: Fontana, 1970), 114.
26 The major example is the rediscovery of a previously lost defense of *History of Class Consciousness* against its Soviet critics. The publication of this work has inspired several reassessments. See: Georg Lukács, *A Defence of History and Class Consciousness: Tailism and Dialectic*, trans. Esther Leslie (London: Verso, 2000).

does more harm than good. In this section, I suggest that focusing on the issue of racism does provide a way to connect the older Lukács to the younger.

In attempting to link reification to the analysis of racism, I am partially following the work of the French-Hungarian sociologist and psychoanalyst, Joseph Gabel. Much like Gabel, I see traces of Lukács's earlier analysis of reification in his later discussion of racism. Writing of *The Destruction of Reason*, Gabel argues, "All the elements of a reificational interpretation of racism are to be found in Lukács's text: projection into the natural domain of certain interhuman data; denial of the dialectic and History, resignation to the 'natural' inevitable characteristics of the given social context."[27] Racism is a reified form of thought because it "misunderstands and ignores real human history. For ethnocentrism, History is a permanent prehistory, which maintains the illusion of being history; this is one aspect of its false consciousness."[28]

In my view, Gabel is largely correct in drawing parallels between Lukács's discussion of racism and his analysis of reified thought on the basis of an appeal to the "natural laws." As Lukács explains in *History and Class Consciousness*, a feature of reification is the way in which human relations that are sociohistorical products take on the appearance of inviolable laws akin to the laws of nature. Lukács writes, "The view that things as they appear can be accounted for by 'natural laws' of society is, according to Marx, both the highpoint and the 'insuperable barrier' of bourgeois thought."[29] Lukács goes on to argue that classical economics provides a legitimation of capitalism through its attempt to imitate the natural sciences:

> Nor is it an accident that economics became an independent discipline under capitalism. Thanks to its commodity and communications arrangements capitalist society has given the whole of economic life an identity notable for its autonomy, its cohesion and its exclusive reliance on immanent laws. This was something quite unknown in earlier forms of society. For this reason, classical economics with its system of laws is closer to the natural sciences than to any other. The economic system whose essence and laws it investigates does in fact show marked similarities with the objective structure of that Nature which is the object of study of physics and the other natural sciences. It is concerned with

---

27 Joseph Gabel, *False Consciousness: An Essay on Reification*, trans. Margaret A. Thompson with assistance by Kenneth A. Thompson (New York: Harper & Row, 1978), 130.
28 Ibid., 129.
29 Georg Lukács, *History and Class Consciousness: Studies in Marxist Dialectics*, trans. Rodney Livingstone (Cambridge, Mass.: The MIT Press, 1971), 174.

relations that completely unconnected with man's humanity and indeed with any anthropomorphisms – be they religious, ethical, aesthetic or anything else.[30]

Lukács's point is not to reject the natural sciences, but, rather, to argue that reified thought treats social phenomena as though they operate in the same lawlike manner as natural phenomena. And, perhaps more significantly, that this reinforces and legitimates systems of oppression.

Insofar as Gabel advances the claim that the parallels between Lukács's analysis of racism and his analysis of reification rests on this masquerading of socio-historical phenomena as having the lawlike inviolability of the natural sciences, I am in agreement with him. Where Gabel's argument becomes problematic is in its characterization of the racist as displaying a schizophrenic personality:

> The racist perception of human reality is schizophrenic in several ways... It implies a veritable 'deranged perception' of the racial minority in question; the ethnocentrist perceives the colour black as a sort of 'essential characteristic.' It is clear that this essence is not that of the perceived, but rather the perceiver: it is not the Black who is 'essentially' evil, but the racist who is essentially racist and who consequently perceives in this way. It postulates a dichotomization whose equivalent is found in clinical schizophrenia, a dichotomization having as its corollary an actual 'reificational depersonalization' of the individual representative of the minority in question, which is reflected particularly in caricature, the strongest weapon of ethnocentrism.[31]

Such a move is unsatisfactory both as an explanation of racism and in its appropriation of the concept of reification. By treating racism as a type of schizophrenia, it reduces racism from a social phenomenon to an individual pathology. While there certainly may be racist individuals who also display schizophrenic qualities, this does not take us very far in understanding how racism operates in systemic ways. Indeed, as I discuss in the following section, one of the major advances in philosophical and sociological analyses of racism is the discussion of white supremacy as a system.

Gabel's diagnosis of racism as a form of schizophrenia also leaves out an important component of Lukács's concept of reification: its effect on subjectivity

---

30   Ibid., 231–232.
31   Gabel, 123.

and the sense of the self. Reification, as Lukács discusses the phenomenon in *History and Class Consciousness*, is characterized as a consequence of the hyper-rationalizing tendencies of advanced capitalism. With this synthesis of Marx and Weber, Lukács could point to the dehumanizing aspects of the increasing specialization of labor under capitalism, arguing, "there is an even more monstrous intensification of the one-sided specialisation which represents such a violation of man's humanity. Marx's comment on factory work that 'the individual, himself divided, is transformed into the automatic mechanism of a partial labour' and is thus 'crippled to the point of abnormality' is relevant here too."[32] That is, reification entails more than a way of perceiving others. In the context of a social system of oppression, reification affects the sense of self of subjects who are oppressed under that system.

For Lukács, the organization of society affects the consciousness of subjects. Going into further detail about how the rationalization of society under capitalism treats workers as commodities in the production process, Lukács explains,

> The quantification of objects, their subordination to abstract mental categories makes its appearance in the life of the worker immediately as a process of abstraction of which he is the victim, and which cuts him off from his labour-power, forcing him to sell it on the market as a commodity, belonging to him. And by selling this, his only commodity, he integrates it (and himself: for his commodity is inseparable from his physical existence) into a specialised process that has been rationalised and mechanised, a process that he discovers already existing, complete and able to function without him and in which he is no more than a cipher reduced to an abstract quantity, a mechanised and rationalised tool.[33]

Lukács adds, the worker "perceives the split in his being preserved in the brutal form of what is in its whole tendency a slavery without limits. He is therefore forced into becoming the object of the process by which he is turned into a commodity and reduced to a mere quantity."[34] The objectification of the worker is, thus, grounded in the fact that the production process under capitalism alienates the worker from the product of her labor. Of course, Lukács holds out the possibility that the worker can gain insight into her reification if she realizes that she has been reduced to the status of a commodity. Nevertheless,

---

32 Lukács, *History and Class Consciousness*, 99.
33 Ibid., 165–166.
34 Ibid., 166.

what is relevant is that Lukács sees this reification, this stultification of the humanity of the worker, as part and parcel of the social processes of labor under a capitalist system.

Reification is a thoroughgoing phenomenon that is not merely restricted to how people are perceived, but also how those people who become objects of reification think of themselves. In this respect, Gabel stops short in his application of reification to racism when he sees the racist as exemplifying reified thought. Just as it is both the capitalist who is reified by seeing workers as objects in the production process and the worker who is reified by living a stultified life by performing this activity, a proper application of reification to the problem of racism must explain how reification applies to both the racist and the subject who lives under a racist system. Though neither Gabel nor Lukács offer us much guidance in this latter endeavor, it seems to me that the effects of racism on subjectivity were a concern exhibited by one of the most important African-American social thinkers and philosophers, W.E.B. Du Bois.

Much as Lukács characterizes the division of consciousness as a feature of the reification of the worker under capitalism, Du Bois recognizes the splitting of consciousness of the African American in his analysis of double consciousness in his *The Souls of Black Folk*. For Du Bois, the history of enslavement and the social reality of racism have the effect of the denial of self-consciousness of the African-American. The legacy of slavery and racial prejudice leads to "a world which yields him no true self-consciousness, but only lets him see himself through the revelation of the other world. It is a peculiar sensation, this double-consciousness, this sense of always looking at one's self through the eyes of others, of measuring one's soul by the tape of a world that looks on in amused contempt and pity."[35] Du Bois, of course, stops short of linking this to a theory of objectification. Nevertheless, one is implicit here. That is, the subject is split by the fact that she is compelled by the social system of white supremacy to measure herself by the standards of that system. That is, she views her humanity through the lens of a system that denies that humanity.

Both Lukács and Du Bois are keenly aware of the ways social systems of oppression can form the framework through which subjects evaluates themselves. As the philosopher Frank Kirkland has noted, there is good reason to see Du Bois (and, quite possibly, Lukács) as a legatee of Jean-Jacques Rousseau and his analysis of *amour-propre*, the way individuals measure themselves against

---

35 W.E.B. Du Bois, "Of Our Spiritual Strivings" in *The Souls of Black Folk* (Oxford: Oxford University Press, 2007), 3.

others, as a foundation of inequality and the distortion of subjectivity.[36] Similarly, both Lukács and Du Bois can agree that the processes by which individuals develop their sense of self and self worth are mediated (not determined) by the social systems under which they live. In the case of Lukács's worker, the sense of self is mediated through the labor process under capitalism. In the case of Du Bois' "Black folk," the sense of self is mediated through the American system of white supremacy. Both yield peculiar forms of dehumanization.

For Du Bois, the dehumanization manifests in the contradictions of the socio-political status of the African American. The African American is an American citizen, but, at the same time, systemically denied the dignities of citizenship because of the color of her skin. As Du Bois argues, the African American "simply wishes to make it possible for a man to be both a Negro and an American, without being cursed and spit upon by his fellows, without having the doors of Opportunity closed roughly in his face."[37]

Du Bois insists upon the ways that the system of white supremacy in the United States reinforced a self-questioning of the humanity of the African American:

> But the facing of so vast a prejudice could not but bring the inevitable self-questioning, self-disparagement, and lowering of ideals which ever accompany repression and breed in an atmosphere of contempt and hate. Whispering and portents came borne upon the four winds: Lo! We are diseased and dying, cried the dark hosts; we cannot write, our voting is vain; what need of education, since we must always cook and serve? And the Nation echoed and enforced this self-criticism, saying: Be content to be servants, and nothing more; what need of higher culture for half-men?[38]

Of course, Du Bois never suggests that double consciousness is reification. Nevertheless, his argument directs our attention to the ways the sense of self

---

36 See, Frank M. Kirkland, "On Du Bois' Notion of Double Consciousness," *Philosophy Compass*, 8, 2 (2013): 137–148. By linking double consciousness to *amour-propre*, Kirkland importantly gestures at the issue of the social basis of the sense of self. This stands in contrast to more existentially oriented readings of the concept in Du Bois. I should note that Kirkland has voiced valuable criticisms about my use of his interpretation to forge a connection to Lukács and I take responsibility for taking his insights in this different direction. Still, I am indebted to him for opening this avenue of interpretation and his scholarly generosity in encouraging me to take his interpretation in my own direction.
37 Du Bois, *Souls of Black Folk*, 3.
38 Ibid., 6.

are mediated by society and the ways a social system based on oppression can distort the sense of self.

Despite the fact that Lukács himself never directly draws a connection between his analysis of racism and his analysis of reification, both rely on accounts of the way social relations of oppression are naturalized. In the cases of both the social system of capitalism and the social system white supremacy, the naturalization of the condition of the oppressed group has been crucial the system's legitimacy. And, it is clear that, at least from the standpoint of the Lukács of *History and Class Consciousness*, this naturalization, in its denial of history and the developing nature of social relations, constitutes a contributing factor to reification. Further, it is in this theoretical claim that we find the deepest connection between the Lukács who articulated the phenomenon of reification and the Lukács concerned with the development of racist thought.

Gabel is, therefore, partly correct, in my view, when he draws the parallel between reification and racism based on a denial of the historical forces that explain the social condition of the worker and that of a person of color in a racist society. What he neglects is an analysis of white supremacy as a system that mediates the sense of self and affects consciousness in the way Lukács portrays the relation between capitalism and the worker. For this, we have to turn to Du Bois. Du Bois gives us the beginning of an analysis that, in my view, suggests strong parallels with Lukács.

3   Lukács and the Contemporary Terrain

Despite Lukács's explicit confrontation with racism in *The Destruction of Reason*, of the three figures associated with founding Western Marxism, theorists concerned with white supremacy have more readily employed the work of Antonio Gramsci. This is because of the more obvious applicability of his concept of hegemony.[39] I have argued that a connection can be drawn between reification and racism. My primary aim has been to suggest that this connection contributes to a larger effort of reassessing the richness of Lukács's thought. But this begs the question as to whether or not the connection warrants further exploration. Indeed, the very suggestion that racism is a form of reification might be alarming to some. Lukács's argument about the reification of consciousness appears so damning that it seems to banish any prospect for the full recovery of human agency. It was this concern that informed Jürgen Habermas's

---

[39]   See, for example, Stuart Hall, "Gramsci's Relevance for the Study of Race and Ethnicity," *Journal of Communication Inquiry* 10, 5 (1986): 5–27.

critique of Lukács in his *The Theory of Communicative Action*.[40] Nevertheless, there are several reasons why a reconsideration of Lukács might speak to the concerns of the rich tradition of African-American and Africana thought as well as the historiography of slavery and colonialism that has developed in the decades after Lukács's death in 1971.

The first relates to the longstanding enterprise on the part of African-American and Africana philosophers and social theorists to coordinate their analyses with Marxian theory to confront racism and racial oppression. This effort, at the very latest, emerged in historical works, most notably Du Bois' *Black Reconstruction in America*, C.L.R. James' *Black Jacobins*, and Eric Williams' *Slavery and Capitalism*. This project was carried forward in various ways in the works of thinkers like Angela Davis, Walter Rodney, the members of the Combahee River Collective, Cedric Robinson, Stuart Hall, Manning Marable, Cornel West, Adolph Reed, Charles W. Mills, and a host of others. From the standpoint of an intellectual history of the ways Marxism has been used to inform the study and critique of racism, I suggest that Lukács deserves greater consideration. His concern with the issue of racism, which as I suggested at the outset has been largely overlooked, holds the potential to further this still vibrant project of using Marxist thought to enrich our understanding of racism and vice versa.

Further, there is the historical matter of the role of capitalism in the slave and colonial systems that form the material setting for the development of racism.[41] In recent years, renewed attention has been given to capitalism's relation to slavery.[42] This work is based on innovative research to which Lukács may have little to offer. Still, his claim that racism emerges to legitimate capital's interest in colonization and enslavement gives him a place in the historiographical agenda of showing how capitalism contributed to the growth of racialized systems of oppression. It also serves as a reminder that, ultimately,

---

40 The critique can be found in Jürgen Habermas, *The Theory of Communicative Action, Volume One: Reason and the Rationalization of Society*, trans. Thomas McCarthy (Boston: Beacon Press, 1984), 355–365.

41 One of the pioneering works on the relation between capitalism and slavery is Eric Williams, *Capitalism and Slavery* (Chapel Hill: The University of North Carolina Press, 1994). A major study of the relation between capitalism and colonialism is Walter Rodney, *How Europe Underdeveloped Africa* (London: Verso, 2018).

42 Important works include: Walter Johnson, *River of Dark Dreams: Slavery and Empire in the Cotton Kingdom* (Cambridge: Harvard University Press, 2017); Edward Baptist, *The Half Has Never Been Told: Slavery and the Making of American Capitalism* (New York: Basic Books, 2016); Sven Beckert, *Empire of Cotton: A Global History* (New York: Vintage, 2015); and, Caitlin Rosenthal, *Accounting for Slavery: Masters and Management* (Cambridge: Harvard University Press, 2018).

Lukács situates the rise of racist ideas in the history of the development of capitalism.

Even if Lukács has less to offer to the work of more recent historical works, there is a deeper way in which Lukács might be responsive to the concerns of theorists working within the black radical tradition. Capitalism's historical role in shaping the colonial and slave systems aside, an ongoing question posed by these theorists has centered on the persistence of the relation between race and class, even after the abolition of race-based enslavement and decolonization. Specifically, theorists have explored the ways in which racial and class-based oppression intersect. As many theorists, in my view correctly, have stressed, class status and racial status can reinforce forms of oppression. This was certainly a concern that informed Du Bois's study of Reconstruction era relations between emancipated slaves and poor Southern whites. It has also informed the more recent work of Keeanga-Yamahtta Taylor who argues, "To claim, then, as Marxists do, that racism is a product of capitalism is not to deny or diminish its centrality or impact on American society. It is simply to explain its origins and persistence. Nor is this reducing racism to just a function of capitalism; it is locating the dynamic relationship between class exploitation and racial oppression in the functioning of American capitalism."[43] Taylor is right to point to the dynamic relationship as well as the origins of racialized systems of oppression in capitalism's development, but her ultimate emphasis is on the role of the capitalist system today. If capitalism becomes the privileged system of oppression, the significance of the system of white supremacy and the ways it operates independently of capitalism is necessarily diminished. Moreover, we are left with the somewhat oversimplified conclusion that members of the white working class who are racist are simply racist because racism is necessary to capitalism. The danger can be to analyze racism as a kind of false consciousness promoted by capitalism without attending to the ways white supremacy operates in accordance with its own logic.

While I am sympathetic to the case for solidarity and recognize that class and race can overlap to enhance oppression, I am of the mind that, despite the ways white supremacy and capitalism overlap, it is crucial to keep them analytically distinct. Here, I am in agreement with the work of Charles W. Mills. Though Mills is deeply influenced by Marxism insofar as he makes the case that racism, like capitalism, is a system, he clearly breaks with Marxian attempts to understand racism under the rubric of the capitalist system. Mills argues that his position

---

43 Keeanga-Yamahtta Taylor, *From #BlackLivesMatter to Black Liberation* (Chicago: Haymarket Books, 2016), 206.

constitutes a repudiation of the too-often epiphenomenalist treatment of race in the most important Western theory of group oppression, Marxism. Instead of treating race and racial dynamics as simply reducible to a class logic, this approach argues that race, though biologically unreal, becomes socially real and causally effective, since it is institutionalized and materialized by white supremacy in social practices and felt phenomenologies through constructions of the self; proclaimed ideals of cultural and civic identity; decisions of the state, crystallizations of juridical standing and group interests; permitted violence; and the opening and blocking of economic opportunities.[44]

That the two systems of oppression can operate independently of one another is testified to by the very history of racist ideas and the ways in which the racialized slave system in the American South was portrayed as superior to the capitalist "wage slavery" of the American North. One need only read the works of defenders of slavery like John C. Calhoun and George Fitzhugh (albeit in different ways) to see how easily capitalism can be rejected and racism can be upheld.[45] There are, therefore, good reasons to be skeptical of arguments that imagine that class exploitation can lead to interracial solidarity or that, ultimately, place too great an emphasis on framing the debate within the boundaries of class analysis.

The notion of reification provides a valuable tool for analyzing the effects of social systems of oppression. We can link the concerns of theorists focused on class exploitation and theorists focused on racism by proposing that both capitalism and white supremacy entail reification. The dehumanization may occur in different ways and for different reasons, but what they have in common is that they reify subjects. In both cases, the unique agency and autonomy of the subject is denied; the subject is sublimated under purported characteristics of the group as a whole; and, the socio-historical factors that actually explain the legitimation of the group's oppression are ignored.

At the same time, the sources of reification, e.g., capitalism and white supremacy, can be kept analytically distinct even if they have historically

---

[44] Charles W. Mills, "White Supremacy as Sociopolitical System" in *From Class to Race: Essays in White Marxism and Black Radicalism* (Lanham: Rowman & Littlefield Publishers, 2003), 184–185.

[45] For an example of Calhoun's argument, see: John C. Calhoun, "Speech on the Reception of Abolition Petitions" in *Union and Liberty: The Political Philosophy of John C. Calhoun*, ed. Ross M. Lence (Indianapolis: Liberty Fund, 1992), 474–475. For a summary of Fitzhugh's argument, see: George Fitzhugh, *Cannibals All! Or, Slaves Without Masters*, ed. C. Vann Woodward (Cambridge: The Belknap Press of Harvard University Press, 1960), 19.

coincided and aided one another. We can accept that they intersect.[46] An individual can be reified as a worker, as a person of color, or both. Still, it enables us to potentially avoid the problem of which system takes priority in society as a whole. Additionally, it removes the bedeviling question of why white workers and workers of color do not necessarily forge solidarity despite the fact that they are oppressed by the same capitalist system. The white working class can contribute to the reification of workers of color on the basis of race. Racism among the white working class can also inform reified views of elites of African descent (and, for that matter, elites of African descent can reify working people). Further, white workers can themselves be reified by adopting the reified mode of thought on which the notion that there are racial hierarchies or, at the very least, salient racial differences is premised.

A final implication of the utility of the concept of reification is that it forges a middle ground between two extremes. On the one hand, there is, as I have already noted, the tendency to engage in class reductionism. On the other, there is the ever-growing impulse to identify multiple forms of oppression, which insists on the absolute distinctiveness of each and, thus, rejects identifying a common theoretical vocabulary for analyzing oppression writ large. This comes at the expense of developing social explanations for how oppression operates and its actual effects. Criteria for what counts as oppression can fall by the wayside. And, while my focus has been on linking reification to racism, in an age where patriarchy, ethno-nationalism, anti-Semitism, homophobia, and transphobia are globally resurgent, I am of the mind that these phenomena might usefully be analyzed through the lens of reification.

Even if Lukács himself failed to fully appreciate the prospective applications of his theory, it is one that holds potential for understanding and analyzing how oppression operates both on the oppressor and the oppressed. The contemporary political terrain – one in which we are reminded regularly of the realities of capitalist exploitation and white supremacy as well as a host of other reinvigorated bigotries and systemic forms of oppression – speaks to the need for conceptual tools for understanding systems of oppression.

---

46   I have in mind intersecting oppressions not in the way the notion of intersectionality has been employed by thinkers influenced by poststructuralism, but, rather, more along the lines that Claudia Jones discussed triple oppression. See, for example, Claudia Jones, "An End to the Neglect of the Problems of the Negro Woman" in *Words of Fire: An Anthology of African-American Feminist Thought*, ed. Beverly Guy-Sheftall (New York: The New Press, 1995).

CHAPTER 13

Reification and Neoliberalism: Is There an Alternative?

Tivadar Vervoort

In 1999, Rahel Jaeggi wrote in the *Lukács-Jahrbuch* that "Weder in der philosophischen Debatte noch in soziologischen Zeitdiagnosen oder politischen Bewegungen spielt die Verdinglichungsdiagnose zur Zeit eine nennenswerte Rolle."[1] Although the concept "reification" (*Verdinglichung*) returned on the philosophical stage with Axel Honneth's reinterpretation of the concept from the perspective of his philosophy of recognition,[2] it remains an open question to what extend a *diagnosis* of reification as a structural societal problem is stuck in the margins of philosophy.[3] Such social critique of reification was introduced by Hungarian philosopher Georg Lukács in his magnum opus *Geschichte und Klassenbewußtsein*.[4] "Reification" must be understood as a critical philosophical concept, elaborating further upon Marx's analysis of commodity fetishism as the "universal" category of objectivity in capitalist societies. Lukács's further elaboration of Marx's idea of commodity fetishism understands the commodity form (*Warenform*) as the "second nature" of modern societal existence. Lukács stresses that the economizing tendency of market societies has a determining influence on all social relations, so that his understanding of the commodity form goes beyond Marx's critique of political economy: the commodity form expresses the *historical a priori* – the category of objectivity – of late capitalism. With Lukács's analysis of reification, therefore, an accurate critique of contemporary neoliberal reality can be formulated, since the neoliberal doctrine suggests an "'economization' of political life and

---

1 Rahel Jaeggi, "Verdinglichung – ein aktueller Begriff?," *Lukács-Jahrbuch* (1999), p. 67.
2 Axel Honneth, *Verdinglichung – Eine anerkennungstheoretische Studie* (Frankfurt a.M.: Suhrkamp Verlag, 2005).
3 As Raymond Geuss points out in his reflections on Honneth's *Tanner Lectures:* "If care (or recognition) is a precondition of everything and anything, including hatred or indifference, it cannot be the basis of an ethics or social criticism." Raymond Geuss, in *Reification: A New Look at an Old Idea,* by Axel Honneth (Oxford: Oxford University Press, 2006), p.127.
4 Georg Lukács, *Verdinhlichung und Klassenbewußtsein* (Darmstadt/Neuwied: Luchterhand, 1970 [1923]).

of other heretofore noneconomic spheres and activities."[5] Against Honneth's use of the concept, according to which the distinction between things and non-things points towards a normative or moral distinction,[6] Lukács's actual use of "reification" can ground an immanent critique of neoliberal pathologies such as precarization, flexibilization, and the economized treatment of more and more (private, public, ecological, digital) spheres of social life. The omnipresence of the reified presentation of social actors – *flex offices* instead of colleagues (as if office chairs would work by themselves), *Big Data Management* replacing the possibility of social change, and the necessity to *valorize* every "investment" – underlines this development. Market laws, austerity, deregulation, and privatization form the current schemata of social reality: not only objects appear as commodities, individuals as well are conceived according to this logic.

The question, to what extent Lukács's concept of reification is relevant to understand the alleged determined character of neoliberal reality, must be answered affirmatively. Lukács's analysis of the reified totality of society, in which facts of history appear as objects of eternal unchangeable natural laws, allows for an effective critique of the seemingly all-embracing "There is no alternative" that forms the "natural law" – the "second nature" – of neoliberal governing.[7] By connecting Lukács's critique of reification with critical analyses of neoliberal governmentality, an important but underdeveloped centre of gravity for a contemporary critique of neoliberalism can be broached, namely early critical theory. Uncoincidentally, Jameson pointed out that Theodor Adorno's critical theory reached a highpoint in its relevance after "the end of history," as "in this decade [...] Adorno's prophecies of the total system' finally came true, [...] he may turn out to have been the analyst of our own period."[8] Similarly, the relevance of Lukács's diagnoses is undeniable thirty years *after* the end of history. The challenge therefore is to bring Lukács's philosophy and any further critical-heterodox discourse on the ongoing economization of society together.

Even within the tradition of critical theory, "reification" is used in different senses. As such, a clear-cut separation from similar (Marxian and Marxist)

---

5   Wendy Brown, *Undoing the Demos: Neoliberalism's Stealth Revolution* (Cambridge MA: MIT Press, 2015), p.17.
6   Titus Stahl, "Verdinglichung als Pathologie zweiter Ordnung," *Deutsche Zeitschrift für Philosophie* 59, No. 5 (2011): 731.
7   Georg Lukács, *Geschichte und Klassenbewußtsein*, p.122.
8   Fredric Jameson, *Late Marxism* (London/New York: Verso Books, 1990, p.5).

vocabulary often falls short.[9] Here, the claim will be made that a critique of reification makes the *most* urgent problem of modern market-based societies visible, namely the undeniable omnipresence of the commodity form and the social barriers and oppressing subjectivations following from it. By bringing the reified "nature" of capitalist societies under the radar of contemporary critiques of neoliberalism, and by simultaneously bringing Lukács's analysis in contact with post-structuralist and postmodern theorems, I hope to make plausible Lukács's relevance *beyond* the exhausted dichotomy between German Critical Theory and (post-)structuralist *French Theory*. A contemporary reading of Lukács's concept of reification from the perspective of a critical-radical political philosophy could then as well replace the heavily mortgaged dialectical solution Lukács himself proposed for the problem of reification.[10]

In the following, I will first introduce the distinctive qualities of Lukács's concept of reification and elucidate its deviations from supposedly similar concepts in the tradition of Marxism and critical theory. In a second section, I will close in upon the similarities between "reification" and the young Marx's notion of alienation, as a continuous entanglement of these concept remains prevalent in many social and political philosophical works. After setting up these resemblances, I will shift to their differences, ultimately claiming that reification allows for a systemic critique of contemporary capitalism, whereas reliance on the concept of alienation brings along a normative-moralistic treatment of societal problems and even promotes essentialist account of the human condition. Finally, then, attempts will be made to integrate the concept of reification into contemporary critiques of neoliberalism stemming from the tradition of post-structuralism.

---

9   See for example Rahel Jaeggi and Titus Stahl, "Schwerpunkt Verdinglichung," *Deutsche Zeitschrift für Philosophie* 59, No. 5 (2011): 731–746. There, the everyday (*alltagsprachlich*) use of the concept is separated from its complex philosophical history (p.697). Nevertheless, in her study on alienation, Rahel Jaeggi does not distinguish strictly between the concepts of alienation and reification – despite the effort to move beyond an essentialist understand of the concept of alienation. Rahel Jaeggi, *Entfremdung* (Berlin: Suhrkamp, 2006).

10 Jaeggi und Stahl ("Schwerpunkt," pp.697–8) point out why Lukács's *solution* for the reification of reality should be rejected: "Erst wenn die Einheit des historischen Subjekts, des Proletariats, mit der von ihm geschaffenen Welt philosophisch und politisch eingeholt wird, so Lukács, kann sich dieses Subjekt die Gesellschaft und die Geschichte als Totalität wieder aneignen. Sowohl dieses Bild eines „identischen Subjekt-Objekts", das die Verdinglichung überwinden kann, als auch seine politischen Konsequenzen versperren jede Möglichkeit einer unkritischen Aneignung dieser Theorie."

1 Reification: a Still-relevant Concept

To recognize the relevance of the diagnosis of reification of reality under current late capitalist circumstances, it is necessary to first delimit the concept of reification from other, similar concepts. Although *"Verdinglichung"* is mentioned *en passant* in the third volume of Marx's *Das Kapital,* the task to introduce reification as a genuine philosophical *concept* clearly and distinctively remained preserved for Lukács's *Geschichte und Klassenbewußtsein*.[11] There, Lukács lays one of the most important conceptual groundworks for western Marxism and critical theory – Adorno, for example, used forms of *Verdinglichung* 746 times in his yet published oeuvre.[12] Nevertheless, in most current-day non-exegetic publications, concepts such as reification, commodity fetishism and alienation are frequently used as synonyms. To understand the characteristic meaning of Lukács's concept, it is necessary to revisit Lukács's first acquaintance with Marxian philosophy. To investigate Lukács's "Road to Marx" we can rely upon a vast amount of (auto)-biographical notes and interviews that examine this point in Lukács's intellectual development. Meanwhile, these primary sources can help to put the eclectic psychologizing explanations for Lukács's conversion to Marxism between brackets.[13]

---

11   Both Marx's uses of *"Verdingliching"* are to be found in Karl Marx, *Das Kapital: dritter Band, Marx-Engels Werke,* Volume 25 (Berlin: Dietz Verlag, 1963): "Es sind zwei Charakterzüge, welche die kapitalistische Produktionsweise von vornherein auszeichnen. Erstens. Sie produziert ihre Produkte als Waren. [...] Es ist ferner schon in der Ware eingeschlossen, und noch mehr in der Ware als Produkt des Kapitals, die Verdinglichung der gesellschaftlichen Produktionsbestimmungen und die Versubjektivierung der materiellen Grundlagen der Produktion, welche die ganze kapitalistische Produktionsweise charakterisiert" (p.887); "Im Kapital [...] ist die Mystifikation der kapitalistischen Produktionsweise, die Verdinglichung der gesellschaftlichen Verhältnisse, das unmittelbare Zusammenwachsen der stofflichen Produktionsverhältnisse mit ihrer geschichtlich-sozialen Bestimmtheit vollendet: die verzauberte, verkehrte und auf den Kopf gestellte Welt, wo Monsieur le Capital und Madame la Terre als soziale Charaktere und zugleich unmittelbar als bloße Dinge ihren Spuk treiben" (p.838).

12   This includes all variations starting with *verdinglich-*, and is based upon Theodor W. Adorno, *Gesammelte Schriften* (Frankfurt am Main: Suhrkamp, 1997).

13   Because of his turbulent political career, Lukács was forced to publicly rewrite his vita many times. In his final years, he commenced with reconstructing his life through conversations with journalists and academics. See Wolfgang Abendroth, Hans Heinz Holz & Leo Kofler, *Gespräche mit Georg Lukács* (Reinbek bei Hamburg: Rowohlt Verlag, 1967); Georg Lukács, "Lebenslauf," *Deutsches Zeitschrift für Philosophie* 48, No. 3 (2000), 529–530; Georg Lukács, "Mein Weg zu Marx," in, *Schriften zur Ideologie und Politik* (Neuwied: Luchterhand, 1967); Georg Lukács, *Record of a Life: An Autobiographical Sketch* (London: Verso Books 1983).

In 1940, Lukács himself identified two intellectual epochs in his life before arriving at his final Marxist position; a first, bourgeois-intellectualist period, and secondly an idealist period.[14] Following his opposition to the First World War he ended up in conflict with his milieu. Opposed to his tutors Max Weber and Georg Simmel, Lukács did not perceive wartime heroism as a means to replace the existing order: on the day of the Russian Revolution, Lukács left for Budapest. Subsequently, Marx's works became his central intellectual focal point. Lukács himself, however, categorises *Geschichte und Klassenbewußtsein* into his early idealist period. His philosophical texts from that period itself however rather suggest that his conversion from idealism to Marxism occurred more gradually. Although the works he produced between 1916 and 1923 prove of a radical break with all his former 'bourgeois' intellectual presuppositions, the influence of Hegel remains a permanent ingredient of his thought, so that Hegel became Lukács's chaperon during his transformation from idealistic cultural criticism to and Marxist social critique. In *A bolsevizmus mint erkölcsi probléma* (*Bolshevism as Moral Problem*), a text that appeared right before Lukács's "leap of faith into communism," Lukács contrasts Marx's "sociological" method with communism's ethical ideal of a free society of the same thinker.[15] According to Lukács, Bolshevist politics were unable to resolve the tension between a descriptive analysis of society and the political ideal of freedom, as violent political action is necessary and harms both a purely sociological view and its ethical ideal. In *Taktika és ethika*, which appeared a year later, Lukács resolved this problem.[16] There he claims that "the decisive criterion of socialist tactics [is] the philosophy of history." From that perspective, "adherence to the correct tactics is in itself ethical."[17] For comrade or *elvtárs* Lukács, the class struggle is justified by the congruence of the means and ends of the proletarian struggle. He claims that Marxism transformed Hegel's ethical system by "merely positing other 'values' than the Hegelian ones."[18] Hegel's continuous presence thus cannot be underestimated. Whereas most biographers understand Lukács's early aristocratic existentialism and eschatological diagnosis of the modern world as *the* prerequisite for the idealist tone of his earliest Marxist texts, it rather seems to be Hegel's *philosophical* influence that shaped Lukács's perspective on Marxism. *Geschichte und Klassenbewußtsein* should be read from that perspective.

14 Lukács, "Lebenslauf."
15 Georg Lukács, *A bolsevizmus mint erkölcsi probléma*, in *Történelem és osztálytudat* (Budapest: Magvető Kiadó, 1971): pp.11–17.
16 Georg Lukács, *Tactics and Ethics* (London: Verso Books, 2013).
17 Lukács, *Tactics and Ethics,* p.28.
18 Ibid.

In *Geschichte und Klassenbewußtsein,* Lukács discusses his understanding of the commodity form as the original source or *Urbild* of appearances in modern societies. He understands the commodity form as the structuring category – the neo-Kantian inspired *Gegenstandsform* – of *all* modern forms of life, through which all societal phenomena are united under a thinglike form: „das Warenproblem [erscheint] als zentrales, strukturelles Problem der kapitalistischen Gesellschaft in allen ihren Lebensäußerungen."[19] The problem of reification then manifests itself through the vicious circle of an ever-increasing presence of commodify fetishism. When objects just as subjects appear as commodities, unavoidably the web between these commodified phenomena can only reproduce the form of objectivity that determines them. As such, the commodity form not only defines the entire structure of society, but the thinglike elements of that society retroact upon that very structure as well. In a reified society, the commodity form characterizes the structure that reproduces itself through all things – objects and subjects – that are its products. Lukács therefore formulates a radically executed social-constructivist theory:

> Der qualitative Unterschied zwischen Ware als einer Form (unter vielen) des gesellschaftlichen Stoffwechsels der Menschen und zwischen Ware als universeller Form der Gestaltung der Gesellschaft zeigt sich aber nicht bloß darin, daß die Warenbeziehung als Einzelerscheinung einen höchstens negativen Einfluß auf den Aufbau und auf die Gliederung der Gesellschaft ausübt, sondern dieser Unterschied wirkt zurück auf Art und Geltung der Kategorie selbst.[20]

The problem of reification thus follows from the apparent universality of the commodity form. As a capitalist market economy can only function when social relations are relations of commodities, the capitalist world has an inherent drive towards the universalisation of the identity between commodity relations and social relations. What follows, is that, not only commercial products are considered as exchangeable commodities, but any kind of societal relation shows itself increasingly to be understood as if it naturally exists in a thinglike manner: "[die] Beziehung zwischen Personen [erhält] den Charakter einer Dinghaftigkeit und auf diese Weise eine »gespenstige Gegenständlichkeit«."[21]

At first sight, Lukács's analysis remains close to Marx's characterization of commodity fetishism in *Das Kapital* – and this *topos* indeed forms Lukács's

---

19   Lukács, *Geschichte und Klassenbewußtsein,* p.170.
20   Ibid., p.173.
21   Ibid., p.171.

point of departure. Marx's famous contrast between the triviality of the use-value of an object and its *sinnlich übersinnliche* exchange value, that appears for the first time when that object enters the sphere of the market, forms the basis of both analyses. Market commodities entail something that is not perceivable sensually, yet *is* regarded as their essential characteristic – their price or exchange-value. Marx considers exchange-values is something *übersinnlich,* something transcending perception in the perceptible world, because exchange introduces a form of equivalence grounded in *abstract and social* amount of labour time, that becomes incorporated into the object as a natural quality; a transcendent abstraction of the human productivity shows itself as a characteristic of the object. Put otherwise, activity of its producer is abstracted and naturalised into an essential characteristic of the commodity itself:

> Das Geheimnisvolle der Warenform besteht also einfach darin, daß sie den Menschen die gesellschaftlichen Charaktere ihrer eigenen Arbeit als gegenständliche Charaktere der Arbeitsprodukte selbst, als gesellschaftliche Natureigenschaften dieser Dinge.[22]

As the division of labour is only thinkable if the products of labour are exchangeable, the double character of the commodity – as use value and exchange value – is a necessary correlate of market economies. Subsequently, the value of a product is expressed in the aforementioned *Form der Glechheit* of socially necessary labour time, as if it would be a characteristic of the product itself. The quantitative exchange value of commodities manifests itself as if it belongs to the commodities naturally, but as Marx underlines, "es ist nur das bestimmte gesellschaftliche Verhältnis der Menschen selbst, welches hier für sie die phantasmagorische Form eines Verhältnisses von Dingen annimmt."[23]

In Marx's critique of political economy, the commodity appears *as if* its exchange value is part of its identity – but this "as if" remains a mere phantom.[24] Lukács, however, asserts that in contemporary capitalism reality and appearance intertwine more and more. Capitalism does not merely produce a "phantomlike objectivity," the phantom *is* increasingly the only reality of social life that is in fact available. The commodity form penetrates more and more fields

---

22   Karl Marx, *Das Kapital, Marx-Engels Werke,* Volume 23 (Berlin: Dietz Verlag, 1962): p.86.
23   Ibid.
24   See for instance: "Die Personen existieren hier nurfüreinander als Repräsentanten von Ware und daher als Warenbesitzer. Wir werden überhaupt im Fortgang der Entwicklung finden, daß die ökonomischen Charaktermasken der Personen nur die Personifikationen der ökonomischen Verhältnisse sind, als deren Träger sie sich gegenübertreten." Ibid. p.99f.

of social life and forms the universal category of societal existence.[25] The commodity form produces a second nature of things, as it naturalizes the commodity form into the essence of all things, which then together build a reified society. The problem of reification thus points at a society in which commodity relations produce the only thinkable and seemingly natural social order. This view shows its urgent relevance strongly in the realm of politics. One of the ill-fated consequences of the problem of reification is the "contemplative" subjectivity it produces, which subsequently regards social reality as a static nature instead of as a politically transformable construct. Lukács was able to see this process, which now, almost a hundred years later, sounds painfully familiar. The continuing economization of a manifold of social spheres under neoliberal government underlines the relevance of Lukács's analysis.

2 Reification: the Late Capitalist Comrade of Alienation

The concept *Verdinglichung* does not merely refer to a "false consciousness" that accompanies consumerism in an affluent capitalist society; the relevance of Lukács's reification does not lie merely in the ideological realm. Reification rather affects society in its *ontological* realm. Due to the ever-increasing rationalisation of societal processes – first the bureaucratization and rationalization of administrative and labour process, later the further liberalization and privatization of the state, and more recently the state-organized forms of precarization of both citizens and non-citizens – the reified, thinglike form of appearance becomes the sole real available mode of existence to remain member and part of society. As such, it seems as if the unity of objectivity and subjectivity that Lukács searched for in class consciousness, today became real in the self-understanding of neoliberalism: subjectivities have to understand themselves as part of the objective rationality of society to survive. Here I will argue that this phenomenon does not designate an alienation from an authentic human self-understanding and genuine human relations, but rather that the problem reification grows from and inhabits the principles of modernity itself – to which a political answer must continuously be formulated.

Although Lukács's concept of reification shows strong resemblances to Marx's notion of alienation – Lukács wrote his essay on *Verdinglichung* nine years before Marx's *Parisian Manuscripts* on were rediscovered – these analogies can only be explain with respect to both their relations to Hegel's philosophy. As Marcuse underlined immediately after the rediscovery of Marx's

---

25   Lukács, *Geschichte und Klassenbewußtsein*, p.174.

manuscripts, the rediscovery of the *Parisian Manuscripts* presented the first critical scholarly work on Hegel that focused specifically upon Hegel's notions *Entfremdung* and *Entäußerung*.[26] In Hegel's *Phenomenologie des Geistes*, objects are understood as substances externalised by the (productive) subject: "seine Substanz ist also eine Entäußerung selbst, und die Entäußerung ist die Substanz."[27] For Hegel, "*Entäußerung*" follows from the discrepancy between subjective impressions and their objective counterparts, which can only be relinquished in the fulfilment of absolute spirit. In the *Phänomenologie*, Hegel seeks to resolve the regressive and circular epistemological contradictions that follow from the disconnection between things in themselves and for themselves: "ist das Erkennen das Werkzeug, [...] so fällt sogleich auf, dass die Anwendung eines Werkzeugs auf eine Sache sie vielmehr nicht lässt, wie sie für sich ist. [Ist] das Erkennen nicht Werkzeug unserer Tätigkeit, sondern gewissermaßen ein passives Medium, [...] so erhalten wir auch so sie [die Wahrheit] nicht, wie sie an sich [...] ist."[28] Following Chris Arthur, I understand Hegel's *Entäußerung* to designate the externalisation (*ausser* meaning ex-, or outer-), of an object through subjective action, or Spirit's "positing of itself in otherness."[29] Hegel understands the totality of objects, or nature, as a product of spirit. Therefore, the formal separation of object and subject, introduced and legitimized by Kant's critical philosophy, must be overcome, as Schacht's study on alienation shows as well: "In the Preface [Hegel] suggests that experience requires the object to alienate itself and then return to itself from this alienation: we can, e. g., comprehend phenomena only by invoking abstractions which initially seem remote from the phenomena themselves."[30] Although the physical externalization of objects cannot be prevented according to Hegel, he does not merely seek to overcome this separation, but rather argues for a renewed unity between the object and its producing subject through the self-conscious recollection of the object's former externalisation.[31]

---

26 Herbert Marcuse, *Neue Quellen zur Grundlegung des historischen Materialismus* (Frankfurt a.M.: Suhrkamp Verlag, 1932).
27 Georg W.F. Hegel, *Phenomenologie des Geistes* (Hamburg: Felix Meiner Verlag 1988): p.320f.
28 Ibid, p.57.
29 Chris Arthur, *Dialectics of Labour* (New York: Basil Blackwell, 1968): p.174f.
30 Richard Schacht, *Alienation* (New York: Anchor Books, 1971): p.37f.
31 As Sean Sayers argues: "For Hegel, the overcoming of alienation is not an unattainable or even a distant ideal; it can be, and is being, achieved in the present. Work is an essential part of the process of spiritual self-development: it is a process of objectification – of alienation and its overcoming – leading to self-realisation. The central theme of the Hegelian system is the story of human self-development, culminating in the spiritual achievements – the art, religion and philosophy – of his own age. Thus, in Hegel's system,

Hegel thus argues for *Er-Innerung* as answer to *Entäußerung*, that is, "recognizing them precisely as spirit's own work."[32] Hegel's end thus is "da, wo es nicht mehr über sich selbst hinauszugehen nötig hat, wo es sich selbst findet und der Begriffe dem Gegenstande, der Gegenstand dem Begriffe entspricht."[33] In Hegel's account, then, *Enfremdung* merely means the alienation as secondary societal consequences that is produced by the epistemological externalization (*Entäußerung*) of objectivity.

Marx's critique of Hegel aims at the abstract end of Hegel's perspective on the problem of externalization. Instead of *social* alienation, Hegel's stages the epistemological separation between object and subject as the central problem. Marx argues that in Hegel, "Die ganze *Entäußerungsgeschichte* und die ganze *Zurücknahme* der Entäußerung ist [...] nichts als die *Produktionsgeschichte* des abstrakten, des absoluten Denkens."[34] Therefore, Marx turns Hegel's understanding of objectivity, lying in his concept of externalization, against himself. The young Marx does suggest an ontological role for the producing human just as Hegel did; the human's intellectual power of imagination reduplicates itself into the objective world: "Das Große an der Hegelschen Phänomenologie und ihrem Endresultate [...] ist also einmal, daß Hegel die Selbsterzeugung des Menschen als einen Prozeß faßt, die Vergegenständlichung als Entgegenständlichung, als Entäußerung und als Aufhebung dieser Entäußerung."[35] Marx however designates this reduplication with *Vergegenständlichung* instead of *Entäußerung*: in his case a subjective image reduplicates itself in an objective form – as an objectification through the human's productivity, not as an externalization. For Marx, labour signifies "ein Mittel zur Befriedigung eines Bedürfnisses, des Bedürfnisses der Erhaltung der physischen Existenz."[36] As such, labour objectifies (*vergegenständlicht*) an intellectual capacity of the human: "Der Gegenstand der Arbeit ist daher die Vergegenständlichung des Gattungslebens des Menschen: indem er sich nicht nur eine im Bewußtsein intellektuell, sondern werktätig, wirklich verdoppelt und sich selbst daher in einer von ihm geschaffnen Welt anschaut."[37] Marx's critique is not so much aimed at

---

labour is often presented in positive and uncritical terms, as playing an essential role in a story of spiritual development and progress." Sean Sayers, *Marx and Alienaton* (New York: Palgrave Macmillan, 2011): p.26f.

32   Arthur, *Dialectics of Labour*, p.56.
33   Hegel, *Phänomenologie*, p.62.
34   Karl Marx, *Politisch-Ökonomische Manuskripte* (Hamburg: Meiner Verlag, 2008): p.131
35   Ibid., p.133.
36   Ibid., p.62.
37   Ibid., p.63. Hegel uses the metaphor of reduplication as well: "Die Welt dieses Geistes zerfällt in die gedoppelte; die erste ist die Welt der Wirklichkeit oder seiner Entfremdung

Hegel's understanding of the genesis of objectivity, but at Hegel's philosophical abstraction of the problem of alienation. Here, Marx's early critique of political economy intertwines with his critique of Hegel's philosophy: "Hegel steht auf dem Standpunkt der modernen Nationalökonomen."[38] Therefore Marx can argue that objects (*Gegenstände*) produced following the principles of capitalism are alien beings (*ein fremdes Wesen*) to their producers, as they are brought about as commodities being property of the buyer of the producer's labour power. Although the realisation of labour always encompasses the objectification of a productive activity – Marx's *Vergegenständlichung* –, his critique stresses that this realisation (*Verwirklichung*) under capitalist mode of production goes at the expense of the worker, who then is "derealized": "Die Verwirklichung der Arbeit ist ihre Vergegenständlichung. Diese Verwirklichung der Arbeit erscheint in dem nationalökonomischen Zustand als *Entwirklichung* des Arbeiters, die Vergegenständlichung als *Verlust und Knechtschaft des Gegenstandes*, die Aneignung als *Entfremdung*, als *Entäußerung*."[39] Hegel's *Zurücknahme* of externalization (*Entäußerung*) though self-consciousness thus leads to the reduction of the worker into an object of the chain of production: "Sie produziert Geist, aber sie produziert Blödsinn, Cretenismus für d[en] Arbeiter."[40] Marx thus separates humanities' creative – objectifying – *capacity* from the social phenomenon of alienation (for him: *Entäußerung*), the latter being the externalisation of the former capacity.[41] Under capitalism, the immediate kind of productive objectification is objectified itself and as such externalized – *entäußert*. Externalization shows itself in the alienation between the wage labourer and his productive capacity: "Die *Nationalökonomie verbirgt die Ent-fremdung in dem Wesen der Arbeit dadurch, daß sie nicht des* unmittelbare *Verhältnis zwischen dem* Arbeiter (der Arbeit) *und der Produktion betrachtet*."[42] Such political-economical externalization is accompanied by social alienation for Marx, which can only be overcome through a real, that is, a practical overthrow of the abstractions of economy.[43] Still, alienation

---

selbst; die andre aber die, welche er, über die erste sich erhebend, im Äther des reinen Bewußtseins sich erbaut" Hegel, *Phänomenologie*, p.323.
38   Marx, *Manuskripte*, p.133.
39   Ibid. p.56.
40   Ibid., p.59.
41   For instance: "Das Produkt der Arbeit ist die Arbeit, die sich in einem Gegenstand fixiert, sachlich gemacht hat, es ist die Vergegenständlichung der Arbeit. Die Verwirklichung der Arbeit ist ihre Vergegenständlichung" Ibid., p.56.
42   Ibid., p.58.
43   This, for Marx, is fundamentally at odds with Hegel's position: "Bei Hegel ist die Negation der Negation daher nicht die Bestätigung des wahren Wesens, eben durch Negation des Scheinwesens, sondern die Bestätigung des Scheinwesens oder des sich entfremdeten

(*Entfremdung*) in the first place signifies the relation between society and its individual members, since it points out the separation between individual identities and society as the processes, structures and categories that allow for these phenomena. In Lukács, we find on the one hand an anticipation of the rediscovery of this motive in Marx's oeuvre, but on the other hand his concept of reification allows for a critique on a societal instead of an individual level, without necessarily having to rely on a productivist anthropology – as Marx and Hegel do. Marx's *Hegelian* concept of alienation relates to this problem from a subjective and essentialist point of view – regarding productivity as the essence of the human – whereas Lukács transforms Marx's macro-diagnosis of capitalism of *Das Kapital* into a critique on the formative structures that since increasingly saturated every realm of society.

Lukács as well understands the worker as deprived of its capacity to produce. The worker is transformed into an isolated particle inside a self-governing productive system without insight into the overarching end of that system, forcing the worker to regard its capacity to produce as an "ihm 'gehörende' Ware," as "ein Ding, das er 'besitzt.'"[44] Even those who do not necessarily commodify their labour comply to the same "kontemplative Attitude zu dem Funktionieren seiner eigenen, objektivierten und versachlichten Fähigkeiten."[45] Where Hegel sought the reunification of objectivity and subjectivity under consciousness, Lukács shows that this unity is already actualized under the commodity form. Capitalist reification achieves the unity Hegel sought for in the commodity; the commodities become the "true representatives" of societal life.[46] Exactly this critique is highly urgent in the era of neoliberal individualism.

3   "There Is No Alternative" and Reification

In his 1967 preface to the republication of *Geschichte und Klassenbewußtsein*, Lukács re-evaluates his own book as being too Hegelian, as it would wrongly equate objectivity with reification, leaving no possible way out of capitalism: "Denn die Vergegenständlichung ist tatsächliche eine unaufhebbare Äusserungsweise im gesellschaftlichen Leben der Menschen."[47] Lukács's reflection

Wesens in seinen Verneinung oder die Verneinung dieses Scheinwesens als eines gegenständlichen, außer dem Menschen hausenden und von ihm unabhängigen Wesens und seine Verwandlung in das Subjekt." Ibid., p.142.

44   Lukács, *Geschichte und Klassenbewußtsein*, p.181.
45   Ibid., p.179.
46   Ibid., p.185.
47   Ibid., p.26.

shows his advancing insight into the different meanings of these concepts in a Marxian sense, thereby rightly dismissing his Hegelian *solution* to the problem of reified social totality. Still, the *problem* of reification as sketched by Lukács cannot be understood as a mere critique of objectification. When we bracket Lukács's dialectical understanding of class struggle, that is, when emancipation from a reified society is not understood as emerging from self-consciousness of the proletariat as the identical subject-object of history, what rests is a refined immanent critique of the totalitarian force of the market economy: Lukács shows that the principles of the market not guarantee autonomy and self-determination, as liberal theoreticians argue, but that these principles mean as well the tendential penetration of the commodity form into all spheres of interhuman relations. Instead of arguing for a social critique of *Entfremdung* starting from some presupposed human essence or *Gattungswesen*, as humanist Marxism tends to do,[48] Lukács's analysis provides a structural critique of the dominant form of objectivity. Based on his theory of reification, it is possible to discuss the exploitive organisation of society from a macroscopic and sociological point of view. As such, the ideology-critical perspective of German critical theory can remain, or become, an important element for any critique of the economization and governementization of societal life; tendencies that up to today are mostly analysed from the perspective of the Foucauldian tradition.[49] More specifically, Lukács's critique of reification as form of objectivity could be brought together with Foucauldian concepts such as "truth regime" and "episteme," which as well point at the dominance of a form of rationality, especially since both carry along a neo-Kantian moment.[50] If the end of an immanent but emancipatory critique of capitalism is fundamental to critical theory, such

---

48   For example, Erich Fromm, *Marx's Concept of Man* (New York: Frederic Ungar, 1961); but also Herbert Marcuse, *One Dimensional Man* (Boston: Beacon Press, 1964).

49   For example, Wendy Brown, *Undoing the Demos*, (Cambridge MA: MIT Press, 2015); Isabell Lorey, *Die Regierung der Prekären* (Vienna: Turia + Kant, 2012); Pierre Dardot & Christan Laval, *The New Way of the World: on Neoliberal Society* (London/New York: Verso, 2014).

50   For Lukács's relation to neo-Kantianism see for instance Tom Rockmore "The specific link between his Marxism and German neo-Kantianism lies in his extension of their assertion of the epistemological incapacity of certain forms of historical knowledge to classical German philosophy in general. In sum, although Lukács was trained and influenced by some of the leading neo-Kantian scholars, the decisive reason for its influence on his Marxism lies in his concern to employ neo-Kantian forms of argumentation to grasp and finally to discredit classical German philosophy in general." Tom Rockmore, "Fichte, Lask and Lukács's Hegelian Marxism," *Journal of the History of Philosophy* 30, No. 4 (1992): 557–577. Foucault on his turn sought to renew the Kantian "Ethos" and at the same time builds on the French epistemological tradition Bachelard, Canguilhem, Cavaillés, which via Leon Brunschwicq was influenced by neo-Kantianism. Michel Foucault, "What is Enlightenment?" in Paul Rabinow (ed.) *The Foucault Reader* (New York: Pantheon Books,

a critique remains more actual than ever, since precisely the lack of collective emancipation has led critical to its reflexive perspective on social totality. Although thinkers such as Axel Honneth today rather aim at a normative justification of critical theory, the ferment of critical theory is still made up by immanent analyses of the totality of society. As both Lukács as the Frankfurters were well-aware, such sociological observations and judgements have the tendency to formalise and reify societal phenomena itself, so that they are as well doomed to reproduce the existing forms of society they aim to emancipate society from. The most recent depolitization of socio-economic challenges and the critique of the neoliberalization of governing demand, however, an active integration of the reflexive-emancipatory ends of critical theory into philosophical discourses on neoliberal society. There lies an important role for Lukács's analysis problem of reification, as it precisely points at the form of rationality that depoliticizes society.

As we have seen, Lukács's theory of the proletariat as identical subject-object of history sought to conceive emancipatory change from within the development of reified society itself. Lukács explained change as arising from of the uttermost loss of individual subjectivity of the worker: when the proletariat as class would become aware that it forms the object of history, being the object of value-creation in capitalist production, through class consciousness it could reveal itself as a revolutionary subjectivity. Today, such a conception of social struggle seems not only estranged from reality, but also politically hardly feasible, especially taking the far-reaching fragmentalization of the socio-political organization of classes into consideration, as well in their intersection with other – racist, sexist, etc. – axes of oppression. These cannot be understood from one antagonistic dichotomy any more. Precisely this moment – the atomizing isolation and depolitization of elements of society – Lukács sought to theorize with is concept of reification. The value of the Lukácsian *critique* of society must therefore be brought into relation with other conceptions on social change, otherwise Lukács might end up in the same *Grand Hotel Abgrund* where he situated the later generation of critical theory. Such a connection might go against the grain of Lukács's orthodox-Marxist readers. I want to argue that their orthodoxy itself cannot provide a relevant philosophical critique anymore, not in the least place because of fundamentally contingency at play in reality – as Lukács argues as well. An immanent critique of reified totality must in the end find an emancipatory potential *in* reified totality itself. Despite the self-determined capacity of the "second nature" of capitalist society, based

---

1984): pp.32–50; See also David Webb, *Foucault's Archaeology* (Edinburgh: Edinburgh University Press 2013).

on a self-reflexive critique of society a potential for change must be thought, without falling back on normative or even "natural" grounds: "Das qualitative Sein der ‚Dinge', das als unbegriffenes und ausgeschaltetes Ding an sich, als Gebrauchswert sein außerökonomisches Leben führt, das man während des normalen Funktionierens der ökonomischen Gesetze ruhig vernachlässigen zu können meint, wird in den Krisen plötzlich (plötzlich für das verdinglichte, rationelle Denken) zum ausschlaggebenden Faktor."[51] Not only does Lukács's thesis of reification show the problem of a reified social totality, Lukács points out that that totality itself remains too irrational to be understood, as Jameson implies as well: "Lukács applies to the realm of philosophy the method that Marx himself had already practiced in his critique of middle-class economics. [...] [F]or the Lukács of *History and Class Consciousness*, the limits of middle-class philosophy are signalled by its incapacity or unwillingness to come to terms with the category of totality itself."[52]

Fully in line with Marx's sixth Feuerbachian thesis, Marx's philosophy redefined the greatest social-emancipatory power of that discipline. Marx appropriated those elements of idealist philosophy and bourgeois economic thought that allowed him to critique reality and to understand reality as fundamentally variable. In line with other the political realism of thinkers such as Macchiavelli and Spinoza, Marx recognized that social reality is not absolute, but only *relatively* determined by structural circumstances. The Marxian critique of political economy does not broadcast a historical determinism, but a radical social constructivism, in which the world remains apt to change, making a critical attitude towards reality necessary for an emancipatory praxis. Lukács's critique of reification carries on this attitude: his analysis shows the rationalizing and totalizing effects of capitalism on all domains of society; nevertheless the isolation and atomization of individuals produced by the form of rationality of capitalism remains mere semblance, "Aber dieser Schein ist als Schein notwendig."[53] Although the "second nature" of society manifests itself as a necessary illusion, this illusion is always and fundamentally temporally and limited:

> Diese scheinbar restlose, bis ins tiefste physische und psychische Sein des Menschen hineinreichende Rationalisierung der Welt endet jedoch ihre Grenze an dem formellen Charakter ihrer eigenen Rationalität. [...] Daß

---

51 Lukács, *Geschichte und Klassenbewußtsein*, p.281.
52 Fredric Jameson, *Marxism and Form* (Princeton: University Press, 1974):183f.; see also Jameson, Fredric, "The Case for Georg Lukács," *Salmagundi* 13 (1970): 3–35.
53 Lukács, *Geschichte und Klassenbewußtsein*, p.103.

der – in der Unmittelbarkeit des gedankenlosen Alltags – fest geschlossen scheinende Zusammenhalt der ‚Naturgesetzlichkeit' dieses Lebens plötzlich aus den Fugen geraten kann, ist nur darum möglich, weil das Aufeinanderbezogensein seiner Elemente, seiner Teilsysteme auch bei dem normalsten Funktionieren etwas Zufälliges ist.[54]

At that point it is possible and necessary, to harmonize the critical attitude of the Lukácsian tradition with those critical enquiries that aim for an analysis of the supposed unchangeable neoliberal reality, in which there allegedly are "no alternatives." As opposed to the dialectical tradition of German critical theory, analyses of neoliberalism building on post-structuralist thinkers could offer a dynamical understanding of change and emancipation that can consolidate the all too objectively determined appearance late capitalist society that Lukács was able to predict. In these studies late capitalist society is understood from a neoliberal governmentality creating, through self-discipline, an "entrepreneurial self" as in the Foucauldian tradition; or the omnipresence of capital is rooted into its "detteritorializing" drives following Deleuze and Guattari.[55] It is striking that this tradition engaged more explicitly with the problematics of neoliberalism than the newest generations of Frankfurter critical theory. Without taking over all premises and arguments of any of these traditions, the challenge here is to include Lukács's critique of reified reality into these debates. As such, the kinship between Lukács's analyses of the thinglike forms of objectivity and subjectivity with the forms of rationality analyses of neoliberalism lay bare can be made clear. As both traditions developed a conceptualization of the subject in which its meaning is stipulated by the laws of the market, there lies an urgent opportunity in their converge to criticize social reality today.

At the same time, there are stark contrasts between the dialectical tradition of German critical theory and the focus on difference in French post-structuralism.[56] Still, both traditions recognize the possibility of political resistance: as a multitudal potency, in the non-identical, as *contre-conduites*. Lukács's allusion to the irrationality of the commodity form shows that the

---

54 Ibid., p.276.
55 See Michel Foucault, *The Birth of Biopolitics* (New York: Palgrave Macmillan, 2011); Antonio Negri & Michael Hardt, *Empire*, (Cambridge MA: Harvard University Press, 2002); 2003; Isabell Lorey, *Regieren der Prekären*, Wendy Brown, *Undoing the Demos,*; Ulrich Bröckling, *Das unternehmerische Selbst* (Frankfurt/Main: Suhrkamp, 2007).
56 Jean-François Lyotards *Économie libidinale* (1974), Gilles Deleuze' und Félix Guattaris *L'Anti-Oedipe* (1972), und Jean Baudrillards *Le Miroir de la production* (1973) not only marked the contrast between dialectical thought and post-structuralism, but between the latter and Marxism tout court.

totality of reified reality should be conceived as the real but illusory product of such powers. Even when the image of a reified objectivity is accepted, dynamical forces on different microscopical and macroscopical levels remain at play, arising in-between and inside the objectivity of things; a totality of thing-like realities cannot exhaustively congeal the forces at play inside, underneath and behind it. Indeed, Lukács takes that when "das richtige Handeln zu einem wahrhaften und richtigen Regulativ wird, [es] muß sich das Klassenbewußtsein über seine bloß wirkliche Gegebenheit erheben."[57] An emancipatory politics, even when considered from the viewpoint of history, always cultivates something contingent and non-given, that must become real nevertheless: "Contingency is as it were the inner blind-spot of bourgeois consciousness, or of the existential experience of capitalism."[58] Still, theories that merely adulate the accidental birth of political events, run the risk of boiling down to all too abstract metaphysical trickeries if they give all primacy to the potentially revolutionary dynamics of modernity. The post-structural tendency to reify to possibility for social change into abstract philosophical concepts shows the necessity the work out their critique of neoliberalism under consideration of Lukács's critical theory. Even Negri and Hardt, who present an eclectic mix of ideas stemming from all areas of philosophy and radical theory, hardly refer to Lukács work and reject his theory of reification in their *Empire*-series. Post-Marxists thinkers such as Chantal Mouffe and Ernesto Laclau, who explicitly work around the theme of neoliberalism, as well reject categories such as ideology and reification.[59]

Still, Lukács was first to diagnose the contemplative, inert state of being of central modern-day capitalism that is so characteristic for neoliberal power techniques. Therefore, post-structural forms of analysis of neoliberalism must be brought together with Lukács's conception of reified reality. Such reification shows itself as well in post-structuralist reflections on late capitalism in which always one form of potentiality (power, desire, libido, etc.) determines the entire social construct. Again, Jameson was aware of this opening: "[the] negative and methodological status of the concept of 'totality' may also be shown at work in those very post-structural philosophies which explicitly repudiate such 'totalizations' in the name of difference, flux, dissemination,

---

57 Lukács, *Geschichte und Klassenbewußtsein*, p.51.
58 Fredric Jameson, "History and Class Consciousness as an 'Unfinished Project.'" *Rethinking Marxism* 1, No.1: p.58.
59 See Chantal Mouffe, "Critique as Counter-Hegemonial Intervention," *transversal* (2008); http://eipcp.net/transversal/0808/mouffe/en (accessed September 30st, 2018); Ernesto Laclau, "Why Constructing a People Is the Main Task of Radical Politics," *Critical Inquiry* 32, No.4 (2006): 646–680.

and heterogeneity."[60] And even if political conflict is a product of such dynamic processes, or if reality itself is a "process," there is always the challenge to explain why this totality appears as reified, objective and inert: How does "the *reification* into which the outside world had frozen" follow from dynamics and fluidity?[61] Lukács's concept of reification already pointed towards the depolitization of such dynamics. To move away from both the compulsive omnipresence of market forms and institutionalised repression, a redefinition of the seemingly determined character of this reality is needed. To use post-structuralist jargon to express this moment: there is need appropriate the alienating, derooting and deterritorializing dynamics to move its effects beyond the reified second nature of reality, so that "everything that is solid melts into air." As such, the reification of reality could melt into air as well. Since commodity fetishism is the way in which capitalism disenchants and remystifies society, it might be this "chanting" flux that should be reappropriated politically: if critical theory wants to preserve its emancipatory thrust, it not only needs immanent-reflexive criticism, but also an imagination that can form another world from within reified reality itself. Social change must be sought for without having to fall back into a essentialist anthropology. Still, even such an attempt must deal with Lukács's prerequisite of political action: contingent forces will need to find some form of collective organisation or some reified identity to become effective beyond the reified atomisation of late capitalism.

60   Fredric Jameson, *The Political Unconscious* (Ithaca: Cornell University Press, 1981): p.39.
61   Fredric Jameson, "The Case for Georg Lukács," *Salmagundi* 13: p.22.

CHAPTER 14

Populism and the Logic of Commodity Fetishism: Lukács's Theory of Reification and Authoritarian Leaders

Richard Westerman

Almost a century after the publication of *History and Class Consciousness*, we seem farther than ever from the transformative social revolution that Lukács envisaged. The faith he seemed to vest in the proletariat's capacity to produce the conditions of emancipation already seemed misguided ten years after its publication, when large swathes of the German working classes turned to National Socialism rather than revolutionary Bolshevism. The contemporary international political scene unsettlingly echoes the 1930s. The continuing crisis stemming from the 2008 collapse has produced worldwide anger with globalized capitalism. But instead of a revolutionary class consciousness, much of this has been manifest in the rise of authoritarian populism, characterized by rejection of supranational organizations such as the EU and NAFTA, racism, anti-immigrationism, diminution of civil rights, primordialist nativism, and – above all – the rejection of so-called metropolitan elites in favour of larger-than-life, quote 'strong men' leaders such as Donald Trump. Nearly fifty years after his death, Lukács himself has not been able to rest easy: the Fidesz government of Hungary's Viktor Orbán, one of several such leaders now tightening their grip on power, has of course begun to dismantle the Lukács Archive housed at the philosopher's apartment, and the party has at the same time allied with the even-farther-right Jobbik at the city level to remove a statue of him from the centre of Budapest.[1] But Orban's attacks are not confined to Lukács and those on the Marxian left: his government has also attempted to shutter the Central European University, castigating its patron George Soros – hardly a socialist – as an outsider bent on undermining Hungary, in clearly anti-Semitic terms. Needless to say, Muslim refugees have fared even worse. Orbán's rhetoric, awash with images of a nation under threat from outsiders, is typical of this contemporary breed of authoritarian populism: it summons mass support by

---

1 Jerome Warren, 'The Erasure of History: Lukács Forgotten,' February 7, 2017, http://www.look-leftonline.org/2017/02/the-erasure-of-history-Lukács-forgotten/ (accessed 10 March, 2018).

dividing the world into the honest and authentic People on the one hand, and the scheming internationalist outsiders on the other.

There have been two kinds of political counter-movement in response. On the one hand, left-wing populist movements, such as Bernie Sanders in the US, Jeremy Corbyn in the UK, or Podemos and Syriza in Europe, have gained widespread support for policies that might have been beyond the pale a decade earlier. These movements offer a curious mirror-image of right-wing populism. They are not altogether unalike in their attitudes towards the institutions of global capitalism: Syriza was obliged to rally the Greek people in an ultimately-futile referendum against the terms imposed on repayment of national debts by the 'Troika' of the European Commission, the European Central Bank, and the International Monetary Fund, while Corbyn has a long record of scepticism towards the European Union as a vehicle of neoliberalism. In other respects, they differ sharply: neither Podemos nor Syriza is driven by the image of its leader, and both Corbyn and Sanders could be said to have an anti-charisma as unpolished elderly figures, far from magnetic as public speakers, who had loitered on the fringes of politics for decades.[2] What makes them populist, though, is that they share the same rhetoric of a People assailed by elite or transnational forces as their right-wing counterparts.

However, at the same time, the established elites have dug in, offering their own technocratic competence in contrast to the erratic buffoonery of these *soi-disant* 'strong men.' The 2016 US Presidential election is a case in point. Hillary Clinton presented herself as a competent, experienced politician, whose realistic plans for secure, incremental change were based on careful study of what was possible. Against her, Donald Trump not only made no effort to appear politically qualified – he went out of his way to situate himself as an outsider, determined to 'drain the swamp' of Washington: much of Clinton's campaign focused on Trump's unpreparedness and unpredictability. In France, the *énarque* and former banker Emmanuel Macron took on the xenophobic Marine le Pen. Despite his electoral rhetoric in defence of liberal democracy as a set of values, his policies since assuming power are more typical of a neoliberal fetishization of efficiency and economic productivity – as shown, for example, by his labour

---

[2] Mudde and Kaltwasser have rightly noted that many of the right-wing populist parties in Europe have similarly eschewed charismatic leadership. See Mudde, Cas and Cristóbal Rovira Kaltwasser, *Populism: A Very Short Introduction*, (Oxford: Oxford University Press, 2017). My concern here is primarily with those movements that *are* focused on a leader figure – though I would argue that these are simply the purest form of the same tendencies as the movements Mudde cites.

market reforms. While le Pen and Trump present themselves as combative defenders of the people and their values against the blows of globalization, then, the likes of Macron and Clinton claim expertise and technical know-how that enable them to steer the best course through a painful but fundamentally unalterable economic reality.

These elections presented a contrast between, 'on the one hand, great individuals viewed as the autocratic makers of history, and on the other hand, the natural laws of the historical environment' – each representing a different error, that of 'irrationalizing the hero,' or 'mechanizing the masses.'[3] These are not my words – but those of Lukács, for whom they characterized the antinomy in the bourgeois view of history that tended to treat it as a matter of either so-called 'great men' or of impersonal forces. This view of history, he insists, is a product of the commodity structure and the reification associated with it: capitalist social relations generate such contradictory forms of subjectivity that social and historical events come to be understood in these two ways. I will go further: Lukács's account of reification helps explain the particular appeal of today's nationalistic authoritarian populists, with their homogenising narratives of a unified People. The structure of social being under capitalism is such that groups can only be conceived either in terms of absolute abstraction, as individuated exchangers of commodities, or as an undifferentiated mass bound together in immediate similarity.

Furthermore, Lukács's theory of the revolutionary Party suggests some ways to combat such populisms. In this respect, I will disagree with those who suggest that populism is a viable strategy for progressive movements – in particular, Ernesto Laclau, who argues that populism is not inherently harmful, and that, properly understood, it could be turned to progressive ends. A Lukácsian explanation of the social conditions that generate populism suggests Laclau is wrong, and that *any* movement relying on populist tropes has ultimately regressive effects. I shall therefore begin by adumbrating Laclau's account, pointing particularly to his understanding of social unity as the source of danger. I shall then outline Lukács's account of social being and reification, before turning to an explanation of populism in those terms. Finally, I shall argue that his theory of organization can be detached from his immediate goal of Bolshevik revolution to offer useful insights in to the kinds of movement that might have a genuinely emancipatory effect.

---

3   Georg Lukács, *History and Class Consciousness: Studies in Marxist Dialectics* (*HCC*), trans. Rodney Livingstone (London: Merlin, 1971), p.158; p.217 n13.

1 Laclau's Theory of Populism

I have thus far described populism in terms that imply it is obviously and unquestionably dangerous. There are many who would agree. Jan-Werner Müller, one of the leading contemporary scholars of populism, interprets it as an unequivocal threat to democracy.[4] For Müller, the parallels between populism and fascism are simply too close: both rely on images of a homogeneous People undermined and assailed by nefarious outsiders, in a Schmittian dichotomy of Friend and Enemy. As John Abromeit argues, this verdict stems from his definition of democracy, which, for Müller, can *only* mean *liberal* democracy oriented towards the protection of individual rights.[5] From this perspective, the homogenized mass implied by a People obviously appears anti-democratic – whereas a definition of democracy focusing on the notion of popular sovereignty and the unity of the *demos* as a whole would be less threatened by it. Other liberal democrats have seen some use for democracy: Cas Mudde and Cristóbal Rovira Kaltwasser suggest that 'populism in opposition can have a positive effect on the quality of democracy since it helps to give voice to groups that do not feel represented by the political establishment.'[6] In this case, while certainly not endorsing populist governments, and taking care to note the real threats that it poses, Mudde and Kaltwasser see it as a useful corrective to poorly-functioning democracies – with the implication that it could lead to a better-functioning and more liberal democracy, posited as the ideal form of government.

Not all theorists of populism share with Müller or Mudde and Kaltwasser this assumption that liberal democracy is the *telos* of political development. Certainly this is not the case for Ernesto Laclau, who offers perhaps the most sophisticated argument that populism can serve progressive ends – and may even be necessary to achieve radical social transformation. Laclau is particularly relevant given his influence on major left-populist movements: a number of key figures in Spain's Podemos or Syriza in Greece were students of his thought.[7] Moved by his own experience of Peronism in Argentina, Laclau has argued for the rehabilitation of populism. He takes issue with the common

---

4 Jan-Werner Müller, *What is Populism?* (Philadelphia: University of Pennsylvania Press, 2016).
5 John Abromeit, 'A Critical Review of Recent Literature on Populism,' in *Politics and Governance* 2017 Vol 5, Issue 5, 177–186, p.183.
6 Cas Mudde & Cristóbal Rovira Kaltwasser, 'Populism: corrective *and* threat to democracy,' 205–22 in Mudde & Kaltwasser eds., *Populism in Europe and the Americas: Threat or Corrective for Democracy?*, (Cambridge: Cambridge University Press, 2012), p.209.
7 Dan Hancox, 'Why Ernesto Laclau is the intellectual figurehead for Syriza and Podemos,' in *The Guardian*, Mon 9 Feb, 2015; https://www.theguardian.com/commentisfree/2015/feb/09/ernesto-laclau-intellectual-figurehead-syriza-podemos, accessed January 15th, 2018.

accusation that populism relies on vague, ill-defined ideas of the People, and that it depends on basely irrational instincts, tracing such rhetoric to elitist nineteenth-century accounts of the 'crowd' or 'mob.'[8] Both vagueness and emotion, he insists, are in fact important elements in the success of any broad political movement. Taking issue with those who equate populism solely with ethnocentric or nationalistic movements, Laclau argues there is nothing within it that leads necessarily to such right-wing expressions. Indeed, there is no ideological content common to all previous populisms. On the contrary, many different movements – including socialist ones – have taken on populist dimensions. Thus, '[a]n ideology is not "populist" in the same sense that it is "conservative," "liberal" or "socialist," for the simple reason that, whilst these three terms allude to the articulating principles of the respective ideologies considered as a whole, "populism" alludes to a kind of contradiction which only exists as an abstract moment of an ideological discourse.'[9] Populism should therefore be understood more as a discursive resource than a particular content: it represents a possible dimension of revolutionary demands that consist of 'interpellating the People as opposed to the elites *en masse*.'[10] By 'interpellation,' Laclau means the way a varied band of the disadvantaged, whose interests and values might objectively differ quite sharply, are represented as a single, unified whole; individuals and groups identify as members of the People, however it may be described. A successful populist politics will rely on a symbolic image of the People with which broad sectors of the populace can identify.

Laclau makes his case in two major works, thirty years apart. Though related, they differ in ways that are important for the Lukácsian theory of populism I will present below. The first version appears in *Politics and Ideology in Marxist Theory* (1977), wherein he seeks to move beyond conventional Marxian analyses of class politics. He bases his argument on a Gramscian and Althusserian notion of hegemony, which consists in the successful articulation of the aspirations and perspectives of subaltern sectors of society within the frame of the ideology of the dominant group; for insurrectionary socialism to achieve such hegemony, it must incorporate the perspective of multiple sectors of society within its own ideological paradigm. Thus, hegemony does not mean that all parts of society have *identical* beliefs, values etc; rather, the dominant elites remained so as long as they were able to articulate the various needs, values,

---

8   Ernesto Laclau, *On Populist Reason* (OPR), (London: Verso, 2005), 1–64.
9   Ernesto Laclau, *Politics and Ideology in Marxist Theory: Capitalism – Fascism – Populism*, (London: New Left Books, 1977), p.176.
10   Laclau, *Politics and Ideology*, p.126.

and aspirations of other sectors of society within their own discursive language. A revolution too narrowly focused on the interests of the industrial working class could never hope to win over the sufficient support to achieve its goals. Instead, it must challenge the hegemony of the elites by articulating a common identity capable of enfolding far more than just the proletariat. 'The People' is therefore larger, more diverse, and considerably less exact than a 'class': rather than being overcome, such vagueness of terminology is *necessary* if socialists are to succeed in leading a broad-based movement.

Much of this useful analysis survives in Laclau's much later return to the theme, *On Populist Reason* (2006). There is, however, an important change. As Abromeit notes, Laclau's early theory still retains 'the primacy of the "social"' over the political; in the later version, the order of priorities has been thoroughly reversed.[11] In parts, *On Populist Reason* reads like Carl Schmitt garbed in Lacanian robes: Laclau claims that '[t]he political is, in some sense, the anatomy of the social world, because it is the moment of institution of the social.'[12] The significatory division of society in to two opposed camps is what produces the People and organizes society. Laclau's explanation begins with the notion of the *demand* addressed to the elites by subalterns who expect it to be answered. There is no inherent unity between such demands, as they stem from a range of positions; they are by definition distinct. At this point, society is governed by a logic of *differentiation:* its disparate parts are related in chains of distinction from one another, such that there is no unified People but rather a multiplicity of coordinated groups. Such demands are not yet counter-hegemonic, nor do they seek to overthrow the dominant elites; rather, the very expression of the demand implies the expectation that it could be met within the existing system. But when elites deny or fail to respond to these demands, cracks and gaps begin to appear within the dominant ideology; driven by a Lacanian 'ontological' need for fullness and completion, the masses turn elsewhere for something to replace that failed totality. In this case, the assorted demands come to be united by *one* difference – that of being opposed to the elites; relative to this dominant distinction, they are unified in a logic of *equivalences,* their differences flattened out and each alike in rejecting the dominant powers. They are brought together by an empty signifier – 'empty' in that it represents the gaps within the system. Such a signifier is always overdetermined in that it becomes the locus of a multiplicity of often-contradictory demands, but this is necessary if so many different elements are to be brought

---

11   Abromeit, 'Critical Review,' p.183.
12   Laclau, *OPR*, p.154.

together.¹³ 'Ordinary hardworking Americans' can mean many things to different audiences; demanding clarity would limit its potential to gather people together. Moreover, unity is facilitated by a *leader* figure with whom the masses can identify in certain ways: Laclau draws on the authority of Hobbes to argue that a single leader is more effective in this respect, stating that '[t]he less a society is kept together by immanent differential mechanisms, the more it depends, for its coherence, on this transcendent, singular moment.'¹⁴ Through the reduction of differences to equivalences, their opposition to the dominant elites, and their representation by an empty signifier, the masses are interpellated as a single coherent entity. It is this that begins "at a very incipient level, to constitute the 'people' as a potential historical actor."¹⁵ Crucially, it is only *in being named* as the People, oriented by a symbol of their unity, that this motley crew actually *becomes* the people: populism is not the ideology of a group already constituted, but rather the ideology that constitutes the group.¹⁶

Laclau's argument for populism, then, rests on the claim that effective progressive political action cannot be understood as the expression of a preexisting class. At one level, this could be understood as a matter of practical politics: a narrow class interest alone could never attract sufficient support to be effective. But Laclau offers a more ambitious claim. In arguing that the political generates the social, he offers an image of society held together semiotically. No underlying structures or regularised social relations pre-exist the moments of identification with signifiers that form politico-social groupings such as 'the People.' Ultimately, the most effective of such signifiers are those that are sufficiently vague enough that a range of differences can be united socially to the degree that they are made homogeneous – rather than acting to coordinate heterogeneity.

2   Lukács and the Intentional Structure of Social Being

It is Laclau's drive towards undifferentiated homogeneity and group formation through immediate identification that means his model of populism remains open to the dangers of reactionary, exclusionary authoritarian populism. The problem lies in his theorization of the social: at best, his reliance on identification suggests an extremely broad claim about some of the ways groups in

---

13   Ibid., p.105.
14   Ibid., p.100.
15   Ibid., p.74.
16   Ibid., p.73.

general come together; at worst, his claims depend on the Lacanian notion that humans have a transhistorical 'ontological need' for completeness – a claim both too vague to be of any explanatory use, and also entirely unsubstantiated, no more persuasive than arguing for the universality of (one kind of) rational self-interest or an innate love of colourful design leading us all to follow flags. This claim explains nothing: as Benjamin McKean puts it, Laclau's 'ontological need' merely 'redescribes' what happens.[17] Its generality offers no way to distinguish carefully between different forms of social organization, beyond such broad, unhistorical categories as logics of equivalence or differentiation. The *kind* of equivalence or differentiation in each case remains unspecified.

In contrast, Lukács's account of reification provides a fuller, more historically specific account of the rise of populism – one that, moreover, suggests the kind of social organization required to avoid the dangers of authoritarianism. Of course, Laclau dismisses Lukács, presenting reification as entailing no more than a misunderstanding of more 'real' social circumstances underneath, and treating Lukács's theory of revolution as an account of the tactics to be pursued by one pre-existing class.[18] As Slavoj Žižek rightly noted in a rather acrimonious exchange with Laclau, this dismissal is a 'standard, almost ritualized rejection' that oversimplifies and fundamentally misreads *History and Class Consciousness*.[19] Indeed, Laclau's treatment of his straw-man Lukács is of so little scholarly merit that it is not worth rebutting it directly. Rather, I shall show its weaknesses indirectly, by outlining Lukács's own account of social being, clarifying his account of reification, and showing how this explains certain features of contemporary populisms rather more specifically than Laclau. Where Laclau aims at immediate unity, Lukács defines social relations as the

---

[17] Benjamin L. McKean, 'Toward an Inclusive Populism? On the Role of Race and Difference in Laclau's Politics,' in *Political Theory* 2016 Vol 44(6), 797–820, at p.815.

[18] Laclau, *Politics and Ideology*, p.63.

[19] Slavoj Žižek '*Schlagend, aber nicht Treffend!* Rejoinder to Ernesto Laclau,' *Critical Inquiry* 33 (Autumn 2006):185–211, at 188. The exchange occurred after Žižek offered a largely respectful disagreement with Laclau in the course of an article on populism more generally. Laclau responded with fury, in a rather aggrieved and petulant article that opened by complaining that Žižek had not spent longer responding to Laclau's earlier criticisms of his work; Žižek replied by pointing out that his own article had not said more about Laclau because, surprisingly, its main focus was not a debate with Laclau. Laclau's other criticisms included the complaint that Žižek was unorthodox in his Lacanism, which he had corrupted with Hegelianism. Žižek's thoughtful (if sometimes ironic) rebuttals are indeed a surprise to those of us who had mistakenly assumed he was mostly about showmanship. See also Slavoj Žižek, 'Against the Populist Temptation,' *Critical Inquiry* 32 (Spring 2006): 551–74; Ernesto Laclau, 'Why constructing a People is the Main Task of Radical Politics,' *Critical Inquiry* 33 (Summer 2006): 646–680.

systematic interactions of distinct particulars, such that their differences can be coordinated through a common framework. The same thought, I will argue, underlies his account of the revolutionary party.

As I have argued elsewhere, the 'Reification' essay at the heart of *History and Class Consciousness* tacitly offers a social ontology that draws in various ways on both Hegel and Husserl.[20] Things exist socially in the sense that they have a *meaning* that cannot be reduced to their bare material properties: their meaning is the basis of their interactions with other entities. For example, when people react to a crown, their response is defined by the meaning of this symbol of authority, not the physical properties of the hunk of metal; the same is true when subjects interact with other subjects, such as the relation between professor and student. Lukács's concern in the 'Reification' essay is with one particular complex of meanings, albeit a complex that (he claims) has come to dominate contemporary society – the *commodity*. Following Marx's analysis of commodity fetishism, he points to the double-face of the commodity as both a use value and an exchangeable Value. Because use values are incommensurable, there can be no regularised social interactions on that basis; instead, by treating commodities as Values, they have a common language in which they can be related. In other words, the social being of commodities is *as values*: it is how they exist in society and interact with other objects. Of course, as I shall explain shortly, this means that social being is circumscribed: when objects enter social relations, certain of their properties are excluded (such as use value), defined as outside this particular relational complex and hence not rising to social existence. But Lukács repeatedly and explicitly states that the social being of an object – the way it exists in consciousness, as something meaningful – is its real existence, not merely an illusion. Thus, he cites approvingly Marx's rhetorical demand, "Didn't the Moloch of the Ancients hold sway? Wasn't the Delphic Apollo a real power in the life of the Greeks?"[21] Rather than mere errors, these meaning-complexes existed in a certain sense: they attained a level of being that made them effective forces in their society. The same is true of the commodity structure: it is the decisive form of social being (*gesellschaftliche Dasein*) under capitalism. The social meaning of an object, the way it is mediated, 'is not something (subjective) foisted on to the objects from outside...

---

20 I rely here on arguments I have made more fully in earlier articles. See Richard Westerman, 'The Reification of Consciousness: Husserl's Phenomenology in Lukács's Identical Subject-Object,' *New German Critique* 111 Vol. 37, No. 3 (Fall 2010), 97–130, and Richard Westerman, 'Spectator and Society: Lukács, Riegl, and the Phenomenology of the Individual Subject,' forthcoming in *New German Critique* 135 (Fall 2018).

21 Lukács, HCC, p.127.

[*i*]*t is rather the manifestation of their authentic, objective structure.*'[22] It is not some kind of epistemic error to see objects as commodities, beneath which more real objects are hidden. To the extent that they are social objects, they are commodities; this meaning-structure is what governs the way they behave.

In this respect, Lukács's account somewhat parallels Laclau's logic of differentiation: social relations entail the translation of objects into a shared form that allows and governs their interaction. However, Lukács is not simply concerned with the substantial meanings of social objects: he offers instead a formal account of the structures governing those meanings. There are two important aspects to Lukács's account: firstly, meaning entails specific *intentional practices*; second, these meanings are defined *relationally*. The first of these echoes the concept of intentionality developed by Franz Brentano and Edmund Husserl. Brentano uses it to refer to the peculiar characteristic by which mental phenomena are distinguished from inert, extra-mental objects: every experience, he suggests, entails 'direction toward an object,' such that our knowledge of these entities is inextricably tied up with the way we grasp it – knowing it, judging it, or loving it, for example.[23] It was presumably Husserl's use of the concept with which Lukács was most familiar: he cites the *Logical Investigations* and *Ideas* in his pre-Marxist drafts towards a philosophy of art, which are liberally sprinkled with Husserlian terminology.[24] For Husserl, intentionality is tied up not just with a psychological disposition towards the object, but with its very meaning or sense. As he explains, 'an act of meaning is the determinate manner in which we refer to our object of the moment.'[25] In his *Ideas*, therefore, he distinguishes between the raw data of intuitions – which he terms *hyle* – and the richly significant entities of consciousness, or *noema*. A given mass of *hyle* may be the source of different *noema*, depending on the way consciousness is directed towards it. Thus (to use his example) Napoléon is both 'the victor at Jena' and 'the vanquished at Waterloo': both are *true* ways to think about the same being and so equally *real*, but they are quite distinct phenomenological objects.[26] Our stances towards them are, moreover, bound up with their meaning: we might regard the triumphant Bonaparte with

---

22   Ibid., p.162.
23   Franz Brentano, *Psychology from an Empirical Standpoint*, (London: Routledge & Kegan Paul, 1973), 88–89.
24   Georg Lukács, *Werke*, ed. György Márkus & Frank Benseler, (Darmstadt & Neuwied: Luchterhand, 1962–86), vols. 16 & 17 of 19.
25   Edmund Husserl, *Logical Investigations*, trans. J.N. Findlay, 2 vols., (London & New York: Routledge, 2001), 1.198.
26   Ibid., 1.197.

fear, envy, or admiration, while the defeated Emperor evokes perhaps pity or a sense of the tragic hero. Corresponding to every *noema*, therefore, is *noesis* – the mental act or attitude by the subject that is presupposed by the meaning-complex of the object. Much of Husserl's phenomenology, then, tries to explain the transcendental presuppositions governing the construction of such meanings and their corresponding mental acts.

Lukács's analysis of social being echoes Husserl's noema-noesis dyad. He introduces his analysis of reification by stating that the commodity structure entails 'both an objective form and also... a subjective stance corresponding to it.'[27] This same motif appears throughout the 'Reification' essay. To give one example, he distinguishes between two different stances towards legal systems: for 'the historian (who stands "outside" the actual process),' Lukács argues, the '"law" of primitive societies,' might seem static and unchanging over centuries, while for 'someone who experiences the effects of the social order in question,' it appears 'flexible... renewing itself with every new legal decision.'[28] The same intuitions appear as quite different but equally valid meaning-complexes depending on the stance taken towards them. Where Lukács goes beyond Husserl is in transferring the latter's account of purely mental acts to social practices: intentionality is manifest in activity. As Andrew Feenberg has argued, Lukács uses the term 'consciousness' (*Bewußtsein*) in ways that closely parallel the modern anthropological notion of a culture comprising sets of *practices*.[29] Such social practices, I suggest, should be understood through the phenomenological notion of intentionality: they are oriented towards objects as meaningful complexes rather than simply as brute entities. Lukács's use of the term 'consciousness' to signify practices indicates that they are to be understood phenomenologically, as inherently meaningful. Our social practices of production thus genuinely intend objects *as* commodities – as Value – rather than as use-values. He offers a number of instances of such practices at the individual level. The factory worker under Taylorist work processes, for example, intends their labour only as a strictly-regulated performance of set actions within a definite quantity of time, while the journalist intends their very 'knowledge, temperament, and powers of expression' as a mere commodity to

---

27 Ibid., p.84
28 Ibid., p.97.
29 Andrew Feenberg, *Lukács, Marx, and the Sources of Critical Theory* (Lanham MD: Rowman & Littlefield, 1981); see also Andrew Feenberg, 'Culture and Practice in the Early Marxist Work of Lukács,' in *Berkeley Journal of Sociology*, Vol. 26 (1981), 27–40, and Andrew Feenberg, *The Philosophy of Praxis: Marx, Lukács, and the Frankfurt School*, (London: Verso, 2014), p.70.

be disposed of.[30] These are not just beliefs – they are actual practices that constitute their objects as meaningful in this way. Intentionality is thereby materialized, such that the meaning of an object cannot be dismissed as merely an ideological illusion masking more real social structures underneath. The social meaning of the commodity, the way it is mediated, 'is not something (subjective) foisted on to the objects from outside... [*i*]*t is rather the manifestation of their authentic, objective structure.*'[31] It is not an error to understand capitalist social being through the commodity structure, for it is indeed 'the real principle governing the actual production of commodities': when we practically intend objects as commodities, our social actions are governed by that meaning.[32]

Lukács's insistence that meaning is not subjectively thrust on to objects has a second implication. The significance of a social object cannot be determined in isolation; rather, it is defined relative to other entities, by the terms of its connection to or distinction from them. Social meanings are therefore relational. Here Lukács tacitly echoes the theory of social forms of his earlier mentor Georg Simmel. Take, for example, the latter's famous account of 'The Stranger' as social form. The Stranger is the foreigner or outsider who comes to join a group: Simmel points to the merchant from abroad, or the Jewish community in Europe. The Stranger is therefore 'in the group but not of it.'[33] They are the person who 'comes today and stays tomorrow,' embodying a 'unity of nearness and remoteness.' The Stranger is 'no owner of the soil,' and is thus 'fundamentally mobile.'[34] Crucially, these characteristics are not essential properties of the individual designated as Stranger, or qualities understood as intrinsic to them. Rather, the Stranger is determined by their relation to the rest of the group: they are both inside and outside of it at the same time. This in turn defines the way other group members relate to the Stranger: they may, Simmel suggests, be a recipient of confidences, or be called on to act as arbiters in disputes between settled group members.

Lukács's account of the commodity as a social form follows the same Simmelian logic: the meaning of an object is defined by the relationships within which it stands rather than by some essential properties it may be supposed to have. But where Simmel offers a number of transhistorical social forms, Lukács

---

30   Lukács, HCC, p.100.
31   Ibid., p.162.
32   Ibid., p.87.
33   Margaret Mary Wood, *The Stranger: a study in social relationships* (New York: Columbia University Press, 1934).
34   Georg Simmel, 'The Stranger,' in Kurt H. Wolff ed. & trans., *The Sociology of Georg Simmel*, (Glencoe, IL: Free Press, 1950), 402–408.

argues that capitalism has seen, for the first time, the total domination of society by one single formal structure, that of the commodity. What distinguishes it is the abstraction with which it treats all objects, reducing them to homogeneity. The commodity structure brings entities in social relations with one another only as commodities – as abstract quantities of value. As Lukács puts it, 'the universality of the commodity form is responsible both objectively and subjectively for the abstraction of the human labour incorporated in commodities.'[35] The same structure, he insists, is found across capitalist social institutions: in law, for example, we are related as legally identical citizens, entitled to the same rights and processes. Contrast this, with, say, the relationship between parent and child, founded on affectual bonds, on particular relations of blood or formalized adoption, on specific duties and expectations between the two. What each one is, is shaped by quite *substantive* relations, in which each remains distinct in its meaning. In contrast, the commodity structure specifically excludes such substantiality from social relations. Capitalism is constitutively abstract: it is a mode of social being grounded on the exclusion of content and particularity in bringing entities into practical relations with one another. It is therefore no mere error when we see society and our fellow-subjects as commodities. Abstraction of this kind genuinely is the principle of a society governed by commodity relations, and thus defines the real social being of its members.

3 Reification and the Interpellation of the Subject

It is the intentional structure of the commodity that produces reification, for Lukács: the social meaning of objects comes to be defined in a way that forecloses spontaneous activity, and reduces the subject's interactions with society to largely spectatorial passivity. Capitalist social relations are manifest as a hermetically sealed whole, over which we can have no control, and into which we cannot enter in any substantial way. What makes this so is that social being comes to be defined in a thoroughly *immanent* fashion. The meaning of every object is defined by its abstract comparability to other such objects. Like the commodity itself, the individual is split on the one hand in to an empty social existence, the determinants of which have no relation to their substantial 'private' life on the other. It is this that absolutely excludes any real contribution by the individual, leaving us as mere passive spectators of a fixed social reality rather than its active co-constitutors.

---

35   Lukács, *HCC*, p.87.

Lukács's argument may be clarified by drawing on a distinction made by the art historian Alois Riegl: the commodity structure can be said to have *internal* rather than *external* coherence. Riegl's importance in Lukács's intellectual development has been seriously neglected, despite the Marxist naming him as one of three 'really important historians of the nineteenth century' in the 'Reification' essay, and drawing heavily on the historian's terms in his early aesthetic drafts.[36] Riegl's formalist approach to art is distinguished by his consistent concern with the position of the viewing subject as part of the compositional whole of the work of art: for example, he distinguishes between *Nahsicht* and *Fernsicht*, or 'close view' and 'far view' to describe works of art that must be viewed from near or from further away respectively to make sense.[37] The ideas that help make sense of reification are found in his *Dutch Group Portraiture*, wherein he explores the particular formal structures of sixteenth and seventeenth century civic group portraits of the Netherlands. They are distinguished, he argues, by a particular form of coherence – one that is *external* rather than *internal*. The latter is typical of Italian Renaissance art. Consider Raphael's *Transfiguration*. Here two biblical scenes are depicted on the same canvas, but compositionally unified by the positions and interactions of the figures with one another. The significance of Christ is shown by placing this figure at the apex of a triangle towards which all the other figures are oriented: whatever action they are involved in, they look or gesture towards this peak, bringing together all the different elements in a single semantic whole. Though Raphael obviously deploys perspective, there is otherwise no reference to the spectator of the painting: the disparate parts of the image cohere solely in reference to one another, exhibiting *internal* coherence. Riegl contrasts this with Dutch group portraits of the time, distinguished by the way their figures look out towards the viewer, making the percipient a part of the image. This reaches its pinnacle in Rembrandt's *Syndics of the Draper's Guild*, depicting a group of Dutch burghers gathered around a table, listening to a seated figure who appears to be their leader as he comments on a book of cloth samples.[38] But at the same time, they are looking out towards the spectator, implying that the viewer of the painting is the one who has brought the samples. In other words, the audience is included in the semantic construction of the painting: they are presupposed active participants in the scene, not merely

---

36   Ibid., 153; for a more detailed account of Lukács's debts to Riegl, see Westerman, 'Spectator and Society.'
37   Alois Riegl, *Late Roman Art Industry*, trans. Rolf Winkes, (Rome: Giorgio Bretschneider, 1985), 24–27.
38   Alois Riegl, *The Group Portraiture of Holland*, trans. Evelyn Kain & David Britt, (Los Angeles: Getty Publications, 1999), 253–264.

passive observers. This is *external* coherence: the meaning-structure of the painting posits a spectator *within* it. In rather Hegelian vein, Riegl sees this as exemplifying the 'democratic' spirit of Dutch society, supposedly including all citizens as equal co-creators of their civic space.

Riegl's account may be described as phenomenological *avant la lettre* in that he explains meaning in relation to specific subjective orientations towards it, echoing the Husserlian connection of intentionality and the intentional object (or noema and noesis). In this light, his distinction between internal and external coherence helps to explain reification as a problem of the meaning-structure of commodity fetishism. Other social forms may not only permit but even require the incorporation of personal substance within social relations: the relationship between two lovers, for example, is predicated on a very specific connection between two particular individuals, whose unique characteristics are an integral part of this relationship. Though the precise nature of their interaction may be structured by cultural traditions and practices, they retain some spontaneity in the way they interact. Moreover, they are integrated in to these relations as definite, non-fungible individuals: one does not simply replace one lover by another within a set relationship structure! Such relations are externally coherent, incorporating the individual fully into their meaning-structure – both in the formal sense as subjective agent, and substantively, as *this* person in particular.

In contrast, the formal structure of social reality under capitalism is one of *internal* coherence, excluding active subjective participation. Entities (objects and people) come in to social relations with one another as commodities – that is, their social meaning is defined as a quantity of Value, which can itself be divided into ever-smaller fragments. But this Value is determined purely in relation to other commodities: the Value of one commodity is defined in terms of the other commodities it permits us to purchase, and has no inherent connection to the use value or other significance of the object or its owner. In the first place, this means that 'for the individual, the commodity structure of all "things" and their obedience to "natural laws" is found to exist already in a finished form, as something immutably given.'[39] We have little or no control over socially-meaningful objects: their determination as Values and the rise or fall of this Value are entirely independent of anything we may actually *do*; it is governed instead by shifts in the Value of other commodities. Consequently, the individual's perspective on society is that of an outsider – which explains 'the *contemplative* nature of man under capitalism.'[40] Moreover, since the

---

39   Lukács, *HCC*, p.92.
40   Ibid., p.97.

commodity form is not just the social form of *objects*, but also of *people* in social relations, we lose any connection to our own social being: as Lukács puts it, we become not only 'the passive observer of society,' but also take on 'a contemplative attitude' to our own reified faculties.[41] The only interactions we can have are those of 'rational and isolated acts of exchange between isolated commodity owners.'[42] As such, the subject's particularity is excluded from society: their social being takes the form of abstraction, rather than any substantive relations between people, and we appear within formal social relations shorn of every content. Socially, we are by definition infinitely fungible. This is the core of reification: it is not simply a case of treating others coldly, like objects, but rather entails the transformation of social practices such that the individual feels powerless to control a society that offers them only the most abstract social existence, entirely bereft of any particularity.

What is significant here is the source of such a limited subjectivity. For Lukács, it is not the subject who labours to create the commodity from which it subsequently becomes alienated. Rather, it is the commodity structure that alienates the individual: it produces forms of subjectivity that deny and exclude substantive relations between people. It defines us, therefore, as isolated individuals – a theme to which Lukács repeatedly returns throughout the 'Reification' essay. This may be described as the way the subject is interpellated under capitalism. This reference of 'interpellation' requires some explanation, given its origin in the work of Louis Althusser, who sharply (if with wild inaccuracy) criticized Lukács. Moreover, my sense here is somewhat different from that of Laclau, to which I have already referred. In Laclau's usage, the term is more substantive: it describes the presentation of particular signifiers (such as a given determination of 'the People') which individuals may identify, and so acquire an image of themselves. I am using the term formally, to refer to the circumscription of the subject in terms of the practical input expected by the meaning-structure of social objects. It is this structure that determines what the subject *is*. By limiting us to relations based on commodities, reification determines our substantial existence – all our distinct experience, feelings, and peculiarities – as '*mere sources of error*,' elements that are excluded from social relations.[43] Only our most universal aspects are socializable. Consequently, as real, living individuals, we have few options for coming in to relations with others – and so are isolated from one another. It is for this reason that Lukács describes the overcoming of reification as meaning 'the *abolition of the isolated*

---

41   Ibid., p.100.
42   Ibid., p.92.
43   Ibid., p.89.

individual' by the full integration of the subject in to more substantial social relations.[44]

4 Inclusion and Exclusion: the Dichotomy of Capitalist Social Being

This double existence of the individual – as a substantial, living being excluded from social relations on the one hand, and a formally-constituted component of the circulation of commodities on the other – that epitomises the contradictory semantics of capitalism. The commodity structure may formally exclude substance, but at the same time it depends on that which it casts out of social relations. Social relations draw a border around the social and the non-social: society is defined by what it excludes as non-social as much as by what it includes. As Marx noted, commodities have a double existence – as well as exchangeable Value, they must also have a use value, something that serves someone's needs sufficiently for them to want to buy it. This use value is obscured when the object is sold as a commodity: it is reinscribed exclusively as a repository of abstract value, ignoring its determinate, substantial properties. But the object will only in fact be sold, its value realized, because it has a use for someone. The logic of the commodity thus depends on its circulation and its perennial translation across the border between abstract, quantitative exchange value and particular, qualitative use-value. The problem is echoed, Lukács notes, in the epistemology of classical German philosophy, which is able to derive the rational forms of knowledge, but for which the actual existence of the objects it knows must remain a matter of irrational chance.[45] In both cases, substance and quality are both presupposed and denied by abstractly rational forms. It is this that constitutes the antinomic character of 'bourgeois' thought, the focus of the second section of the 'Reification' essay: extended to culture and philosophy, the commodity structure creates oppositions and contradictions within its central categories.

This border is manifest in the classic public/private divide of bourgeois society. The subject is defined as both a concrete individual and as a citizen. Publicly, we are related to one another through standards of universalization and equality. This is clearest in the legal system correlated with bourgeois society: everyone is granted the same rights, defined as identical, their relations taking the strictly-delimited form provided by the legal system. Indeed, such relations must *by definition* exclude anything particular or substantial about

---

44   Ibid., p.171.
45   Ibid., pp.111–121.

the individual: gender, religion, ethnicity, or sexual orientation cannot be factors in legal relations. Of course, eighteenth century declarations of the Rights of Man were precisely that: in practice, they covered only European males. Nevertheless, the logic of such claims demanded their extension over time so as to include everyone. Publicly, then, every individual is defined in terms of every other, and as a purely rational being. But this very exclusion leaves as its extrasocial residue everything substantial, personal, and emotional. On the side of the 'private' lies the so-called 'soul,' '*Seele*.' Contrary to those such as Gareth Stedman Jones who read *History and Class Consciousness* as romantic anticapitalism, urging the claims of the passionate soul against an austere and mechanical social system, Lukács does not in fact present the 'soul' as any kind of more fundamental or real human essence.[46] In fact, he is careful throughout the 'Reification' essay to place the word in scare-quotes, distancing himself from any quasi-Romantic notion of an expressive, creative, feeling 'soul' defined by some eternal essence. Rather, the 'soul' is in this case the residue of the individual, that which is excluded from social being by the abstraction of the commodity form. It is thus the byproduct of societal rationalization: rather than a Romantic subject expressing itself in the creation of social structures, it is the very abstraction of the commodity form, designating drives, desires, and passions as private, that produces the interiority of the soul as the supposed locus of 'authentic' human existence. At the same time, it determines these elements as both irrational and irrational*izable*. Excluded from social relations, they cannot take on any consistent form: they remain immediate and incoherent from the perspective of society, incapable of being represented in the ordered, coherent forms of social being. The rational, ordered system of society is placed in conflict with everything particular and individual, by the very logic of the commodity structure.

It is not only the individual that is determined in this contradictory form. Nature too is defined antinomically for Lukács. He points to the two contradictory definitions of nature emerging from the eighteenth century onwards. On the one hand, following the likes of Kant, Kepler, and Galileo, 'natural' comes to refer to law-governed, predictable, and fixed systems – ones rather like capitalism. As Lukács explains, '"nature" has been heavily marked by the revolutionary struggle of the bourgeoisie: the "ordered," calculable, formal and abstract character of the approaching bourgeois society appears natural by the

---

46 Gareth Stedman Jones, 'The Marxism of the Early Lukács,' in Gareth Stedman Jones ed. *Western Marxism: A Critical Reader*, (London: New Left Books, 1977) 11–60. See also Michael Löwy, *Georg Lukács: From Romanticism to Bolshevism*, trans. Patrick Camiller, (London: New Left Books, 1979) on Lukács's overcoming of Romantic anti-capitalism.

side of artifice, the caprice, and the disorder of feudalism and absolutism.'[47] In this case, it refers to the formal, abstract validity of intelligible and rational systems: nature designates that which is ultimately explicable. But on the other hand, in the likes of Rousseau, 'Nature' becomes a 'value concept' referring to the exact opposite: it 'acquires the meaning of what has grown organically, what was not created by man, in contrast to the artificial structures of human civilization. But at the same time, it can be understood as that aspect of human inwardness which has remained natural, or at least tends or longs to become natural once more.'[48] It is the very antithesis of abstraction, mechanization, and reification – and it thus identified with our authentic humanity. Once again, reification expels this substantial content from social relations, producing on the one hand an abstract system laying claim to validity and rationality, and on the other, a formless, immediate fog of sensation.

Lukács's statement of his own position in this case is revealing. He insists that 'what seems to be the highpoint of the interiorization of nature really implies the abandonment of any true understanding of it. To make moods into the content presupposes the existence of unpenetrated and impenetrable objects (things in themselves) just as much do the laws of nature.'[49] Neither sense of the word 'nature' can claim exclusive truth; what is important is that they exclude one another. In fact, the problem more generally is the separation of valid or rational form from substantial values or contents by the commodity structure. (In his concern with the relation of validity and value, Lukács remains very much within the ambit of Neo-Kantianism.) Social being is rational in the sense that it comprises an ordering system of relations, organizing particulars in a coherent, manner: every interaction between particulars happens the way it does for good reason; it is intelligibly meaningful. That which is not thus organized is irrational: its behavior seems to follow no consistent rule. Rationality need not be entirely abstract, such that its rules are defined *a priori* and only then imposed '*post festum*' on contents. A painting, for example, can be described as 'rational' in that its elements are organized and composed by a definite rule or principle – but the specific rule is defined through and in interaction with its contents; except in the case of certain *avant garde* works, the artist does not create according to abstract rules. For this reason, Lukács points to art as an idealized reconciliation between the antinomies of soul and form, or the contradictory senses of nature – albeit a reconciliation that, he insists, can never be socially realized, for we do not create society in the manner of an

---

47   Lukács, *HCC*, p.136.
48   Ibid., p.136.
49   Ibid., p.214 n47.

artist creating a work.[50] In contrast, the constitutive abstraction of capitalism defines its rationality independently of any particulars. Excluded from a society governed by the commodity form, contents are placed in absolute opposition to form, defined as that which must be spontaneous and direct, undifferentiated and untrammelled by the demands of coherence. If everything that is particular and substantial is excluded from rationalized social relations, then so too must rationality be expelled from particularity: rationalization or the imposition of form comes to felt as an artificial restriction of spontaneity, feeling, and authenticity. The 'soul' feels trapped by social institutions whose shapes are determined separately from them. Lukács's argument implies that this need not be so – and that it is possible to conceive of a rationality that incorporated substance and significance in its very structure, rather than one aiming at an entirely immanent coherence. It is the failure to achieve this that produces the characteristic conflicts of capitalism.

5   The 'Deplorables'

What, then, does all this have to do with populism and its authoritarian forms? For liberal theorists of populism, whether those such as Müller who see it as an unmitigated threat or those such as Mudde and Kaltwasser who suggest it might be a corrective to non-functional democracies, the appearance of authoritarian populist movements within politically functioning liberal democracies is hard to explain. Abromeit rightly argues that this is in part due to their focus on the political, without regard to the broader social factors that contribute to its rise. Lukács's account of the semantic dichotomies of social relations produced by the commodity form suggests that the emergence of such movements may be an inherent part of the structure of capitalist social relations: they are the form of anti-establishment movements dictated by the logic of the commodity.

The antinomy Lukács describes in the concept of nature mirrors that which he identifies in bourgeois views of history – as either a process of mechanistic laws, or transformed by the action of 'great men.' On the one hand, the past is so ordered and predictable that spontaneous subjectivity can make no mark on it; on the other, all that is needed is expressive spontaneity from a leader capable of bending the masses to their will. It echoes too the opposition painted by contemporary authoritarian populists in rallying support for their movements: on the one hand, elites, 'experts,' bureaucrats and technocrats, the

---

50   Ibid., 137–140s.

unalterable laws of the global economy, and the depersonalized rules imposed by transnational institutions; on the other, direct action by figures who promise to overturn international trade deals and protect the interests of the American, French, British People conceived as a homogeneous mass under assault by those elites. The opposition of rationality and spontaneity is perhaps most strikingly illustrated by the plummeting trust in scientific expertise or established media organizations and the rise of conspiracy theories. Take, for example, those who insist that the wave of mass shootings in the US has been staged by actors, and that these events never in fact occurred: such fantasists believe that these massacres were concocted in order to justify further control by a bureaucratic state, to the degree that they confront the bereaved and aggressively deny that those who died had ever existed.[51] The same can be seen in the anti-vaccination movement or climate skepticism, both of which reject rigorous scientific study as merely more evidence of a plot against them. There is literally no use in arguing with such people, because reasoned debate itself is understood as simply a tool used by conspiratorial elites to baffle and distract from the exercise of their power. Rational debate as such *is seen as the enemy*, because it is so associated with the elites – and this opposition is one determined, in Lukács's paradigm, by the logic of the commodity.

I want to point here to four manifestations of this opposition in authoritarian populist movements. In each case, I suggest, authoritarian populist movements are defined by their opposition to the reified social life of the commodity structure. First, the 'strong men' populist leaders symbolically negate the powerlessness of the individual under reification. Second, the appeal of these leaders can be understood not in spite but because of their irrationality and lack of coherence. Third, populism's recourse to the notion of an immediate, undifferentiated 'People' purged of heterogeneity is the antithesis of the articulation of difference promised by rational social forms. Finally, contemporary populism's definition of this 'People' as virtuous producers – what John Abromeit has termed 'producerist populism' – can also be understood in relation to the public/private divide posited by the commodity.

The primary experience of reification, Lukács argues, is one of powerlessness. The internal coherence of the commodity structure leaves us powerless in the face of a system allegedly constructed by humans: it is hermetically sealed against creative intervention, and all we can do is watch. Modern consumer society is the logical extension of the commodity form to absurdity: the

---

51   See, for example, Matthew Iglesias, 'The Parkland conspiracy theories, explained,' February 22, 2018, https://www.vox.com/policy-and-politics/2018/2/22/17036018/parkland-conspiracy-theories,(accessed March 10, 2018).

individual is absolutely free as private consumer to choose from the myriad offerings of the market – but has no sway whatsoever over what is on offer, or how the system bringing these things to market functions. It is this exclusion of intervention, the presentation of social interactions as necessary, depersonalized processes that has been the target of much populist rage, even in wealthy, industrialized nations. Over the past few decades, neoliberalism has become economic and political orthodoxy, and it has grown ever harder to contemplate alternatives; this is summed up in the Thatcherite slogan, 'There Is No Alternative' to market capitalism (TINA), embraced since the 1990s even by social democratic parties such as Tony Blair's New Labour or Bill Clinton's reorientation of the Democrats. International trade agreements such as NAFTA or transnational organizations such as the EU have operated on the same logic, seeking to facilitate the removal of obstacles to global trade as an inevitable and necessary step forward. At the same time, the decline of labour unions in many industrialized nations since the 1980s – and in particular the move by ostensibly labour-oriented parties such as the Democrats or New Labour in the UK to reduce the influence of unions within their party – excludes even this limited opportunity for action. Rather than a battle of competing interests – in which even if one loses, one *might* have won – politics has become a matter of administration and management. In Lukács's words, all that is left is 'the recognition and the inclusion in one's calculations of the inevitable chain of cause and effect in certain events – independently of individual caprice. In consequence, man's activity does not go beyond the correct calculation of the possible outcome of the sequence of events... and beyond the adroit evasion of disruptive "accidents."'[52]

This neutralization of opposition *within* social and political being means that opposition must instead be *to* the system as a whole – and to systematization as such. This reaction can be seen in the 'strong men' of authoritarianism. In this light, the fact that Trump, Putin, Duterte, Erdogan, or Orban – reject precisely these limiting institutions, flaunting their attacks on such laws and norms, means they seem able to stand up against the reified system of social relations. Rodrigo Duterte's response to widespread drug usage in the Philippines exemplifies this. Widespread misperceptions (fostered, in fact, by Duterte) that the nation was being overrun by drug addiction led to calls for action; in such an 'emergency,' normal legal procedures seemed too slow and ineffective.[53] Duterte's 'death squads,' responsible for thousands of deaths in

---

52 Lukács, HCC, p.98.
53 In fact, the Philippines has a relatively low level of drug use compared to global averages – as has effectively been conceded by government officials. See Clare Baldwin & Andrew

their extrajudicial efforts to stamp out widespread drug use, can be understood as appealing precisely because they reject the limitations imposed by legal processes that seemed to limit the human capacity to take action. The purported strength of such 'strongmen' appears on the side of the substantial, irrational, or individual and opposed to the minatory structures of society.

Second, the internal coherence of the commodity structure claims a monopoly on reason that posits spontaneity, irrationality, and incoherence as its deadliest opponents. Of course, for Laclau, irrationality (in the form of libidinally-driven identification) is an important part of politico-social groupings as such. As a result, one of his first tasks in describing the potential of populism is to rebut criticisms of the 'irrationality' of the mob, to show that such epithets are typically the product of elitist disdain for the masses. But Lukács's argument suggests that Laclau is too conservative in his ideas here: he still operates with notions of rationality and irrationality defined within commodified social forms. By contrast, Lukács's account implies that the very concept of reason itself is socially determined. Libidinal impulses are not inherently 'irrational' because there can be no single, fixed, transhistorical definition of reason; it is because the commodity form excludes them from social relations that such drives are categorised in opposition to reason. The exclusion of the 'irrational' from social forms is itself a historical product of reified social relations.

In consequence, the rejection of global elites goes hand-in-hand with the rejection of rationality. This is exemplified by the claim by one particularly contemptible leader of the Brexit Leave campaign that 'the British people have had enough of experts.'[54] Voting to leave the European Union could be portrayed as a way to thumb their noses at the eggheads. Or consider once more the Clinton-Trump opposition. The former presented herself as the epitome of rationality; her outstanding résumé was evidence of her unquestionable competence for the job. Both in her primary campaign against Sanders and in the general election, she attacked her opponents for being unrealistic and unprepared; her own policies were supported by reams of research. In contrast, Trump himself unrepentantly embraced the role of the irrationalist, even attacking Clinton's supposed strength, her lengthy experience in Washington. His obscene, misogynistic remarks were excused as 'locker room talk': he

---

R.C. Marshall, 'As death toll rises, Duterte deploys dubious data in "war on drugs,"' October 18, 2016, https://www.reuters.com/investigates/special-report/philippines-duterte-data/ (accessed February 25, 2018).

54 Henry Mance, 'Britain has had enough of experts, says Gove,' June 3, 2016, https://www.ft.com/content/3be49734-29cb-11e6-83e4-abc22d5d108c, (accessed 10 March, 2018).

stepped forth as pure Id, unrestrained by quote 'political correctness,' just acting 'naturally' and without artifice. None of his bizarre actions caused serious, lasting damage to his popularity – because it was precisely his apparent uncalculated irrationality that was central to his appeal. By acting this way, Trump signaled his absolute opposition to the demands of coherence and rationality of the elites – and hence his alliance with those left outside the system, the 'deplorables' who so alarmed Clinton.

There are yet more sinister consequences. Recall: this same implacable system is supposedly the locus of social being, the way humans come in to determinate relations with one another despite their substantial differences. Difference is actualized and mediated; heterogeneity is presupposed by the formalization of social relations that govern it. But when these relations become so thoroughly depersonalized as to threaten everything substantial about us, the rational mediation of social relations necessarily collapses. Instead, social unity must appear to subsist in precisely those things *excluded* by the commodity structure. It takes on the immediate, unreflective, and self-consciously irrational form of a direct group identity predicated on homogeneity. Lukács, of course, criticises attempts to attribute immediate forms of existence to class consciousness, suggesting they lead to something as mysterious as Hegel's *Volksgeiste*.[55] Such immediacy entails a unity based on pure similarity – those with identical values or lifestyles, the defence of a quote 'Christian' West, of quote 'ordinary Americans,' and so on. Obviously, such immediate and superficial particularism tends towards racialized or culturalist group identities. Rather than a structure that coordinates heterogeneity, society comes to be identified with immediate homogeneity. Nativism and xenophobia surge: rejecting the rationalized social relations that might have coordinated our particularities, we cannot relate to those who are 'different.' At the same time, we see emphasis on the direct expression of the 'will of the people' without any attempt to give this immediate subjectivity a coherent form as such, and indeed the rejection of any demand for coherence as an imposition. In this way, capitalism symbolically defines its own antithesis – not, unfortunately, a revolutionary proletariat, but a mystical nationalism based on belief in a 'spiritual' unity.

Of course, this notion of a mystical unity has often taken a very particular form – something missed by Laclau's dehistoricized account of populism. As John Abromeit has brilliantly shown, since the eighteenth century it has been expressed in a discourse of 'producers' versus 'parasites' – that is, of a virtuous, hardworking but oppressed majority whose labour produces wealth on the

---

55 Lukács, HCC, p.173.

one hand, and an exploitative, unproductive ruling class on the other.[56] In an analysis relying tacitly on Moishe Postone's reinterpretation of Marx, Mark Loeffler has similarly argued that such producerism is the result of abstracted social relations such as those of finance or bureaucratic administration seem to overwhelm the concrete everyday lives of ordinary individuals.[57] The division between abstract social relations and everyday life, Loeffler argues, makes producerist narratives plausible – however impossible it would be in practice to remove such abstract domination from complex modern societies. This has been a distinct feature of much recent populism. Before the 2008 crisis, steadily rising living standards and relative economic stability led many to picture themselves as the 'isolated individuals' Lukács describes: believing that their independent hard work earned them their place in society. The recession turned this upside down, revealing them to be at the mercy of a globalized market over which not even the wealthy had any control.

Lukács's account clarifies the problem further: it is not just that abstract social relations seem distant from daily life. Rather, the commodity form determines labour and production as private and even moral matters in opposition to an amoral, depersonalized system of relations. Of course, Lukács has himself often wrongly been read in somewhat 'producerist' terms, accused of identifying the proletariat as the 'subject' of history by virtue of their labour, and hence as the supposed creators of commodities.[58] On such a reading, a transhistorical form of labour would pre-exist a society that it created. In fact, his account of the commodity form implies exactly the opposite: it suggests that an extra-social labour is in fact simply a necessary illusion (*Erscheinung*) produced by capitalism's exclusion of labour from the form of commodity. Labour, Lukács states explicitly, is always social – but under capitalism it *appears* as a private, transhistorical category, its social determinants obscured in a way that would not be the case with, say, feudal forms of labour, or hunter-gatherer tribes.[59] The individual is interpellated within social relations as a private vendor of a commodity that happens to be labour – but whether it is or not is irrelevant. That aspect, like all substantial questions, is excluded from

---

56 John Abromeit, 'Transformations of Producerist Populism in Western Europe,' in John Abromeit & Bridget Marie Chesterton, Gary Marotta, & York Norman eds. *Transformations of Populism in Europe and the Americas: History and Recent Tendencies*, (London: Bloomsbury Academic, 2016), 231–64.

57 Mark Loeffler, 'Populists and Parasites: On Producerist Reason,' in Abromeit et al, *Transformations of Populism*, 265–92.

58 See, for example, Moishe Postone, *Time, Labor, and Social Domination: A Reinterpretation of Marx's Critical Theory* (Cambridge: Cambridge University Press, 1993), p.73.

59 Lukács, HCC, p.83–88.

the commodity form. Thus, labour itself comes to seem extra-social: it is that which is deemed to pre-exist society – and indeed (in Locke, Smith, and others) is cited as the source of property rights, which are thereby equally cast as private. Labour and property are thus determined as natural, not defined by social relations; they are the 'irrational given' that society is expected to protect in classic social contract theory. They are not further rationalisable. As Abromeit has shown, many such discourses – including those of *soi-disant* Marxists such as Sorel – have envisaged a removal of the political and the restoration of a society directly produced by the laboring majority, without the oppression of reified social and political institutions.[60] This vision of an undifferentiated, immediate, and hence irrational unity is, I suggest, a direct product of the exclusion of labour from differentiating social relations.

At the same time, this labour is supposedly the nexus of the interaction of individual and society – or the way in which the individual is an agent within society. But such agency is effectively nullified: the individual cannot change social relations allegedly created by them by their own individual labour. The problem here parallels that which Lukács found in ethics under the Kantian and Fichtean system. Unable in fact to explain how the moral will could in any way affect the external world of necessity, they turned to an 'inwardly-turning form' of mere good intentions.[61] Ethics becomes 'a mere *point of view from which to judge* internal events.'[62] Something similar happens with labour: unable in practice to effect any change on social reality, it becomes simply an ethical demand, the *Beruf*, carried out because it is to be deemed good in itself. Excluded from manifest social practices, it is a matter of private virtue: the individual works, not because labour is in any way socially effective, but to answer the inner voice of morality. In this way, labour as a whole becomes valorized as intrinsically morally-worthwhile, rather than revealed as the drudgery necessary to make one's way in the world – and those who do not labour are condemned as parasites.

6 Populism or Party?

How, then, can we respond? Here, I think, Lukács's diagnosis of the *formal* problems of the commodity structure – the way it composes and manifests social being – is telling. First, and most directly, it rules out the technocratic

---

60   Abromeit, 'Transformations of Producerist Populism.'
61   Lukács, *HCC*, p.124.
62   Ibid., p.124.

approach of so-called 'Third Way' politics of the nineties, which Hillary Clinton's presidential run harked back to. Indeed, such approaches are at least partly responsible for our current predicament: when the Clinton Democrats or Blairite New Labour began to detach from their traditional bases in organized labour and social movements in the 1990s, they lost one way – however flawed – to incorporate individuals in to social action. As Lukács put it in warning against a revolution carried out on behalf of the worker, this reduces them to quote 'a purely *contemplative*' attitude that leads to 'the voluntaristic overestimation of the active importance of the individual (the leader) and the fatalistic underestimation of the importance of the class (the masses).'[63] In other words, such parties reproduce the same externalization of the individual as the commodity structure: rather than being integrated as active participants in social relations, people were fully externalized as private consumers, and so all the more in opposition to those relations when things went awry. These methods were a source of the problem – not its resolution.

At the same time, we should not be tempted to turn with Laclau towards our own populist solutions. True, his embrace of the leader principle does not directly fall prey to the same form of problems as the administrative/technocratic solution: the libidinal identification with the leader that he describes might at least allow some illusion of agency by proxy to the followers. Moreover, there are in fact several points of similarity between Lukács and Laclau. For example, Lukács too insists that the representative of the movement – in this case the Party – is not an expression of something already existing, but is rather how the proletariat is raised to conscious existence as a class, paralleling Laclau's claim that the signifier creates the signified, rather than representing a People that already exists without it. Moreover, Lukács acknowledges that any successful revolution will not be carried out by the proletariat alone, but 'must indeed carry out the revolution *in league* with the other classes that are in conflict with the bourgeoisie.'[64] In this, of course, he was quite in line with Lenin's willingness to work alongside nationalist independent movements if the tactical needs of the moment demanded it: Laclau was hardly the first to recognize that transformative social struggles must incorporate numerous different strata.

But Lukács's model suggests that Laclau's approach is too limited. The weight he lays on a People formed as an undifferentiated, homogeneous mass simply reproduces the problems of reified social relations in mirror-image. Even as he selects the opposite pole, Laclau remains within the antinomies of the

---

63   Ibid., p.318.
64   Ibid., p.286.

commodity structure rather than surpassing them. In opposition to abstract mediating form, he proposes substantive immediate content, a night in which all cows are black. This may be expressed simply as outright rejectionism. To take an example from left-wing populism: in 2015, the Syriza government in Greece called a national referendum on whether to accept the terms of a debt bailout proposed by the so-called 'Troika' of the European Commission, the European Central Bank, and the International Monetary Fund. The electorate resoundingly rejected these terms – but was obliged to submit to even harsher ones imposed by the Troika in punishment. The Greek όχι was exactly that – an indeterminate negation, a flat 'no!' without any coherent alternative. It could not in itself overcome the contradictions that produced this crisis.

This lack of differentiation produces a number of problems. In the first place, it leaves any populist movement unstable and excessively reliant on contingency. This is vividly illustrated by the case of Hugo Chávez, Venezuela's late socialist strong-man. Despite his introduction of purportedly-democratic councils, his regime rested heavily on his own personality in the same way as right-wing authoritarianism – a big enough problem itself, made worse when his untimely death led to his replacement by the wretched Nicolás Maduro.[65] Maduro's abject failure to routinize Chávez's charisma in rational institutions has left the *chavista* movement in tatters, the national economy in ruins, and his regime only able to engage in futile fist-shaking at internal and external enemies in order to shore up support. The problem here lies in the failure to develop differentiating relations that hold together the People in the absence of a unifying leader figure: the overdetermination of any single signifier means that it is all too likely to come tumbling down beneath this weight at crucial moments of transition, lacking any good reason for its different parts to hold together.

Of course, Laclau's reason for embracing indeterminacy is to allow as wide a spread as possible to identify with populist signifiers. But united by their rejection of the dominant system in a logic of equivalences, such groups have no way to mediate their own internal elements in a way that produces progressive outcomes. Consider the Five Star Movement in Italy. Ostensibly a left-populist movement, it includes numerous reactionary elements: its founder, Beppe Grillo, has called for the exclusion and expulsion of all immigrants.[66] Grillo's

---

65 Carlos de la Torre, 'The Contested Meanings of Populist Revolutions in Latin America,' in Abromeit et al, *Transformations of Populism*, 330–344, p.342.
66 See, for example, ANSA, 'Grillo calls for mass deportations,' December 23, 2016, http://www.ansa.it/english/news/politics/2016/12/23/grillo-calls-for-mass-deportations-2_c2583737-0f97-4157-a2f3-d2a9137728b6.html (accessed 10 February 2018).

stance is fully in line with the exclusionary logic of a populism that counterposes a homogenous 'Us' against a hostile, heterogeneous 'Them.' Similarly, the Syriza government has found itself in coalition with ANEL, a highly-conservative faction seeking to limit immigration and proposing an Orthodox education system. A direct and immediate unity of equivalences such as Laclau proposes offers no way to scrutinize, select, or transform the signifier: it is an irrational social form, not because of any supposed psychological dispositions of the individuals involved, but because the elements held together in this way interact without any coherence or valid form – that is, for no good, consistent reason.

While Lukács's own account of party organization is obviously a product of very different historical circumstances and opportunities, the theoretical presuppositions that underlie it can offer some suggestions may offer some suggestions as to the kind of social movement that could counter the effects of reification. Two points stand out: first, any such movement must establish clear organizational forms, rather than rely on an immediate homogenizing unity; second, this movement must aim at the full social integration of its members through common practices that both incorporate them in a more than formal sense, and are externally coherent and open to change.

At one level, the first of these is simply a matter of political practicality: without clear organization, it is all too easy for progressive elements to be swept up by regressive forces in a populist coalition. Lukács predicted this danger: the very fact that the proletariat would necessarily be part of a broader insurrectionary coalition made the need for it to maintain its own organizationally-independent party all the more pressing.[67] Without it, truly revolutionary elements might be swamped by the conservative rage of the peasantry or petit bourgeoisie. We need not look to Bolshevik revolutions for a concrete example. Take the vast popular uprising that overthrew Hosni Mubarak in Egypt. Here a disparate band stretching from secular liberals to the Muslim Brotherhood united, just as Laclau might urge, in one common front against a decaying regime. But it was the Muslim Brotherhood, with their long-standing organizational structure, who were best able to take advantage of the situation: their candidate, Mohamed Morsi, was thus able to win the democratic Presidential election – and the secular liberals who had stood alongside them against Mubarak were obliged to fall behind the military autocrat General Sisi, whose coup overthrew Morsi in turn. But such a practical concern assumes a more fundamental theoretical point. Party organization, for Lukács,

---

67 Lukács, HCC. 307ff.

is the way the proletariat can 'see its own class consciousness given historical shape.'[68] Repeatedly rejecting any reliance on a revolution headed by a leader figure or run by a small cadre of professional revolutionaries, he clarifies that the Party should not seek to *instruct* the workers on their interests, as if holding superior objective knowledge. Rather, it is the formal organization of the Party itself that serves the role of fostering class consciousness. Organization is an intentionally meaningful social practice: it signifies the way a group is directed towards its situation. The clarification of organizational forms, therefore, provides a conscious and determinate social form for a group's opposition to hegemonic powers; in governing the relations between the parts of a movement, it helps explain when they may pull in contradictory directions. Lukács's model thus suggests that grassroots organizational efforts, in which group members are forced to clarify their position by giving it organizational form, is essential for progressive forces to ensure that their goals are not overrun by reactionary tendencies.

If organisation is understood as an intentional social practice, it follows that such practices shape the social being of those engaged in them: through them, the members of a movement can be fully integrated as members of the group. Lukács's rejection of a party administered by experts is instructive here: those seeking to act on behalf of the revolutionary movements would become 'isolated from the mass of ordinary members who are normally give the role of passive onlookers.'[69] In other words, this would reproduce what I have described as the internal coherence of the commodity structure by reducing the bulk of party members to participation in practices that were determined independently of them. Instead, the party's organizational forms must be the product of the workers' own progressive struggles towards consciousness. There is no single form that can be imposed on the organization – and it would be wrong, Lukács argues, for the Party to move directly to one supposedly-ultimate form of organization; rather, there must be a steady 'dialectical interaction between theory, party, and class,' such that collective practices emerge out of ever-changing practical situations as the means by which they are clarified. They can thereby be characterised as externally coherent, to the degree that organizational practices by definition interpellate those who perform them as subjects active in the constitution of their own social being. Moreover, the openness and fluidity of such forms in Lukács's account even presupposes differentiation in the popular movement. As the Party grows, he suggests, it reaches out to new and distinct strata; its organizational forms must change to

---

68   Ibid., 326.
69   Ibid., 336.

reflect and incorporate these elements in turn. For Laclau, of course, differentiation must be eliminated; as McKean has argued, this emphasis on homogeneity and the exclusion of difference is all too liable to become racialized.[70] By placing organization at the centre of his account, Lukács aims instead to recognize and coordinate heterogeneity in a way that includes as many different elements as possible in the movement. Open, constantly-renewed organizational practices are necessary to hold together a variegated coalition if it is not to lapse into chauvinistic exclusion.

It is such active, substantial inclusion of members in the movement that is at the heart of Lukács's theory. It is necessary that 'party members enter with their whole personalities into a living relationship with the whole of the life of the party,' if the movement is to hold their loyalty. Where commodified social forms divide us in to public and private being, Lukács aims to socialise the entire person, offering a substantial and not merely a formal kind of social being in the movement. Once again, the Muslim Brotherhood offers an instructive example: much of its success has been attributed in part to its long-developed networks supporting various religious charitable organizations among the poor. Going beyond merely political ends, it developed more substantial social bonds through such works. While we may not wish to adopt such a religious dimension, the example is useful: by incorporating and drawing together its members in this way, it became (as Lukács puts it) a 'world of activity' for members who were fully integrated within it.[71] If such substantive social being can be manifest in externally-coherent organizational forms that fully incorporate individual members in to the movement, then an insurrectionary coalition can do more than replace one hegemonic power with another; it might genuinely transcend the problematic structures of contemporary social relations.

7   Conclusion

It is easy to dismiss Lukács's theory of revolution because it seems to have failed. If *History and Class Consciousness* predicted the necessary rise to consciousness of the proletariat, and the collapse of capitalism as its inevitable consequence, then indeed the book's central contention would have been mistaken. But such a reading is mistaken. As Žižek points out, Lukács does not offer a deterministic theory of any kind, but rather insists on 'the utter

---

70   McKean, 'Toward an Inclusive Populism?.'
71   Lukács *HCC* 337.

undecidability and contingency of the revolutionary process.'[72] Lukács's diagnosis of the problems of social relations on the commodity form is not, therefore, a prediction that these will necessarily lead to a revolutionary consciousness. Rather, it explains what sort of contradictions may be produced by such reification: the abstraction through which capitalist social relations are constituted produces antinomies of form and content, while isolating the individual as a substantial private being left only to look on passively at a public realm over which they have no control. In times of crisis, this might be turned to genuinely progressive purposes – but there is nothing in the problems themselves that leads directly to their solution. In the absence of any organized progressive bodies (including, but not limited to, a Party), it is equally possible that such a crisis will lead to conflict between the two poles of the dichotomies of reified social relations: irrationality against rationality, spontaneity against order, immediate homogeneous social unity against mediated and differentiated social relations. Such circumstances are ripe for populism, with its reliance on narratives of a unified People against an elite detached from the masses; they are ripe too for its descent into authoritarianism and ethnic chauvinism.

For this reason, Laclau's embrace of populism is ill-advised: the homogeneity and vagueness he endorses have no inherent way to protect against descent into reactionary forms – and the very centrality of setting the People against an Enemy drives it that way. From the perspective of Lukács's analysis of social forms, such a social unity would be irrational. But rationality and irrationality should not be understood here as properties of the individuals coming in to social relations. Laclau is right, I think, to criticise elitist characterizations of the 'crowd' as an irrational, animalistic mass, in which individuals' capacities to reason are overcome by their passions: in such critiques, irrationality refers to the people who make up the crowd, who are thereby signified as something less-than-human. In contrast, in Lukács's analysis, it is social relations that can be rational or irrational: they are rational to the degree that they are explicit, ordered, formalized, and susceptible to comprehension; they are irrational to the degree that they are immediate, direct, substantial, and accepted as natural without question. Only the former is able to recognize and incorporate diversity by devising structures that coordinate the relations of substantial particulars.

Of course, such structures must, for Lukács, be fluid and open: they must exhibit external, rather than internal coherence. Organization is a matter of practice: to be a member of such a movement means building one's relations to others, rather than remaining as a private individual who merely dips a toe

---

72   Žižek, 'Schlagend, aber nicht Treffend!,' p.188.

in the public realm. Brought together as co-constitutors of society, directly related to one another, citizens may feel less powerless in the face of social reality; they might too be less susceptible to those who seek to unite them instead through some nebulous national 'essence,' reinforced by the exclusion of the Other – left-wing Jewish philosopher or Muslim refugee. If the electorate is taught only to observe passively as technocratic experts run matters on their behalf, it is little wonder if, when those technocrats err, they turn to more brash and confident leaders who promise to do the same, only better. What populist and technocrat share is the assumption that the particular individual is isolated and hence powerless; perhaps the abolition of that isolation is, after all, the most effective defense against illiberal authoritarianism.

Index

1968, Generation of   2, 5, 163, 167, 213, 279

Abromeit, John   292, 294, 308–309, 312–314, 316
Adorno, Thedor W.   13, 28, 39, 130–131, 135–136, 139–141, 143, 169–170, 183, 211, 272, 274
aesthetics   7, 29, 130–131, 145, 164, 175, 204–205, 253
alienation   2, 16, 22, 48, 50, 52–57, 62–63, 67, 116–121, 128–129, 136, 144–146, 156, 162, 174, 177, 180, 182–184, 190, 198, 203, 210–212, 214–215, 223, 240, 249, 273–274, 278–282
Althusser, Louis   3, 53, 95, 117–120, 128, 145, 170, 304
Appiah, Kwame Anthony   259
Arendt, Hannah   90
Aristotle   42, 76, 80, 183

Bacon, Francis   155
Badiou, Alain   36, 215
Baudelaire, Charles   129, 136–138, 143
Benjamin, Walter   109, 116, 120, 128–143, 170, 215, 296
Berger, Peter   4
Bernstein, Eduard   162
Bloch, Ernst   130–131, 145, 166, 168, 170
Bolshevism   49, 51, 150, 164, 275, 289, 306
Borkenau, Franz   108–112
Bourdieu, Pierre   128
Brecht, Bertolt   130, 132, 143, 181
Brentano, Franz   298
Brunschvicg, Léon   113
Bukharin, Nikolai   52, 105–107, 166
Bürger, Peter   167

Calhoun, John C.   269
Chamberlain, Houston Stewart   257–260
Civil Rights   2, 171, 289
colonialism   252, 267
Combahee River Collective   267
Comintern   2, 166, 260
commodification   53, 68, 99, 125, 184, 193

commodity fetishism   15, 52–54, 56, 72–73, 100, 105–108, 116–117, 119, 127, 133–134, 142–143, 146–147, 238, 271, 274, 276, 288–289, 291, 293, 295, 297, 299, 301, 303, 305, 307, 309, 311, 313, 315, 317, 319, 321
commodity-form   91–93, 99–101, 103–105, 108, 114–115, 156, 238–239
communicative action   4, 267
Communist Party   49, 60–62, 94, 108, 195, 204, 212, 214, 217
Comte, Auguste   153
constructivism   30, 144–145, 147, 149, 151, 153–156, 285
Corbyn, Jeremy   290
Cunow, Heinrich   105–106

Darwin, Charles   52, 153, 166, 257
Davis, Angela Y.   252, 267
de Beauvoir, Simone   203
Deborin, Abram   132
Deleuze, Gilles   286
democracy   22–23, 51, 87, 150–151, 179, 208, 255, 290, 292, 308
Derrida, Jacques   215, 222
Descartes, René   92, 109–114, 154, 167–168
Destruction of Reason   121, 128–129, 252–255, 257–261, 266
Dewey, John   161, 173
Dilthey, Wilhelm   16
Dostoevsky, Fyodor   164, 184
double consciousness   253, 264–265
Du Bois, W.E.B.   252–253, 264–268
Duns Scotus   40, 42, 44

Engels, Friedrich   96–100, 116, 118–119, 144–145, 147, 149–150, 152–153, 163, 168, 190, 196, 274, 277
Enlightenment   83, 90, 133, 160, 177, 283
epistemology   21–22, 26, 38, 42, 73, 97, 188–189, 200, 205, 218, 228–230, 249, 254, 305
ethics   25, 76, 184, 205, 218, 230, 271, 275, 314
European Union   290, 311

existentialism 128, 180, 203, 205, 211–212, 218, 275

fascism 133, 142, 160, 292–293
Feenberg, Andrew 5–7, 13–14, 16, 18, 20–22, 24–26, 29, 60, 70, 77, 80, 82, 102, 165, 228, 259, 299
feminism 21, 188, 227–229, 232, 247–248
Feuerbach, Ludwig 49, 52, 127, 144, 149, 152, 180–181, 242
Fichte, J.G. 6, 36, 47, 96, 128, 146, 153, 155, 164–165, 283
Firmin, Anténor 256–259
Foucault, Michel 22, 283–284, 286
Frankfurt School 2–3, 7, 13, 25–26, 31, 59, 77, 92, 109, 128, 130, 135, 142, 169, 174, 180, 205, 299
Fraser, Nancy 68
French Revolution 161, 255
Freud, Sigmund 134

Gabel, Joseph 253, 261–262, 264, 266
Galileo 110–111, 306
Gobineau, Arthur 255–259
Goethe, J.W. 164
Goldmann, Lucien 3, 128, 164, 203
Gramsci, Antonio 181, 266
Grossmann, Henryk 91–94, 108–115

Habermas, Jürgen 3–4, 25, 28, 90, 170–171, 173–174, 176–177, 266–267
Haitian Revolution 255
Harding, Sandra 22, 188, 227–230, 251
Hartsock, Nancy 21, 188, 227–237, 241–243, 246–248, 251
Hegel, G.W.F. 6, 25–27, 30, 33–35, 37–38, 42, 44, 51, 76–77, 118, 120, 128, 133, 145–146, 149, 151–155, 160, 164, 168, 170–171, 176, 195–196, 211, 213–214, 216, 218–219, 222, 227–229, 235, 241–242, 275, 278–282, 297, 312
Heidegger, Martin 3, 25, 27, 32–34, 36–40, 42–45, 80, 128–129, 134, 141, 173, 176, 180, 203, 206, 216–218
Heine, Heinrich 152
Hobbes, Thomas 110–111, 149, 154–155, 295
Honneth, Axel 5–6, 8, 28, 49, 57, 60, 71, 90–91, 159–162, 170–177, 181, 183, 185, 271–272, 284

Horkheimer, Max 13, 26, 92, 109
humanism 92, 118, 146, 170, 242
Hungarian Revolution 2
Husserl, Edmund 7, 27, 43, 112, 164, 297–299

idealism 6–7, 26, 71–72, 77, 95–98, 136, 145, 152, 205, 211–212, 242, 275
ideology 13, 16, 53, 77, 116, 119, 139–141, 149, 166, 170, 173, 179, 182, 188, 231, 237, 253, 259, 283, 287, 293–296
imperialism 94, 180, 244
Industrial Revolution 138, 149
irrationalism 154, 253–255, 257–259

Jaeggi, Rahel 54, 63, 171, 174, 271, 273
Jaggar, Alison 227–228, 251
James, C.L.R. 252, 267
Jameson, Frederic 22, 53, 188, 227–228, 232–233, 248–250, 272, 285, 287–288
Jung, C.G. 139
Jünger, Ernst 135, 138–142

Kant, Immanuel 6, 18, 26–28, 30, 37, 39, 41–42, 76, 83, 104, 149, 152–155, 164, 168, 176, 183, 211, 239, 279, 283, 306
Kautsky, Karl 162, 166
Kendi, Ibram X. 254–255, 260
Kierkegaard, Søren 133, 152, 203, 212, 216–218
Kirkland, Frank 264–265
Klages, Ludwig 139
Korsch, Karl 2, 26, 54, 144, 150, 166
Kouvelakos, Konstantinos 25, 29, 40–41, 45

Laclau, Ernesto 287, 291–296, 298, 304, 311–312, 315–317, 319–320
Lask, Emil 27, 34, 36–47, 80, 164, 283
Lassalle, Ferdinand 128
Lefebvre, Henri 128
Lenin, Vladimir 60–62, 93–99, 115, 145, 150, 164–165, 195, 206–209, 213–215, 315
Locke, John 55, 314
Lohmann, Georg 38, 41, 43, 49–50, 54, 57–58, 159
Löwy, Michel 51–52, 164–165, 184, 306
Luxemburg, Rosa 150, 164, 194, 199, 206, 209, 213, 215–216

INDEX

Mach, Ernst   95
Marcuse, Herbert   2, 13, 20, 25, 81, 278–279, 283
Marx, Karl   2, 6–7, 13, 15–16, 20, 22, 25, 27, 29–31, 33, 37–38, 40, 43, 46, 48–60, 62, 68, 72–73, 76–77, 80, 90, 97, 100, 106–107, 109–110, 116–122, 127–129, 131, 133–134, 142, 144–156, 160–168, 170, 176, 180–181, 183–185, 190, 195–196, 198, 205–206, 210, 217–222, 228–232, 234–238, 240, 252, 259, 261, 263, 271, 273–278, 280–283, 285, 297, 299, 305, 313
materialism   21, 93–99, 102, 104–105, 107–108, 130, 150, 152, 188, 230, 232, 242, 246, 248
Merleau-Ponty, Maurice   3, 128
metaphysics   7, 22, 26, 38, 76, 99, 176, 198
Mills, Charles W.   229, 267–269
Mouffe, Chantal   287
Mudde, Cas   290, 292, 308
Müller, Jan-Werner   292, 308

Negri, Antonio   95, 215, 286–287
neo-Hegelianism   170
neo-Kantianism   7, 13, 26, 38, 40, 42, 72–73, 164, 204–205, 283, 307
neoliberalism   225, 271–273, 275, 277–279, 281, 283, 285–287, 290, 310
Nietzsche, Freidrich   133, 152
norms   67–71, 73, 75, 77–87, 89–90, 310
Novalis   130
Nussbaum, Martha   60, 172, 175–176

objectification   45, 54, 57, 91, 119, 121, 123, 129, 144, 146, 156, 167, 171, 175, 178, 194–195, 197, 249, 263–264, 279–281, 283
ontology   3, 13, 25, 27, 31, 37–38, 42, 70–72, 76–77, 80, 82, 88–90, 129, 162, 166, 168, 170, 177, 180, 185, 203, 205, 217–218, 297
Orbán, Viktor   3, 289
Orthodox Marxism   26, 50, 52, 72, 173–174, 231–232

Parmenides   153–154
Parsons, Talcott   80–82
perspectivism   249
Petrovic, Gajo   52, 146

phenomenology   7, 26–27, 37–38, 40, 42–44, 112–113, 120, 151, 164, 168, 173, 181, 204–205, 213–214, 230, 269, 297, 299
Phenomenology of Spirit   26, 120, 151, 168, 213–214
Pitkin, Hanna   4
Plato   151
Podemos   290, 292
Pollock, Freidrich   92
populism   225, 289–293, 295–297, 299, 301, 303, 305, 307–309, 311–317, 319–321
positivism   136, 153, 180
post-structuralism and postmodernism   148, 229, 273, 286
Postone, Moishe   211, 222, 313
praxis   6–8, 13, 25, 48, 57, 72, 74, 76–77, 80, 82, 87, 116, 127, 136, 140, 172, 174–175, 180–181, 185, 203, 211, 215, 217, 219, 227, 235, 242, 285, 299

racism   173, 181, 229, 252–270, 289
rationalization   17, 58–59, 73–74, 81, 83–85, 111, 168–170, 238, 263, 267, 278, 306, 308
Raz, Joseph   78–79, 82
recognition   5, 22, 72, 91, 97, 161, 172–173, 198, 271, 310
relativism   30, 249
Rickert, Heinrich   38, 40, 164
Riegl, Alois   297, 302–303
Rousseau, Jean-Jacques   54–55, 149, 174, 264, 307
Russian Revolution   150, 204, 208–209, 275

Sanders, Bernie   290, 311
Sartre, Jean-Paul   3, 128, 203
Schelling, F.W.J.   253
Schmitt, Carl   294
Scholem, Gershom   130
Science of Logic   26, 213–214
Searle, John   71, 82–83
Simmel, Georg   1, 25, 30, 73, 135, 164–165, 171, 275, 300
slavery   240, 252, 263–264, 267, 269
Smith, Dorothy   227–228, 230, 243, 248
social Darwinism   257, 259
social movements   22, 67, 90, 228–229, 249, 315
Sohn-Rethel, Alfred   188
Soul and Form   164, 307

Soviet Union   2, 22, 94
species-being   55, 116
Spengler, Oswald   139
Spinoza, Baruch   154, 285
standpoint theory   187–188, 227–233, 235–237, 239, 241–243, 245, 247–251
subjectivity   7, 18, 67, 73, 79–80, 86, 139, 175, 177, 179, 182, 191, 196, 198, 203, 207, 211–215, 220, 241, 264–265, 278, 282, 284, 286, 291, 304, 308, 312
Suzuki, D.T.   14, 20
Syriza   290, 292, 316–317

Taylor, Keeanga-Yamahtta   268
Taylorism   57, 103, 238
technology   15–17, 20–22, 24, 93, 105–108, 115, 140, 178, 228
Theory of the Novel   50, 164, 204
Thompson, Michael J.   6, 8, 119
totality   20, 25, 30, 34–36, 46–47, 51–52, 70–78, 88–90, 92, 102–104, 115, 128, 133–134, 136, 160, 166, 168, 181, 187–188, 193, 195, 199–200, 210–211, 213, 215, 217–219, 221–223, 227–228, 239, 241, 272, 279, 283–285, 287–288, 294
Trump, Donald   289–291, 310–312

values   3, 67, 69–73, 75, 77–79, 81, 83–87, 89, 126, 196, 201, 220–223, 228, 234, 275, 277, 290–291, 293, 297, 299, 303, 307, 312
Vico, Giambattista   154–155, 167

Weber, Max   1, 17, 25, 30, 58–59, 73, 85, 164–165, 168, 170, 263, 275
Western Marxism   171, 203, 213–215, 218, 266, 274, 306
white supremacy   259–260, 262, 264–266, 268–270
Williams, Eric   267
World War I   2, 51, 130, 140

Žižek, Slavoj   98, 120, 296, 319–320

Printed in the United States
By Bookmasters